Photo: Emery Walker, Ltd.

CHARLES, SECOND EARL GREY, K.G.,
1764–1845

*From the Painting by* Sir THOMAS LAWRENCE, P.R.A., *in the National Portrait Gallery*

# RECENT HISTORICAL WORKS

PAGEANT OF THE BIRTH, LIFE, AND DEATH OF RICHARD
BEAUCHAMP, EARL OF WARWICK, K.G. (1389-1439). Edited by Viscount
DILLON, D.C.L., F.S.A., and W. H. St. JOHN HOPE, Litt.D., D.C.L. Photo
engraved from the original Manuscript in the British Museum by EMERY WALKER,
F.S.A. Bound in boards with linen back. 4to (11 in. × 8 in.), 21s. net.

### EXTRACT FROM INTRODUCTION.

The Warwick Pageant is a Cottonian MS. (Julius E IV) and in a series of fifty-three outline
drawings portrays the chief events in the life and death of Richard Beauchamp, Earl of Warwick,
the father-in-law of the kingmaker.·
This MS., which it may be presumed from various evidences was done between 1485 and 1490,
presents to the armour student and to the artist a most rich series of authorities for the costume of
that period. It was rather imperfectly reproduced in Vol. II of Strutt's *Horda Angel-cynnan* in
1775 and again in facsimile in a very limited edition for presentation by the late Earl of Carysfort to
the Roxburghe Club. The present work places within reach of students and others at a moderate
price a reproduction as accurate as that of the Roxburghe Club, but without the meticulous details
as to paper and tone. A short list of the chief events recorded has been added with some explana-
tory notes to each plate. The MS. consists of 28 leaves of vellum, measuring 11 inches by 8 inches,
and this work is practically on the same scale as the original, being reproduced by photography, so
that every detail may be shown in its present state.

A HISTORY OF ENGLAND. From the Defeat of the Armada to the
Death of Elizabeth. With an Account of English Institutions during the Later
Sixteenth and Early Seventeenth Centuries. By EDWARD P. CHEYNEY, Professor
of European History in the University of Pennsylvania. In 2 Vols. 8vo. Vol. I.
16s. net.

THE LIFE OF WILLIAM PITT, EARL OF CHATHAM. By BASIL
WILLIAMS. With Portraits and Maps. 2 vols. 8vo, 25s. net.

THE LIFE OF CHARLES THIRD EARL STANHOPE. Com-
menced by GHITA STANHOPE. Revised and Completed by G. P. GOOCH, Author
of *History and Historians in the Nineteenth Century*, &c. With Illustrations. 8vo.
10s. net.

THE ECONOMIC ORGANISATION OF ENGLAND. An Outline
History. By W. J. ASHLEY, M.A., Ph.D., Professor of Commerce in the University of Birmingham.

THE REIGN OF HENRY VII FROM CONTEMPORARY SOURCES.
With an Introduction by A. F. POLLARD, M.A. Three Volumes. Crown 8vo.
Vol. I., Narrative Extracts, 10s. 6d. net. Vol. II., Constitutional, Social, and
Economic History, 10s. 6d. net. Vol. III., Diplomacy, Ecclesiastical Affairs, and
Ireland, 10s. 6d. net.

HENRY VIII. By A. F. POLLARD, M.A., Litt.D. Crown 8vo, 4s. 6d. net.

CUSTOMARY ACRES AND THEIR HISTORICAL IMPORTANCE ;
being a Series of Unfinished Essays. By the late FREDERICK SEEBOHM, Hon.
LL.D. (Edin.), Litt.D. (Camb.), D.Litt. (Oxford). 8vo, 12s. 6d. net.

THE CONFEDERATION OF EUROPE. A Study of the European
Alliance, 1813-1823, as an Experiment in the International Organisation of Peace.
Six Lectures delivered in the University Schools, Oxford, at the invitation of the
Delegates of the Common University Fund, Trinity Term, 1913. By WALTER
ALISON PHILLIPS, M.A. 8vo, 7s. 6d. net.

THE AGRARIAN PROBLEM IN THE SIXTEENTH CENTURY.
By R. H. TAWNEY. With Reproductions of Plans (1590 to 1620). 8vo, 9s. net.

THE VILLAGE LABOURER, 1760 to 1832. A Study in the Government of England before the Reform Bill. By J. L. HAMMOND and BARBARA
HAMMOND. Second Impression. 8vo, 9s. net.

---

LONGMANS, GREEN AND CO.
LONDON, NEW YORK, BOMBAY, CALCUTTA, AND MADRAS

\*

# RECENT HISTORICAL WORKS—*(continued)*

**HISTORY AND HISTORIANS IN THE NINETEENTH CENTURY.** By G. P. GOOCH, M.A. (Cantab.) 8vo, 10s. 6d. net.

**THE FATE OF EMPIRES:** Being an Inquiry into the Stability of Civilisation. By ARTHUR JOHN HUBBARD, M.D. (Dunelm). 8vo, 6s. 6d. net.

**STOLEN WATERS: A page from the Conquest of Ulster.** By T. M. HEALY, K.C., M.P. 8vo, 10s. 6d. net.

*This narrative is based on unpublished MS. State Papers, and historical trials or inquisitions. It brings to light the hitherto unknown frauds practised on the Crown and the City of London in the times of James I, Charles I, Cromwell, and Charles II. The narrative is woven round the controversy as to the title to two great fisheries in Northern Ireland—The River Bann and Lough Neagh.*

**THE FIRST TWELVE CENTURIES OF BRITISH STORY: A** Sketch of the Social and Political Conditions of the British Islands from the year 56 B.C. to 1154 A.D. With 20 Sketch Maps and 3 Photographic Reproductions of Medieval Maps. By J. W. JEUDWINE, LL.B. (Camb.), of Lincoln's Inn, Barrister-at-Law. 8vo, 12s. 6d. net.

**ESSENTIALS IN EARLY EUROPEAN HISTORY.** By SAMUEL BURNETT HOWE, A.M., Head of the Department of History in the Plainfield High School, Plainfield, New Jersey. With Coloured Frontispiece, 168 other Illustrations, 31 Maps and Plans (10 Coloured), and 8 Charts and Genealogical Tables. Crown 8vo, 7s. 6d. net.

**A HISTORY OF EUROPE.** By ARTHUR J. GRANT, M.A., King's College, Cambridge, Professor of History at the University of Leeds. With Maps and Coloured Chart. Large crown 8vo, 7s. 6d. net.

**INDIAN HISTORICAL STUDIES.** By H. G. RAWLINSON, M.A., Professor of English Literature, The Deccan College, Poona. With Illustrations and Map. Crown 8vo, 4s. 6d. net.

CONTENTS.—Gautama Buddha—Asoka—Indo-Greek Dynasties of the Panjab—Chinese Pilgrims in India—Ibn Batuta—Akbar—Sivaji the Maratha—Robert Knox—Ranjit Singh and the Sikh Nation—Foreign Influences in the Civilisation of Ancient India.

**ORGANISED DEMOCRACY: An Introduction to the Study of American** Politics. By FREDERICK A. CLEVELAND, Ph.D., LL.D. Crown 8vo, 10s. 6d. net.

**A HISTORY OF WALES FROM THE EARLIEST TIMES TO** THE EDWARDIAN CONQUEST. By JOHN EDWARD LLOYD, M.A. With Map. 2 vols. 8vo, 21s. net.

**THE RISE OF SOUTH AFRICA: A History of the Origin of South** African Colonisation and of its Development towards the East from the Earliest Times to 1857. By GEORGE EDWARD CORY, M.A., King's College, Cambridge, Professor in the Rhodes University College, Grahamstown, South Africa. In 4 vols. 8vo.

VOL. I. FROM THE EARLIEST TIMES TO THE YEAR 1820. With Map, Plans, and Illustrations. 15s.

VOL. II. From 1820 to 1834. With 38 Illustrations and 2 Maps. 8vo, 18s.

**THE FIRST DECADE OF THE AUSTRALIAN COMMON-** WEALTH: A Chronicle of Contemporary Politics, 1901-1910. By HENRY GYLES TURNER. 8vo, 9s.

**THE MAKING OF THE AUSTRALIAN COMMONWEALTH** (1899-1900). A Stage in the growth of the Empire. By the Hon. B. R. WISE, formerly Attorney-General of New South Wales. 8vo, 7s. 6d. net.

**THE MAID OF FRANCE: Being the Story of the Life and Death of** Jeanne d'Arc. By ANDREW LANG. With 3 Maps and 3 Portraits. 8vo, 12s. 6d. net. Cheap Edition. With 3 Maps. Crown 8vo, 6s. net.

**NAPOLEON I.** A Biography. By AUGUST FOURNIER, Professor of History in the University of Vienna. Translated by A. E. ADAMS. With 2 Photogravure Portraits and 7 Maps. 2 vols. 8vo, 21s. net.

---

LONGMANS, GREEN AND CO.

LONDON, NEW YORK, BOMBAY, CALCUTTA, AND MADRAS

# THE PASSING OF
# THE GREAT REFORM BILL

# THE PASSING OF THE GREAT REFORM BILL

BY

## J. R. M. BUTLER

FELLOW OF TRINITY COLLEGE, CAMBRIDGE

WITH ILLUSTRATIONS

## LONGMANS, GREEN AND CO.

39 PATERNOSTER ROW, LONDON

FOURTH AVENUE & 30TH STREET, NEW YORK

BOMBAY, CALCUTTA, AND MADRAS

1914

All rights reserved

TO MY FATHER

# PREFACE

IN spite of recent changes in its letter, and a great and growing modification of its spirit, the Constitution as we know it wears, to all intents and purposes, the shape it assumed in 1832. To parody a famous phrase, that year is now the limit of constitutional memory. The passing of the Great Reform Bill takes us suddenly into another air ; we leave the remote world of the eighteenth century, peopled by the heroic ghosts of Pitt and Fox and Canning, for the era of Peel and Palmerston, of the corn-laws and the Crimea. The old aristocratic system begins to crumble, and the feet of the nation are set in the path that leads to democracy. It is generally known that this mighty change in our polity was not carried through without a struggle, and it is lightly said that the country was brought to the verge of revolution. But the actual facts of the struggle are not well known. When Roebuck and Molesworth wrote, the private letters of the time were not available, and they were unable to check the oral traditions they received. Since their day most of the important documents have come to light, but the story of the Reform Bill has never been fully told.

This book was mainly written in the summer of 1912 as a dissertation for a Trinity fellowship. It is more concerned throughout with negotiations behind the scenes, and with the working and effect of popular opinion, than with the course of events in Parliament. The endless debates have been exhaustively quoted and described in various books, and except in the last weeks of the contest do not seem to require detailed treatment. I have thought it better to gather together the ideas and opinions they express in a separate chapter, and to set beside them other political views of the time. I have also omitted to follow the course of the Scotch and Irish Reform Bills. Important as they were, their fate was always bound up with that of the English bill, which on each occasion was introduced first and bore the brunt of attack.  In the third chapter, which deals mainly with the condition and desires of the working class, I have tried to escape the snares that beset one who without any knowledge of economics ventures to lay hands, however gingerly, on the " perilous question " of prices and real wages, by avoiding controversial questions.  But it seemed necessary to make some such attempt, since the demand for Reform [1] was often closely connected with the complaints of labour.

By the great kindness of Lord Grey, Lord Durham, and Lord Spencer, I have been allowed to use the valuable papers at Howick, at Lambton, and at Althorp ; I have also drawn on the Broughton, Place, and Wilson MSS. in the British Museum, and on the Home Office papers in the Public Record Office. Besides these, my chief authorities have been the published correspondence of Lord Grey with William IV and with Princess Lieven, and the published papers of Lord Melbourne, Sir Robert Peel, Lord John Russell, the Duke of Wellington, and Christopher Wyvill.  Other important letters can be gleaned from biographies, and there are various memoirs of the time. [2]  In dealing with the early Reforming societies I have been much helped by the appearance of Mr. Veitch's *Genesis of Parliamentary Reform*. For the later history of the Reform movement in the classes outside Parliament there is no source to compare with the materials collected and arranged by Francis Place ; his continuous account of the struggle from the point of view of a Radical wire-puller includes many valuable documents in the form of letters, manifestoes, and newspaper cuttings.  Any student of the industrial and political condition of England in the early nineteenth century must owe a great debt of gratitude to Place's tireless labours in the service of posterity, without which it would be hardly possible to reclaim that waste-land of history.

For many and various points I am indebted to conversations with Mr. J. H. Clapham, Mr. and Mrs. J. L. Hammond, Mr. W. T. Layton, Mr. H. W. V. Temperley, and Mr. Graham Wallas.  I

---

[1] I have spelt Reform with a capital letter when it means Parliamentary Reform.

[2] See the bibliographical note at the end of the book.

also owe much to the criticism of my friends Mr. R. V. Laurence and Mr. D. A. Winstanley, of Trinity College ; I have to thank Mr. Winstanley in particular for his great kindness in reading through the proofs. Above all I am grateful to Mr. George Trevelyan, who first generously suggested that I should write this book, and ever since has been in every way its unfailing friend. It owes to him more than I can say, and is fortunate in the hope that his promised Life of Lord Grey will correct its many faults.

Finally, I am further indebted to Lord Durham and Mr. Graham Wallas for allowing me to reproduce portraits of the first Lord Durham and Francis Place.

*February* 1914.

# CONTENTS

# ILLUSTRATIONS

# THE PASSING OF
# THE GREAT REFORM BILL

## CHAPTER I

### 1769–1829

" The distempers of Monarchy were the great subjects of apprehension and redress, in the last century ; in this, the distempers of Parliament."—BURKE.

THE statesmen who in 1688 readjusted the balance of the Constitution in favour of Parliament did not do more than settle the difficulty which immediately faced them. Content with destroying the prerogative as they knew it, they took no measures to prevent Parliament itself becoming an instrument of despotism, and ignored the hint by which Clarendon commended the reform of the House of Commons, so boldly handled by Cromwell, to the wisdom of a less distracted time. By this omission their successors were enabled to create a system of Whig predominance untrammelled by popular control. In spite of the criticisms of such Tories as Swift and Bolingbroke, the Constitution acquired a prescriptive sanctity, behind which venerable screen Walpole and Newcastle advanced their party's interests by money and influence not withdrawn from the Crown by the Revolution settlement. But the system had one weak spot. It depended on the compliance of a king fearful for his crown and ignorant of the maze of British politics. The accession of George III was fatal to the old methods ; here was a prince firm on the throne, quick to learn all the arts of corruption, and determined not to rule by proxy alone. Profiting by the divisions of the Whigs, the result of nearly fifty years of unbroken and un-challenged power, he turned his face to the Tories, whom he found not unwilling to transfer their loyalty to a king who could reward it. Within a few years one of the strongest of English administrations was completely shattered. Pitt, the hero of the people, was ignominiously driven out of office, and the great Whig oligarchy found themselves a hopeless and discredited faction, while the King's influence, which they had themselves fostered, seemed now permanently turned against them and likely to increase.

Driven back upon themselves, the Whigs were forced to reconsider their methods and restate their creed ; defeat in the rather sordid warfare they had hitherto waged led them to look for less perishable weapons in the armoury of ideas.   The result was a new party which, though it retained much that was unprogressive and ridiculous, has yet contributed to English political thought many noble and truly liberal principles.   Of these new Whigs the founder was Newcastle, the leader Rockingham, and the prophet Burke.[1]   In the politics of their day they stood for the assertion of party government against the personal rule of the King, and were led as by accident to assault the outworks of corruption behind which the King lay securely entrenched.   In this endeavour they found a powerful ally in their great rival and late colleague, Chatham, who, however much he might disapprove of the Whig theory of government, yet shared the Whig disgust at the tyranny of George III.   A notable instance of this tyranny, in the case of John Wilkes, ranked all the democratic feeling of the country on the side of the Opposition.

Nothing was so favourable to the maintenance of the royal power as the freedom of members of Parliament from popular control, and from henceforward the demand for a reform of the House of Commons is of constant importance.   But this demand was neither united nor uniform nor continuous.   It was long before the Whigs as a party were pledged to Parliamentary Reform ; and between them and the less exalted votaries of the cause there was for many years little sympathy and no joint effort.   In spite of Burke's lofty defence of aristocratic government, it must be admitted that the Whigs tended to behave as an oligarchic clique ; they appear to have been conscious of this defect themselves, and the ill-success of their various attempts to win the nation to their support was rather due to failure to understand the popular mind than to any lack of good-will.   The democrats, on the other hand, often showed little regard for what was practical at the moment.   It was not till the several currents

---

[1] See Winstanley, *Lord Chatham and the Whig Opposition*, pp. 16-22.

were to some degree united that the Reform Act was passed. Nor were Reformers even of one party agreed on any particular measure. Proposals varied widely according to circumstances, and by the time the victory was at length won the enemy was no longer the same. And, finally, it was no smooth, ever-broadening river that bore the Reformers on to their triumph. Rather it was a turbid stream, running at first narrow and deep, broken at times by rocks and rapids, and for a season flowing unseen beneath the earth, but gathering volume all the while, and at length emerging with irresistible rush.

This space of sixty years falls naturally into two periods, divided by the war with revolutionary France, which stifled the demand for Reform. When the days of stress and panic passed, a new start had to be made. Each of these periods has again a former and a latter part, making four stages in all, though logically perhaps the second and third should be looked upon as showing one continuous development in the days of repression. The one strand which runs through the whole web, and gives it a unity, is the faith in Reform of a section of the Whig party, at times the merest remnant, and it is no accident that, when the Reform Bill was at length carried, it was carried by men who boasted their political descent from Rockingham and Fox.

From the Middlesex election to the outbreak of the French Revolution the Reformers were bent mainly on the curtailment of royal influence. As a rule they accept the existing Constitution as the basis of moderate change ; divisions run on non-party lines ; the subject is rather academic and makes no appeal to the mass of the people.

The atmosphere of the period between 1790 and 1800—years covered by the Revolution and the great war—is very different. Those faithful to the cause are an aggressive and persecuted band ; many are republicans, most desire a large change in the democratic direction, and all are deeply inspired by the mighty events in France. The people is against them and they are met with hatred or contempt. Popular feeling was hardly more tolerant when the question was revived after Pitt's death. Reformers were still held to be tainted with Jacobinism, and the distressful years after Waterloo were the bitterest of all.

From after the Queen's trial in 1820 to the days of Catholic Relief, men are in a milder mood. The times of cruel strain are over, and ideas are less crude. There is a growing belief in the necessity of reform in various parts of public life. At length in 1830 the fuel is ready for the sacred spark which the Whigs have cherished through their wanderings of forty years in the wilderness of distrust.

The year 1769 is taken by Lecky as dating the origin of Radicalism in England ; it is also the birth-year of the movement for Parliamentary Reform.[1] The tyranny of the Court in the affair of Wilkes and the Middlesex election not only united the various sections of the Opposition in furious protest in Parliament, but in taverns and coffee-houses started discussions which opened a new line in English politics. The action of a corrupt House of Commons in condemning an elected member to perpetual exclusion from its walls, virtually for an offence against the Court, was to many a last outrageous proof of the dependence of the Commons on the King. Another instance of their indifference to popular sympathies was the continued impotence of Chatham, the only statesman of the time who had touched the imagination of the classes outside Parliament. The remedies suggested were various. That proposed in 1770 by Chatham himself, as the leader of his party, was to strengthen the independent remnant of the House of Commons by the addition of an extra member for each county. The disfranchisement of those boroughs which were entirely under royal influence he mentioned as a possibility, but hesitated to approve. " The limb is mortified, but the amputation might be death." In May 1771 Chatham announced his acceptance of the proposal for triennial parliaments, but he admitted that his Reform schemes were not popular.

The Rockingham Whigs were stirred to equal indignation ; in his *Thoughts on the Present Discontents* Burke assailed the Court and the servile Commons, holding out once for all his theory of representation. " The virtue, spirit, and essence of an House of Commons consists in its being the express image of the feelings of the nation. It was not instituted to be a controul *upon* the people, as of late it has been taught, by a doctrine of the most pernicious tendency. It was designed as a controul *for* the people." And conversely : " The House of Commons can never be a controul on other parts of Government,

[1] See Lecky, *History of England in the Eighteenth Century*, iii. 174–220.

unless they are controuled themselves by their constituents; and unless these constituents possess some right in the choice of that House, which it is not in the power of that House to take away." But though Burke agreed with Chatham as to the evil, he held his proposed reforms to be mere palliatives. A Triennial Act would only handicap the poor honest candidate yet further in his contest with the Treasury; a Place Bill would disfranchise important interests. He trusted to the restoration of freedom of election, and to the elector's conscientious influence on his member. However, in 1771 Burke too complained that apathy in the country had followed on the excitement of which so much was hoped.

But apart from the doings of the governing class, the Wilkes affair made a deep impression on an order of men not as yet much connected with active politics.[1] These were little more than a left wing of the Whigs, mainly middle-class theorists in London and its neighbourhood, of small influence with the people. In 1769 was founded the Society of Supporters of the Bill of Rights, primarily for the purpose of paying Wilkes' debts, but resolutions were passed in favour of shorter parliaments and a fairer representation. The strength of the society was soon sapped by the secession of Horne Tooke and his adherents, but its formation is important as the first organised attempt to put pressure on Parliament from without. Though the cause languished, Reform pamphlets with arguments based on " natural right " and " Saxon principles " were issued from 1774 onwards by such men as Cartwright,[2] Jebb,[3] and Price,[4] and in 1776 Wilkes himself made a motion to the same effect in the Commons. The doctrines of the Radical pamphleteers were altogether alien to

[1] See Kent's *English Radicals*, p. 41 ff.; Veitch, *The Genesis of Parliamentary Reform*, p. 29 ff. Mr. Veitch's book gives a full and detailed account of the Reform movement in the eighteenth century.

[2] Major John Cartwright (1740–1824) gave the last fifty years of his life to the cause of Parliamentary Reform. In 1776 he published *Take your Choice*, the first of many pamphlets on the subject. His creed was : " I ought to have a vote because I am a man."

[3] John Jebb, the son of an Irish dean, born in 1736, was forced to give up his living and college lecturership on account of a change in his religious views, and became a doctor. He took an extreme line in politics, and held strongly the delegate theory of representation.

[4] Richard Price (1723–1791), a Nonconformist minister, is chiefly known for his *Observations on Civil Liberty* and for his sermon on the *Love of our Country*, which drew famous replies from Burke.

those of Chatham, and Burke called their authors " the bane of the Whigs, who do us infinite mischief by persuading many sober and well-meaning people that we have designs inconsistent with the Constitution left us by our forefathers. The machine itself," he said, " is well enough to answer any good purpose, provided the materials were sound."

The excitement which had died down after 1770 was raised to a higher and more sustained pitch by the mismanagement of the American war in its later years by Lord North's government. This wave of discontent carried the Reformers' prospects to a mark not reached again till 1830. As the former agitation was centred in Middlesex, the call to Reform now sounded out of Yorkshire. Late in 1779 a county meeting was held at York, supported by the great Whig landowners of the north—Rockingham, Devonshire, Fitzwilliam, Lowther, Savile,—to petition the House of Commons for economic reform in view of the distress caused by a wasteful war.[1]  " As men of property," the great nobles desired to lessen the Crown's influence ; Lord Fitzwilliam declared that the country was united on this point, if on this only.  On the suggestion of Christopher Wyvill, a Yorkshire clergyman with a genius for organisation, a committee was appointed to consider the basis of a proposed association of the county for the purposes of Reform. Several other counties followed suit, and a meeting of deputies was held in London. On March 28, 1780, the committee reported to a second meeting at York. It was now maintained that besides economic improvement reform of the House of Commons was necessary ; the addition of 100 knights of the shire and the shortening of parliaments were advised. The committee had originally recommended one year as the term, but three years was substituted in the vain hope of conciliating the nobles. Rockingham refused to attend the meeting, and Lord John Cavendish, who was present, spoke strongly against the inclusion of Parliamentary Reform among the objects of the association. " The absence of the Lords alluded to," writes Wyvill, " was a sufficiently plain intimation to the popular agents that the assistance of the great Whig aristocracy in any more effectual reform than that held out in the economical petition was not then to be expected." The

---

[1] *Wyvill Papers*, i. 4. The five volumes of the papers collected by Christopher Wyvill are an invaluable original source for the Reform movement of the eighties.

proposals were attacked by Burke alike in the country and in Parliament, though supported by Shelburne, the leader of the Chatham Whigs.

The doctrines made way, however, in the south, especially at Westminster, where an association was formed on the York-shire model, with Charles Fox, an ally of Rockingham, as its chair-man of committee. As early as March 1780 the committee advised annual parliaments and the addition of 100 county members ; in May they received a " very intelligent report " from a sub-committee converted to the necessity " of reviewing the whole plan of delegation," as the only security against the influence of the Crown. The report favoured annual parliaments, universal suffrage, the ballot, payment of members, the abolition of property qualifications, and the division of the country into 513 equal electoral districts. Seven days later, the Duke of Richmond, influenced, it may be, by ideas born beyond the Channel or the Atlantic,[1] brought forward in the House of Lords a motion for Radical Reform. His speech was interrupted by the tumult of the Gordon mob outside, and indeed the terror caused in the country by these riots brought the Reformers into great discredit and afforded the King much needed support amid the disasters of the American war. Partly for this reason, Reform made little impression on the country at the general election. Even in Yorkshire, where Sir George Savile made it a feature of his address, Burke found no enthusiasm on the matter.

The Reformers, though disheartened, were not hopeless. The more advanced among them, headed by John Cartwright, the lifelong champion of the cause, had formed in April the Society for Promoting Constitutional Information. Its subscription was a guinea, and its original members included Richmond, Sheridan, Sawbridge,[2] Jebb, and Price. They proceeded to issue Reform literature, sometimes going so far as to demand annual parlia-ments and universal suffrage. In the meantime Richmond pressed Rockingham eagerly, but in vain, to take up the ques-tion, urging that it might be made a winning cause, especially in the event of union with Shelburne.[3] The Yorkshire com-

---

[1] Veitch, p. 43.

[2] Alderman John Sawbridge, brother of Catherine Macaulay, sat in three successive parliaments as member for the City.

[3] Barré gives the Duke's words in a letter to Shelburne, dated De-cember 1780 : " ' I was much hurt with L^d Fitzwilliam's opposing with

mittee issued addresses to catch the economic reformers, and co-operated with the other associated counties ; in 1781 a second meeting of delegates was held in London, and a proposal to disfranchise certain nomination boroughs " with adequate compensation " was discussed. There was an idea, suggested by Wyvill but never realised, of possible union with Rockingham and the Whig nobles on this basis. " And thus, the cities and the sounder part of the boroughs, co-operating with the augmented representation of the counties, under a triennial duration of Parliament, would form an effectual barrier against the ambition of the Crown." [1]

In the spring of 1782 the aspect of affairs was changed by the formation of a coalition Whig government under the headship of Rockingham. The administration was short-lived, but it succeeded in passing into law several important measures of economic reform. Nevertheless it refused all but the most insignificant reform of the representation, and accordingly Wyvill, though he welcomed its general policy, would not offer it the support of the Yorkshire association. There was indeed more to be hoped from the Chatham wing of the coalition. Shelburne states that he actually proposed Parliamentary Reform to the Rockingham party as one of the three planks of their common platform, but that the Cabinet rejected the idea.[2] In June Wyvill had interviews with the two leaders separately ; Shelburne pledged his support to the measures of the Yorkshire

so much warmth the proposition of 100 Knights in the Westminster Committee yesterday. . . . I have worked night and day with Lord Rockingham ; I have told him repeatedly the mischievous consequences of his not adopting this measure ; that it must come forward : and that the loss of it (if it should be lost) will be laid at his door ; and he will besides have the mortification of seeing most of his best friends quitting him upon the division.' All that he says in answer is that he is sure the measure is not popular without doors, to which the Duke replies, ' You and we can soon make it so ' " (Fitzmaurice, *Life of William, Earl of Shelburne* (second edition), ii. 67).

[1] *Wyvill Papers*, iii. 295.

[2] " Though Lord Shelburne had the confidence of the King from March 27, . . . yet from the influence of the Rockingham party, their number in the Cabinet, and their numbers in Parliament, it was impossible for him to do much good. . . . He made to them three propositions : (1) for a Reform of Parliament, (2) for a general reform of the receipt and expenditure of the Publick Revenue, (3) to bring Lord North to a Publick Trial " (Shelburne in Lansdowne House MSS. ; Fitzmaurice, ii. 104).

body, but Rockingham would say no more than that he had promised Richmond an opportunity for the discussion of the question. Indeed the Whigs were not sufficiently united, and on Rockingham's death in July Fox explained to Richmond, who had hoped to succeed to the leadership, that they had both lost their chances by their too decided advocacy of Reform ; [1] the King had singled them out in the same way in 1780, when he wrote to North of Richmond's " strange conceit."

But the main assault of the Reformers in 1782 was led by a private member, a Shelburne Whig of little over a year's standing ; on May 7 William Pitt proposed in the House of Commons the appointment of a committee to inquire into the state of the representation. He maintained that the practice of the Constitution was untrue to its theory, the representatives being no longer connected with the people. The control established over boroughs by the Treasury and private individuals made urgent the need of limiting the corrupt influence of the Crown. He was supported by Mr. Secretary Fox, who disowned the theories of Richmond but demanded an addition of county members to strengthen the respectable landed and moneyed interests against the Crown. The motion was opposed mainly on the ground that its vagueness was dangerous while wild ideas were abroad, and it was lost by 141 votes to 161. The Reformers decided to reintroduce the question next session, and in the meantime urge the country to send petitions. The Yorkshire committee, now becoming converted to the total disfranchisement of some at least of the nomination boroughs, sent out a circular suggesting some measure of this nature. The Society for Constitutional Information also issued an address appealing to mechanics and artisans, an experiment in the direction of democracy.

Within the year events of vital importance to the cause of Reform occurred. The King's selection of Shelburne to succeed Rockingham broke up the Cabinet. Rockingham's followers left the administration, and Fox and Shelburne were henceforth open enemies. The Reforming forces were divided, but Shelburne, an avowed Reformer, was at the head of the Government. In the autumn the new Prime Minister declared to Wyvill his firm adherence to the principles of the Yorkshire association, but pointed out the difficulty of carrying any scheme

[1] Sir G. C. Lewis, *Administrations of Great Britain*, p. 29.

of disfranchisement, " against the manifest interest of many powerful members of Parliament." [1] Wyvill was not contented with the limited plan " which the Cabinet seemed disposed to promote," and the large Yorkshire meeting held in December, which sent to the Commons a petition for general reform with 10,000 signatures, declared for the disfranchisement of at least fifty boroughs with compensation. Sympathetic messages were received from many associations of counties and towns in the three kingdoms, though, according to Fox, the Westminster committee were averse to any specific proposals at the present time.

But any hopes raised by the Shelburne Cabinet perished on its defeat by the Coalition of the Portland Whigs and the Tories —the consequence of Fox's personal quarrel with Shelburne. The new Government left Reform an open question, and so shelved it as a practical matter. Francis Place testifies to the blasting influence of the Coalition of 1783 on Westminster politics, and in the country it certainly dealt a ruinous blow to confidence in Whig principles. When Pitt again on May 7 brought in the resolutions he had discussed with Wyvill, he was foredoomed to failure in spite of the support of Fox and a mass of petitions from England and Scotland. The other Secretary of State, Lord North, raised the cry of danger to the Constitution, and denied the responsibility of Parliament for any general distress ; the motion was lost by 144 votes in the fullest House known for many years. The damage was increased by the events of the session ; the bitterness connected with the East India Bill, and Pitt's defiance of the Coalition majority in the Commons, made it difficult for men opposed on those matters to join hands over anything else. This was fully seen at a meeting held at York in March 1784 ; a strong address condemning the Coalition was carried against the opposition of Lord Fitzwilliam and Lord John Cavendish. Many speakers openly declared their preference for the influence of the Crown to that of a corrupt aristocracy. How could the Whigs maintain without hypocrisy their exalted theory of party, when they were willing, apparently for the sake of office alone, to consent to the very negation of party government ? If this view could be maintained in the stronghold of Reform, the question was as good as settled ; it had lost its one popular argument. The

[1] *Wyvill Papers*, ii. 29.

meeting resulted in a large secession of members from the committee of the association.

The dissolution of 1784 disarmed the Rockingham Whigs for a generation ; the only hope lay in Pitt, now First Minister of the Crown. Encouraged by his promise of persevering support, the Yorkshire Reformers renewed their efforts in February 1785. The absence of rumours of Cabinet dissensions gave Wyvill grounds for hoping that Pitt would have the Government as a whole at his back when he came forward in April " to exert his whole power and credit as a man and as a minister " in favour of his main and final resolutions for Reform. These had been carefully discussed with Wyvill beforehand ; thirty-six boroughs were to be disfranchised with their own consent, giving up their members to London and certain counties. The members of any decayed boroughs beyond the thirty-six, which might apply for disfranchisement, were to be transferred gradually to growing towns. An automatic progressive system was thus established. A million was to be set apart for compensation. Dr. Holland Rose suggests that this last feature was the idea of Dundas,[1] but it is noteworthy that similar proposals were made by the delegates at London in March 1781, and by Wyvill to the Yorkshire committee in the summer of the same year. The vote was also to be extended to copyholders in counties. Again supported by a vast number of petitions, Pitt defended his scheme largely on the ground of its finality ; it " would comprehend all that a rational Reformer would think it necessary now or at any time to do." But all the glamour of Pitt's official position failed to carry the plan. Fox, soured by his treatment over the Westminster scrutiny,[2] joined with Burke in objecting to the principle of compensation, while North asked in vain for any signs of popular eagerness for the bill. It was lost by 74 votes, and even a meeting of the friends of Reform held shortly afterwards refused to endorse it. Reform was not again brought forward by a minister of the Crown till 1831, when the conditions, the causes, the objects, and the nature of the measure were completely different.

[1] *William Pitt and National Revival*, p. 200 *n*.
[2] " The contest greatly increased the personal animosity which divided the two great rivals, and it shook the confidence of Parliamentary Reformers in the sincerity of Pitt " (Lecky, *History of England in the Eighteenth Century*, v. 60).

This was the death of the Yorkshire Reform movement, though the association was not dissolved till next year ; Wyvill himself was forced to admit the uselessness of bringing up the question again in 1786, when returning prosperity and Pitt's purer government had disinclined the people to change. The same decrease of interest is visible in the Radical societies founded, at the same time as the more aristocratic bodies, to protest against the same grievances but on different principles.

Early in 1780 Constitutional Societies were formed at Cambridge and Nottingham. The assertion by the Cambridge society of all men's " natural right to life, liberty, and property " has a distinct smack of the Declaration of Independence. Admitting the theoretical excellence of the British Constitution, it demanded Reform to secure the practical emancipation of the Commons. The Nottingham society favoured radical Reform after the plan of Cartwright, the founder of the Society for Constitutional Information, which issued three addresses to the people, before it too succumbed to the prevailing languor. These Reformers were not yet definitely separated from the Whigs ; they differed from the main body chiefly in attaching less value to the Constitution as such, and more to abstract principles ; but they had not, any more than the orthodox Whigs, the ear of the country.

The Reform movement of the eighties failed because its ostensible objects were attained by other means. As it owed its rise to the mismanagement and corruption of George III's personal government, it sank with the mitigation of those abuses by the administrations of Rockingham and Pitt. Those grievances removed, there seemed no crying need for Reform while England was still predominantly agricultural. " Where the will of the nation is almost entirely homogeneous there is no injustice in selecting representatives by the haphazard methods then in use." [1] The farm labourers indeed were wholly unrepresented, but they had not yet reached the stage of political consciousness. Outside London democratic feeling hardly existed. Burke admitted that where the will of the people is clearly known it must of right prevail, but he had the country behind him when he rebuked those who would disturb the venerable stability of institutions in which they could prove

---

[1] J. H. Rose, *William Pitt and National Revival*, p. 11.

no practical defect. He complained that nine-tenths of the Reformers of his day stood on the ground of natural right and personal representation ; as long as this was so they could have no hope of carrying the country. The forces which later on made Reform a vital question had at this time scarcely passed out of their infancy in the great towns of the north ; until they reached their strength Reform was but one of several expedients for curbing royal domination, or an abstract conclusion drawn from premises not generally accepted. We may fairly believe that Pitt looked upon it in this light ; certainly for his own justification in dropping Reform he might plead the unfriendly, or at least apathetic, attitude of the King, the Cabinet, the country gentlemen who formed the House of Commons, and the nation as a whole. Only a few years passed before Fox too learnt to his cost that you cannot force liberty on a people.

Even before the full thunders of the French Revolution burst upon Europe, Reformers' ears were awake to its first rumblings. The interest which had never wholly died was revived in 1788 by the centenary of the English Revolution. Naturally enough the various Revolution Societies did not eschew politics at their anniversary dinners, and in April 1790 a general meeting of the friends of Reform was held in order to renew exertions in the country. In the Commons too, while the nation was still listless and unterrified, Henry Flood proposed to forestall revolution by the moderate but novel measure of adding 100 members elected by the resident householders of counties. The arguments by which it was supported were symptoms of a change in thought ; they were based not on the need of resistance to monarchy but on the knowledge of the people since the Middlesex election that they were not duly represented. However the request of Pitt, now strengthened by the unnatural attitude of the Whigs in the Regency debates, was enough to secure the withdrawal of the motion. Six years of office had made Pitt the resolute champion of the established order ; but cynics may speculate on what would have happened if the Prince of Wales had become king or regent in 1789 and brought the Whigs into power. Is it possible that Fox would have kept himself in office by borough patronage and Pitt have renewed his advocacy of Reform ? Such questions cannot be solved by history, and in any case the whole trend of English politics was soon changed by the course of events in France.

At first, however, the general sentiment was one of neutrality, if not of sympathy, towards those who would give France a constitution. Fox's exultation at the fall of the Bastille is well known, and even Pitt was favourably inclined. The more advanced Reformers went further, and entered into communication with the French ; an address of congratulation, drawn up by Dr. Price, was sent to the National Assembly by the London Revolution Society, fresh from their centenary rejoicings. Delighted by the cordiality with which the address was received at Paris, the English society proceeded to exchange sentiments of admiration and eternal friendship with various French bodies, among them the famous Jacobin Club, which at this time and for some time to come was pledged to constitutional monarchy. Many similar societies were formed in the towns of England and Scotland, in the fond hope that an age of international peace and love was beginning.

But in the meantime English sympathy was quickly changing into alarm and disapproval. Each successive development in France drove all parties to adopt positions more extreme and intense than before. Almost before the revolution was a fact, Burke had launched at it the fulness of his anger, and Pitt seemed willing to sacrifice everything for the sake of order and security. At Norwich and Birmingham fierce anti-revolutionary riots broke out, and the house and laboratory of the famous scientist Priestley were gutted by the mob.

All who were not shocked by the new principles were inspired by them with renewed zeal for Reform. Burke's *Reflections* were promptly answered by a host of pamphlets, of which the most famous were the reply by Mary Wollstonecraft, the mother of Mary Shelley, James Mackintosh's *Vindiciæ Gallicæ*, and the First Part of Tom Paine's *Rights of Man*. The last of these had far the greatest influence, and was in fact for at least the next forty years the main political literature of the working classes of England, among whom it won an enormous circulation. Paine cared nothing for the official Whigs, believing Parliament to be incapable of reforming itself ; he looked forward to a National Convention. However, associations with more orthodox views were being formed in very different levels of society. In January 1792 Thomas Hardy, a shoemaker, founded the London

Corresponding Society for the reform of parliamentary representation, with a subscription of a penny a week ; this claims to be the first political club formed by English working men. As early as October 1790 a Constitutional Society was organised at Manchester, whose members paid half a guinea yearly. Highest in the scale, with a subscription of five guineas, was a society formed in April 1792 by the left wing of the Whig party in Parliament, and known as the Friends of the People.

Among those responsible for this bold venture were Charles Grey, W. H. Lambton, George Tierney,[1] and Samuel Whitbread,[2] but even such advanced Whigs as Fox and the Duke of Bedford held aloof. The Friends of the People ran risks not less from would-be allies below than from enemies above ; soon after their foundation they received through Cartwright a letter of friendship from the Society for Constitutional Information, advocating a declaration of rights with full radical paraphernalia on the model of Tom Paine. Wyvill and his friends speak of the alarm to moderate Reformers caused by Paine's book, and the new society thought it wise to renounce his abstract principles and to reject Cartwright's overtures. The Friends of the People were essentially Whig in their acceptance of the 1688 settlement.

They were accordingly indignant, as were the other Reform societies, at Pitt's proclamation against seditious meetings, issued in May 1792, which they regarded as aimed against themselves and intended to split up their party. It was certainly successful in doing so. When Fox and Shelburne, now Marquis of Lansdowne, defended the society and attacked the proclamation in Parliament, they were looked upon with horror by the majority of the Whigs. In December there followed a second proclamation against sedition ; the Government were alarmed at the addresses of various English bodies to the French Convention, and had convicted Paine of seditious libel. Certainly all their disclaimers of revolutionary intentions served the Friends of the People little when, after a last vain appeal to Pitt

---

[1] George Tierney (1756–1830) led the Opposition during Fox's secession from the Commons, and later between 1818 and 1821 ; he is best known on account of the duel he fought with Pitt.

[2] Samuel Whitbread (1758–1815), a Nonconformist, succeeded to his father's brewery. In 1789 he married the sister of Charles Grey, and soon afterwards entered politics as a Whig. Eventually he became one of the leaders of the advanced wing of the party.

by Wyvill to meet the people's eager hopes by a measure of Reform, they laid before Parliament on May 6, 1793, a document which Burke described as an "infamous libel" on the whole system of representation. As Pitt's scheme of 1785 gives the best idea of the views of Reformers before the revolution, so this petition of 1793, based on an elaborate report, is the manifesto of the men who welcomed the great change. The petitioners, who had chosen for their spokesman Charles Grey, the young member for Northumberland, declared their readiness to prove that 71 peers and 91 commoners procured between them the return of 306 members of Parliament—an easy majority of the House. This "criminal impeachment" of the existing order was followed by a motion for a committee. By rejecting the motion by 282 votes to 41 the House showed the effect of the French Revolution. In 1797 another huge majority defeated the definite plan of Reform suggested by the Friends of the People, including the addition of twenty-one county members and the extension of the vote to copy, lease, and householders, with triennial parliaments and the abolition of plural voting.

There had indeed appeared a fundamental difference of temperament between the two wings of those who had united to carry economic reform eleven years before. The opinions of these post-Revolution Reformers are more democratic; they base their measures rather on the claims of the people than on the iniquities of the Crown or borough mongers. Fox spoke the true democratic note when he said: "If the King and the House of Lords were unnecessary and useless branches of the Constitution, let them be dismissed and abolished, for the people were not made for them but they for the people."[1] Burke, on the other hand, said: "Neither the few nor the many have a right to act merely by their will, in any matter connected with duty, trust, engagement, or obligation. The Constitution of a country being once settled upon some compact, tacit or expressed, there is no power existing of force to alter it, without the breach of the covenant or the consent of all the parties."[2]

Shortly before these words were written Burke had broken personally from Fox; he was followed by that once ardent Reformer, the Duke of Richmond. In 1794 the great schism in

[1] Hansard, *Parliamentary History*, xxx. 921.
[2] *Appeal from the New to the Old Whigs.*

the Whig party took place ; Portland, Fitzwilliam, Spencer, and Windham rallied to the standard of authority and threw in their lot with Pitt. They held with Burke that when men act from imagination and ideas there can be no bound to their passions and no hope of their halting within the limits of constitutional government.

The influence of the secession of the conservative Whigs on the prospects of Parliamentary Reform was so great that it is in danger of exaggeration. The remnant were ludicrously small in numbers, but they were united under a leader of compelling attraction, and pledged as a party to the cause. The secession was made from them, not by them, and when the reaction began after the time of stress it was to the Foxite Whigs and their principles that stragglers came in. Their very isolation had made their position conspicuous. The Whigs of the early nineteenth century derived in apostolical descent from Fox, not from Burke. Is then the Whigs' support of Reform when Canning and the followers of Pitt were against it to be traced to the secession of the Portland section in 1794 ? Before an answer is given, it should be remembered that, though the Foxites held up the banner of Reform in the tempest, it became much soiled and tattered in their misfortunes. By 1810 even Grey had retreated from his bold position of 1793, and as the years went on his hopes and energies sank. After the war, though the leaders were sound at heart, the reconversion of the Whig party to Reform was a necessary, and not a short or easy process. This being so, it appears doubtful whether, if some or all of the more conservative Whigs had remained in the party ranks, they would have seriously delayed the adoption of Reform when the eagerness of manufacturing and middle-class England made it, as it had never been before, a practical and profitable cry.

On the other hand it is hardly possible to exaggerate the importance of the part played by Fox and his little band in Parliament. On divisions they were of no account ; in the eyes of the country they had forfeited all reputation for patriotism and even sanity. The value of their work lay in the open witness they bore to a faith which Pitt might smother but could not utterly stamp out. They preserved a link between the governing class and the inarticulate political sense of the populace, and in the evil days after the war, when this sense found passionate

B

voice, it was of vital importance that the cry for Reform without should find an echo within the walls of Parliament. Except for these few aristocrats, there was no channel for the will of the people to force itself upon a House of Commons packed with the nominees of landowners and peers. Privileged bodies are not in the habit of reforming themselves, and borough-mongers laughed at a general election. Finding every constitutional means of agitation blocked, English Liberals must have followed their brothers on the Continent in the dark ways of conspiracy and intrigue. The struggle for Reform would have become a class war waged with lawless violence. From such a catastrophe the Foxite Whigs saved the country. They stood between the living and the dead, and broke the shock of revolution.

Yet it was not an easy nor a pleasant task to uphold principles which to the rest of upper-class Europe seemed blasphemous and indeed ungentlemanly. Cut off from power and honour, these men of fashion must have been grievously tempted to retire from the hopeless conflict and drown their convictions in the pleasures of the brilliant society they could so well appreciate. Their firmness was only made possible by those qualities at which their critics jeer. Party spirit, pride, and indifference to opinion, often marred the fortunes of the Whigs, but to an unpopular and derided minority they proved a priceless boon. The storms of obloquy which assailed them only stiffened their obstinate resolve.

In 1792-1793 repression was highly popular. It became difficult for the Reform societies to find rooms where they could assemble in peace, and county meetings were impossible. " The impression made on the publick by the execution of Lewis XVI was so deep and so universal," wrote Lord Holland, " that an Englishman was hardly permitted, in publick or in private, to express any opinion on politicks without first pronouncing an anathema against the French Convention." [1] Naturally then those who were known or believed to have been in correspondence with the Convention had little mercy to hope for from British juries when the Government chose to prosecute. Scotland was the first to feel the new temper. Here the basis of the representation was even narrower than in England ; in 1788 forty-six of the sixty-six royal burghs had petitioned for Reform, and had

[1] *Memoirs of the Whig Party*, p. 28.

found a champion in Sheridan.[1]  But under the despotic though
beneficent rule of Henry Dundas their cause was hopeless.  The
lairds who nominally returned the thirty county members were
his obedient tools ;  the whole patronage of the country seemed
concentrated in his hands, and, save for a few Edinburgh lawyers,
the diminutive party of opposition was without leaders or spokes-
men.  The Government, in the words of Cockburn, " engrossed
almost the whole wealth, and rank, and public office of the
country, and at least three-quarters of the population. . . .
Jacobinism was a term denoting everything alarming and hateful, and every political objector was a Jacobin." [2]

By the end of 1792 Dundas felt apprehensive of the rise of
Reform societies in many of the towns of Scotland ; information, bought and unbought, poured in.  Prosecutions for sedition
began in 1793, obscure pamphleteers and publishers being first
attacked.  By Scotch law the juries were chosen by the judge
and sheriff, and often the prisoners, who had no right of per-
emptory challenge, preferred not to face their accusers ; many
of the cases were tried before Lord Justice Clerk Braxfield, the
savage original of Weir of Hermiston.  At length a sentence
of transportation for fourteen years was secured against Thomas
Muir, a young advocate whose main offence was having formed
societies in aid of Parliamentary Reform.[3]  In the trial of a
Unitarian divine called Palmer, the judge actually advised the
jury that, as universal suffrage tended to subvert the Constitution, it was for them to consider whether agitation to
promote it did not in itself constitute sedition.[4]  Palmer was
sentenced to seven years' transportation.

In England several other trials followed on the conviction
of Paine.  The actual Reform associations, however, among
which the London Corresponding Society, under the guidance
of its founder Thomas Hardy, was the most conspicuous, continued to escape official prosecution by extreme caution and
by repeated assertions that their aims were limited to reform
of Parliament.  But proposals were made in the summer of 1793
which led in October to the meeting at Edinburgh of the so-called
British Convention, an assembly of delegates from about fifty
English and Scotch Reforming bodies.  A similar step had been

[1] Veitch, p. 243.      [2] *Memorials of His Time*, p. 82.
[3] *State Trials*, xxiii. 118 ;  Veitch, pp. 255 ff.
[4] Veitch, p. 261.

taken in calmer times by the gentlemanly Reformers of the eighties, but the word convention now had an ugly sound, and the assembly was forcibly dissolved. There is no evidence that the Convention proposed anything more deadly than Radical Reform ; nevertheless a new series of sedition trials began, and three of the delegates were sentenced to transportation for fourteen years. The only two prisoners against whom treason was proved were a government spy and his dupe. " It was by these proceedings," wrote Lord Cockburn, " more than by any other wrong, that the spirit of discontent justified itself throughout the rest of that age. It was to them that peaceful Reformers appealed for the practical answer to those who pretended to uphold our whole Scotch system as needing no change." [1]

The English associations were not long spared. Indeed the London Corresponding Society invited attack by its expressed approval and intended imitation of the Edinburgh Convention, as did the Society for Constitutional Information by an unwise address and toasts, though both still protested their perfect legality. On May 12, 1794, the secretaries of the two bodies were arrested, and their houses raided for papers. The same day the House of Commons appointed a Committee of Secrecy to investigate the suspected plot. Hardy and Horne Tooke and eleven others were interrogated by the Privy Council, and eventually three of them were put on trial. Against none of them, though confronted with masses of documents, could a conviction be obtained.[2] The Government had failed to find evidence of the great conspiracy. Nevertheless Pitt, who had been called as a witness by Horne Tooke, had broken the offending societies. The Society for Constitutional Information collapsed almost at once ; the London Corresponding Society maintained itself till 1797, but before that the burst of loyalty resulting from the attempt on the King's life, together with the two Treason Acts of 1795, had made Reform yet more hopeless. Lastly, in 1799, the Corresponding Society and some others were specifically suppressed by Act of Parliament.

Pitt's defence for his repressive measures was that in view of the European situation nothing like disaffection could be tolerated at home. To justify him, it is necessary that something more than mere constitutional agitation should be proved

[1] *Memorials*, p. 102 ; Veitch, pp. 288–294.
[2] Veitch, pp. 309–317 ; *State Trials*, xxiv.

against the proscribed societies. Lack of evidence long entitled Pitt to the benefit of the doubt. But of late the documents of the Reformers have been ransacked ; we know what information was at Pitt's disposal ; and on the strength of our knowledge we must decide against him. The proceedings of the various societies were frequently unwise and sometimes culpable ; but nothing whatever of the nature of an attempt at organised insurrection has been discovered. After Pitt's first proclamation, Talleyrand, no obtuse observer, wrote to his Foreign Office : " Those curiously deceive themselves who regard England as on the eve of Revolution. . . . The truth is that the mass of the nation is generally indifferent to all those political discussions which cause so much stir amongst us. . . . It is pretended that beneath the mask of a reform, long demanded by justice and reason, there can be seen the intention of destroying a Constitution equally dear to the peers whose privileges it consecrates, to the rich whom it protects, and to the entire body of the nation to whom it assures all the liberty that a people, methodical and slow by character, can wish to enjoy, a people which is occupied without intermission by its commercial interests, and does not wish to turn aside from them to occupy itself with public affairs." [1]

By the suppression of the Radicals the Foxite Whigs were left as the only open adherents of Reform. With the Radicals indeed they had little sympathy, though they protested against the cruelty of their punishment. Their own troubles were sufficient. Lord Holland gives the strength of the Opposition as forty in the Commons and four in the Lords, and their influence in the country was no greater. Disgusted by the hopeless struggle, several of them for a time abandoned the farce of attendance in Parliament. Their utterances are generally despondent, and they look rather to the future than the present ; but Reform seems a constant item in their suggested programmes, and it is likely that the faith was deeply burnt into their minds by this time of fiery trial.

The new century opened more brightly. Pitt's long reign was broken by difficulties with regard to Ireland, and his suc-

[1] Despatch of May 23, 1792. See Veitch, p. 209. The opinion given above is that of Mr. Veitch himself, the greater part of whose book is devoted to the question. See also chap. vii. of Dr. Holland Rose's *William Pitt and the Great War*.

cessor Addington looked favourably on the Whigs. Both on this occasion, however, and in 1804, when Pitt wished for a fusion of parties, the King's dislike of Fox was the stumbling-block. Still the negotiations led to a rapprochement with the Grenville Whigs, and Fox was able to write to Grey in October 1804 : " Opposition seems now restored, at least to what it was before the Duke of Portland's desertion and the other adverse circumstances of the times." [1]

The short-lived administration of All the Talents gave the Whigs little opportunity of showing their mettle, and none of introducing Reform. To say nothing of the presence in the Cabinet of such anti-Reformers as Grenville and Sidmouth, the dying leader's hands were sufficiently full. " The Slave Trade and Peace are two such glorious things," he wrote to Holland, " I cannot give them up even to you. If I can manage *them* I will then retire." The deaths of Pitt and Fox began what Mr. Sichel well calls the age of the Epigoni, and deeply affected the prospects of Reformers. The nature of the fascination and influence exercised by Fox on his colleagues and followers is peculiarly hard to estimate and understand from the mere written record of what he said and did. We remember some few generous words, some chivalrous actions, which haunted even his enemies throughout their lives, but the real force of his attraction must have depended so much on his warm living personality,—the jolly gallant bearing and the lazy smile. His early and his later extravagances, his frequent lapses of judgment, were as nothing beside these human touches of broad sympathy which gave the memory of his opinions an almost religious sanction to the minds of several generations of Whig statesmen. His nephew, Lord Holland, spoke of him as " the best and greatest man of our time," and long afterwards Lord Grey and Lord John Russell, standing respectively at the consummation and the beginning of their careers, were both proud to speak of his example as the stimulus and guide of their political lives. Most of his followers were naturally much more bound than Fox by the ordinary Whig prejudices of birth and clique, and it is likely that his influence was a powerful factor in keeping many of them true to democratic principles, and so in maintaining the tie between Parliament and people.

[1] *Life and Opinions of Charles, 2nd Earl Grey*, p. 94.

After the loss of their one chief of genius, the leadership of the Whigs in the Commons now fell in due course to Charles Grey, who from his first entrance into Parliament in 1786, at the age of twenty-two, had been the admirer and firm friend of Fox. The eloquence of which his maiden speech had shown brilliant promise in the judgment of all was constantly exercised in opposition to the Government's foreign and domestic policy. Nevertheless he seems to have soon regarded the venture of the Friends of the People, whose spokesman he had been in the Commons, as premature and mistaken ; certainly in later life he regretted it, and by temperament he was anything but a hot-headed revolutionary. The secession of 1797 was a far more characteristic step. Great as his parliamentary talents were acknowledged to be, Grey's inclination was all for the intimate circle of his relations and friends, who bear witness to his warm and generous nature. To others he seemed often irritable and supercilious, and, if we may trust the Holland House tradition, was never really popular. Subject to fits of deep depression which took the life out of his beliefs, he was found fickle and unsatisfactory, and himself complained that he was judged by an unreasonable standard of consistency. His life was doubly affected in 1801 by his father's acceptance, without his own previous knowledge, of a peerage from Addington, and by the removal of his home to Howick, his uncle's house in Northumberland. Henceforward the distance from London, together with his natural distaste for strenuous political life, served to keep him away from Westminster more than his party liked. At the time of the Peace of Amiens his distrust of the French Consular government cut him off to some extent from whole-hearted sympathy with Fox, but in the years which followed the two acted together, Grey refusing to entertain the idea of taking office without his chief. In 1806 he was given the post of First Lord of the Admiralty, which the requests for preferment he received from place-hunters almost persuaded him to resign. On Fox's death, although his succession to the Earldom was expected shortly, and in fact occurred next year, he was promoted to be Foreign Secretary and leader of the House of Commons. The position was one of extreme discomfort, owing to the scruples of the half-demented King, the growing indifference of the Prince of Wales, and the divisions in the Cabinet.

The sacrifice of principle involved in the Coalition of 1806 had been regretted by some Whigs, and when the Government fell after little more than a year the division between the two sections of the party was plain. At the general election the Whigs were completely discomfited ; much of their unpopularity was attributed to the conduct of Sheridan, who was defeated at Westminster by Burdett owing, it was said, to his arrogant defiance of the aristocracy and the Reformers alike. The Whigs had all the vested interests against them ; except for their one great measure which abolished the slave-trade, their venture of 1806 had failed entirely and left them in nearly as discredited a condition as in 1784. It was their impotence in office which decided William Cobbett, now turning his vast energies to politics, that nothing in the way of Reform was to be hoped from Parliament.

The loss of Grey in the House of Commons, followed in 1809 by that of Lord Henry Petty, the son of Shelburne and heir to the traditions of his name, was a further blow to the party, and George Ponsonby by no means filled his place. Some energy was supplied by an advanced wing, which began to act about this time under the headship of Whitbread and Romilly, and included certain among the new generation of the great houses, such as Lords Tavistock and Althorp, but the real force of the Opposition was Henry Brougham, brought into Parliament in 1809 by the Duke of Bedford, after his good services in working the press during the general election. Brougham was never popular with the House, but his immense activities both within and without it soon marked him as one of the foremost figures of the country. His keen vulgar features, shown in the picture in the National Portrait Gallery, testify to his weakness and to his strength. The rise of Brougham was also important as forming a link with Edinburgh, where a small but very able group of Whigs, distinguished in law and literature alike, had lately raised their capital to a high pitch of eminence by the foundation of the *Edinburgh Review*. Anything of the nature of a public meeting to spread Reforming opinions was as yet unthinkable, and the *Review* articles were rarely political, but the Whig point of view was put before the world with a brilliance that defied mere contempt.[1]

The inner politics of these few years are tangled and paltry.

---

[1] Cockburn, *Memorials*, pp. 166, 260-263.

Some five times before the end of the war communications of a more or less official character were opened with the Opposition, with a view to their joining the Government ; all were futile. This result was due partly to the fickleness and insincerity of the Prince Regent, partly to the inevitable stumbling-block of Catholic Emancipation, and largely to the unconciliatory behaviour of the Whig leaders. For their determination, often repeated, to hold by their party they are worthy of praise, but on at least one occasion their refusal to take office was based on trivial grounds and was certainly not encouraging to any whc might have hoped for a stable administration from Grey and Grenville. A by-product of these feeble negotiations was the increasing distaste felt by the Prince for Grey, a sentiment of more than temporary importance.

Such discussion of Reform as took place in these years did not correspond to any enthusiasm in Parliament or in the country. In 1807 Francis Place revived democratic politics by organising the Westminster electorate, Fox's old constituency, to bring in Sir Francis Burdett, a Radical baronet of great wealth, who had witnessed some of the scenes of the French Revolution. To borrow a famous phrase, Burdett had a heart of gold but a head of feathers. The carefully staged scene, in which the officers who came to arrest him found him expounding Magna Carta to his child, caused general ridicule ; he was sometimes no better appreciated by the Radical meetings at which his tall, graceful, aristocratic figure looked strangely incongruous. He appeared in 1809 as the spokesman of a school of thought in little sympathy with ears attuned by Burke to the prescriptive glories of the Constitution. In Parliament Burdett showed bitter dislike and contempt for the orthodox Whigs, and the failure of his motion for household suffrage and equal electoral divisions was all that he could expect. The official demand for Reform was made by Grey, who expressly limited himself to moderate proposals, and disclaimed in his own name and that of Fox all merely speculative opinions. Two other motions in the Commons for moderate Reform were also lost by large majorities and excited little interest.

Grey's speech of 1810 was taken by Place as the mark of his apostasy. This was natural ; but Holland had also to defend it to a youthful Whig who might have been expected to look with more reverence on the head of his party. In a most interesting letter to Lord John Russell, then just eighteen years old, Holland discusses Grey's right to be considered " a *Whig* or a friend of Liberty," especially on the question of Reform. Admitting that his early zeal had cooled, he claims that his leader's views are all that a good Whig should hold, and professes his own very moderate creed. With this Russell should have been satisfied, for in 1811 he spoke of Holland as " the only remaining Whig in England," to the amused distress of his father, who as an old Friend of the People claimed to share the title, and, if we may believe Whitbread, with good reason. But in fact, as Holland himself agreed, there was so much dissension in the party that it is impossible to say what the orthodox view was. Perhaps three articles of Jeffrey's in the *Edinburgh* come as near it as anything else, and they are mild in the extreme.[1] Declaring his loyalty to the general frame of the Constitution, the writer eschews all merely theoretical perfection. It may be desirable to extend the scope of popular election, but not at the risk of disturbing " the balance of the Constitution," which now means that the monarchy, the aristocracy, and the people should all be represented in the Lower House, so as to avoid a deadlock. Placemen and nominees of the great houses should therefore not be wholly excluded. " We are not much afraid of the influence of noble families. It is not in general a debasing or ungenerous influence." Nevertheless knowledge is increasing among the people, and if they desire it, " the people must be the keepers of their own freedom." " The great body of the nation appears to us to be divided into two violent and most pernicious factions ;—the courtiers, who are almost for arbitrary power—and the democrats, who are almost for revolution and republicanism. Between these stand a small, but most respectable band—the friends of liberty and of order—the Old Constitutional Whigs of England. . . . It is to the popular side that the friends of the Constitution must turn themselves. . . . We laugh at the idea of there being any danger in disfranchising a few rotten boroughs, or communicating the elective franchise to a great number of respectable citizens. . . . The people have far more wealth and far more intelligence now, than they had in former times ; and therefore they ought to have, and they must have, more political power."

---

[1] *Edinburgh Review*, July 1807, July 1809, January 1810.

Such was the torpid condition of the question during the continuance of war with France. High rents and profits combined with patriotic fervour to disincline the country for innovation. Desire for constitutional change seemed almost treasonable while the Constitution was waging a struggle of life and death against the Republic or the Empire. Only two counties were contested at the general election of 1812. This year, however, the advanced Reformers of the nineties, including Wyvill and Cartwright, at last thought it safe to emerge from their retirement, and the Union and Hampden clubs were founded to propagate Reform. Both of these were highly respectable, and branch societies were founded about the country. In 1813 the unwearying Major Cartwright set out on a missionary tour, visiting thirty-five towns ; in a similar tour in 1815 he included Edinburgh, where, Cockburn tells us, no paper dared report his lecture. Nevertheless even in Scotland things were changing, and the fact that an anti-slavery meeting could be held in 1814 was considered a great event ; it was the " first assembling of the people for a public object that had occurred for twenty years." [1] In England, too, the rise of the great manufacturers, Tory though most of them were, challenged the power of the old aristocracy, and even their despised operatives were making themselves felt. [2] At last in 1815 the final peace settlement transferred the tension from foreign to home affairs, and a complete change of spirit took place, not least in the matter of Reform. In the course of the next few years it was vehemently canvassed from many points of view with a zeal, a bitterness, and a passionate sense of reality, such as it had never aroused before. The temporary distress, which might have been in any case expected to follow on the dislocation of industry in a time of transition, was aggravated by a succession of bad harvests. The general dissatisfaction meant a revival of strength to the powers opposed to Government. In 1816 began a popular agitation for Radical Reform which in three years almost rose to revolution point, and then subsided as suddenly as it had sprung up.

The forces of opposition were of the most various descrip-

---

[1] Cockburn, *Memorials*, pp. 282, 309.

[2] See Halévy, *Histoire de l'Angleterre au XIXe siècle*, pp. 118, 126, 192 : " De 1810 à 1815 à Londres et dans les provinces, l'émeute est permanente."

tion, ranging from the official Whigs by gradual stages down to Jacobins and republicans, and lower still to the Manchester "Blanketeers" and the wretches concerned in the "Derbyshire insurrection." Though occasionally working together for definite and temporary ends, none of these sections ever really united or indeed showed the least cordiality to one another. Probably the greatest power was William Cobbett. Born of a labourer's family at Farnham, he had served in the army in America long enough to feel a deep disgust for the stupidity and corruption of the public service. Disillusioned by the events of 1806–7 of any hopes of rational improvement on parliamentary lines, he joined the extreme Radicals and applied himself to the political education of his own class by means of the *Political Register*, a paper started by him as early as 1802. Besides an intense hatred of corrupt government, on which subject his ideas were often of the wildest and most exaggerated, Cobbett's ruling motive was a passionate love of the soil of England and all that he associated with it. The rescue of the agricultural population was the darling object to which he devoted the splendid, though unscrupulous, vigour of his written and spoken eloquence. The misery of 1816 awoke in him indignation against the governing class and a keen desire for Parliamentary Reform as a root of blessings to the poor. He proceeded to tour the country, urging his hearers to petition for Reform, and in November lowered the price of his *Register* to twopence. The effect of this at a time when ordinary newspapers cost not less than sevenpence was most startling. The Middlesex election had shown one latent force in English politics; the agitation aroused by Cobbett revealed another not less full of possibilities. "The labouring classes," he wrote, "seemed as if they had never heard a word on politics before."[1] By March 1817 he had made the country too hot to hold him, and left for America, a fugitive from the combined terrors of the laws of sedition and of debt.

But though Cobbett was a demagogue of the first water, he was by no means a revolutionary. He urged the people to enrol themselves in Hampden clubs about the country and eschew violence, and he was actually a moderate Reformer

[1] *Political Register*, August 2, 1817; quoted by Carlyle, *Life of Cobbett*, p. 194.

compared with such men as " Orator " Hunt and Bamford.[1] The main demonstration of these extremists, who stood for universal suffrage and the whole Radical programme after the fashion of Paine, not excluding certain Spencean doctrines of land-nationalisation, was held in the Spa Fields in December 1816. Their resolutions were passed in spite of the protests of Burdett and even Cartwright, representatives in the eyes of Hunt of " a faction composed principally of petty shopkeepers and little tradesmen "—" a privileged class above the artisans." [2] But the " faction " itself was not idle, for in 1817 delegates from the country branches of the Hampden Club met in London to consider the drafting of a Reform bill. Highly respectable as were these bourgeois clubs, to the Government of the Regency all forms of associations seemed equally dangerous, and in the spring the Habeas Corpus Act was suspended and an Act passed against seditious meetings. In Scotland, too, there was a revival of State trials, and one prosecution for administering unlawful oaths aroused great excitement.[3] To those who considered the decline in strength of the Radicals since the early years of the war, it might appear that the authorities were creating disaffection by their efforts to prevent it. .

Burdett himself, with Cochrane, the brilliant but unlucky sea-captain, and a few others, was the imperfect spokesman in Parliament of that very efficient group which sat at the feet of Jeremy Bentham, the friend of Shelburne, and framer of constitutions for two continents. Bentham had long been pounding the world with his pregnant universal theories, but it was not apparently till 1809 that he turned his mind to Parliamentary Reform. The *Catechism* of that year, which insisted in characteristic fashion on Probity, Appropriate intellectual aptitude, and Appropriate active talent, as the necessary qualifications for members of Parliament, was followed in 1817 and 1819 by the more elaborate *Plan of Parliamentary Reform* and *Radical Reform Bill*. Bentham cries out at the degraded state of the country ; corruption is everywhere, the King is Corrupter General. It was this pervading deadening corruption which

[1] Samuel Bamford, a Lancashire weaver, author of *Passages in the Life of a Radical*.

[2] *Memoirs of Henry Hunt*, ii. 75, 82 ; quoted in Kent's *English Radicals*, p. 265.

[3] Cockburn, *Memorials*, p. 325 ff.

stirred the Utilitarian soul to fury ; its desire was an efficient business Government. " Honourable House incorrigible," Bentham quaintly complains. " Sole remedy in principle— Democratic Ascendency. Remedy in detail—Radical Reform." Self-interest generally governs individuals, classes always. The only hope for democracy is in the accidental coincidence of its advantages with those of the Whig party. " The Tories are the people's avowed enemies. Man must change his nature ere, to any radically remedial purpose, the Whigs—the great body of the Whigs—can be their friends." [1]   But real sympathy is not necessary ; a temporary community of interests may suffice. " On no occasion, under the ever-increasing weight of the yoke of oppression and misrule, from any hand other than that of the parliamentary Whigs can the people receive any the slightest chance—(talk not of relief—for that is at all times out of the question) but for retardation of increase." There were coming to be many at this time who would reply that, if this was the best that Parliament could offer, the people had better take their relief into their own hands. But the Utilitarians were essentially pacific. In his *Reform Bill* Bentham states the four principles he himself favours, comprised in the formula—" secret, universal, equal and annual suffrage." The second principle he qualifies by the exclusion of women, children, lunatics, and confined criminals. To soothe the nervous he declares that " in Pennsylvania, for these forty years, Radicalism has been supreme ; Radicalism without Monarchy or Aristocracy : Radicalism without control, and not any the slightest shock has property there ever received." . . . " Life is not worth more to yawners than to labourers." He prefers an educational qualification. The ballot alone would be a great part of Reform. " Mr. Brougham would second the motion, or a laugh would run through Westmoreland as often as his eloquence ventured to indulge itself in a complaint of Lowther influence." [2]

The Benthamites were as yet too isolated to exert any great influence on the political thought of the time. As far removed from Rousseau's point of view as from Burke's, they despised and were despised by the Radical extremists, while they had no

---

[1] *Plan of Parliamentary Reform*, p. cccxxvii.

[2] The parliamentary representation of Cumberland and Westmorland, Brougham's own county, was in the hands of Lord Lonsdale, who was said to return eight members.

sympathy with Cobbett's bludgeon methods, though recognising his great importance. With the official Whigs they hardly came into contact except through their own parliamentary section. Such a case arose in 1817, when Lord Grey and his followers decided to oppose the suspension of the Habeas Corpus Act, at the price of breaking up their long alliance with the Grenville Whigs. Seeing that Grey was himself inclined to believe in " the existence of a very extensive conspiracy and plan of insurrection," his confidence in the power of the ordinary law was a courageous assertion of principle. His young critic's verdict on the situation was that " the Opposition have succeeded in shaking all confidence in Ministers, but have obtained none for themselves." [1] For the confidence of the extreme Reformers they had little desire. Far from grateful to those who might at times consider a Whig government as a least of evils, they bitterly complained of the damage done to the cause of constitutional Reform by seditious agitators who " availed themselves of the elaborate blunders of Major Cartwright, the able mischief of William Cobbett, and the brawling eloquence . . . of Hunt, to promote the cry for universal suffrage and annual parliaments, among a class whose sufferings give to the prospect of change, whatever name it may assume, the pleasing colours of improvement." Such feelings, as described in retrospect by Lord Holland, were not a hopeful basis on which to unite a party of Reform, even had Whig pride allowed it. " Parliamentary Reform, however, was not yet adopted as an indispensable article in the Whig creed ; nor did the Burdettites pledge themselves to act as a party in bringing Whigs into power." [2]

The dissolution of 1818 was followed by a general election, at which, if the sense of the people had been at all adequately represented, it is hardly possible to believe that Lord Liverpool's Government could have been returned to power, considering the unpopularity of the Sidmouth circular and other measures of the preceding year. This lends colour to Disraeli's assertion that in the ordinary course of things the Whigs should have come in in 1819 ; finding that the existing electorate could never give them a majority, they were, he says, for the first time converted as party to Reform. [3]

[1] *Early Correspondence of Lord John Russell*, i. 189, 190.
[2] Holland, *Further Memoirs*, pp. 249, 254.
[3] *Coningsby*, Book II. ch. i.

Whether this bold statement be true or not, the year 1819 is. in any case of great importance in the growth of the Reform movement. Events occurred which forced Reformers to declare themselves, and differences of opinion become clearly marked. The first incident of note was the Westminster by-election, made necessary by the death of Samuel Romilly, which led to an open clash between the two wings of the Opposition. Romilly himself was when he died leader of the Whigs in the Commons, and at the same time one of the more advanced group, though even he was objected to by Bentham " as a lawyer, a Whig, and a friend to only moderate Reform " ; [1] still his constant and merciful reforming energies had won him the respect of all parties, so that his loss at this moment was in any case serious to the cause of peace. Shortly before the election Grey and his son-in-law, J. G. Lambton, had forcibly denounced the Radical Reformers ; Hobhouse, the popular candidate, replied with such violence that the Whigs put up George Lamb against him. Hobhouse was beaten ; he lost some votes by the rivalry of Hunt, but his defeat was due to the aristocracy.

The first session of the new Parliament showed the width of the cleavage. The vague suggestions of Tierney, now leader of the Opposition in the Commons, and a timid attempt to check bribery, after flagrant corruption at Grampound, contrast vividly with the keenness of the Radicals on the motion brought forward by Burdett on July 1. Burdett declared that he had waited vainly for the Whigs to introduce their moderate and rational measures, and protested against the corrupt abuses of the parliamentary system. At the late election, it was asserted, many members had promised to support Reform, and Lord John Russell expressed his belief in triennial parliaments and the disfranchisement of corrupt boroughs. But the damning arguments on the other side were the divisions among Reformers and the visionary schemes of the Radicals. The motion for a committee was lost by 58 votes to 153 : the year before Burdett had been in a minority of one on a proposal of Radical Reform. But numerous petitions, and the very fact of the debate, showed that the question was attracting serious interest, and when Parliament rose it was kept alive in the country by crowded meetings. On August 16 was the famous " massacre " of

[1] *Life of Romilly*, iii. 364.

Peterloo ; it arose from the folly of the Manchester magistrates in sending the Yeomanry to arrest Hunt, at the moment when he was addressing a vast and closely packed assembly on the subject of Reform. Though several lives had been lost, the Government did not wait for an inquiry before thanking the parties concerned in effecting the arrest. Their tactlessness raised a storm of indignation. Lord Fitzwilliam protested, and was dismissed from his lord-lieutenancy. Parliament was summoned to pass repressive measures, and met at a crisis of great excitement.

This was in many ways an excellent opportunity for the Whigs to come forward and lead a general assault on the hated administration. The Benthamites were anxious to co-operate with them ; Francis Place tried for their help in organising a monster protest meeting, but declared that no eagerness was shown to meet him half-way.[1] Such reluctance, however, was by no means shared by all the Whigs. Tierney, now their leader in the Commons, was most anxious that the party should adopt a strong line. " I take it to be our duty to do so," he wrote to Grey, " but, putting that aside, it seems to be our interest, for if everything is left to the Radicals, as they are called, they will be sure to spoil a good cause, and by the time it comes to our turn to take it up in Parliament they will have managed to disgust or alarm all those from whom we might hope to derive countenance or assistance." He believed the Radicals' appearance of strength was largely due to their having the field to themselves. " So far from thinking that they are at this time peculiarly formidable, my conviction is that this is the precise moment when the Whigs might resume the popular lead, and reduce them to their original insignificance."[2] So, too, Sir James Mackintosh, while wishing to proclaim " irreconcilable war against the Radicals," wrote to urge Lord John Russell not to miss the beginning of the session. " Your reform must be immediately brought forward, if possible, as the act of the party, but at all events as the creed of all Whig reformers."[3]

It was only the personal influence of Grey and other Whig magnates which restrained the keener spirits from a bold course. We are told that " Fox used always to say that he did not like

---

[1] Graham Wallas, *Life of Francis Place*, p. 143.
[2] Tierney to Grey, September 6, 17, 1819 ; *Howick Papers.*
[3] *Early Correspondence*, i. 205.

C

to discourage the young ones." [1]   Lord Grey was of a different stamp.   In point of fact he was in any case little suited to act as the leader of a popular movement ; still less so when the affair of the Westminster election had touched his pride.   In March he had assured the Radical General, Sir Robert Wilson, that nothing could ever induce him to act in unison with the Burdett party after their recent behaviour ; he must " avoid even the intercourse of private society with them whom I consider as having degraded themselves from the character of gentlemen." [2] A letter to the same friend, dated Howick, October 24, deserves fuller quotation, as giving the views of the Whig leader at this juncture on the kindred subjects of the Radicals and Reform itself.

" I see in the exaggerated tone which you take upon all that has lately happened, in your disposition to see only the culpable conduct of the Government and those who have acted under their influence on the one hand, and to shut your eyes not only to the dangerous practices but to the mischievous designs (which cannot be doubted) of the Ultra-Reformists and of their leaders on the other, too alarming symptoms that but a short period of the coming session can pass without showing that we act with views so extremely different, as to leave no possibility of publick union."

He goes on to profess " equal hostility to the Government on the one hand and to the Radicals on the other.   I shall certainly with all my power urge the necessity of enquiry and satisfaction for the proceedings of August 16 ; and this satisfaction I am persuaded will be obtained, if those who are still enough under the influence of popular feelings to partake in the general impulse, or at least to yield to it, are not driven from the course they would be inclined to take by intemperate language and violent measures. . . .

" I will not now go into an examination of the principle of Reform which is the only one which will be tolerated by the leaders of the popular party, or rather of the Mob, or of the means by which they are endeavouring to effect their object, which certainly is not Reform but Revolution.   But I will desire you to look at the men themselves. . . . They may use Burdett for their instrument for a time, and you also . . . but if a con-

[1] *Life and Opinions of Charles, 2nd Earl Grey*, p. 11.
[2] British Museum, Add. MSS. 30,109, f. 9.

vulsion follows their attempts to work upon the minds of the people, inflamed as they are by distress, for which your Reform would afford a very inadequate remedy, I shall not precede you many months on the scaffold. . . .

"My line must therefore be a line of moderate and cautious policy and of gradual improvement formed on those Whig principles, which will not allow me to submit to an invasion of popular rights because bad men have abused them, but will not allow me either to give any countenance or support to them or their proceedings." [1]

Nothing was therefore done till the meeting of the " Savage Parliament " in November, and even then the strenuous protests of many Whigs failed to prevent the passing of the notorious Six Acts. On the subject of Reform, Tierney, while dissociating himself from the Radicals, declared " it was now almost universally admitted that the great mass of the people did not feel that the present state of the representation was beneficial to them." Russell, however, found little support when he proposed the transference of the franchise of corrupt boroughs to growing towns. Nevertheless Lambton, in the spirit of his father, an original Friend of the People, gave notice of a comprehensive measure after the recess, to deal with what he described as " the most important question that ever existed." " In the present state of the public mind," he wrote to his father-in-law, " we should sink ' ten thousand fathom deep ' if we were to hold a meeting, and not make Reform a principal and leading topic." [2] But Grey had little faith, and feared above all things to break up the party. Once again he threw his influence into the unheroic scale.

" In a public view I think the preservation of the Whig party in Parliament of the utmost importance. It is really in practice the only defence for the liberties of the country. . . . You say a change of Ministers by means of the Whig party is hopeless. Is the accomplishment of a Reform of Parliament more certain ? From all I hear I believe that the public opinion in favour of that measure is greatly increased, but I have great doubts whether it is so increased, especially amongst those whose influence will always be greatest on such questions, as to afford any reasonable hope of its being carried during my life or even yours. The result of all this is, though I think it highly desirable to

[1] Add. MSS. 30,109, f. 57.    [2] *Howick Papers.*

endeavour to raise the character of the House of Commons in the opinion of the public, by uniting the representative more closely with the constituent body, I would have that object pursued individually by those who are favourable to it, in such a manner as may neither divide the Whig party, nor pledge them to it in such a way as may make their acceptance of office —if so improbable an event as its being offered to them should occur—a reproach to them without it." [1]

Grey's eyes were strangely holden. Even the Tories were beginning to feel their foundations giving way. " Don't you think," wrote Peel to Croker, " that the tone of England is more liberal than the policy of the Government ? Don't you think there is a feeling, becoming daily more general, in favour of some undefined change in the mode of governing the country ? " Croker himself had suggested to Lord Liverpool the wisdom of enfranchising at least four large towns, as the best policy of resistance, and Peel now doubted if Reform could be delayed for seven years. He almost expected a coalition of Tories and moderate Whigs to carry it. [2]

The dark years after the war, shadowed by famine, strikes, and unemployment, and finishing a period of unnatural stress and tension, had opened the eyes of the governing class to dangers hitherto considered almost fabulous. " The year 1819 closed," wrote Cockburn, " and the new one opened, amidst the popular disturbances called, gravely by some, and jocularly by others, ' the Radical War.' The whole island was suffering under great agricultural and manufacturing distress. This was taken the usual advantage of by demagogues, and consequently there was considerable political excitement. Quite enough to require caution, and even to justify alarm. Its amount in Scotland was contemptible. But it was first exaggerated, and then exhibited as evidence of a revolutionary spirit." Accordingly Edinburgh was put in a state of defence against the expected march of forty or fifty thousand Glasgow weavers—a false alarm ending in an absurd fiasco. [3] In England nothing more terrible occurred than the attempt to assassinate the Cabinet, known as the Cato Street conspiracy. But a true rebellion took place in the realm of ideas, and its bitter spirit found voice in the satire of Byron and Shelley. The

[1] Grey to Lambton, January 3, 1820 ; Reid, *Life of Durham*, i. 129.
[2] *Croker Papers*, i. 170.          [3] *Memorials*, p. 363 ff.

distressed country had sent up a great cry for sympathy, and Parliament had not responded to the call. There had come about, in the words of Mackintosh, " the alienation of the working classes from the proprietors and the Constitution." [1]

Before Reformers could fairly return to the charge in 1820, George III was dead ; his death demanded a general election. Hardly had the new House of Commons set to work, when the proceedings consequent on Queen Caroline's arrival in England shelved all questions of ordinary interest. The sordid details of the new Queen's so-called " trial " aroused in the entire nation an extraordinary excitement, due partly to curiosity, partly to a sense of the injustice of the hated King, and partly to more questionable motives. The enthusiasm of the people, and the virulent pamphlets which deluged the country, showed a spirit which ignored usual party distinctions. The Utilitarians must have been thoroughly disgusted by such a sidelight on the Springs of Action. Had the elections occurred a trifle later in the year, the results would probably have been strikingly different ; as it was, though the Government had secured an adequate working majority, they decided to drop the measures against the Queen in face of national protest. Here once more was a chance for the Whigs, without sacrifice of principle, to capture and direct the popular imagination. To a certain extent they availed themselves of it. Lambton and the advanced section took up the Queen's cause eagerly, and the party generally gained by the reflected glory of Brougham, who, as the Queen's counsel, became the hero of the day. Nevertheless Place sneered at their lukewarm lack of enterprise, and Grey and Lansdowne refused to make party capital out of such a matter. A letter of Grey's at this time shows his fundamental distrust of popular movements except when implicitly following the guidance of the aristocracy.[2] In spite, however, of much half-hearted behaviour, the party had gone some way toward winning the confidence of the poorer classes. " The Queen's business has done a great deal of good," wrote Lord John Russell, " in renewing the old and natural alliance of the Whigs and the people, and weakening the influence of the Radicals." [3]

[1] *Early Correspondence of Lord John Russell*, i. 210.
[2] Add. MSS. 30,109, f. 140.
[3] Spencer Walpole, *Life of Lord John Russell*, i. 122, quoted by Wallas, *Life of Place*, p. 152.

At least ordinary disputes had been interrupted, and, when the excitement sank, politics were found in an altered condition.

The fierce strain of the five years after Waterloo gave place to a period of "truce between Parliament and people." Trade improved, and the "Condition of England" question, as Carlyle called it, began ; economic problems were discussed, by which all classes felt themselves intimately touched. It was now that the current in the direction of Reform set in, which, gaining steadily in volume and force, burst at length upon the country in 1830. Liberal-minded men like Sydney Smith recognised the people's desire, and proceeded to convert themselves and others. Place traces much of the increase in democratic feeling to the events of 1820, which lowered royalty and the aristocracy of privilege in the eyes of the middle and lower classes, by exposing their disreputable and unromantic privacies to public comment.[1] The champion at whose side the Queen entered the capital was no highborn cavalier but a Radical alderman. Removed from the jar of active struggle, Whigs and Radicals were able to work for the common principle, and even their disputes, as when Grote crossed swords in 1821 with Mackintosh, the repentant author of *Vindiciæ Gallicæ*, were useful as an advertisement.

The task of reconciling the two sides lay with the left wing of the Whigs, and especially with Lambton, at once the confidant of Lord Grey, whose daughter he married as his second wife, and the headlong exponent of views which earned him in Durham the name of Radical Jack. Spoilt as a child after his father's early death, and subject to constant illness, Lambton was greatly handicapped in his political career by a short and peevish temper, particularly unfortunate in one meant for the delicate position of peacemaker between men of very different minds and circumstances. He was a born Radical of unfailing energy and keenness, and his generous quixotic nature rose to fierce indignation at all oppression or injustice. But the dashing enterprise which induced him at the age of nineteen to throw up a commission in the 10th Hussars for a Gretna Green marriage often led him into difficulties when applied to public life. His insight was greater than his judgment, and petulance and vanity made him difficult to work with. For all his defects, he saw

[1] Add. MSS. 27,789, f. 123.

much more clearly than the majority of his party the need of making a far more democratic appeal, if the Whigs were to enlist the help of the people in carrying the practical reforms they desired.[1] The old idea of a grateful populace blindly obeying a clique of hereditary legislators was out of date ; the people would only exchange its support for power. The American Minister said in 1821 : " The Whigs are a party of leaders with no rank and file—accomplished men, but as aristocratic as the Tories. They have lost their strong ground, the Reformers have taken it from under them." [2] In the hope of winning something back, Lambton in the spring of the same year proposed to the House of Commons an extensive scheme of Reform, including equal electoral districts, household suffrage, and triennial Parliaments. In the debate much was said of the mandate for Reform given by many constituencies, and several speakers were struck by the contrast between the votes of the Commons and the overwhelming popularity of the Queen in the country the year before. But Lambton's scheme was of too sweeping a nature, and was rejected in a thin house.

More orthodox were the persistent endeavours of Lord John Russell, representative with his brother Lord Tavistock of the great Bedford branch of Whiggism. From 1819 onwards Russell was the recognised champion of the Whigs in the cause of Reform. Never was a great career more consistent or more appropriate. Son of an original Friend of the People, and nephew of Fox's Duke of Bedford, he thrived in Whig principles from his earliest years, and made haste to apply them at home and abroad. Even had the atmosphere of Woburn failed to nurture him aright, he must have drawn the true milk of the word from Lord Holland, with whom he travelled much in Spain during the Peninsular War. He was thus familiar with the most liberal strain of Whiggism, and sympathy with the constitutional aspirations of the Spaniards inclined him to a more democratic form of government at home. At Edinburgh University he trained himself by speeches before the " Spec " ; as early as 1810 we have seen him distressed by the lukewarmness of Lord Grey. Lord Sefton speaks of the future Prime Minister as " a conceited little puppy," and he may well at this time have shown some of the defects of the serious young

[1] See Harris, *The Radical Party in Parliament*, p. 153.
[2] S. J. Reid, *Life of Durham*, i. 150.

Liberal.  But to those who knew him well his keen and affec-
tionate nature was entirely charming, and his early letters
show lightness of touch.  His pen too, however, was consecrated
to the Whig cause ;  in 1819 he had just finished a life of his
ancestor, William Lord Russell, who suffered for his opinions
on the scaffold.  But to the interests of his class and clique
Russell added others not usual among the Whigs of noble birth.
In 1811 his father with wise foresight sent him on a tour to
visit the great towns of the industrial north, whose will was in
time to supply the driving force for his own Reform Bill.  We
can gather from the pages of *Coningsby* what impression those
great towns could make thirty years later on the mind of a
young politician.  In 1811 the idea of their greatness was less
familiar and their cry less urgent to statesmen ; it was therefore no small thing that one Whig member, and he young and
able, should have some first-hand acquaintance with those to
whom Reform was no mere catchword but the removal of a
personal and intimate wrong.  Russell was thus admirably
qualified for the work to which Bedford, like the Carthaginian
father, at length devoted his son—an eternal warfare on behalf
of Liberty in Church and State.[1]  He was anxious, he tells us,
to make Reform the test of popular principles in the Whig
party ;  but the pendulum had not yet swung over far enough,
and Tierney, though himself a strong Reformer, did not feel
justified in allowing him the official party whip for this purpose.[2]

Nevertheless in May 1821 Russell followed up Lambton's
sweeping measure with a proposal to transfer members to large
towns from convicted boroughs.  This was lost by only 31 votes ;
but when, next April, in view of " the present state of external
peace and internal tranquillity," and fortified by numerous
petitions, Russell presumed to suggest to disfranchise 100 small
boroughs partially and give their members to counties and
large towns, he was beaten by 105.  It is a telling sign of the
new spirit that, whereas Pitt had proposed in 1785 to divide the
available members between London and the counties, Russell
assigned two-fifths of them to the towns.  On this occasion he
at least succeeded in drawing a clear statement of the case
against Reform from its arch-enemy.  In a Burke-like speech,
whose eloquence long sounded in the ears of Parliament, Canning

---

[1] *Early Correspondence*, i. 149, 199.
[2] *Recollections and Suggestions*, p. 41 ; *Recollections of a Long Life*, iii. 32.

declared that Reform on principle, other than the remedy of definite grievances, would destroy the Constitution ; to establish one uniform right would be to exclude some important interests. He went further : " I do not believe that to increase the power of the people—or rather to bring that power into more direct, immediate, and incessant operation upon the House—would enable the House to discharge its functions more usefully than it discharges them at present." [1] It was felt that Canning's speech had sealed the fate of Reform for some years. Only the disfranchisement of Grampound, for notorious corruption, broke the charmed security of the old system, and even this Lord Eldon abhorred, as bound to plunge England in " the whirlpool of democracy." Russell himself realised that the Commons were only reflecting the apathy of the country, and complained that some of the Whig leaders had succumbed to its deadening weight.[2] Grey indeed, discussing party prospects on the death of Castlereagh, was now prepared to make Reform a condition of accepting office, but his views were distinctly moderate.[3] For the moment Russell turned to literature ; he published in 1822 his *Essay on the English Government*, in which the principle of representation was treated in a judicial manner. His periodical motions in the Commons were of hardly more practical importance.

All attempts to secure a change in the Scottish system were also futile ; it was something that they were again being made. " There is nothing too base," wrote Campbell, the future Chancellor, " for the freeholders of a Scotch county. Were I in Parliament, there is no project I should support more earnestly than the reformation of the representation in Scotland. . . . The county members must almost of necessity support the Minister for the time being, or lose their seats. An unspeakable reproach is thus brought upon the country. The very worst possible number of electors is between fifty and three hundred. If the voters are very low, and will take five or ten guineas a man, as in the English boroughs, the evil is considerably mitigated, because a man may hold the seat, and act upon independent principles ; but if they look only to government

---

[1] *Hansard*, April 25, 1822.
[2] Russell to Moore, February 26, 1822, January 24, 1824 ; *Early Correspondence*, i. 223, 236.
[3] *Brougham Memoirs*, ii. 444 ff.

patronage, the members are inevitably dependent on the Court.
. . . If you look at the late divisions, you will find a majority
of English county members in the minority. Of Scotch there
are none besides Maule and Lord Archibald [Hamilton]—a
greater show of independence than we can always boast of."[1]
But if petitions and motions were ignored, political gatherings
were no longer forbidden. Annual Fox dinners were a first
step towards emancipation, and were followed by ordinary
public meetings.[2] The conversion of the country was a mere
question of time.

In fact there can be no doubt that the accession of Canning
and Peel to positions of authority in the ministry, and the
ensuing readjustment of the political situation, were indirectly favourable to the movement. Not only did their
liberal policy at home and abroad seem to give a foothold for
innovation generally, but the junction of Lord Buckingham and
the Grenville Whigs with the Tories did, at this stage, tend to
unite the Opposition more closely on the basis of Reform. The
surrender of their traditional leaders is worth noting. Creevey
remarks on the conversion of the Duke of Devonshire ; Croker
on that of Lords Fitzwilliam and Darlington, " two of the largest
borough-holders in England."[3] If Lord Spencer had retired
from politics, his eldest son had long been among the more
advanced of the Whigs. Reform was rapidly becoming a practical topic in the country in a way it had never been in 1794,
and the philosophic and parliamentary Radicals stood to the
Reforming Whigs in a relation very different to that of the
obscure and fanatical sectaries of old.

The Benthamites, whose views on Reform had been power-
fully expressed in 1820 by James Mill's article on Government
in the *Encyclopædia*, marked a definite step of their advance
into the political field by the institution in 1824 of the *Westminster Review*, prepared to meet the publicists of the *Edinburgh*
and *Quarterly* on equal terms.[4] In these lists the Utilitarians
were constantly running courses with such Whigs as Jeffrey
and Brougham, himself an acquaintance, if not a disciple, of
Bentham. Whatever the result of these skirmishes, the plausible

---

[1] *Life of John Lord Campbell*, i. 393.
[2] Cockburn, *Memorials*, p. 425.
[3] *Creevey Papers*, p. 348 ; *Croker Papers*, ii. 52.
[4] Leslie Stephen, *The English Utilitarians*, i. 224.

dogmatism of the Westminster school, with their universal utilitarian standard, became widely ventilated and wrought on many minds that would have scorned to own their influence. It is amusing to find Macaulay, who spared no terms in his insolent attack on James Mill's philosophy, claimed by Professor Dicey as a Benthamite.[1] The general dislike which these dismal prophets incurred by their grey unattractive common-sense and contempt for antiquity did not prevent their tenets from becoming the informing principles of Liberalism.

The financial crisis of 1825, preceded by the strikes which attended the repeal of the Combination Acts, and followed by distress in manufacturing districts, created an atmosphere of unrest contrasting strongly with the optimism of the last five years. On the one hand Tories, strengthened by Canning's assertion that his opposition to Reform was based not on temporary circumstances but on unalterable principle, might plead the folly of mooting such a question at a time of disturbance ; while Hobhouse, speaking to a motion introduced by Russell just before the dissolution of 1826, found in " the reverses of the present day " strong proof of the financial incapacity of an unreformed House of Commons. But he saw no hope of carrying such a measure from the Opposition benches. The general election of this year, fought mainly on the subjects of Corn and Catholic Emancipation, made little change in party strength.

Vastly different was the effect of the change brought about by Canning's promotion, in the spring of 1827, to the place so long filled by Lord Liverpool. The arrangements made broke up both great parties and left politics in a fluid condition in which anything might happen. The central difficulty was to find a statesman to lead the two wings of the Tory party, as Liverpool had done with considerable success, on a basis of neutrality on the subject of Catholic Relief. Peel and Wellington would not serve under a " Catholic " head, nor Canning under one pledged against Emancipation. But here, as elsewhere in the career of Canning, the personal motive must not be disregarded.

Deserted by the High Tory wing, the King's minister had

---

[1] *Law and Opinion in England*, p. 181. Macaulay describes the Utilitarian philosophy as a pursuit " not much more laughable than phrenology, and immeasurably more humane than cock-fighting."—*Edinburgh*, January 1829.

recourse to the Whigs; it remained to see what attitude they would adopt.  Catholic Relief and Parliamentary Reform were barred subjects, and it is remarkable that many of the more advanced Whigs accepted the invitation, while the staid prudence of Lord Grey declined.  To the former Canning's liberal foreign policy, his acknowledged genius, and the loftiness of his ideals, made a strong appeal; [1] though an awkward colleague, as a leader he was a glorious figure, and appeared as the last splendid representative of the men who had fought with gods of an earlier age.  Still a critic could draw a cynical contrast between " Canning, the sneering Tory, who objects to the repeal of the Test Acts, leaves Catholic Emancipation in abeyance, and detests Reform," and the combination of " Lansdowne, the moderate Whig, calling the Catholic question a vital one and complaining of Lisbon jobs," with " Burdett, the Radical Reformer, who called Canning the ass that knew his crib . . . who abused Fox for coalescing with the Grenvilles without making a stipulation in favour of Reform." [2]  But the compelling reason which induced Lansdowne, Holland, Tierney, Russell, Brougham, Lambton, and even Burdett, to support Canning, most of them without office, was the hope of breaking up the Tory party, and by a strong and enlightened administration making it impossible in the future for a ministry to be formed on reactionary lines.  The advantage of winning the support of the King was also a factor. [3]

Lord Grey, on the other hand, with Lord Althorp and the Duke of Bedford, held back.  It was said indeed that Grey's refusal arose from personal pique at some delay in asking his opinion. [4]  But if the personal note was important, this was no momentary spleen on Grey's part, but the result of a deep-rooted distrust of Canning's character felt by the whole Whig

---

[1] Brougham to Wilson, March 26, 1827, Add. MSS. 30,115, f. 36 ; Reid, *Life of Durham*, i. 172.

[2] Colonel Napier to Lord F. Somerset, May 13, 1827; *Despatches, Correspondence, and Memoranda of Arthur, Duke of Wellington*, Civil Series (henceforward cited as *Despatches*), iv. 30.

[3] Brougham to Creevey, April 21, 1827: " My principle is—*anything* to lock the door for ever on Eldon and Co."  Sefton to Creevey, May 28, 1827: " I *do say* the junction is justified by the exclusion of Eldon, Wellington, Peel, and Bathurst.  It could have been brought about by no other means."  *Creevey Papers*, pp. 456, 459.

[4] *Recollections of a Long Life*, iii. 186.

party. This feeling was shared on the Tory side by those who looked with dismay on his liberal ideas ; in Grey's case it was at least twenty years old. To say nothing of Canning's " turning his jacket " in early youth, and his apparent readiness to join either side in 1807, Grey, his predecessor at the Foreign Office, accused him of downright lying in the Copenhagen affair. His later career had done nothing to lessen the old suspicion.[1] Noble as were the ideals which guided Canning while in power, something of a cloud hangs over his struggles to attain it. If we reject the common taunt that he was entirely without principles, we cannot acquit him of a degree of self-seeking and lack of straightforwardness. It was a similar distrust which crippled the career of Shelburne, a man whose great talents and originality of outlook may well be compared with Canning's. But besides the personal motive there was another no less potent.

It is indeed curious that no one but Althorp seems to have considered the abandonment of Reform decisive, though Tierney made the right to vote for it a condition of entering the ministry.[2] Lord Grey made his own position plain in the violent attack he launched in the House of Lords on May 11 against Canning's whole career. " I will not dwell on [Canning's] known opposition to parliamentary reform, on the ground of which some of my noble and honourable friends have been accused for giving their support to the new administration ; for that is not a question to which they are pledged, nor on which the party to which they belong are agreed. . . . The question of parliamentary reform is not so uniformly supported, nor has it at present the public opinion so strongly in its favour, as that it should be made a *sine qua non* in forming an administration. There was a time when the expression of my opinion of parliamentary reform exposed me to obloquy. But I still adhere to the opinion I always entertained on this subject. I have always maintained that reform ought to keep pace with the march of human intellect—that its progression should be gradual. . . . It is not then, I repeat, because of the right hon. gentleman's opposition to parliamentary reform that I object to him as one opposed to civil liberty." [3] To many moderate Reformers this definite

[1] *Lady Holland's Journal*, i. 217, ii. 217 ; *Life and Opinions of Earl Grey*, pp. 99, 195 ; *Creevey Papers*, pp. 108, 460.

[2] Russell, *Recollections and Suggestions*, p. 54 ; Le Marchant, *Memoir of Viscount Althorp*, p. 216.

[3] *Hansard*, N.S., xvii. 732.

repudiation of Reform as an official article in the Whig creed thus late in the day must have been matter for sorrow. Silently tenacious of his own principles, Lord Grey seemed to lack every capacity of a popular leader for coming forward at a dramatic moment and risking a little by a bold declaration of opinion. He almost despised any popular appeal; it was impossible to drag him into the open.

We must seek yet further for Grey's real motive. He wrote to Creevey in August: " My objections were not merely personal to Canning, but applied principally to the manner in which the Government was composed "; he spoke to Russell of " the original and fatal mistake of joining Canning at the expense of ' a negligent and unnecessary sacrifice of the importance of the Whig party.' This I never would have consented to, even for the sake of keeping out the old Tories—their return would, in my opinion, have been a much less evil." [1] Here lies the secret of Grey's attitude. A Whig to the backbone, his pride forbade him to merge the tradition of the party which he led in the policy of a mongrel Tory; even had the coalition been on equal terms, it would have meant a loss of dignity to the genuine line of Fox. A material blow to a party can be remedied; but a shock to its prestige, to the fictitious entity which represents it in the imaginations of men, wounds it more than many adverse by-elections or divisions. By withholding his support, Grey preserved the ancient personality of the Whig party, and later on, after Canningites and Tories had tried their hand and failed, when a Reforming government was to be formed on traditional lines, he stood out as its obvious head.

For the moment, however, this difference as to strategy, as usually happens, led to extreme bitterness. Grey's conduct was spoken of as " very atrocious," and a definite breach created between the majority of the party and their former leader. In any case the matter was reopened by the death of Canning at Chiswick in August. The instinctive feeling in Liberal circles was naturally one of despair at the great loss; on second thoughts it was hoped that, supposing the administration could be con-

---

[1] *Creevey Papers*, p. 467; *Early Correspondence*, i. 263. Althorp (*ibid.*, i. 271) complained that " the Insurrection at Brooks's and Lord Lansdowne's weakness did the great injury of destroying Party in the country." Grey's followers spoke of the deserters as " The Malignants." Brougham is " The Arch Fiend."

tinued on the same principles, the removal of its chief might
not be an unmixed evil. "In the Lords he did us mischief,"
wrote Brougham, "*e.g.*, keeping Lord G. aloof. In the
country, little more good than evil came from him, for the
Reformers and the High-church folks hated him about equally." [1]
Suggestions of every kind were made ; there were ideas of a
conservative coalition between Wellington and the aristocratic
Whigs, and it was rumoured that Lord Grey would accept the
Foreign Office.[2] Eventually, in spite of Brougham's endeavours,
nothing better could be patched up than the Goderich ministry,
and the Whigs resigned themselves to look for better things in
a new reign.

In January 1828 George IV reshuffled the cards. Rumours
of a Lansdowne Cabinet, to include Holland and Brougham,
had been current, when the King sent for the Duke of Wellington
and commissioned him to form a government. "He had no
objection to anybody excepting to Lord Grey." [3] The new
ministry was on the lines of Lord Liverpool's ; the Lansdowne
Whigs crossed back into opposition, the pure Tories taking their
places ; the Canningites joined in a body. Grey's own following
were neutral, if not friendly to the Duke ; even his conversion
to the cause of Catholic Relief did not seem impossible, and
at any rate he would restore at least the semblance of party
government.[4] For the last few months England had been
ruled by the group system. Each of the two great parties
was split into a right and a left section. Canning was to the
Tories what Brougham, in a less degree, was to the Whigs—a
brilliant but rather dangerous champion, much too clever to
be trusted, and suspected of perpetual intrigue. Wellington's
administration embraced the two Tory groups ; Canning's and
Goderich's the advanced wing from each party. It was not
till both sections of the Whigs united with the Canningites under
Lord Grey that a stable ministry was formed, and then not
for long. The Duke said in January 1828: "Peel is quite

---

[1] Viscountess Knutsford, *Life of Zachary Macaulay*, p. 445.

[2] Lambton to Grey, August 15, 1827; *Howick Papers. Despatches*,
iv. 79 ; *Croker Papers*, i. 384 ; *Recollections of a Long Life*, iii. 232.

[3] Wellington to Peel, January 9, 1828 ; *Despatches*, iv. 184.

[4] Grey to Princess Lieven, January 25, 1828 : "I wish personally well
to the Duke of Wellington, and I should be glad to see a Government
established by him that might rescue us from all the disgrace of the last
eight months."—*Lieven Correspondence*, i. 103.

right—those who are for an exclusive ministry expect me to go into the House of Commons with half a party to fight a party and a half."

For all that, to half a party he was soon reduced. Reform was again in the air of Westminster in March, the occasion being the proposed disfranchisement of Penryn and East Retford for notorious corruption. On the necessity of this step the Tories were agreed ; but the Cabinet were divided as to whether the four members thus secured should be given to two large towns or merely to the hundreds of the offending boroughs. Lord Dudley, Palmerston writes, was for adopting the bolder plan "and thus getting rid of the great scandal of the present state of our representation." Croker was of the same opinion, thinking now as in 1819 that prudence counselled throwing a sop to Reformers.[1] A compromise, however, was agreed upon, on the ground that the manufacturing should not be favoured at the expense of the agricultural interest. The Commons resolved to transfer the franchise of Penryn to Manchester, and, if the Lords agreed to this, that of East Retford to the surrounding hundred. But the Lords amended the bill, so as to enfranchise the hundred of Penryn. Whereupon Huskisson in the Commons, believing that he was following the plan prearranged by the Cabinet, voted against his party for the total disfranchisement of East Retford. Touched by conscience, he wrote that night to Wellington a letter which the Duke not unnaturally took as a definite resignation of office. With unnecessary promptitude he showed it to the King, and, when Huskisson attempted to explain personally and by proxy that he had only meant to give the Duke an opportunity of dismissing him, declined to consider the resignation cancelled unless Huskisson would withdraw his original letter. This Huskisson refused to do, and the result of the absurd incident was the retirement from the Cabinet of the entire Canningite section. There is little doubt that the Duke was tired of his allies, whose general outlook differed widely from his own, and was not sorry to lose them.

Weakened by the defection of their ablest supporters, the Duke and Peel were now called upon to carry on the Government in the face of disturbances calculated to overwhelm a stronger ministry. First they had the mortification to see the

[1] Bulwer's *Palmerston* (3rd edition), i. 234; *Croker Papers*, ii. 15.

repeal of the Test Act carried in their teeth by Lord John Russell, as the firstfruits of his father's charge ; the second shock was severer still. The reconstruction of the ministry on the flight of the Canningites had made necessary a by-election in the County Clare. As a rule the Irish constituencies of forty shilling freeholders voted obediently for their landlords' nominees ; on this occasion Daniel O'Connell, organiser of the renowned Catholic Association, and himself, as a Catholic, disqualified from sitting in Parliament, appeared as candidate and was triumphantly elected. The Catholic Association had defeated the Government ; the revolt successfully raised in Clare might be repeated in all the counties of Ireland. Henceforward Catholic Emancipation, for some years the main point of contention between the parties, became a matter of life and death to the administration. The Opposition leaders admitted that the minister who could succeed in passing the bill so urgently needed would deserve and secure the support and approbation of all parties. Early in 1829 there were rumours that surprising developments might be looked for ; these were confirmed by the King's Speech and by Peel's resignation of his seat for Oxford University ; on standing again he was defeated by Sir Robert Inglis, the "Protestant" candidate. Acting avowedly on imperious necessity due to the imminence of civil war, the Government brought in and carried, with the assistance of the Whigs, the long-sought measure of Catholic Emancipation, linking it however with the disfranchisement of the forty shilling freeholders. As far as the Government were concerned, the temporary conciliation of the Whigs was dearly bought at the price of the bitter hostility of the extreme Tories, headed by the Duke of Cumberland, most hated of all the sons of George III ; this faction acted with High Churchmen throughout the country, and assailed their betrayers with a virulence which only inconsistency can provoke, and only religious hatred supply. One furious Tory actually urged Lord John Russell to bring in his Reform Bill to spite the Duke, and Croker told Lord Hertford that "the old Duchess of Richmond had a number of stuffed *rats* under glass cases on her drawing-room table, to which Her Grace affixed the names of all the apostates."[1] The Duke of Wellington's duel with Lord Winchelsea is notorious, and was justified by the challenger as the only means of checking

[1] *Croker Papers*, ii. 15.

D

the flow of libellous abuse. Such was the origin of that fierce cleavage in the Tory ranks, at a time when the stoutest union was needed to stem the rising tide of democratic feeling.

The Whigs, on the other hand, who for nearly thirty years had toiled in fair and foul weather for Catholic Relief, and for its sake had sacrificed place and power, though bound not to oppose the successful intervention of allies however tardy and reluctant, could not escape a pang of cruel disappointment at seeing how completely others had entered into their labours. Baulked of the one great measure on which they were agreed, it is not surprising that they turned with keener zeal to that other great measure on which indeed they were not agreed, but which came to them recommended alike by the pleading of their leaders in the past and by the growing voice of the people. But the rift in the party still existed, and those who had condemned the ill-fated venture of 1827 were inclined to prefer the existing Government, especially in view of possible invitations to join it, to any likely alternative. The Duke, on the other hand, was advised not to divide his power with men who might claim the lion's share. Indeed there was no cause to fear them, for though a combination of factions might overthrow him, the party of Grey and Althorp stood to gain nothing by his fall; distasteful as they were to the King, they would yield precedence to the Ultra-Tories, the Canningites, or even their Lansdowne cousins.[1] In this opinion Lord Grey himself concurred, and the year ended leaving the Whigs without immediate hope of office, but rather disposed to maintain in power the Government which had settled the burning question of the day.[2]

[1] Arbuthnot to Wellington, October 5, 1829; *Despatches*, vi. 198.
[2] Grey to Princess Lieven, November 4, 1829, *Correspondence*, i. 348; to Russell, December 13, *Early Correspondence*, i. 299; *Life of Lord Campbell*, i. 472; *Recollections of a Long Life*, iv. 3.

# CHAPTER II

## THE FALL OF THE TORIES

"I most heartily wish that the deliberate sense of the kingdom on this great subject should be known. When it is known, it *must* be prevalent."—BURKE.

THE condition of English politics at the end of 1829 was one of unstable equilibrium. The rapid changes following on Lord Liverpool's retirement had dislocated the natural working of the party system. The Tories had lost most of their ablest men over a petty incident which a little goodwill and concession on either side must have prevented. Further to shatter their solidity came the startling events of 1829. The good Church and State men were amazed by the sudden inexcusable treachery of their leaders, by which their opponents had won all the fruits of their long endeavour without its odium. The cleavage was complete, and the High Tories henceforth were numbered as part of the professed Opposition, assailing the Government with more than party rancour and making as much capital as possible out of agricultural discontent. The ministers, reduced by the double defection to dependence on little but the firmness of Wellington and the ability of Peel, turned their eyes to Eastern diplomacy, and hoped to tide over the difficulties of the time by a policy of general inoffensiveness and the dissensions of their opponents.[1] The Whigs, excited for the moment by the prospect of effective union with all that was liberal and progressive among their opponents, had seen their hopes dashed to the ground by the death of Canning and the incapacity of his successor. The manœuvres from which they hoped so much had done little more than break up the party.

Not yet prepared to adopt Reform as their official object, they gnashed their teeth helplessly, and tendered to ministers a lukewarm and not altogether disinterested support. Their embarrassment is described by Campbell, their future Chancellor, now a moderate Whig : " The Catholic Relief Bill having passed in 1829, it hung in the balance whether the Duke of

---

[1] Arbuthnot to Wellington, October 5, 1829 ; *Despatches*, vi. 198.

Wellington's Government was to be progressively *Liberal*, or . . . was to return to the old principle of *Toryism*.  In the hope of its adhering to the cause of religious liberty, and even listening to some small commencement of parliamentary reform . . . the Whig party approved of Lord Rosslyn, Lord Jersey, and Scarlett holding office under the Duke." On the other hand, Althorp wrote to Brougham in June : " Ministers are so weak that they are quite unfit to govern this or any other country, and I am doubtful whether it might not be expedient to say that, with every wish not to oppose them, yet that unless something is done to strengthen their hands before next session, we shall feel it our duty not to allow the country to remain any longer in such inefficient hands, if we can prevent it.  A great deal depends on the real wishes of the Duke of Wellington.  If he wishes to form a junction with us, and is only prevented by the bad humour of the King, it is perhaps the most prudent thing to say nothing." [1]

Their veteran leader was at this time in splendid isolation, lamenting over the disruption of the Whig party, which he had tried so hard to keep together.  Distasteful to many of his reputed followers,[2] he saw little prospect of any invitation to join the ministry, to which some even of his own personal adherents were transferring their allegiance.  The Duke of Bedford had actually entrusted his proxy to Lord Rosslyn, now a member of the Government, and that without any stipulation for his leader's inclusion.[3]  That the possibility of overtures from the Prime Minister to the head of the Opposition should have been the subject of constant rumour may well appear surprising, even if we take into account the Duke of Wellington's conscious weakness and Lord Grey's isolated position, which would remove the difficulty of admitting his " party " with him.  It is important, however, to remember the severity of the blows dealt in 1827 and 1829 to rigidity of party connection ; ever-varying combinations of political groups had reduced public affairs almost to that complexity which makes of the end of George II's reign a kaleidoscope so dazzling to the mind.  The Duke and Lord Grey had both been in opposition to Canning, both were believers in aristocratic government, and the session

[1] *Life of Campbell*, i. 472 ;  *Althorp Papers*.
[2] *Creevey Papers*, p. 538.
[3] Bedford to Grey, January 1, 1830 ;  *Howick Papers*.

of 1829 had removed the chief question at issue between them. Aberdeen, the Tory Foreign Secretary, denied that there was any difference in their opinions, and Grey fully realised that continued isolation might induce Wellington to strengthen himself by alliance with either the High Tories or the Canningites, whose grounds of offence might well be considered only temporary, or to extend a much desired invitation to the remnant of the Grenvilles. But whether such considerations, backed by the urgent advice of Princess Lieven, his would-be Egeria, would have prevailed on Lord Grey to abandon his lonely furrow for office under " the Great Captain," must remain a matter for speculation, for the overtures never came.[1] Early in January Grey was distinctly apprised that they would not, and after this the grapes might well look sour ; the reason given him was the inveterate hostility of the King, but Grey, while disclaiming any desire for office, spoke bitterly of the all too ready acquiescence of the Duke, and even of his own friends, in his exclusion on such grounds.[2]

It is no doubt well for Lord Grey's political reputation that he did not join the Duke. Apart from the inevitable widening of the breach with the excluded Whigs, and the consequent difficulty of forming a harmonious union with them in the autumn of 1830, it would have entailed a certain lowering of what Princess Lieven called his " great moral position " in the eyes of the people. As it was, on various occasions in the Reform struggle their confidence in him was strained almost to the breaking point. Had he been open to the added taunt of having joined the Tories for the sake of place alone, abandoning Reform, it is hardly possible to suppose that he could have retained their respect. The middle classes must have believed the Radicals' assertion that Whig and Tory were but meaningless names adopted for carrying on the ancient game of oligarchic rule. Lord Grey could not have come forward, as he did, on the fall of the ministry, and pointed to an exile from power of three-and-twenty years, endured in the cause of liberty.

It is possible, on the other side, to blame Grey for not coming forward at the end of 1829 as the leader of the Reforming Whigs, boldly adopting Reform as the natural successor to Emancipation, and exploiting the growing interest of the country in the

[1] See *Lieven Correspondence*, vol. i. chaps. vi. and vii.
[2] Grey to Howick, January 8, 1830 ; *Howick Papers.*

question. But, to say nothing of the extreme unlikelihood of his obtaining a parliamentary majority to pass any such measure, such a part was entirely alien from Grey's character and cast of mind. A perfect Whig, he combined subtly the aristocratic traditions of Newcastle and Rockingham with an enthusiasm for popular liberty derived from Fox. If his earlier career manifested more of the democratic spirit, in later life he recurred rather to the older principles. He declared in his place in the Lords in 1827 : [1] " If there should come a contest between this House and a great portion of the people, my part is taken, and with that order to which I belong I will stand or fall." But this was not mere pride of birth, nor is it to be concluded that Grey's liberal principles were nothing but a high-sounding profession or a weapon to overthrow the Government. His whole career cries out against such a view. He sincerely felt, as he wrote in 1820, " a good deal of apprehension of the ultimate success of any measures which are not supported by that class which ought to lead in any expression of public opinion." [2] Though he honestly put the good of the people as the end of government, he by no means accepted the democratic principle that the people should work out their own salvation ; political liberty did not mean political equality. It was far better that they should receive from their hereditary rulers just and beneficent measures than that they should be forced to agitate for them themselves, running the risk of awakening a spirit that could not be restrained within the bounds of constitutional safety. This conviction led him to regret at the end of his life that Fox had not dissuaded him from joining even so unrevolutionary a body as the Friends of the People ; [3] it kept him aloof from the popular movement in 1817 ; it sanctioned the cruel suppression of the insurgent labourers in 1830 ; it was also at the root of his distrust of the Political Unions, whose co-operation in the cause of Reform some of his younger colleagues were joyfully willing to accept. Grey loved the people, but he loved them at a distance. It was therefore hardly to be expected that he would stand out in 1829 as the demagogue of a half-formed public opinion in a cause bound to arouse violent antagonism from more parties than one.

In these circumstances, he declared his attitude to the Govern-

---

[1] *Hansard*, N.S., xvii. 1261.    [2] Add. MSS. 30,109, f. 140.
[3] *Life and Opinions of Earl Grey*, p. 11.

ment to be one of "friendly neutrality."[1] Such a course was not a heroic one ; but, apart from his age, his desire for quiet, and his extreme isolation, Grey's was a character far more calculated to excel in power than in opposition.[2] It will be shown later with what amazing tactical adroitness, supported by no little firmness and force of will, he piloted the Reform Bill through the dangers which beset it ; he had then a definite object to work for and a recognised position of authority from which to act ; greatness was thrust upon him by stress of circumstances. It was another thing to create opportunities, to weld together jarring elements, and win his way to power. His failure in this respect, confirming the Whig reputation for ineffectiveness, is visible in the early negotiations with the Prince Regent, as well as in the critical years after the peace. His very straightforwardness and dread of appearing in any but his true colours made it difficult for him to submit to that compromise of non-essentials which is the secret of collective action.[3] This appears strongly in his discouragement of Tierney and Lambton in 1819, and in his condemnation of the alliance with Canning ; even in 1830 he was doubtful of the very necessary union of some of the younger Whigs under Althorp, for fear they might find themselves pledged to measures of which they disapproved. The group system inaugurated in 1827 was against his experience and his theory of politics ; to maintain the Whig party unbroken and uncontaminated was to him an almost sacred duty.

Besides this great defect as a popular leader—the unwillingness to secure allies by a slight broadening of the party basis—Grey suffered from moods of profound dejection which deepened as he advanced in age. Often in his correspondence he breaks out in despair at the hopeless prospects of his party and himself. This is perhaps not altogether surprising, seeing that, when Grey at last entered into his kingdom, he had enjoyed only a few months of office out of a political life of forty-

[1] Grey to Howick, January 8, 1830 ; *Howick Papers.*

[2] Burdett is reported to have said of Grey : " He should not have been a patriot; he should have been a minister ; that was his line " (*Recollections of a Long Life*, iii. 79).

[3] His son wrote : " Nor was it enough . . . that there should be no real abandonment of political principle for the sake of place ; there must not be even such an apparent compromise of it, as might lead the public to doubt for a moment the purity of the motives on which he had acted " (*Life and Opinions of Earl Grey*, p. 386).

four years. The result was a lack of enterprise and yearning desire for quiet. Never really happy away from Howick and the family gatherings he associated with it, Grey perfectly fulfilled Plato's qualification for a statesman, that none are fit to rule save those to whom ruling is hateful.

This distaste for office under any conditions was heightened by the change of front which had come over English politics since the war. More and more, dismal questions of economics were superseding the "tangled secrets of high policy" which composed the splendid game of eighteenth-century statesmanship. Currency, tariffs, corn-laws, seemed poor stuff to the survivors of the days when the map of Europe was the board on which Napoleon and Pitt played for mastery. There is an amusing correspondence between Grey and his eldest son on the economic situation at the beginning of 1830. Lord Howick, full of youthful zeal, writes at some length of free trade and a possible property tax. The father, stoutly opposed to State interference with the individual's privacy, answers in cautious strain, divided between fear of dangerous innovation and desire to encourage his hopeful son in so serious an enthusiasm for political questions. At length he breaks away to speak of foreign policy—"so much better and pleasanter a subject for debate than dry matters of finance." [1] Here lay alike his interest and his reputation. A High Tory paper, in announcing a visionary administration to be formed by the Duke of Richmond, declared that the Cabinet was to consist exclusively of "Protestants," with the exception of "the first diplomatist of the day." [2] For the moment, however, such fascinating matters had little grip of the country as a whole, and minds were turned to the distress at home, while many saw in it the seeds of final victory for Parliamentary Reform.

Cobbett and the Radicals were first in the field. Even while the excitement over the Catholic question was at its height, which indeed was never very great outside the parliamentary classes, Cobbett gave the need for Reform a foremost place in the doctrines of class antagonism he was now preaching. "Great numbers of the people, in the labouring and middle rank of life, trace all the degradation and suffering of the country to

---

[1] Grey to Howick, January 8, 16, 1830; *Howick Papers.*
[2] *Standard*, January 7, 1830.

a want of Parliamentary Reform ; they cannot, if my Lord Grey can, perceive that the House of Commons is sufficiently under public opinion." [1] Any enthusiasm for Catholic Relief they might feel arose simply from seeing the same party which bullied them in 1817 bullying the Catholics now. If the Tories had granted Reform twenty, or even ten, years back, they would never have heard of the Catholic question. Full of contempt for alike the orthodox Whigs and the " Westminster Rump," Cobbett called for Reform as a protection against the Papists, who might use their wealth to buy up rotten boroughs. If the distress would bring Reform, he hoped it would continue. " In short, the game is up unless the aristocracy hasten forward and conciliate the people." [2]

This class feeling comes out strongly in the proceedings of the London Radical Reform Association, founded in July with a " Radical rent " of a penny; [3] in October it issued an Address to the People, urging the country to form local societies to promote the cause of Annual Parliaments, Universal Suffrage, and the Ballot. No administration, no party, is guilty of the present misery ; the nation is divided into two castes, alien in interests, habits, and sympathies. Of the rich all interests are represented—the Land, Commerce, Shipping, East India merchants and West India planters, Brewers, " Saints," Sport, and Science. The people alone has no representation, and as a result the country is on the verge of beggary. The Reform movement among the working classes, the revival of which since the days of Peterloo seems to spring from this society, began and continued as a demand for social revolution, ignoring any distinction between the aristocratic parties. A Scotch mower, forbidden to ply his scythe near the laird's house in the morning for fear of disturbing the ladies, shakes his fist at the " lazy Tories " and says they will have a bad time when Burdett gets among them. [4] The Radicals of this class were usually indifferent to the Constitution, if not avowed republicans. Cobbett, however, to whose imagination the past of England meant much, said approvingly that the middle classes would always hold by King, Lords, and Commons.

The defence of the Radical Reform Association was taken

---

[1] *Political Register*, February 28, 1829.   [2] *Ibid.*, June 13, 1829.
[3] The " Catholic rent " had been a feature of O'Connell's Irish agitation.
[4] Alexander Somerville, *Autobiography of a Working Man.*

up by the *Westminster* reviewers, lately engaged in a battle-royal all along the line with the *Edinburgh*, and therefore cherishing no friendship for Whiggery. The Whigs, they declared, " are men who profess to do everything for the people and nothing by the people, and who are at this moment pushing a not over-wise Government into persecution of the press." [1] Though the poor might not be themselves equal to the task of government, they knew enough to use the little power they had to obtain more, and " in this pursuit the classes whose personal suffering takes the most substantial form are naturally foremost. The wonder is that the classes next above, in whom has been truly said to reside the preponderating portion of the momentum of the public, should be so long in joining." [2] The duty of intelligent men was to exorcise the spectre of revolution raised by the inflammatory speeches of irresponsible demagogues. " Sensible men are not to endure an evil for ever, through a vague fear of its removal being something they have not tried before." Long ago Lord John Russell had agreed with Bentham that nothing could be done till the bogey was laid. For some years now the Radical quarterly had been coming out with an appearance of spotless respectability, and showing that Utilitarians did not confine their appeal to the *sans culotte* of Westminster. They had never ceased to keep Reform in a prominent position, and in 1827 James Mill had contributed an article on the subject to the *Parliamentary History and Review*.

By the beginning of 1830 Reform had become a familiar topic to the minds of the middle classes ; the discontent following on the bad winter was likely to make it practical. Cobbett, who beyond question had a wider influence in the country at this time than any other single man, had delivered a course of lectures at the Mechanics' Institute in London. In December he started on his Northern Tour, with a view to collecting information as to the real state of the people, besides addressing meetings and urging his hearers to agitate for Reform. He proceeded first to Birmingham and thence in a northerly direction. In Manchester, where in 1819 and 1826 he was treated with little courtesy, he was delighted by his receptions at four meetings, each of which he estimated as numbering not less than a thousand. At Cambridge only he complains that the Vice-Chancellor

---

[1] *Westminster Review*, October 1829.
[2] *Ibid.*, January 1830.

refused him permission to lecture in the theatre on Radical Reform of Parliament.

The London papers were taking the same line. One Whig journal, finding the question raised in *Blackwood's Magazine* whether education is calculated to make the lower classes better subjects, supplied the paraphrase : is it "calculated to add to their affection for rotten boroughs, licensing, game and corn laws," and the other results of an unreformed Parliament ? [1] The libel prosecutions by Sir James Scarlett, the Attorney-General, also caused much bitterness. The general feeling was that the Government always played the people with loaded dice. It was the cue of the High Tory organ no less to emphasise the distress of the country and cry out against the scandalous composition of a House of Commons which could pass Catholic Relief by an act of sheer despotism over the heads of a Protestant nation.[2] The country districts followed suit. Several county meetings were held in a spirit more or less hostile to the Government ; in view of the distress alleged to be nearly universal in agricultural England, a lightening of taxation, especially on beer and malt, was demanded, and many speakers laid the blame on Peel's decision to resume cash payments in 1823. But on the remedies needed, and on the nature of the disease, the two great interests were sharply divided in opinion. Manchester did not believe in county meetings got up by ultra-Tories and a few ultra-Whigs ; reduction of rents and taxes was the true policy. London and the manufacturing districts would not co-operate with men who wanted prices artificially raised.[3] Reform was usually mentioned, but rather as a matter well worthy of consideration than as an article to be included in a petition—a phase that recalls the early days of Wyvill's agitation of the eighties. These distress meetings held in different parts of the country culminated in a vast assembly of between ten and fifteen thousand people, held at Birmingham on January 25, and the formation there of the Birmingham Political Union, to whose energies even Whig statesmen largely attributed the passing of the Great Reform Bill.

At Birmingham, as at many other places, the Reform movement originated in the miseries of 1817, when a mass meeting

[1] *Morning Chronicle*, January 1, 1830.
[2] *Standard*, January 1, 1830.
[3] *Manchester Guardian*, January 23, 1830.

of ten thousand supporters was held ; two years later the Reformers brought trouble upon themselves by their presumption in appointing Sir Charles Wolseley to proceed to London as their Legislatorial Attorney and Representative, in protest against the exclusion from representation of so great a town, a place with a population of 100,000 and the centre of the hardware industry.  Here as elsewhere efforts slackened after the repressive legislation of 1819 ; however, in 1823 a "Birmingham Union Society of Radical Reformers," on the principles of Henry Hunt, was in existence, and in 1827–8 Tennyson's endeavours to transfer to Birmingham the tarnished franchise of East Retford were followed by the townsmen with warm interest and support.  The desired enfranchisement was spoken of as a " sacred trust to be exercised with the soundest discretion," and petitions for it with 4000 signatures were sent up.[1]  In the space covered by the great war the centre of gravity in England had been shifting from the agricultural south to the northern seats of manufacture, where the Industrial Revolution had caused a vast increase of population.[2]  Agriculture no longer enjoyed an unchallenged pre-eminence ; Manchester was already forging the weapons which won the battle of Free Trade, but it was becoming clear that another contest must be waged first. The efforts of pre-revolution Reformers had centred on an addition to the county representation as a check on the Crown.  Now the King's influence was not feared, but that of the squirearchy was, and when the cry for Reform revived after its suppression during the war the enfranchisement of the great new towns was the main demand, and remained so till 1830.

About this time there came forward as a leader of the movement a remarkable man, who eventually reached a position which made him one of the arbiters of the nation's fate and, in the eyes of many, its saviour.  Thomas Attwood, born in 1783, was a member of a great banking family, who had risen to be chief magistrate of Birmingham.  Always interested in politics as they touched the industrial classes, he had been pre-

[1] Langford, *A Century of Birmingham Life*, vol. ii.

[2] A table of growth in population, as given by the Census, may be useful :

|  | 1801. | 1811. | 1821. | 1831. |
|---|---|---|---|---|
| Manchester | 84,020 | 98,573 | 133,788 | 182,812 |
| Birmingham | 73,670 | 85,753 | 106,722 | 146,986 |
| Leeds | 53,162 | 62,534 | 83,796 | 123,393 |

sented by the operatives of the town with a medal for his
exertions on their behalf. He had a large family to which he
was devoted, and enjoyed at Birmingham a kind of patriarchal
reverence. He was a typical merchant prince of the early
nineteenth century, full of energy and common sense, with an
emotional disposition readily touched by large ideas of liberty,
and a great sense of the dramatic. In April 1829 he had spoken
at a town's meeting called to consider the distress of the country,
the cure for which he religiously believed to be a large issue of
Bank of England notes to neutralise the effects of the resumption
of cash payments. The currency was Attwood's pet subject,
and there is reason to believe that his despair of obtaining any
improvement such as he desired from the unreformed House of
Commons convinced him of the necessity of Reform. The fact
that Cobbett, whose views on the currency were as radical as
his, but in the exactly opposite direction, decided to pass through
Birmingham first, on his tour of the northern counties, out of
respect to Attwood, says much for the strength of his personality.
In December 1829 Attwood formed a small society of friends,
which he called a Political Union, for the protection of public
rights ; but it was not till January 1830 that the agitation with
which his name is associated began.

On January 5 an appeal signed by many of the most distinguished men of Birmingham was issued to the High Bailiff,
requiring him, in view of the lamentable state of public affairs
and the consequent need of Reform, to call a town's meeting
for the formation of a Political Union.[1] On the refusal of the
High Bailiff to do so, a meeting was arranged by the Reformers
for January 25, to assemble in Beardsworth's Repository, a vast
covered building ; and there, with Attwood in the chair, the
Birmingham Political Union was formed, its first resolution
being, " to obtain by every just and legal means such a reform

---

[1] " Sir, We the undersigned being of opinion that the General Distress
which now afflicts the country and which has been so severely felt at
several periods during the last fifteen years is to be entirely ascribed to
the Gross Mismanagement of Public Affairs, and that such mismanagement can only be effectually and permanently remedied by an effectual
Reform in the Commons' House of Parliament, and being also of opinion
that for the legal accomplishment of this great object and for the further
redress of public wrongs and grievances it is expedient to form a General
Political Union between the Lower and Middle Classes of the people, do
request you will call a meeting . . ." (Add. MSS. 27,789, f. 134).

in the Commons' House of Parliament as may ensure a real and effectual representation of the lower and middle classes of the people in that House." In the course of a long speech the chairman said that, though he had always been for Reform, he should not have wasted his energies in proposing it at a time of prosperity. Now, however, when the trade of Birmingham had been progressively decreasing for the last four years, when the decrease could be directly attributed to the financial ignorance and excessive taxes of a corrupt Government, it was madness not to come forward. For effectual action union was necessary ; he therefore proposed the formation of a Political Union, under the guidance of a Political Council.

The proceedings at Birmingham were excellently advertised in the papers and created a great impression throughout the country. Cobbett looked for great things from the long delayed union of the middle and lower classes, and even Lord Grey, writing from his retreat in Northumberland, prophesied that the new spirit rising in the country would result in some force potent for evil to the Government.[1] The *Times* indeed maintained that the whole thing was nonsense and would probably die away quickly, but none the less gave the account of the meeting four and a half columns. As a rule Attwood's currency ideas were treated with amused contempt, but interest in the general question of Reform was stimulated. The *Morning Chronicle*, giving the proceedings five and a half columns, agreed on the necessity of Reform, but expressed its fears " that no great measure will ever be carried by the agency merely of high-minded and disinterested men ; that interest, and interest alone, in the vulgar sense, determines nineteen out of twenty, or rather ninety-nine out of a hundred men in the course they pursue." Such Benthamite cynicism did not, however, lead to despair of success. Capitalists were forcing up the price of boroughs and the expenses of elections almost beyond the reach of the aristocracy. The *Standard*, representing the country party, was willing to sacrifice rotten boroughs, and, declaring that the aspect of the question was completely changed by the events of the last year, if not by the gradual rescue of Reform from the exclusive hands of the Radicals, expounded a scheme of Tory Reform, by which a judiciously generous treatment of

[1] Grey to Princess Lieven, January 29, 1830 ; *Lieven Correspondence*, i. 423.

the agricultural districts could not fail to return at least a three-fourths majority of good Church and King men to Parliament ; it were better to enfranchise no large towns at all than multiply mere workhouse and alehouse votes. " If the Tory nobility and gentry imitate Mr. Attwood by early taking a lead in the popular cause, there will be no ' crisis ' whatever." No one could now maintain that the Constitution worked well in practice ; from all shades of opinion Reform could claim approbation, at least in theory. The Radicals would abandon it when it ceased to be their exclusive property ; as to the Whigs, on Sheridan's own confession, they only adopted it as a perennial and irremovable grievance.[1] But for the English Jacobins of 1793, Parliament would have been reformed long ago, and by the Tory party, whose leaders, from Bolingbroke onwards, had always been its advocates. Even if they had not, a hundred popish legislators created a new danger, for neither the Crown nor the aristocracy as a whole had any influence in the Commons. If a definite grievance were demanded, Peel's return for Westbury, after his rejection by High Church Oxford, was in itself sufficient.[2]

In less official political circles the Birmingham meeting had acted as a powerful stimulus to Reform. The Metropolitan Association for Radical Reform, apparently connected, if not identical, with the society which issued the appeal in October, discussed its resolutions with approval, though regretting their moderation ; and from now onwards an impulse was given to the formation all over the country of societies to promote Parliamentary Reform.[3] The importance of these unions, as providing channels for the communication of Reforming ideas and centres for organised effort, can hardly be exaggerated, though before the introduction of the Whig bill they had no definite objective. Many indeed were founded to support it, and many again after its rejection by the Lords. It will be seen later that

[1] *Standard*, January 27–29.
[2] *Ibid.*, February 24.
[3] *E.g.* on March 25 a political meeting was held at Stow-on-the-Wold, Gloucestershire, to form a " Union of the Middle and Lower Classes of Society " on the Birmingham model ; the rules and manifesto of the parent body were quoted. Reform was desired as a step to reduction of taxes. " By this great measure, the general state of prosperity which existed in the years 1824 and 1825 may yet be restored " (Public Record Office, *Home Office Papers* (henceforward *H. O.*), 44. 19).

they fall naturally into two distinct classes, but the inspiration of nearly all came from Birmingham. Attwood wished to have inscribed upon his grave, " Here lies the founder of Political Unions," and was usually recognised as such.[1] As a matter of fact the associations of the Reform movement in the eighties, and especially the Yorkshire Association, provide very close parallels in object and organisation : the delegates sent by the committees in 1780 and 1781 to the central meetings in London played just such a part as excited the horror of strict constitutionalists fifty years later. The reason that Wyvill escaped the odium incurred by Attwood is that his activities were mainly concerned with country gentlemen of like passions and sympathies with the Government. The unionists of 1831 were of a different class and outlook ; their behaviour was unintelligible, and therefore suspicious, to those in power. Those who enrolled themselves in military organisations of course went a step further ; but extremely few unions proceeded to this length. The intention of most was the same—the compassing of a political end by extra-parliamentary, but not unconstitutional, means.

The stir created by the Birmingham Union and the county meetings had hardly subsided, when Parliament met for the King's speech on February 4. The condition of parties had changed little since the end of last session. Apart from the Ministerialists, represented in the Commons by Peel and Goulburn, and the slender remnant of the old Whig Opposition, there were the High Tories led by Cumberland and Eldon, the Canningites under Huskisson, and the young Whigs and Reformers, as yet without an acknowledged chief.[2] Distress was very much in the air, and to a lesser degree Reform, in connection with which four notices of motions had been laid down in the Commons.

The Duke of Wellington himself expected a difficult session, but hoped to weather it by a straightforward course, trusting that the country gentlemen would think better of their opposition and " not seriously endeavour to break down the establishments of the country because the getting in of the harvest has

[1] Wakefield, *Life of Attwood*, p. 151.
[2] *Morning Chronicle*, February 4, 1830.

been expensive to their tenants." [1] Nor had he anything to fear from the manufacturers, so long as they might expect a remission of taxation. The *Manchester Guardian*, a champion of Free Trade and afterwards of the Reform Bill, offered him its full support.[2] The divisions, too, between the four sections of the Opposition looked too deep to be easily healed, and the Duke saw no reason for making advances to anyone at present. The High Tories, who a month before had been excited by rumours of a possible administration to be formed by the Duke of Richmond, seemed void of any motive save a passion to overthrow the Duke ; to gain which end most of them were prepared to unite with the Whigs, who at least had never betrayed them, to adopt Reform, or to take any other step. An opportunity was promptly afforded them by Sir Edward Knatchbull's factious amendment to the Address, declaring that the distress in the country was not partial but general. The Brunswickers, as Cumberland's following were called, mustered in force, and only the votes of a few Whigs saved the Government from a premature defeat, to which Huskisson, Althorp, and Brougham would have alike contributed. The Whigs would have indeed gained little from such a victory, as they themselves realised ; the Duke would be forced, if not to give way to a High Tory Cabinet, at least to divide his power with that section or with the Canningites. Neither prospect was pleasing to the Whigs, who preferred, in Hobhouse's phrase, a good weak Government. Many indeed of them appear to have voted for the amendment simply as a truer statement of fact, though they must have known the possible result of their votes.[3] Certainly Althorp and Brougham and Tavistock meant to give the ministry a fair chance ;[4] Althorp admitted that they had done more good to the country than any former administration, and many Whigs thought any change would be for the worse. The Opposition henceforward played a cat and mouse game with the Government, partly from contemptuous tolerance of the mouse

[1] Wellington to Maurice Fitzgerald, January 19, 1830; *Despatches*, vi. 424.

[2] *Manchester Guardian*, January 23, 1830.

[3] Lord Broughton's *Recollections*, iv. 8 ; *Broughton Correspondence*, Add. MSS. 36,466, February 13, 1830.

[4] Tavistock wrote to Hobhouse on February 13 : "I am for the Duke with his wings clipped, because I see nothing better to look to" (Add. MSS. 36,466 ; Le Marchant, *Memoir of Viscount Althorp*, p. 234).

E

and partly from dislike of the other cats. Howick at least had hopes that the Duke's extremity might mean an offer of place to his father, and voted accordingly to keep him in ; he deeply resented that the Duke, who was generally supposed to be kept in office simply because he was the one man who could manage the King, should confess his failure even in that, by bowing to royal caprice in the matter of Lord Grey's exclusion.[1]

A test of parliamentary opinions on Reform was provided on February 11 by the introduction of Calvert's bill to prevent bribery at East Retford, with an amendment by Tennyson to transfer its franchise to Birmingham ; " the general distress had created a great alteration of opinion." The amendment was supported by the Canningites ; Huskisson declared that he considered some such proposal as this, which but for ministerial influence would be by now the expressed desire of Parliament, to be the only barrier " against the growing danger of sweeping reform on principles too general and abstract." The Birmingham Union, with its intention of raising " a universal cry for Parliamentary Reform," seemed to him no less dangerous than the Catholic Association. In spite of such conservative arguments, the view of Goulburn, who " thought that there was a great danger in going even one step towards general reform," prevailed by twenty-seven votes, and the wider proposals of Howick were rejected by a majority of ninety-nine. On the wisdom of moving this amendment, which his impatience at the miserable half-measures proposed had prompted, Howick had consulted his father ;[2] he received an answer from the champion of Reform which might well damp his enthusiasm. Approving of the motion in itself, Lord Grey was doubtful of his son's prudence in mixing himself up with so troublesome a question in a way which might compromise him awkwardly when the distress, to which its present popularity was due, had subsided, and might bequeath to him, like his father, many weary years of effort in the face of a hostile king and an indifferent people.[3]

---

[1] Howick to Grey, February 5, January 12, 1830 : " If he really only owes his power to the King's inability to do without him, his junction with you would make it still more impossible to dispense with your services, and the same necessity which keeps him in the Cabinet ought to introduce you into it " (*Howick Papers*).

[2] Howick to Grey, February 8 ; *Howick Papers*.

[3] " I do not see what advantage you would derive by hampering yourself with a question which will always be opposed by the Crown,

At first sight, counsel of such blatant opportunism appears unworthy of a great man and a great cause, and tends to justify the contention of Radical critics that Reform was forced upon the Whigs as surely as Catholic Emancipation was forced on the Duke of Wellington.[1] Certainly the world-worn politician of sixty-six has lost the quixotic faith of youth, and he betrays a strange ignorance of the change in popular feeling since 1820. But experience had taught him that circumstances are of as much importance in politics as ideas, and had warned him of the danger of exciting false hopes. He once complained to Holland of the unreasonable criticism levelled at the administration of 1806, and drew the moral: "The lesson that I have learnt therefore is to *pledge myself to as little as possible whilst in opposition,* and, when in Government, if ever it should be my lot to be again in that situation, *to do as much as I can.*"[2] When his day came, Grey put the second part of his lesson into practice as strictly as he now put the first; but in the meantime he wished to save his son, and he was not the man to understand the workings of political thought in classes outside his own. The result of the accession of a king less obstinate than George IV was a factor which he had, perhaps, no excuse for ignoring; but the effects of the Three Days of July he could not be expected to foresee, and without them it is perfectly arguable that returning prosperity might in time have killed the desire for Reform. Barring these two considerations, and ruling out the possibility of agitation in the country as alien to Grey's principles, remembering also the small and divided numbers of the Reformers in Parliament, one sees no reason

and on which you cannot rely on the support of the people. Assist in carrying the measure if a fair opportunity should offer, but do not pledge yourself in such a manner as may give ground hereafter, if you should be connected with the Government, as I hope to see you, for reproach in not pushing it. *Experto crede*" (Grey to Howick, February 10; *Howick Papers*).

[1] "The two factions in the State, the Whigs and Tories, had played their game a little too broadly—nothing was said in Parliament of Parliamentary Reform as a remedy, no such remedy was desired by either party, but the people saw no other, and their reiterated demands for Reform soon gave the tone to many members of both Houses, and this coupled with the notions of distress and the dread of the consequences were the causes which on the accession to power of the Whigs compelled them to propose the Reform Bill" (Add. MSS. 27,789, f. 142).

[2] *Life and Opinions of Earl Grey*, p. 164.

why Reform should have been more practicable in 1830 than in the few years before, and why the leader of a political party, not a crank of one idea, should not have been averse to hazarding all on a single throw. Grey was wholly consistent with his own views, expressed at least as far back as 1810, in refusing to legislate ahead of public opinion.

The zeal of younger men, however, renewed the attack ; it was now the turn of the ultra-Tories, and on February 18 the Marquis of Blandford continued his efforts of the last session by bringing in a measure of wide Reform, including a redistribution of seats, a scot and lot franchise in the new boroughs, and payment of members, with repeal of the Septennial Act. This motion was held to prove Blandford's sincerity as a Reformer— he became a member of the Birmingham Union ; it is needless to say that it was lost, as well as an amendment of Althorp's in favour of general Reform. On this occasion Burdett, who for Reform's own sake had kept his hands off it in Parliament for the last few years, gave voice to the feelings of the progressive party, in declaring " that the only struggle really worth making was for Reform in Parliament. He believed that the people of England were at last beginning to bestir themselves." A further opportunity for moderate Reformers was given on February 23. Lord John Russell brought in an extremely gentle bill for enfranchising Manchester, Birmingham, and Leeds, with a £10 or £20 householder qualification ; he recommended it by showing that, as it only proposed to give the vote to places at the head of some particular interest, its principle could not be applied to more than four or five towns in the empire. In spite of this soothing thought, in spite of Brougham's eloquence and the blessing of the Canningites, this, the main effort of the Whigs in 1830 on the subject of Reform, was lost by forty-eight votes in a fairly good House. The result was largely due to the opposition of Peel, who called up the shades of Burke and Canning to cry sacrilege on those who would touch the fabric of the Constitution and violate the Act of Union with Scotland. His uncompromising attitude disappointed the Manchester manufacturers, who had hoped that he, " the reformer of so many abuses," would in this matter too prove the friend of the middle class.[1]   Even this defeat, however, was claimed as a moral victory

---

[1] *Manchester Guardian*, February 27, 1830.

for moderate Reform by the *Times*, which at this time supported the ministry and deeply regretted the attitude of the High Tories ; it was obviously unfair, it said further, to load the transference of the franchise to large towns, with the odium attaching to immoderate measures. Croker, as in 1822, was for giving up four members to the great towns as a sop to irresistible demand.[1] Another motion to transfer the forfeited franchise of East Retford to Birmingham was quashed in March, and so was a demand for a committee of inquiry into the conduct of the Duke of Newcastle, who had shamelessly evicted thirty-seven tenants at Newark in the late election, for voting for a man " of bad political principles," as the *Standard* indignantly declared in the Duke's defence.

A few weeks of the session were enough to make clear to the Whigs the unsatisfactory nature of their attitude. Althorp and Howick soon began to reconsider their position of neutrality to what they considered a culpably inefficient Government.[2] Though still hiding their claws, the party determined to exert pressure by motions for retrenchment in various parts of the civil service ; their foremost speaker in debates of this nature was young Sir James Graham of Netherby, member for Cumberland, who at a county meeting shortly before the meeting of Parliament had called for moderate Reform as a means of infusing more of the spirit of the country into the Commons ; he admired the Duke personally, he had said, but feared the military aspect of his Cabinet ; in one way his unpopularity with the Court and aristocracy was an advantage, as he would only be able to govern by the support of the people. " What a satire upon our glorious Constitution," exclaimed the *Morning Chronicle*.[3] The financial reformers were warmly encouraged by the press, which promised them the people's support.[4] In Parliament, though, the enterprise was one requiring the greatest delicacy of manœuvre ; to stand up for retrenchment was all very well, but if the ministry sustained a defeat by their efforts, it would be the Huskissons or the Brunswickers who would be

[1] Croker to Peel, February 24 ; *Croker Papers*, ii. 54.
[2] Howick to Grey, February 15 ; *Howick Papers*.
[3] January 30, 1830.
[4] " The party which will rally round his Lordship [Lord Morpeth] and Lord Althorp is worth 100 benches of meretricious middlemen, who never vote except for themselves."

called in. So much seemed clear from Lord Grey's continued exclusion. On the other hand, as Grey himself thought necessary to point out, a too obvious reluctance to injure the Government would bring down the contempt of the people on themselves and the whole parliamentary system.[1]

The party was indeed in a lamentable condition. The leadership in the Commons, which since Grey's removal to the Lords had been held by a succession of worthy but undistinguished politicians, had been for some time in abeyance. Tierney lived till January 1830, but of late years Brougham seems to have filled the post in practice, though socially he was hardly fitted for it. For a party of serious intentions such an anarchic state of things was impossible, and that it was tolerated bears witness to the Whig's disorganisation.[2] Then in 1827 came the " Insurrection at Brooks's " and the great schism, the effects of which were such that Althorp in 1828 discouraged any ideas of forming an inner circle of his own allies, preferring " to be absorbed in the general Whig party " in course of time.[3] It was only gradually that a corporate spirit grew up ;[4] common opposition to Government helped it, and at length in March 1830, with a view to strengthening themselves as a party, some thirty or forty of the young Whigs met at Althorp's house to contemplate uniting under his leadership. The points discussed were mainly economic ; fear of currency change kept off some, the idea of a property-tax others.[5] On March 6 Althorp wrote to inform Grey and Brougham that a union for the purpose of securing retrenchment had been formed ; it had been decided not to seek alliance with the Tories or " Huskissonians " and to refrain from compassing the Government's overthrow. Grey received

---

[1] Grey to Howick, February 27 ; *Howick Papers*.

[2] Althorp wrote to Brougham, March 17, 1823 : " Lambton and Duncannon, I believe, have written to you about some plan of a Republican form of government for the Opposition. I think it rather a bad plan, but at all rates, I can't give any answer about it without consulting you. If you approve of it I shall not object, but that must be the full extent of my approbation " (*Althorp Papers*).

[3] Althorp to Russell, January 13, 1828 ; *Early Correspondence*, i. 272.

[4] Devonshire to Russell, December 22, 1829 : " I quite agree with you in trusting Althorp and Brougham, but till there is some strong feeling to unite our friends in one general interest, to prevent their following their own desires as they do now, we shall never be worth much as a party " (*Early Correspondence*, i. 300).

[5] Howick to Grey, March 2, 3, 6 ; *Howick Papers*.

the news of the venture with anything but enthusiasm; he distrusted the new financial ideas, and thought Althorp had not sufficiently allowed for the likelihood of the Government's defeat. But the union being a *fait accompli*, Grey turned his mind towards the best chance of forming a new ministry, and so far the enterprise must be regarded as a step forward. The difficulties of including Huskisson—the Whigs never liked or trusted him—might be removed by the help of Palmerston and the Grants; supposing Peel to be in opposition, Palmerston might lead the Commons.[1] In the letter from which these views are taken Grey spoke of the proposed arrangements entirely in the second person. His son protested. Whether or not the Duke and Peel were members of the new ministry—and such a coalition was not held inconceivable,—Grey must certainly belong; in the one case as the only personality that could check the Duke's autocratic conduct, in the other as Premier to overrule Huskisson.[2] Grey's answer is surprising to those who have gathered from his numerous remarks on the subject that he was pained at the Duke's silence. He announced definitely that in no case could he take an active share in the work of government. He was an old man, and lack of energies of both body and mind forbade him to contemplate more than occasional intervention in the new ministry's behalf.[3] This was no decision of the moment, but his matured judgment. Such an announcement was indeed a shock; all desire for conciliation with the Duke was then, it appeared, the mere caprice of vanity; the aged Reformer would not lead the wanderers into the promised land. No wonder his son refused to accept the renunciation.

It is worth while at this moment of Whig awakening to notice one or two points which present themselves. It was a frequent taunt on the part of the Tory press that the Whigs had favoured and courted the ministry during this session as long as they saw any hope of proposals for comprehension, but adopted instead an attitude of hostility as soon as they were dis-

---

[1] Grey to Howick, March 9. Grey spoke of " that rogue Huskisson," Creevey of " the shuffling, lying Huskisson " (*Creevey Papers*, pp. 487, 494). They disliked him as a Canningite and a *bourgeois*. On the other hand, he was the darling of the manufacturers.

[2] Howick to Grey, March 11, 17; *Howick Papers*.

[3] Grey to Howick, March 14.

illusioned.[1]  These assertions were flatly denied on behalf of the
party by Lord Althorp, most honest of men.[2]  The question is of
course connected with the conduct of Lord Grey, which, as we
learn from Hobhouse's Diary, gave cause of dissatisfaction to his
own side.[3]  It is perhaps fairer to frame an indictment against
a political party than against most other associations of men ;
its policy is of necessity unified and its members live in intimate
contact.  But the Whigs in the first session of 1830 were not
duly organised as a party; on the vital question of supporting
the Government they were divided.[4]  Such concerted action as
eventually took place was a process of time, and one is almost
reduced to an analysis of the behaviour of individuals.  The
principles of Althorp himself stand clear ; originally friendly to
the Government, he had hoped it would repair its weakness,
but, as the session wore on, he was alienated by its incompetent
inaction.[5]  In Howick's case the imputation is proved on his
own showing.  He had wished at first, he writes, to force the
ministry to invite his father.  Events showed that the Duke
would admit no one but creatures of his own.  Howick would
have preferred the Duke and Peel to have retained their places
with his father at the Foreign Office.  This being impossible,
the Government had better give place to one headed by Grey
and Huskisson.  Lord Grey's own position is doubtful ; probably it varied according as distaste for business, party spirit, or
the hope of leading a victorious cause, lay uppermost in his
thoughts.  In January we have seen him resentful, in March
anxious for repose ; " he must indeed know little of Lord Grey,
who hopes that his indolence will be conquered by the ambition
of leading the awkward squad who now sit on the left of Mr.
Speaker." [6]  The surprises of the summer encouraged him to

---

[1] " In their best days they coalesced with Lord North," a pamphlet
puts it ; " most of them fairly hugged the French Jacobins ; they afterwards joined the English Radicals, lastly Mr. Canning.  They are now
perfectly willing to embrace the Duke of Wellington."  And again :
" The Duke of Wellington having politely declined their offers, they now
address themselves to the High Tories."

[2] Althorp to Brougham, October 5, 1830 ; *Memoir of Althorp*, p. 242.

[3] *Recollections*, iv. 31.

[4] *Ibid.*, iv. 10.

[5] Althorp to Brougham, June 17, 1829, *Althorp Papers ;* quoted
above, p. 52.

[6] *The Country Well Governed.*

look for better things. It is not contended that Howick
and those who acted with him played a dishonourable part ;
it must frequently happen that a party decides to support
men in office from the belief that in its own influence on
the ministers lies the best chance of good government, but
as circumstances alter abandons that hope for more direct
methods. Only it must be maintained that some at least of
the Whigs showed a change of front as prospects of office
receded.

Outside Parliament the general lowness of wages and profits
were still complained of in the press and at county meetings.
In the old sequence, the demand for reform of the representation followed on protests against the financial policy of the
Government, and a bitter class feeling was abroad. Not only
was the amount of taxation attributed to the need of providing
for aristocratic beggars, but all the growing degradation of the
working classes during the last few years was laid at the landlords' door.[1] The cry was raised with an intensity which forced
at least Whig noblemen to admit its provocation.[2] A feature
of this spirit was the foundation, at a mass meeting in the City
Road on March 9, of the Metropolitan Political Union for Radical
Reform. Among the speakers were Hunt, who had lately carried
a resolution in this sense at a gathering at the Mansion House ;
O'Connell, now transferring his noisy energies across St. George's
Channel ; Carlile, the Radical atheist ; and Hetherington, stern
opponent of the taxes on knowledge, who later on took a prominent part in the Reform struggle. This body made unsuccessful overtures to the Westminster Reformers ; more respectable
was the Parliamentary Reform Association, started in April by
the Radical Colonel Jones, the friend of Hobhouse and Burdett.[3]
On May 17 the Birmingham Union gave evidence of its flourishing condition by organising a procession estimated at 20,000
men, and striking a medal with a lion surrounded by the im-

---

[1] " The howl set up by the landlords on account of the Poors' Rates
is almost ludicrous. This is not an evil of to-day or yesterday, and they
have either been parties to the creation of it, or they have looked on
with their arms crossed while the farmers throughout the agricultural
districts were reducing the labourers to the condition of bondsmen "
(*Morning Chronicle*, February 26).

[2] Tavistock to Hobhouse, March 29 ; Add. MSS. 36,466.

[3] Add. MSS. 36,466, April 28.

pressive motto, " The Constitution : nothing less and nothing more." [1]

The views which found favour at Radical meetings were less warmly received when, on May 28, O'Connell proposed to the House of Commons a bill for Universal Suffrage. In the course of the debate Althorp declared his approval of the ballot and triennial parliaments, while Lord John Russell now asked for the enfranchisement of a number of large towns, in place of several small boroughs which should receive compensation. O'Connell's bill was lost by 306 votes ; a non-committal resolution of Lord John Russell's by 96. This was the last verdict on Reform of the Parliament of 1826. But though the Reformers still seemed a long way from victory so far as votes were concerned, a great change of feeling had taken place both in the country and the House. At Birmingham a large association had been formed by eminently respectable men, who excluded from their demands those Radical projects which recalled the days of Jacobinism ; at Westminster the innovators were led by the son of a ducal house and the heir to an earldom, both disclaiming any sweeping measure. So great was the effect, that Hobhouse said the House refused to listen to the few speeches in which all Reform was condemned. [2]

As May advanced, the death of the King was known to be a matter of weeks, and the spirits of the Whigs rose at the prospect of a dissolution, with the Government in its present disrepute. Sir George Cornewall Lewis speaks of 1830 as the nadir of the Tory party ; in 1828 William Lamb had said that he knew no young Tory of promise. In Peel alone, as representing the better elements of the Liverpool Cabinet, had the country any real confidence. Probably the ablest of the politicians of his time, unquestionably the most business-like, his enlightened spirit commended him to the middle-classes and, as we have seen, to the Whigs, while even such a cynic as Francis Place recognised his industry and superior knowledge. Nevertheless to the High Tories he was anathema, and his own outlook at this time was dispirited and oppressed by the general dislocation

---

[1] A lady who had been in France in 1789 said to Joseph Parkes of Birmingham : " Your country is on the eve of great political changes. I noticed almost the entire company to be men under forty years of age. So it was in Paris " (Le Marchant, *Memoir of Althorp*, p. 251).

[2] *Recollections*, iv. 24.

of politics. The secession of the Canningites had left him stranded among uncongenial colleagues ; we may well believe with Disraeli that he faced the possibility of defeat at least with equanimity. Early in the month Croker was aware of the Whigs' increase of confidence, and seriously considered their chances of forming an administration, not forgetting to allow for the effects of a new reign. Granted a combination of the Old and Young Whigs, the Grenvilles, and the Canningites, he admitted their internal strength both in Parliament and in the departments, but doubted their power of winning support outside. " I do not think the country would tolerate them a second session, because they must either offend public opinion by pursuing Whig measures, or forfeit it by abandoning their pledged principles." [1] The last words are interesting as an example of the low opinion in which the party of Fox was held by its opponents, and indeed, it may be said, by the country in general. Tories and Radicals were at least consistent ; Englishmen who were not their dependents found it hard to appreciate the principles of these aristocrats, who spoke eloquently of the rights and liberties of the people, but from combined ill-luck and inefficiency never seemed to achieve anything more than a few measures of little public benefit and a few months of family government.

New and more hopeful attempts, however, were being made to take away the reproach and make the Whigs a party once more. No public meeting at Brooks's was yet thought wise, but some sixty Whig members assembled one Saturday in Althorp's chambers in the Albany, and formed the nucleus of a united party to act under his leadership. Lord Althorp's biographer speaks, on the authority of an eye-witness, of Peel's start when the new leader first used the magic " *we.*" [2] Even Grey, who had arrived in town in April, was raised from his constitutional despondency by the aspect of affairs, as he observed the increasing weakness of the ministry and the willingness of their opponents to act with himself.[3] At length, the

[1] Croker to Vesey Fitzgerald, May 3, 17 ; *Croker Papers*, ii. 58 ff.

[2] Le Marchant, *Memoir of Viscount Althorp*, pp. 243–246.

[3] *Lieven Correspondence*, ii. 5, 8, 12. Creevey wrote on May 31 : " To call on Lady Grey. . . . She is all against Lord Grey becoming a politician again, and says she sees people getting round him whom she hates, and never can forgive for their past conduct to him, and whose only object now is to use him for their own interests. She mentioned Brougham in particular " (*Creevey Papers*, p. 553).

day before King George died, he forced a division, on a trifling matter, against the Duke in the Lords, and was only beaten by fifteen votes.[1] The need of comprehension was more than hinted at in a pamphlet which suggested that, while a Board of General Officers might be tolerated in exceptional circumstances, it was impossible for a ministry to continue which enjoyed the confidence of neither the King, the Church, the Nobility, Parliament, nor the country.[2] The Duke himself was well aware of the consolidation of the Opposition likely to result from the King's death, which would involve the political extinction of the Duke of Cumberland and the rise of his party in public estimation. In a letter to Peel he reviews the situation, and finally suggests the inclusion of the Canningites under Peel as Prime Minister.[3] Parts of the letter are worth quoting as expressing the thoughts of the Premier at a time when his probable intentions were widely and vaguely canvassed.

" The course of events, supposing matters to go on as they are, and that the new King should require the services of the existing administration, will necessarily oblige Lord Grey to take a course. He must be informed of the Duke of Clarence's inclination to have the benefit of his services. If the ministers of the day do not avail themselves of this inclination in order to employ him in office, he will consider the objection to be personal to himself ; and he will be as ready to become the leader of the four parties in opposition to the Government, as they will be to act under his lead. . . .

" I do not think that we could take Lord Grey into office

---

[1] *Hansard* (New Series), xxv. 698. There is an allusion to Grey's attitude in Hobhouse's Diary of the same date, June 25. Tavistock and he " agreed as to the strange inconsistency and weakness of Lord Grey's general conduct, sometimes coquetting with ministers, and then undoing all previous courtship by unreasonable hostility. Now, with the prospect of a new reign, this change has much the air of shabbiness. Yet he is not a shabby man ; far from it, only peevish and wayward " (*Recollections*, iv. 31).

[2] *The Country without a Government. The Manchester Guardian* of June 12 notices rumours that a strong opposition is to be got up against the ministry, and admits that several of them are very little qualified for office. " There are no such broad and fundamental differences of opinion between the principal members of the present Cabinet and Lord Lansdowne . . . in the Upper House, and Mr. Huskisson and his followers and the moderate Whigs in the Lower, as should prevent a union." Still the Government is disposed to be " liberal, economical, and reforming."

[3] Wellington to Peel, [June] 1830 ; *Despatches*, vii. 106.

here, still less send him to Ireland. I would infinitely prefer that he should be at the head of the Government to belonging to a Government of which he was a member. . . ." [1]

" We must then count upon Lord Grey as being the head of the Opposition, and upon all the parties joining his lead. Could we go on ? Have we talent ? I should think that we do enjoy the respect and confidence of the country, and that after the general election we should have numbers.

" Lord Grey is certainly in himself a host, and his active opposition in the House of Lords, as the leader, would render others active likewise. . . . The question is, what is to be done in the House of Commons ? . . .

" I do not think that I personally could or ought to sit in a Cabinet again as First Lord of the Treasury with Mr. Huskisson, Lord Palmerston, or Mr. Charles Grant. . . ."

Before, however, any changes in the ministry had taken place, the death of George IV on June 26 turned the eyes of both parties to the constituencies, or at least to the patrons of boroughs. The Act compelling a general election within six months of a demise of the Crown was then in force, but such was the Duke's anxiety to escape from the 1826 House of Commons, that he hurried on the dissolution even before providing for a regency on the not unlikely chance of the new king dying before Parliament met. It is difficult in days after the Victorian epoch, when personal respect for royalty has joined with more democratic government to make republicanism in England hardly more unpopular than irrelevant, to realise the

---

[1] An interesting commentary on this paragraph is to be found among the *Lyndhurst Recollections* given in an appendix to Monypenny's *Life of Disraeli* (i. 388) : " Lord Grey wanted office, and it was known that he would have taken the viceroyalty of Ireland (*e.g.*). Once the intention of the Duke to admit the Grey party. Took a sudden prejudice to Grey. Something happened on a coal committee. Told L[yndhurst] afterwards he had seen enough of Grey that morning to have nothing to do with him.'' This note was written down by Disraeli in 1836. The Duke himself, in a letter dated December 26, 1830, said that, apart from the King's wishes, the Tories would not have consented to the admission of the Whigs as a party. " The Whigs not being admitted into power as a party, and Lord Grey's conduct from the time he came to town last spring having rendered it impossible to make an offer to him and to some of his friends upon the accession of the present king, the union of four parties in Parliament against the Government . . . was prepared " (*Despatches*, vii. 382). All the same, there were some Tories who desired comprehension (Hertford to Wilson, December 24, 1830 ; Add. MSS. 30,112, f. 131).

position of the monarchy before Queen Victoria's accession. The *Times* leading article on the death of his sacred majesty King George IV is a curious witness to the change of feeling with which an institution may be regarded, while its essence remains permanent. The passionate loathing that Shelley and the men of 1820 felt for Swellfoot the Tyrant had some time back turned to a less active spirit of contempt for the heavy-bellied voluptuary, who like a modern Tiberius buried himself in the unlovely magnificence of Brighton or Windsor, out of sight of the world which he never touched except to exact money for his palaces, or perplex his ministers by his caprice. No vindictive cheers such as the crowd raised over the coffin of Castlereagh welcomed his death, but the rare touches of real sorrow for " the kindest of masters," shown by those who had no motive for defending his memory, stand in vivid contrast to the indifference of the country and the hypocrisy of the Court. The nation was not indeed opposed to the monarchy as such at the end of his reign, but the divinity that doth hedge a king did not exist.

The good-will of the middle classes, however, perhaps an equally valuable asset, was gradually won back by the new sailor-king, whose easy eccentric manners became immediately the delight of the London crowd and the prey of wits and diarists. His unattended strolls in the streets, and the amazing indiscretions of his after-dinner speeches, were a nine days' wonder, and justified the expectations of those who knew him.[1] But when the first exhilaration of kingship had passed, he resumed his natural very ordinary character. William IV brought to the throne a reputation for Whig predispositions based on very inadequate grounds, and all the prejudices and honesty of a country gentleman of his time.[2] He was perhaps vaguely inclined to Whiggism as a natural reaction from his brother's despotic views,

---

[1] " The general bet is that it is an even chance that Clarence is in a strait-waistcoat before the King dies" (Sir H. Cooke to Lord Fitzgerald, June 16 ; *Despatches*, vii. 93).

[2] In 1828 he declared himself in favour of a Government based on a union of all parties, on the ground that Whig and Tory were now mere names, whatever they might have meant a hundred years ago (*Croker Papers*, i. 401). In February 1830 he gave his proxy to the Lord Chancellor, and promised Wellington his support " in the event of any peculiar attack on the King's Government " (Clarence to Wellington, February 3 ; *Despatches*, vi. 462).

and was conscientiously determined to do his duty fairly by both parties, but no one could be less of a Joseph II, if such principles were expected of him. Totally lacking, apparently, in a sense of humour, he enjoyed a sound common-sense which filled its place for practical purposes.[1] His worst defect, as a constitutional king reigning at a time of keen democratic aspiration, was that he thoroughly distrusted the people and shared to the full the hostility of the upper classes to labour organised for political or social ends. He might be qualified to keep the ring between Whigs and Tories, but the popular awakening connected with the passing of the Reform Bill was outside his comprehension and his sympathy alike. Made by circumstances in turn the object of the people's keenest enthusiasm and its fiercest hatred, he felt equally uncomfortable in either situation. His wife was a German princess of excellent and amiable character, who lived on the friendliest terms with the King's numerous children by Mrs. Jordan, and enjoyed the respect of the people, till they eventually turned on her with unfounded enmity.

The death of the King inspired the Whigs with new vigour ; no longer would royal caprice make the Duke indispensable. In both Houses they threw off the mask and forced the Government to a division on the question of postponing the settlement of a regency and the Civil List ; in a moment of excitement Brougham called the Treasury Bench " base, fawning parasites of the Duke of Wellington." Grey realised that war was declared, and felt that the other sections of the Opposition were likely to support him.[2] In the Commons success was attending the efforts to form " a systematic opposition " under Althorp's leadership. Advanced Reformers, who had despised the too conciliatory nature of the earlier negotiations, saw in these a

[1] In 1827, four months after the death of the Duke of York, William's elder brother, the Duke of Wellington received the following circular : " At the suggestion of H.R.H. the Duke of Clarence, the General Committee of Management, at their meeting yesterday, (May 8).

" Resolved, that a dinner in the great saloon should be held on the 4th June next in commemoration of H.R.H. the late Duke of York, under the following regulations : Officers to be in uniform, with crape on their arms. The dinner including wine, &c., 30/- a head."

Soon after his accession William tried to induce the Lord Chamberlain's office to buy a valuable set of plate from him for the use of the Crown (*Despatches*, iv. 27, vii. 209).

[2] Grey to Princess Lieven, July 2, 1830 ; *Lieven Correspondence*, ii. 20.

prospect of something more businesslike, and the leaders of the Whigs were urged to make a bolder bid for popular support.[1] The meetings in the Albany still did not number more than sixty, but there was now at least in embryo something like the old Whig party before the split of 1827, and the constitutional Reformers might face the elections with an unbroken front.

The elections were fixed for the end of July, but long before that time politicians had been laying their plans. A great effort was made in various quarters to secure a working alliance between the two wings of the Reformers ;[2] with this object it was decided by the Westminster group to run Joseph Hume, the champion of retrenchment, as candidate for Middlesex, on the retirement of the veteran Samuel Whitbread. The difficulties were considerable ; though Althorp favoured the scheme, Grey gave his sanction with extreme reluctance, and the Duke of Bedford was known to be unpropitious. Scared by the possible expense,[3] the Scottish Reformer hesitated to sacrifice his safe seat in the north, and actually wrote two letters, one accepting and the other declining the offer. But as usually happened in matters where Francis Place was concerned, the scheme was carried through with success.

The Life of Place by Mr. Graham Wallas has revealed the springs of most of the improvements won for working men in the first few decades of last century, and done much to redress the balance of history, so often content to ignore the political interest and importance of all that is not done by statesmen and diplomatists. The proceedings initiated in Place's pamphlet-littered room at Charing Cross had a no less vital effect on the progress of the Reform movement in 1830–2 than the discussions at Downing Street or St. Stephen's. If it were a duty to award the palm to a single man for the successful conduct of that " bloodless revolution," Grey, Althorp, Russell, Durham, Brougham would press no juster claim than Francis Place or

---

[1] *Recollections of a Long Life*, iv. 36, 37. " Hume said unless Grey and Holland and other party men would declare for cutting down places and for more decisive reform than they ever had yet done, the people would not sympathise with any Parliamentary efforts of theirs."

[2] *E.g.* St. Clair Cullen writes from Chichester : " I have united the two parties of the Whigs and the Radicals " (Add. MSS. 36,466).

[3] Shaw Lefevre did not think Hume could get in on £7000 (Add. MSS. 36,466, June 23). Warburton guaranteed £2500.

FRANCIS PLACE

*From a Portrait painted by* G. P. HEALY *in* 1843, *in the possession of*
FRANCIS C. MIERS, Esq.

Thomas Attwood.   Starting life as an operative in the tailoring trade, Place was driven into the ranks of political democracy by disgust at the exploitation of the Westminster scot and lot voters by the aristocracy.   As he rose in his profession to the dignity of a master tailor, he devoted himself more and more to the service of labour, lending his practical advice and organising skill to further the theoretical projects of his friends the Benthamites.   Despising alike the ability and the industry of the Radicals in Parliament, though constantly forced to co-operate with them, he learnt by experience " that to obtain one's ends in that truly infamous place we must demand a great deal more than we can hope to obtain." [1]   He was the founder in one sphere, as the political unionists were in another, of what Mr. Bernard Shaw calls the proper development of English democracy—" the science of putting pressure on Parliament from the outside." [2]   By this means Place was largely responsible for the softening of the Combination Acts in 1824–5, and in the Reform struggle acted as an invaluable link between Parliament and the working class.   Though he gave a long life without thought of rest or praise to the sole cause of the public good, and, undeterred by the contempt of his social superiors or the suspicion of those below him, achieved in obscurity a mass of benefit to the labouring classes which may fairly be set beside the work of Howard, or Wilberforce, or Shaftesbury, few men can have been more irritating to know or live with than Francis Place. [3]   Wise in all the learning of the Utilitarians, he seems the very incarnation of the singularly unpleasing type of rational man on which their theories were built.   If ever a man did good from the motives Bentham believed, it was he ; his mind was intellect naked.   He saw through all the abuses and absurdities of the Constitution, but did not therefore join the Radicals, whose methods of pushing their views were incompatible with the parliamentary government then existing.   With this inflexible common sense he united a vast capacity for organisation of every kind, due to tireless perseverance and a limitation of view which left no room for disillusionment.   His main faults

[1] Add. MSS. 36,466.          [2] Times, March 8, 1912.

[3] Lambton, who knew him, wrote : " Place is a superior man, but why will he always wear a coat of bristles when he is in company with those who, by accident of station, are his superiors in society ? " (S. J. Reid, Life of Durham, i. 346).

F

were an often justified contempt for the sagacity of others, and unreasonable annoyance if his advice was not adopted. He stands as the Arch-Wirepuller of English politics, and, if his efforts have not been appreciated by posterity, that is a matter to which he would have been indifferent.

It was generally understood that seats in the new Parliament would fetch an unprecedently high price, and numbers of old members, as well as new men who might naturally have stood, fought shy of the requisite sum.[1] The last Leicester election, we read in the *Morning Chronicle*, cost Mr. Evans, the member, £19,000 ; for his uncontested seat for Yorkshire Mr. Marshall paid upwards of £30,000.[2] There are estates in England which to this day suffer from the enormous burdens incurred by the elections of those unblushing times. The optimistic view was that " Freeborn Englishmen will at last be forced to be pure, because members are too poor to buy them."[3] The question how far the Government attempted to influence the election is difficult to solve. It was boldly asserted by the author of a pamphlet which became famous that " the Treasury were never more active or less scrupulous."[4] This was categorically denied in the equally notorious *Reply* ; and Brougham, to whom the work containing the attack was generally attributed, states in

[1] Bergner to Wilson, July 23 : " We are on the eve of a general election. I take it, it will be about *the corruptest* which we shall have witnessed in our generation, though every candidate is breathing ' purity ' and ' reform ' " (Add. MSS. 30,112, f. 70). Eldon to Lady F. J. Bankes : " I hear the seats in the next parliament are very high-priced indeed, much beyond any price in former parliaments. So much for corruption ' (Horace Twiss, *Life of Eldon*, iii. 114). Campbell wrote on June 26 : " Seats are said to be scarcer and dearer than ever known : £1500 a year, or £6000 taking all chances." A barrister on his circuit spent £20,000 on being returned for Gloucester (*Life of Campbell*, i. 471, 476. Also Add. MSS. 27,789, f. 155, 158 ; *Standard*, July 28). Cobbett said no honest man could afford to stand a contested election (*Weekly Political Register*, July 31).

[2] *Morning Chronicle*, July 26.

[3] Add. MSS. 27,789, f. 157.

[4] *What has the Duke of Wellington gained by the Dissolution ?* (1830). " Besides the accustomed boards of canvass held at Whitehall, a special commission seems to have sat in Regent Street. Mr. W. Holmes . . . passed many hours a day with a Scottish Earl." The Bank and East and West India interests are also asserted to have been used. The *Reply* states that the Government influence was used at Wendover against two West Indians in favour of two candidates who had opposed ministers as often as they supported them.

his *Memoirs* that the Duke neglected to use the Crown influence.[1] On the other hand, the Duke, in a letter to Peel on the Louth election in May,[2] admitted " that the regular course of the Treasury is to support the interest in possession of the representation, by which the Government is supported in Parliament " ; and the Tory pamphlet mentioned above assumes that the Treasury boroughs now held by ultra-Tory and Canningite supporters of Lord Liverpool will be given to loyal Ministerialists. A few hints are available as to how an Ordnance borough could be worked, but the general question must be left open from lack of evidence.[3]

But if the methods by which the two sides prepared to contest the close boroughs are doubtful, the issues on which the election was fought—where a fight took place—are not. From the Opposition newspapers the ministry and the majority which had supported it came under a violent cross-fire. The *Birmingham Journal* attacked the memory of " the most abandoned Parliament that ever sat." From the *Standard* came a demand for Reform on the best Tory lines, now that money was the sole qualification, and several Ministerialist candidates were the victims of a strong " Protestant " opposition. In Cobbett's hands " the thing became a trumpet," and every week the call for change in the representation, as the only cure for the ills of the country, was sounded in the *Political Register*. Not content to reach the classes that could afford a sixpenny weekly, in July Cobbett started his famous *Twopenny Trash*, designed as a counterblast to Brougham's *Useful Knowledge* tracts, to appear monthly and so evade the act of 1819 against unstamped periodicals. From its inception, the chief notes were distress and the need of Reform. Primed with the evidence he had acquired during his northern tour, Cobbett ascribed the universal wretchedness in a fertile land to " the famous 658 " and their currency infatuation. Laws and taxes were all devised to pay for the extravagant idleness of the rich and to fall on the shoulders of the poor.[4] If revolution was to be avoided, Radical Reform

[1] iii. 48.    [2] *Despatches*, vii. 44.
[3] At Queenborough, a burgage borough, at which seven-tenths of the population did not vote, the Ministerialist out-voters were brought down the river in Ordnance yachts. A question on this subject was asked in the House in November (*Standard*, August 3).
[4] For example, the rich avoided their share of the £2,500,000 raised by the Post Office by the device of franking. The Window-tax of the

must be granted speedily, and to this end he recommended the
formation of Political Unions on the basis of universal suffrage,
triennial parliaments, and the ballot. A considerable fillip to
the cause of the ballot had been given by an article by James
Mill in the July *Westminster*. Mill's ability in lashing all save
Indian abuses Cobbett admitted ; but he distrusted the tedious
argumentations of Bentham, who had been converted to Reform,
he asserted, by Pitt's rejection of his patent prison, the Panop-
ticon. As for Whigs and Tories, there was little to choose between them, and the " Shoyhoys " were mere hypocrites, who
did not even want to obtain the Reform for which they
clamoured.[1] It is true that the class to which Cobbett addressed
his widest appeal enjoyed the franchise in but rare cases ; however, the Westbury election, at which the corporation and the
patron, Sir Manasseh Lopez of evil fame, barely escaped with
their lives, showed the influence which even before 1831 could
be exerted by non-voters. In several cases burgesses and freemen outside the charmed circle of privilege took it upon themselves to vote in defiance of established usage.[2] The associations
also played their part. In London the Westminster party
attended a meeting of the Society for Promoting Reform at the
Freemason's Tavern. At Birmingham a general meeting of the
Union was addressed by Burdett—an incident which lost Attwood
the confidence of Cobbett, who henceforth ranked him as one
of the Shoyhoys.

same amount meant a charge of 2s. on all windows up to 180, and only
1s. 6d. beyond that number. Sir James Graham has shown that 113
of the aristocracy draw £650,000 of public money yearly (*Twopenny
Trash*, August).

[1] In the Radical press Burdett is " the Don," Hobhouse " Sancho,"
and the parliamentary group generally " the Shoyhoys."

[2] At Truro the burgesses claimed by charter of Elizabeth to vote as
well as the twenty-four Capital Burgesses, mainly non-resident, who were in
the habit of returning the members at the nomination of Lord Falmouth.
They insisted, amid a scene approaching a riot, on recording their votes,
and when the poll closed it showed 179-14 in favour of the popular candidates, who stood for Reform. However, the mayor disallowed the votes
of all but the Capital Burgesses, and returned the patron's nominees, one
of whom was Lord Eldon's grandson and heir (Cambridge University
Library, Z. 24. 33⁴). At Hythe also there was a dispute over the franchise, where 400 non-resident freemen supported the two sitting members,
while the popular candidates received the votes of 250 inhabitant householders. However, the ministerialists were declared elected by 270-8.
At Marlborough the candidates promised to work for the restoration to
the borough of its old right of voting (*Standard*, July 30, 31 ; August 3).

The borough elections were yet in full swing, and those in the counties were about to begin, when news arrived from France which changed the course of English history. From the accession of Charles X it had appeared probable that the reactionary views of the King would lead to trouble with the constitutionalists who held to the Charter of 1814 ; the return of Polignac to power turned this belief into a certainty. On March 23 the *Morning Chronicle* said ominously : " The King and people are now fairly at issue, and another problem is also about to be solved, namely, whether monarchy is compatible with a popular representation, not a virtual representation, chosen by the aristocracy." On July 26 it was known that the elections, which followed on the King's dissolution of a refractory Chamber, promised a majority against the Court of 124 ; on July 28 that by royal ordinance the new Chamber was dissolved before it had met, liberty of the press cancelled, and the franchise restricted. It was impossible but that the English people should wait in breathless excitement to learn how the French would take the blow, and augur the fate of their own struggle against an unpopular ministry from such a parallel.[1] Rumours trickled through at the end of the month that the National Guard were arming ; August 1 was Sunday, and on Monday it was known throughout the length and breadth of England that the French middle and working classes had risen, had conquered the troops after a short but desperate struggle, had driven the tyrant from his throne, and had used their victory with moderation as admirable as it was astounding. The feeling of boundless exultation which sprang up in the vast majority of Englishmen is hardly conceivable to us who have known nothing like it. It created a new world. Every class thrilled to it. The staid *Edinburgh* reviewer burst out in passionate hero-worship. " The conduct of the French people on this occasion was truly above all human praise." " The battle of English liberty has really been fought and won at Paris." As for Englishmen, " with an unanimity wholly unexampled they have suffered their delight at the

[1] " It was indeed of immense importance to this country at the time it happened. Had the people submitted to the ordinances, or had they been subdued by the King's troops, the Wellington administration would have been excessively strengthened and would have taken advantage of their own power and the depression of the people " (Add. MSS. 27,789, f. 163).

glorious revolution to burst forth, and to reach all the ends of the earth, in accents of applause, of exultation, of heartfelt thankfulness to the French people." " A well-inhabited street is a fortress no troops can take, if the inhabitants be but true to themselves." [1]

But if the governing class could be thus exalted, the effects on men of obscurer lives was far deeper and more potent. They seemed to live in a new age of the world's history. The peoples that sat in darkness had seen a great light. Hitherto they had been content to take their heroes at second hand. Now from their own midst, as it were—for bars of birth and language were done away—men had arisen to cast down kings and win liberty at the cannon's mouth. The unemotional Francis Place writes that " the impression the events in Paris made on even the least intelligent of the people was such as will never either be effaced or to any extent forgotten by them." [2] " No similar event," wrote Cockburn from Scotland, " was ever so generally hailed in this country." [3] But only the eloquence of Cobbett can do such raptures justice. " But now how will this affair affect us ? No tongue, no pen, can describe how it will affect us. Our feelings are our instructors here. Does not every man of you feel differently from what you did twenty days back ? . . . Do not all the hopes of relief from the efforts of the sham-patriots and sham-reformers sink away out of your minds ? " The application was obvious: " The people of France saw that it was the design of the Bourbons to give them all the blessings arising from an English House of Commons." " This is a revolution made by the industrious classes, and by the working part of those classes ; and will any man now be so impudent as to assert that these people are unworthy of being permitted to vote for representatives ? " [4] " Wild, enthusiastic, and republican

---

[1] *Edinburgh Review*, vol. lii. Brougham wrote : " The French glorious revolution is most advantageous to our cause, because it denounces wrath and destruction on those who would by force withstand the popular opinion " (Lady Knutsford, *Life of Zachary Macaulay*, p. 454). Thomas Arnold called it " a most blessed révolution, spotless beyond all example n history " (Stanley, *Life of Arnold*).

[2] Add. MSS. 27,789, f. 163.

[3] *Memorials*, p. 467.

[4] *Political Register*, August 7, 14. *Cf.* a letter of General Morgan to Wellington, dated August 18 : [La révolution] " est l'ouvrage unique de la classe ouvrière, conduite et dirigée par une jeunesse de 18 à 21 ans,

ideals," proclaimed a Manchester orator, " have yielded to sober
good sense and moderation, which marks the progress of the
mind, and the ' march of intellect.' The comparatively free
institutions, under which the French have been educated for the
last forty years, have actually produced a change of national
character. . . . I also trust that the 154 usurpers, who have
deprived the English people of their just, undoubted, and ancient
privilege of chusing their representatives, will take warning." [1]
The country was not so Frenchified as to omit to celebrate the
event by dinners of joy, where the good cheer prompted enthusiasts to vow every faculty to the service of Parliamentary
Reform. Even the Tories found it difficult to condemn what
had been done, so manifestly was Charles in the wrong ; the
*Standard* saw in the fall of Polignac good material for attacks
on the Duke of Wellington, who was generally believed to favour
his principles, if not to have counselled the ordinances of July.
After this the grave assertion in the *Quarterly* that " the body
of the British nation have done themselves honour by regarding
with stern suspicion the recent progress of events " rings rather
false, though it may be true that " the meetings, dinners, . . .
set on foot by our old established disturbers of the public peace,
have been countenanced by hardly one name which any human
being will dare to call respectable." [2]

The importance which the Reformers attached to the French
revolution may suggest the question why it did not on the
other hand band together the moderates of both parties on the
side of reaction as in 1792. There are indications that some
such union was suggested, and all through the Reform struggle
the Opposition did bitterly reproach Lord Grey with having
wantonly introduced his bill at a time of European unrest.
But the events in Paris were so swift and so complete that they

mais jeunesse pleine de talens et d'activité. Les classes supérieures dans
la bourgeoisie n'y prirent aucune part. . . . Cette classe ouvrière n'étoit
pas celle de la lie du peuple, c'étoit des hommes attachés aux imprimeries,
aux manufactures" (*Despatches*, vii. 187).

[1] *Manchester Guardian*, August 28.

[2] *Quarterly*, October. Lord Francis Leveson-Gower wrote : " I have
always dated the Duke's downfall as Prime Minister, not from the turning-point of the Reform Bill, but from the barricades of July." The
Duke declared that a Hyde Park review late in July " was the last
exhibition of English loyalty and good-humour " (Ellesmere, *Personal
Reminiscences of the Duke of Wellington*, p. 73).

gave little opportunity for panic-mongering; the whole revolution was over in three days; and after the Duke had recognised Louis Philippe, such an attitude would have been rather absurd. Then, too, the movement was so safe and so matter-of-fact, for all the heroics it inspired in England. It has been brilliantly called " a Limited Liability revolution." No dramatic vengeance was taken, no breach was made in the national continuity, no dormant spirits of anarchy were released, as befell forty years before. And for Englishmen, besides being short and safe, the revolution fulfilled every condition of justification which Locke and Burke had required and found in the events of 1688, and which both English parties had by now accepted. Charles X stood before Europe in exactly the position of James II, and his guilt was not denied by those who most regretted it.[1] He had violated the original contract with his subjects—in this case incarnate in the Charter of 1814—and released them from their obedience. Like that which the Whig statesmen had carried through, this was essentially a conservative revolution.

Such a shock had English politics received when the county elections came on. Suffolk was contested for the first time in forty years, and eventually forty-seven knights of the shire were returned in opposition to Government.[2] But the eyes of the country were set beyond all places on Yorkshire, where Henry Brougham, connected in no way with the county, was being run free from any expense as candidate for what was usually considered the fairest prize in the parliamentary field. At this time he was beyond doubt the foremost figure in politics. When the Tories spoke of the Opposition, they thought of Brougham, terrible in debate, but far from a satisfactory colleague to his own friends. His vigorous attitude in the late session had greatly enhanced his reputation, already firmly founded on his pre-eminence at the Bar and the long list of services he had conferred on the public. The repeal of the Orders in Council,

---

[1] " Charles X, having been wholly in the right, managed so as to put himself in the wrong" (*Quarterly*, October). " Confound these French Ministers," wrote Sir Walter Scott. " I can't forgive them for making a Jacobin of an old Tory like me " (*Cockburn's Memorials*, p. 468).

[2] " Those candidates who stood on the support of the Government found no advantage from it, but on the contrary were invariably obliged to abandon such ground for the ground of reform and economy " (W. H. Fremantle to Duke of Buckingham, August 26; *Courts and Cabinets of William IV and Victoria*, i. 45).

elementary education, the instruction of the working classes, the defence of Queen Caroline, the abolition of negro slavery, were subjects he had made specially his own, and all of them matters of more than ordinary popular interest. His hurricane energies were now to be applied to Reform—in itself no trifling symptom of that question's improving chances. He followed up a great speech at Leeds before the election, in which he pledged himself to bring forward a measure on the lines of triennial parliaments, votes for inhabitant householders, and extension of the franchise to large towns, by another, at the opening of the poll, in the very cradle of Reform, the Castle yard at York. Reform was an important plank in his platform, but he admitted that in Yorkshire slavery held the first place.[1] Over all was spread the glamour of the days of July. Brougham's triumphant and bloodless victory was a vast acquisition of strength to the Whigs, presaging ill for Peel and the Duke when Parliament should meet. He received the delighted congratulations of Althorp and Durham, who hoped that now at last, with Canningite aid, the " dictator " might be deposed.

As the elections ended, the framers of Cabinets returned to the welcome game of discussing combinations of parties and their chances in the new Parliament. To the spectators of 1830 the one constant factor on which their descendants of to-day may count was lacking. On the close of the polls nowadays much difference of opinion is possible as to the lines of action the various parties will adopt, but their respective strength is hardly matter of dispute. In 1830 this was not so, for there was no uniformity of policy and effort over the different constituencies. Elections were far more local affairs ; candidates for the most part stood on their known reputations as men of honour and ability, rather than as the representatives of any party, though there were of course exceptions. Their future conduct in the House was often doubtful, and the uncertainty was increased by the number of nomination boroughs where even the formality of an election address could be dispensed

---

[1] Brougham to Z. Macaulay : " The country gentlemen tried in vain to stem the torrent which set in from the West Riding. . . . I have found no reason to doubt that it is an anti-slavery triumph. I have assumed it to be so. . . . I find that all sects and all the old Wilberforce interest is with me except the Evangelical Church party, and they hold back on the avowed ground of London University " (Lady Knutsford, *Life of Zachary Macaulay*, p. 454).

with.  So it was impossible in those times for the daily papers
to publish ladders with the two leaders climbing up them towards
the prize of a majority.

In this instance the party estimates varied widely.  In
English open constituencies the *Annual Register* gave the
Opposition a majority of 142 to 78.  Scotland was of course
strongly Tory, and in Ireland, under the raised franchise,
Peel was assured by a correspondent of a majority of 74
to 9.[1]  In the United Kingdom as a whole, some calculated
on a ministerial gain of 21, others on a loss of 26.  Grey
made the decrease as much as 50, and another estimate, though
granting the Duke a numerical gain, allowed little real improvement of his position.  " It will require a master hand,
such as Pitt had," wrote Eldon, "and such as nobody now
has in this country, to allay what is brewing, a storm for
changes here, especially for Reform in Parliament."[2]  The
*Manchester Guardian*, while friendly disposed to the Duke on
the whole, could promise no undiscriminating confidence on the
part of its readers.  " If the aristocracy wish to maintain their
influence over society, they must not nowadays be mere jockeys
or fox-hunters."  His colleagues were urged to emulate the reforming energies of Peel.[3]  The one hope of many Tories was that
the excesses which might be expected from the Radicals would
drive the lovers of order into their arms.  " We had not more
want at the beginning of the last French Revolution, to augment
and consolidate the force of *all* friends of quiet and good
order."[4]  The *Standard* spoke again of the possibility of a Whig-
Ultra coalition, to comprise such opposites as Grey, Brougham,
Graham, Richmond, and Wetherell, on a basis of moderate
Reform.  At the Cornwall election Sir Robert Vyvyan, a rising
hope of the High Tories, had hinted at such a union, and even

---

[1] *H. O.*, 100. 235.  Mahony gives the figures as follows :—Counties :
for the Government, 45 ; against, 4 ; neutral, 15.  Boroughs : for the
Government, 29 ; against, 5 ; neutral, 2.  He adds the names of the
opposing and neutral members.

[2] Eldon to Lady F. Bankes, August 19 ; *Life*, iii. 114.

[3] *Manchester Guardian*, August 28, September 18.

[4] Fremantle, Lord Londonderry, and Lord Grenville to the Duke of
Buckingham, August 26, 28, September 21 ; *Courts and Cabinets*, i. 45, 48,
69.  Place bears witness to their disappointment.  " The admirable conduct in almost every part of the kingdom silenced the aristocracy and
the clergy, who would willingly have played the game of 1792 " (Add. MSS.
27,789, f. 166).  *Cf.* the report of a spy, *H. O.* 40. 25.

declared that a purely Whig administration might be tolerated.[1] From the other side the *Edinburgh* had agreed in July that, since Catholic Relief was granted once for all, nothing now separated such men as Lord Grey and the Duke of Richmond. Every possible arrangement was suggested and dismissed in the war of pamphlets which raged through the autumn, those in the ministerialist interest accusing the Whigs of a complete change of tactics since the general election, and seeing in Tory reunion the only legitimate settlement.

The rulers of England spent the summer moving from country-house to country-house, imbibing gossip and discussing policy. For the Whigs this was a season of eager preparation. Lord Grey himself had rejoiced at the news from France, and now watched events from his family circle at Howick.[2] It included a very fair quorum of his future administration, among them Lambton, now Lord Durham, and Grey's brother-in-law, Edward Ellice, zealous Reformers both. From a young Tory who visited Howick in those days we hear of warlike plans and dark threats against Tory boroughs.[3] Gladly would we give many letters of the time for a few snatches of the familiar talk of these men among the autumn woods on the windy Northumbrian coast. For we may guess that there and then the scope of the coming Reform Bill was first dimly conceived.

As to the enemy, news was uncertain. Grey knew that Lyndhurst, the Chancellor, wished to strengthen the Government in the Commons, but he thought the Duke was more likely to alter his principles than his Cabinet ;—on the lines of 1829, he might even adopt Reform.[4] In any case, however, Grey would not at this period have accepted an invitation. Wellington himself had lightly borne the Canningites' rejection of his overtures in July, and professed to face the future with confidence, strong in the belief that the King would strain every nerve to support him, and that he had only to lift his finger for any party to join him gladly.[5] In September he had proposed to attend a series of political functions in Lancashire—an arrange-

[1] *Standard*, August 6.

[2] See *Lieven Correspondence*, ii., chaps. i. and ii.

[3] Malmesbury, *Memoirs of an Ex-Minister* (3rd edition), i. 36, 37.

[4] *Lieven Correspondence*, ii. 64, 67, 89 ; *Life of Campbell*, i. 477.

[5] Palmerston's Autobiography, given in Bulwer's *Palmerston*, i. 361 ; *Lieven Correspondence*, ii. 27. Wellington to Vesey Fitzgerald, September 4 ; *Despatches*, vii. 240.

ment which Grey considered hardly worthy of a statesman, and
which the eloquence of Brougham threatened to disturb.[1]  But
his plans were changed by the death of Huskisson on September 15 at the opening of the Liverpool and Manchester
railway, just as he had stepped down from his carriage to shake
hands with the Duke for the first time since the rupture of 1828.

Huskisson's death had a considerable influence on the course
of party affairs.  A stout opponent of any but the most limited
reform of the representation, from the point of view of both
Grey and Wellington he had been for personal reasons a serious
obstacle to union with the Canningites.  Brougham, however,
thought that his loss would lessen the chances of an invitation
to his party ; without him they were worth but little to anybody ;[2]
and the Canningites on their part were less inclined than before
to enter the Duke's Cabinet without the protection and the
weight that Huskisson's character lent them.[3]  Against a Whig
alliance there was to be set the memory of Lord Grey's vehement
opposition to their great founder, culminating in the bitter
onslaught in the House of Lords which almost persuaded Canning
to take a peerage to answer it.  But since that personal attack
much had happened to change their situation.  Very little difference of views separated the Canningites from the conservative
Whigs ;  it was more a question of party prestige, which a prospect of effective combination in office might do much to settle
satisfactorily.[4]  On the matter of Reform, though on principle
opposed to any extensive measure, they had departed some
way from Canning's uncompromising position, and during the
1830 session supported the moderate proposals of Tennyson and
Russell.  It has been seen that in 1828 Dudley and Palmerston
were anxious to satisfy by trifling concessions the demand,
which they felt to be irresistible, for some alteration in the
system that denied to Birmingham and Manchester the franchise

---

[1] *Lieven Correspondence*, ii. 83.
[2] Brougham to Graham, September 17 ; *Life of Graham*, i. 88.
[3] Melbourne to Brougham, September 19 ; *Brougham's Memoirs*, iii. 67.
[4] Palmerston wrote, January 18, 1828 : " I like [the Whigs] much
better than the Tories and agree with them much more ; but still we,
the Canningites, if we may so be termed, did not join their Government,
but they came and joined ours. . . . If we had all gone out, I should
certainly not have sat with them in the House of Commons, but should
have taken an independent and separate position " (Bulwer, *Life of
Palmerston*, i. 220.)

it preserved to Gatton and Old Sarum. In the debate on the introduction of the first Reform Bill Palmerston declared, against Peel's violent protests, that Canning himself would have been a Reformer if he had been living then. Certainly Melbourne, who in 1819 had spoken of the danger of any Reform whatever, and regretted that the subject had to be touched at all, was now convinced of its necessity, as a claim that could no longer be refused with safety.

This conviction was no peculiarity of the Canningites. It was largely agreed in Tory circles in the autumn of 1830 that some Reform was inevitable, and it was held possible Wellington himself might consent to enfranchise the great manufacturing towns.[1] It was not, however, with any such intention that he now, at the end of September, renewed to Palmerston the proposals which Melbourne had rejected in July.[2] Though he had declared earlier in the month that he doubted the expediency of such coalitions, the Duke was forced to some such step by the obvious weakness of the Treasury bench in the Commons, as well as by the unmitigated hostility of the ultra-Tories.[3] Seeing through so obvious a counsel of despair, Palmerston now took a higher line, and refused on behalf of his friends and himself to enter the Cabinet without Lansdowne and Grey. This amounted to a demand for the resignation of the Duke's monarchical position, and was of course rejected. Palmerston writes that Croker considered his determination to vote for Reform decisive, and Peel saw that this was likely to be " the all-important vital question." [4]

Thus thrown back on their own unaided resources, the ministry were suddenly faced by industrial and agricultural disturbances in the north and south, as well as insurrection in the Netherlands and general European unrest. The Belgian revolution had no such dramatic effect in England as the French, but it was far more dangerous to the cause of peace. Besides

---

[1] *What has the Duke of Wellington Gained ?* Princess Lieven to Grey, October 4 ; *Lieven Correspondence*, ii. 100 ; *Life of Eldon* iii. 114. Lord Londonderry complained that the Government had " yielded far too much to liberality, reform, and Hume's supremacy" (*Courts and Cabinets*, i. 49).

[2] Wellington to Clive, September 30, *Despatches*, vii. 281 ; Bulwer, *Life of Palmerston*, i. 361 ; *Life of Eldon*, iii. 118.

[3] Hertford to Wilson, October 17, Add. MSS. 30,112, f. 111 ; *Standard*, October 28.

[4] *Life of Palmerston*, i. 361–3 ; *Peel Papers*, ii. 161.

the strictly constitutional question, the settlement of Vienna was directly violated by the proposed disruption of the Netherlands. It was a faint rustling of the wings of the spirit of Nationality, soon by their full spreading to cast such fearful shade over the thrones of Europe. But, nineteenth century though it was, it was not so much the sympathy of nationality as of class, which inspired Cobbett's harangues to the working people and aroused a torrent of indignation at the thought of war with Belgium, for some weeks an appalling reality.[1]

At home the prospect was no less embarrassing. A friend travelling with the Duke of Wellington in the north at the time of Huskisson's death relates that the spirit of those parts was " detestable " : [2] the Duke was informed at the same time of a plot to assassinate him. In October the political feeling is reported to be " very strong and bad " and to have been inflamed by the events on the Continent.[3] Men were heard to say there was no need to fear the military after the events in Paris and Brussels.[4] In August a strike of cotton-spinners had begun in the neighbourhood of Stalybridge. In October, when the membership of the lately founded Trades Union was estimated at 80,000, and its weekly receipts at £330, the hatters in the Newcastle district were also out, as well as the Oldham colliers. It was feared that the latter strike might extend over the entire north-western coalfield, and the association of the colliers' unions with the General Trades Union gave ground for alarm to Peel, who admitted that legislation to crush it might be necessary. The city of Carlisle was almost in a state of siege. In addition to the troops already in the north, the Prime Minister

---

[1] Attwood proposed an association to collect " the names of persons in London pledging themselves not to pay taxes if ministerial interference should produce the probability of a war with Belgium" (Add. MSS. 27,789, f. 194). Lord Grey, in a letter to his son Charles, dated September 22, speaks of a war as probable (*Howick Papers*).

[2] Ellesmere, *Personal Reminiscences of the Duke of Wellington*, p. 62.

[3] Place wrote : " The whole mass of the working people are essentially republican, a vast many of them scarcely knowing why" (Add. MSS. 27,789, f. 164). With this judgment it is interesting to compare what Hobhouse writes of a conversation he held in June with Attwood, whose experience of the labouring classes was also extensive : " He was convinced that the whole people of England were essentially aristocratic and imbued with respect for their superiors, and hatred of those neighbours raised by accident above themselves " (*Recollections*, iv. 28)."

[4] *H. O.*, 40. 26.

ordered reinforcements of artillerymen to be sent to Carlisle, Chester, and Teignmouth, and advised a reserve of troops to be kept at Manchester.[1]

In Kent and Sussex the revolt of the agricultural labourers was yet more serious. At the end of August began the breaking of threshing machines, which was later accompanied by the firing of hay and corn ricks. By the end of October the south-east corner of England was practically in the hands of the insurgents.[2] It is difficult to say to what extent any political feeling co-operated with actual hunger and social distress. Cobbett, who should have known, asserts that it was a complete mistake to suppose the labourers knew nothing of the political causes of their misery, and of the arch-grievance, the state of the representation. As early as October, he says, when scarcely a petition for Reform had as yet been presented, the labourers of three Hampshire parishes met to draw up a petition for Radical Reform, which one of their number, Joseph Mason, who was afterwards transported for his share in the rising, carried to Brighton to be laid before the King.[3] Certainly the revolutionary feeling incited by the example of the French and Belgians was encouraged by the circulation broadcast of fly-sheets drawing attention to the " nice pickings " of public money received annually by various peers and prelates.[4] For the publication of these often widely exaggerated statements in all parts of the kingdom Cobbett was often responsible.[5] He sympathised heartily with a petition offered to the King in September by " persons belonging to the Industrious Classes of London and its Vicinity," demanding the three points of Radical Reform to remedy the partial and oppressive legislation of the last twenty and forty years. In October he himself issued on the same lines a " Plan of Parliamentary Reform ad-

[1] *Despatches*, vii. 301.
[2] See J. L. and B. Hammond, *The Village Labourer*.
[3] *Twopenny Trash*, July 1832.
[4] " A peasant about to enlist, being dragged away by his companions, exclaimed, ' Why, you fools, can't I come and help you as well when I ha' got a gun, as when I ha' nothing but a stick ? ' Another said, ' See if we ha'nt a bloody good revolution here, as well as in France ' " (*State of Kent, H. O.* 44. 21). Peers and bishops are said to receive £4,199,847 out of the taxes, which would be enough to maintain 83,997 families at £50 a year.
[5] *H. O.*, 44. 21.

dressed to the young men of England." If Cobbett had no direct connection with the insurgent labourers, he was at least the apologist, and in will and spirit the prophet of their cause, which he interpreted as a class war kindled by sheer destitution. Placarding the pension list before the eyes of the nation, he called for the repeal of half the Acts of the last twenty years ; " and then there may be peace and safety until a reform of Parliament can be made."

The thoughts of many of other classes were tending in the same direction. The Political Council of the Birmingham Union petitioned the King in September, and in October 3600 of its members dined together to celebrate the French revolution. The *Edinburgh* came out with an article on Reform, and the *Manchester Guardian* put in a moderate plea for it from the middle-class point of view. " This class . . . is at present notoriously indisposed to any extreme plan of Reform." However, it will be impossible for the Government " permanently or even long to withstand that current of popular opinion which is now strongly running in favour of an adaptation of our institutions to the present condition of society." [1]

In London, at the meeting of Parliament, the air was very full of Reform, as well as of a vague alarm that something was about to happen. It was half expected that the Duke would bring in a moderate measure, or at any rate that he would not oppose one. It was stated that even the enfranchisement of a few great towns would greatly strengthen his Government, and that his consent would win him the adhesion of Palmerston, the Grants, Sir James Graham, and Stanley ; otherwise he must expect the opposition of the powerful Stafford interest.[2] It is doubtful, however, how far, if at all, Littleton, who acted as go-between, was authorised in making these overtures ; Palmerston had had an unsatisfactory interview with the Duke shortly before, and Graham and Stanley were at this time carrying on negotiations with Brougham with regard to the provisions of his promised Reform Bill. In fact on the very day before the letter with the above assurance was written, or perhaps on the day itself, Stanley dined with Brougham, Althorp and Denman being also present, to arrange a date for discussing the measure.

[1] *Manchester Guardian*, October 9.
[2] Arbuthnot to Peel, November 1 ; *Peel Papers*, ii. 163.

Graham was to sound the Canningites, proposing, as main points, the enfranchisement of large towns, the partial disfranchisement of small boroughs, and the possible extension of the vote to householders in the place of non-residents.[1] The resolution to be moved on behalf of the party was actually written out in Brougham's hand, when the Duke of Wellington, in the debate on the address on November 2, made his never-to-be-forgotten declaration against all Reform, on the ground of the present perfection of the Constitution.

" The noble earl," he said in answer to Grey's appeal for moderate Reform, " has been candid enough to acknowledge that he is not prepared with any measure of Reform, and I can have no scruple in saying that his Majesty's Government is as totally unprepared with any plan as the noble lord. Nay, I on my own part will go further, and say that I have never read or heard of any measure up to the present moment which can in any degree satisfy my mind that the state of the representation can be improved. . . . I will go further and say that the legislature and the system of representation possesses the full and entire confidence of the country. . . . I will go still further and say that, if at the present moment I had imposed on me the duty of forming a legislature for any country, and particularly for a country like this, in possession of great property of various descriptions, I do not mean to assert that I could form such a legislature as you possess now, for the nature of man is incapable of reaching such excellence at once ; but my great endeavour would be to form some description of legislature which would produce the same results. . . . I am not only not prepared to bring in any measure of the description alluded to by the noble lord, but I will at once declare that, as far as I am concerned, as long as I hold any station in the Government of the country, I shall always feel it my duty to resist such measures when proposed by others."

The gods plainly meant to destroy the Duke of Wellington, for such a pronouncement was indeed madness. Admitting as he did, wise after the event, that " the country was in a state of insanity about Reform in Parliament," that " there was scarcely an election, even in a corrupt borough, in which the candidates were not called upon to give pledges, and did not

[1] Brougham to Graham, November 1 ; Parker, *Life of Graham*, i. 96.

pledge themselves to vote for Reform," [1] the Duke was utterly unjustified in making such a speech at a time of confessed excitement. Peel, he said, was agreed with him that Reform could not be made a Government measure, but Peel would never have been led into so tactless a declaration of eternal hostility ; [2] to the moderates of the party the shock was totally unexpected, and Aberdeen, the Foreign Secretary, always said that with a moment's warning he could have prevented it. [3] By some contemporaries it was taken as a conscious attempt to conciliate the ultra-Tories ; but that the Duke had any such intention there is no evidence. His methods were more direct, and, seeing that part of that section were known to be in favour of Reform, it would have been a most injudicious form of overture. Probably, as many believed at the time, the Duke, like others, who are not natural speakers and have an imperfect control of language when on their legs, used words far more forcible than he intended. Trained in another school, he lacked that sympathetic understanding of the sense of Parliament, which in Grey and Peel amounted to intuition, and was of the greatest value to them as leaders of its debates.

In the story of the Reform Bill the character of the Duke of Wellington is of deep importance. That character stands as one of the noblest possessions of English public history, and the keenest tests which students of political intrigue can apply serve only to re-establish its essential simplicity and grandeur. Subject to endless misrepresentation and abuse from men whose sympathies and standards were alien to his, and often playing a part which the democratic tribunal of to-day condemns as politically criminal, he never appears for a moment to have failed in what he believed to be his duty, or to have been consciously swayed by selfish or hypocritical motives. When he returned in triumph to the country to which his victories had given lasting peace, it was but natural that the foremost living Englishman should continue in public life, and that amid the

[1] Wellington to the Duke of Buckingham, January 26, 1831 ; to Fitzgerald, December 26, 1830 ; *Despatches*, vii. 399, 383.

[2] *Despatches*, vii. 384. Peel, however, wrote in October 1831 : " Whether the Duke had made his speech in November 1830 or not, we should never have been able to stem the tide that was setting in favour of Radical Reform " (*Peel Papers*, ii. 189).

[3] Sir A. Gordon, *The Earl of Aberdeen*, p. 104.)

crowd of ineffectual politicians much should be expected from the man who had done something great. In war, as in peace, success must largely depend on knowledge of human nature. But the soldier who takes up a definite line in politics rarely succeeds in retaining general confidence and respect. Forced to abdicate at once his absolute command of his own side, and in dealing with his enemies the readiness to push hostilities to the extreme point, he must descend to a weaker position, and, often unfairly, is unfavourably judged by the standard of his former attainment. Few historical contrasts are more pathetic than the mobbing of the Duke of Wellington in Holborn on the seventeenth anniversary of Waterloo. Yet, if political hatreds may be made personal, such an outburst does not seem unreasonable. Courageous and resolute in the face of actual physical crisis, the Duke had little power of seeing consequences beyond the event, and taking a wide view of political probabilities. Indeed he eliminated from his calculations the one force it was most necessary for him to weigh, and even on the brink of revolution seemed unconscious that the people meant anything serious. He was totally unfitted for leadership at a time of democratic aspiration; it cannot be too deeply regretted that he did not trust his better instinct, and refuse the premiership in 1828; he had declared shortly before that he would be " worse than mad if he had thought of such a thing." [1]

The Duke's declaration against Reform, taken with the unpopular tone of the King's speech, violently shook his feeble administration.[2] In the Commons Brougham's motion was already down for discussion. Althorp, also asking for Reform, asserted he should no longer be deterred from opposition by the fear of turning out the Government. The numbers of the Whig members who met at his rooms in the Albany to discuss party

[1] Maxwell, *Life of Wellington*, ii. 210.

[2] " We have for the last two years looked with some favour on the Duke of Wellington's ministry. . . . But we must say that our confidence has been very much shaken by the unexpected and unaccountable course which the Duke of Wellington has chosen to take " (*Manchester Guardian*, November 6, 13). " Never was any administration so completely and so suddenly destroyed ; and, I believe, entirely by the Duke's declaration ; made, I suspect, in perfect ignorance of the state of public feeling and opinion " (Lady Holland, *Memoirs of Sydney Smith*, ii. 313 ; Howick to Charles Grey, November 24, *Howick Papers*).

prospects increased tenfold.[1]  They were now assured by Sir James Graham of Canningite support in their assault on the Government, and possibly in the division on Brougham's Reform resolution.[2]  Sir George Murray, Secretary for the Colonies, said in his place that he was prepared for some Reform, and there were rumours in the City that dissensions in the Cabinet would lead to the Duke's resignation.[3]  Francis Place was delighted. He augured the expulsion of the Tories from office, though anxious to keep them in till the Whigs should have matured a specific plan of Reform.[4]

But if there was a flutter within the walls of Parliament, outside a storm was rising and spreading fear of revolution in many hearts.[5]  Cobbett expressed gratitude for the Duke's straightforward refusal, and amusement at the prospect of a tussle between him and Brougham.   His speech had given offence to ninety-nine hundredths of the people.[6]  It was from the working people of London that danger was feared.   At the very time that Parliament met, their brothers were fighting in the streets of Antwerp, and it was believed that they themselves were spoiling for a battle with the aristocracy.   All this week the Home Office was deluged with warnings and advice.[7]  The steam presses and sawmills of London were to be attacked; the supply of gas was to be cut off ; there was a pile of sharp stones near the corner of Chancery Lane which would be handy to throw at the Duke of Wellington.   The Life-Guards were not to be trusted ; it would be wise to enrol the shopkeepers as special constables ; householders might be instructed to collect bricks on their roofs to drop on the heads of the mob in case of riot.   Joseph Hume actually received a letter inviting him to

---

[1] Le Marchant, p. 256.   Still it is possible that the week before several members were not yet in town.

[2] *Recollections of a Long Life*, iv. 60 ;  Bulwer, *Life of Palmerston*, i. 364.

[3] *Times*, November 5.

[4] Add. MSS. 27,789, f. 176.

[5] " I heard everywhere that a great change had taken place in public opinion since the meeting of Parliament.  The Duke was scarcely safe in the streets, and the King's popularity was evidently on the wane " (Hobhouse, *Recollections*, iv. 57).   The *Standard* of November 8 says stones were thrown at the Duke in the Park.

[6] *Political Register*, November 6.

[7] H. O. 40. 25 ;  44. 22.

take part in an insurrection.[1] The police discovered seditious handbills and tricolour cockades, now to be found reposing in the less excitable atmosphere of the Public Record Office. Place speaks of the " immense increase of the illegal unstamped penny and halfpenny periodical publications." [2] Much inflammation was supplied by the gatherings of Radicals at the Rotunda, a hall in Blackfriars Bridge Road owned by Richard Carlile, where lectures on political and other subjects were given most evenings in the week. Though advocating pressure by moral, rather than physical, force, the lecturers preached a class war and a contemptuous hatred of the aristocracy, which its objects found difficult to distinguish from downright sedition.

The fears of the authorities for the quiet of London were concentrated on Tuesday, November 9, the date fixed for the King and Queen's visit to the Guildhall. A flyleaf picked up in the streets added to the alarm : " Liberty or Death. English-men ! Britons !! and honest Men !!! The time has at length arrived—all London meets on Tuesday—come armed—we assure you, from ocular demonstration, that 6000 cutlasses have been removed from the Tower for the immediate use of Peel's Bloody Gang—remember the cursed speech from the throne. These damned Police are now to be armed. Englishmen, will you put up with this ? " Among the chief causes of the Government's unpopularity was the recent establishment by Peel of the New Police to supersede the old incompetent parish system—an innovation which stirred the bile even of men like Lord Durham. Known as Raw Lobsters or Blue Devils, they were exceedingly disliked as a symptom of military rule, though they had hardly yet acquired their position as a firmament to separate the classes from the masses. It was feared that the irritation thus caused would increase the danger of riot on Lord Mayor's day. The Duke placed a hundred of the Foot Guards in Buckingham

[1] W. Chubb to Hume, November 6 : " We hope you will be ready to take the lead. We intend attacking St. James's as soon as the soldiers are in their barracks. Our friends at Manchester will furnish pikes, and we expect assistance from Kent to the amount of eight or ten thousand. Cobbett's lectures on the French Revolution are attended by thousands, and they have enlightened the people very much."

[2] Add. MSS. 27,789, f. 183.

Palace, and made preparations for the defence of Apsley House.[1] But great as was the general disquiet, London was not prepared for the announcement on November 8 that the royal visit to the City was cancelled. It was supposed that ministers had received some startling information of imminent tumult, and Consols sank 3 per cent. from Saturday. The general suspense was great when Peel rose in the House that evening to explain his letter of the day before to the Lord Mayor elect. It was in answer, he said, to a letter received by the Government, which was taken to intimate that the quiet of the City could not be guaranteed if the procession took place. He defended his action by reading the above-mentioned handbill. The cat was out of the bag. But the Opposition, anxious to pick a quarrel, were by no means satisfied with the evidence adduced ; still less when two Aldermen rose and declared that Key, the Lord Mayor elect, had written without the sanction of the Court of Aldermen, which had actually decided that no danger was to be feared. The feeling, up till now one of approval for the ministers' wisdom, turned to angry ridicule. Why should the King be made the victim of the Duke's unpopularity ? Could the Prime Minister not have let his master go without him to receive the homage of a loyal people ? Such had in fact been Wellington's own suggestion : he was overruled by the Cabinet. For days the caricaturists made merry over the trembling Duke and his Don Key, a joke which seems to have been very warmly received.[2] Many considered the postponement more dangerous than ever the procession would have been. Almost universally it was held that the ministers had proclaimed their own incapacity and must go.

[1] Lord F. Leveson-Gower says that the Duke's anteroom was full of military officers—Lord Hill, the Commander-in-Chief, Lord Fitzroy Somerset, &c. There were, he says, 5000 troops and marines available (*Personal Reminiscences*, pp. 64, 74 ; *Despatches*, vii. 353).

[2] The " Ballade of ye downfall of Kynges " (*Prompter*, January 8, 1831) is worth quoting :

> " Charles the Tenth is at Holie-Rode,
>     Louis Philippe will sone be going ;
> Ferdinand wyse and Miguel good,
>     Mourne o'er the dedes their people are doing ;
> And ye Kynge of Great Britain, whom Godde defende,
> Dare not go out to dine with a frende."

See also the political caricatures of 1830 in the Print Room of the British Museum.

# THE FALL OF THE TORIES

tBut the Home Office were not reassured.  Nor was the information of their spies encouraging.  On Monday night half-hourly reports were sent from the Rotunda, where Cobbett was speaking ; a crowd of 3000 men had assembled outside.  In various taverns there was an expectation that the Duke of Wellington would be killed the next day, and that the troops would refuse to fire on the mob in insurrection.  Eighty thousand men were believed to be ready to rise in the north, and twenty thousand might march from Kent.  Tuesday itself was treated as a holiday, and many labourers were observed flocking into town from the south.  All the evening crowds were moving about London and tiring out the police ; at seven a mob, whose numbers were put at 10,000, was parading the Strand with flags and bands.[1]  However, the Constitution and the Government and even the Duke survived the night ; there seems to have been general excitement and desire to make a demonstration, but little more ; and though much discontent, political and otherwise, continued, a year passed before any crisis of at all the same nature occurred.

The question arises as to how far the Government were justified in their forebodings ; it was not without grave misgivings that they yielded to them.  The Duke afterwards told Lord Glenelg that in the whole of his career, military and civil, the crisis which cost him the most anxious consideration was when at a Cabinet Council he had to consider the question of the safety of the King in going to the dinner in the City, and he felt compelled to say No.  " If firing had begun," he said to Knighton, " who could tell where it would end ? . . . Would this have been well or humane for a little bravado, or that the country might not have been alarmed for a day or two ? "[2]  The wildest ideas were current ; the King was to have been kidnapped and kept as a hostage for Parliamentary Reform.  Lord Wellesley's remark, that his brother's decision was " the boldest act of cowardice he had ever known," is famous.  Place, whose opinion on such a matter is valuable, believed there would have been a riot, and that even at the eleventh hour the ministers did well in avoiding it.  On the whole it seems likely that there would have been a riot, perhaps a serious one, but hardly worse.  The working classes appear to have been little organised and to have lacked leaders.  The speakers at the

[1] H. O. 40. 25.
[2] Ellesmere, *Personal Reminiscences*, p. 64 ; *Courts and Cabinets*, i. 115.

Rotunda would not have led, as they did not advise, a *coup d'état*.[1] Carlile declared that as late as Monday nothing had been arranged, to his knowledge. And even in May 1832, when the National Union of the Working Classes was in being and a revolution was on the lips of men in many different ranks of society, the London Radicals of this class sat on the fence and took no steps. So it is hardly to be believed that any actual revolutionary rising was likely in November 1830.

For a week the " Grand Giraffe Administration " contrived to drag on an ignominious existence amid the increasing contempt of the daily papers, now gathering vulture-like, and the jeers and execrations of Cobbett and his kind, who maintained it was as clear as daylight that Alderman Key's letter was the result of collusion with Peel.[2] As a last desperate stroke the Government had manœuvred to create a panic which should rally the constitutional classes round them. As a practical measure, Reform had now fairly come to its own ; many of those who had most dreaded it were converted by the events of the last few days to see in some moderate measure the only barrier to radical change. As many Conservatives regretted in 1910 that occasion had not been taken by their party, in its decade of power after 1895, to reform the House of Lords in a manner they could approve, so eighty years earlier the Tories began to see the folly of having left Reform of the Commons to their enemies, when during twenty-three years of office it had been within their own power to appease popular demand by a trifling concession. In Parliament petitions for Reform were pouring in from England, Scotland, Ireland. Grey boasted of " 200 sure votes in town," [3] and Brougham's motion was down in the Commons for the 16th. The night before, however, Sir Henry Parnell moved an amendment to the Government's Civil List proposals. All sections of the Opposition united to carry it by 233 votes to 204. The result was entirely unexpected,[4] and perhaps due to chance, but it was generally believed that the ministers' resignation was only a question of days. On Tuesday, November 16, the Duke and Sir Robert Peel announced to both Houses that the administration was

[1] *Prompter*, November 13.

[2] *Standard*, November 11 ; *Political Register*, November 13.

[3] *Lieven Correspondence*, ii. 119.

[4] See Le Marchant, *Memoir of Viscount Althorp*, p. 257.

at an end. They had decided to forestall the evening's probable more serious defeat, and so, in the Duke's phrase, prevent Reform being carried by storm.[1] At Althorp's request, Brougham then consented, with a reluctance that showed signs of insincerity, to postpone his motion till the 25th, but no later. No change, he said, that might take place in the administration in the meantime could by any chance affect him. But on the next evening he made his last appearance in the House of Commons.

[1] Wellington to the Duke of Northumberland, November 17 : " Our resignation prevented the discussion of Parliamentary Reform yesterday. Indeed it was with that view that I thought it best to lose no time in sending it " (*Despatches*, vii. 361).

# CHAPTER III

## UNDERCURRENTS

*" And though the tired waves, vainly breaking,*
*Seem here no painful inch to gain,*
*Far back, through creeks and inlets making,*
*Comes silent, flooding in, the main."*

CLOUGH.

IN the sixty years through which we have followed the varying fortunes and slow advance of the political Reformers, a revolution in the social state of England had been brought about without delay or check. Industry and agriculture alike had been transformed, and the parliamentary representation, which had seemed anomalous to Bolingbroke and Chatham, bore no longer any relation to the facts of the national life. The scattered villages of the north had become mighty cities throbbing with energy ; the predominance of agriculture was challenged, and beside the country gentleman, the merchant, the yeoman, and the artisan who aspired in time to become a master, stood the manufacturer and his operatives. The England of John Bull had vanished in the smoke of the factories, and the England of the capitalist was taking its place.[1]

But though the factory is the obvious symbol of the new order and its consummation, it does not represent more than a single step, and the last step, in the process of change. The industrial revolution did not depend on the introduction of machinery or the crowding of operatives in single buildings. It is the name we give to the confluence of many forces, of which several have their source early in the eighteenth century and long precede the invention of the Spinning-Jenny or the designing of the first model factory. Both to agriculture and to industry the increased knowledge of the eighteenth century

[1] The population of Oldham rose from 400 in 1760 to over 12,000 in 1801 ; Leeds rose from 17,000 in 1775 to 53,000 at the end of the century ; Manchester rose in the same period from 27,000 to 95,000 (P. Mantoux, *La Révolution Industrielle*, pp. 368–371).

106

brought a process of expansion and speeding up, favourable indeed to efficiency but perilous to the stability and sense of confidence which were the best features of the ancient system. In the case of industry, it had been usual for the artisan to work at home and use his own implements ; the merchant would buy the product of his labour from the artisan direct, and sell it in the markets open to his trade. The fateful step was taken when the merchant came to acquire the implements of labour himself, reducing the artisan to a mere worker for a wage. " As soon," writes Monsieur Mantoux, " as the means of production cease to belong to the producer, as soon as there is one class of men which sells labour and another class which buys it, the inevitable antagonism begins. The essential fact, which cannot be too strongly emphasised, is the divorce between the producer and the means of production." [1] The herding together of workmen under the master's eye and the introduction of machinery were further steps in the establishment of the factory system as we know it.

The parallel event in agriculture was the abolition of the old wasteful system of open fields and commons in favour of enclosed estates belonging to a single owner. This was no novel occurrence. The economic history of the sixteenth century is full of " enclosure," and, though it was less practised in the next century, it formed an essential part of the schemes of scientific agriculture put forward by such men as Jethro Tull in the years about 1730.[2] Henceforward intensive farming became more and more popular, first with a few great nobles, and later with the nation at large. The process tended to the growth of large properties, and, whatever may have been the effect of the change on the rural population as a whole, it is certain that many of the old yeomen, or small freeholders, chose to leave the country and seek wealth in the great rising towns.

The isolation of England from the Continent during the Napoleonic wars gave home producers every chance. Some enormous fortunes were made, and by the beginning of the nineteenth century the master manufacturers stand as a class by themselves, ranging from the humblest employers of a few hands up to the great princes of industry, men of the type of Arkwright, Boulton, Wedgwood. Many of these, like Sir Robert Peel the elder, acquired a country estate, and came gradually

[1] Mantoux, p. 54.      [2] *Ibid.*, p. 148.

to share the habits and sympathies of the landed aristocracy. The greater number, preferring to live and rise to positions of dignity in the new towns whose greatness they had done so much to create, remained a separate class, and if they were not successful in purchasing a rotten borough or two, might be trusted to call for Reform of Parliament among the loudest. They regarded the country gentlemen as their natural enemies, and were anxious to rival them in political power as in wealth.

Proud of their abilities and their success, and fearful lest at the least slackening of their efforts their prosperity should vanish as suddenly as it had arisen, these men had little time to think of the welfare of those whose labour enriched them. The industrial revolution took the country so much by storm, and the science of its growth was so little understood, that the working classes were allowed to sink into a condition which ever since has been the shame of the country. " The strife of labour and capital," writes Mantoux, " we cannot too strongly insist, dates from many centuries before the industrial revolution. But never till then had it been so sharply defined." [1] It is difficult to pick out any one industry as particularly brutal. In mines, shops, and factories alike men and women and children were forced to work, with little food or sleep, in loathsome atmospheres for as much as eighteen hours a day. They had no education and no holidays, and many employers, or their foremen, were guilty of revolting cruelty. Up to this period a tradition had survived from mediæval times that to a certain degree it was the function of the State to regulate industry and to maintain a standard of living. But from the beginning of George III's reign onwards Parliament turned more and more to the doctrine of *laisser-faire ;* the vestiges of the ancient safeguards were swept away, and the operatives were left to their own resources. [2] A slight reaction against this policy began in 1819, when an Act to limit the hours of child labour in cotton factories was passed. However, this measure and a similar one in 1825 were of little value, owing to their very narrow scope and defective provision for inspection and control. Neither of them dared so far flout the doctrines of the new economy as to interfere in any way with adult labour. The grim fiction was

[1] Mantoux, p. 436.
[2] S. and B. Webb, *History of Trade Unionism*, p. 48.

that the workman bound himself of his own free-will and could throw up his job if not satisfied.

But it soon appeared that this theory of free contract only applied when it suited the employer ; it would be most awkward if a number of hands should agree to bargain for better terms by withholding their labour. Such a scheme struck at the roots of trade and property, and had to be speedily suppressed. For one compensating advantage the new concentration had—it at least made union possible. Trade unionism dates from long before the industrial revolution, but the growth of collective action in various trades at this time, and the wider outlook it involved, are among the few bright spots in a period dark enough from the point of view of labour, though even they were brighter in promise than in achievement. But feeble as such efforts at protection were, they were too dangerous to be winked at by the governing class ; in 1799 a bill was passed without opposition through Parliament to make a combination of two or more workmen to obtain higher wages or shorter hours of labour a crime punishable with three years' imprisonment.[1] Nevertheless in 1812 a desperate strike broke out, followed by years of rigorous repression. "The effect of this tyranny," say Mr. and Mrs. Webb, " was actually to shield the Combination Laws by turning the more energetic and enlightened working-class leaders away from all specific reforms to a thorough revolution of the whole system of parliamentary representation. Hence there was no popular movement whatever for the repeal of the Combination Laws."[2] When this repeal was finally brought about in 1824, it was due to the labours of two men, Joseph Hume within the House of Commons and Francis Place without ; they carried the measure through a House that hardly understood the importance of the change, almost in spite of the workmen, whose ill-judged violence the year after came near to losing them their hard-won freedom.[3] Henceforward the path of

[1] Professor Foxwell writes : " This seems to have been a turning-point in English social history. The injustice of the repressive policy drove all the best energy and intelligence of England into the party of Reform. Place and the Benthamites, Cobbett and the Radicals, the *Edinburgh Review* and the Whigs, all in their various ways began to prepare a new era" (Introduction to Menger's *Right to the Whole Produce of Labour*, lxxx.

[2] *History of Trade Unionism*, p. 85.

[3] See the account of the struggle in Graham Wallas's *Life of Place*, chap. viii.

labour lay clear, though special causes prevented any immediate progress.

If less dramatic, the plight of the farm-labourers was equally miserable ; they formed in 1831 over one-fifth of the adult male population.[1] As, even apart from the invention of machinery, the labour of bands of operatives was superseding that of the family or the individual in the textile trades, so in agriculture a more productive and economical form of cultivation took the place of the old rather happy-go-lucky system, and a new order of " manufacturing labourers " arose.[2] To this change of method the necessary preliminary was enclosure of all or part of the common land, a practice which, when unfairly or inconsiderately enforced, as it frequently was, proved a cruel blow to the interests of the individual commoner, as well as a total subversion of the old English village life. On the Tory theory of society as composed of graded orders of men, the peasantry were a no less essential and honourable part of the nation than the nobility or gentry. They had a recognised position in the body politic, and until the latter part of the eighteenth century the State had felt itself bound in some way to maintain it. In 1830 this in many ways happy relationship had passed away. Lord Henry Sydney complains in *Coningsby* that the order of the Peasantry " has vanished from the face of the land." Deprived of his rights of common and fuel, and sometimes of the garden patch which grew vegetables to eke out his earnings, the peasant sank into the condition of a mere labourer, without capital or assured rights, depending solely on his precarious wages. Nevertheless it cannot be fairly said that enclosure had a bad effect on either population or employment.[3] Nor was it a unique feature of the time ; it was a progressive movement carried over several centuries, and its necessity was only specially emphasised when the

---

[1] Porter (*Progress of the Nation*, p. 35) says that in 1821 agriculture engaged 33.2 per cent. of the families of Great Britain, while 45.9 per cent. were employed in trade and manufacturing. In 1831 the proportion was 28.2 to 42. Of those connected with agriculture, more than three-quarters were labourers. (New Edition, p. 189.)

[2] *Observations on the State of the Country.* The anonymous author adds that farms have become " a species of manufactory for the production of corn."

[3] E. C. K. Gonner, *Common Land and Inclosure*, p. 437. Professor Gonner's book shows the extreme danger of generalising from single instances on this subject.

great war forced England to be self-supporting. But beyond question in many cases bitter hardship resulted, and too often the interests of agricultural science were less consulted than those of the grasping landowner, and it was natural that the extension of the system should bring in its train the sufferings of a period of transition. No doubt Cobbett and his like were short-sighted, but his " Rural Rides " gave him every opportunity of noticing actual cases of ill-treatment, which he was not slow to make public.

Along with this fruitful cause of distress, and sometimes arising out of it, grew the abomination of the old poor law, a mutilated relic of Elizabethan prudence. It was not till 1796 that the monster reached its final and most hateful form. An Act was then passed enabling Justices of the Peace to allow out-relief at their discretion out of the rates to the able-bodied poor. Of this with sentimental thoughtlessness they took full advantage, and the poor rate rose by leaps and bounds. It was calculated that in 1823 the amount of it would have bought one-fourth of the entire quantity of wheat needed for consumption in England and Wales.[1] Sometimes the relief was granted in kind, as when a magistrate who was also a landlord of pauper cottages would order his own rent to be paid to him out of the rates. More often the paupers were relieved in money by one of several expedients calculated to combine the maximum of waste with the minimum of inducement to the labourer to better his condition. The relief was simply a dole paid by the parish to save the employer from having to give his men reasonable wages ; farmers who paid their men well were penalised by having to pay over again to preserve less generous pockets. If anything, the most disgraceful device of all was the labour-rate system, which compelled ratepayers to provide work for paupers for whom they had no use, at an arbitrary rate of wages, frequently to the ruin of the self-supporting labourer whose place was taken by the paupers the farmer was forced to employ. Sometimes " the parish pay equalled or exceeded the average wage of the district." [2] The scheme produced all the evils of slavery, without the motive a slave-owner felt to take some care of his slaves. As demoralising in another way were the " allowances " given to a labourer according to the number of his children ; men were

[1] T. P. McQueen, *Thoughts and Suggestions*, 1830.
[2] *Poor Law Commission* (1909) *Report*, p. 61.

encouraged, by the increased rate offered, to marry before they could afford it, and in many cases bastards were given an advantage over other children. Thus the labourer had no inducement to support either himself or his family, and his children, who might claim relief in their own names, were strongly tempted to look to the parish as their natural paymaster throughout their lives. Everything was done to keep the labourer helpless and dependent. The sort of service the parish exacted of him was to spend so many hours in a gravel pit, or attend a roll-call at fixed times. The scandal was aggravated by the system of close and open parishes.[1] In the former a landowner who employed labour could pull down the cottages on his estate, so that the wages he allowed should not have to be supplemented out of his own parish. He thus defrauded the next parish by forcing it to pay for his own meanness, and added to the labourers' troubles by giving them an additional walk, perhaps of many miles, before and after their day's work. There were, of course, exceptional parishes where administration was strong and good ; but the general principles of the old poor law were such as put a premium on negligence and violated every rule of wise philanthropy. It was in fact simply an " insurance against revolution."

The iniquities of this system were still in existence when the Poor Law Commission presented their report in 1834, by which time the rate stood at 8*s.* 9½*d.* per head of the entire population.[2] Landlord, farmer, and labourer suffered from it alike, and the papers and letters of the time are full of protests against the ruination of the two latter classes by the paying of wages out of the rates. Farmers, who found it hard enough in any case to make both ends meet in the reaction after the war prices, complained bitterly of the gratuitous burden they were called upon to bear. The tariff on foreign corn no doubt kept much land in cultivation that would otherwise have been wasted, but agricultural produce of various kinds was sadly depreciated.[3] Farming in the north was supposed to be in a more flourishing state than in the southern counties.[4] However, Lord Grey

[1] Thorold Rogers, *Six Centuries of Work and Wages*, ii. 438.

[2] Nicholls, *History of the Poor Law*, vol. ii.

[3] See *A Letter to Sir J. Graham*, by the Rev. R. Warner, dated January 31, 1831 (Cambridge University Library, Z. 24. 33⁵).

[4] See an account quoted in the *Letter to Sir James Graham*. " The armers in general are a very respectable class of men in the four northern

writes from Northumberland that even there farmers are paying rent out of their capital, though to his surprise farms let as high as ever.[1] The bad harvests beginning in 1828 were of course also serious ; in the agricultural riots at the end of 1830 the insurgents as a general rule admitted that the farmers were unable of themselves to raise their wages, but rather urged them to head a general movement of the agricultural population to demand a reduction of rents and tithes.[2]

Tithes were indeed excessively unpopular, and more than anything else were the cause of disaffection to the Church. The feeling was not as strong or as universal as in Ireland, but even in England it was widely held that some reform must be introduced if the Establishment was to be maintained. Many country parsons were, and were admitted to be, true friends of the people, and the fiercest anti-clericals agreed that the mass of curates were shockingly underpaid. But the large incomes of the bishops were blazed on countless handbills throughout the country ; many of them were pluralists, and nearly all appeared rather in the character of princes than pastors ; except in some individual cases, their hold on the people's love and reverence had vanished. The bishops bore the brunt of the odium the covetousness of the Church had provoked ; but there were many rectors and vicars whose tithes, often drawn from several livings held together, were a shameful contrast to the misery of the farmers and labourers around them. The idea that the clergy were battening on the want and degradation of the poor was at the root of most of the anti-Church feeling of the early nineteenth century.

If the condition of the farmers was a cruel change to the prosperity they had enjoyed twenty years or less before, that of their labourers was admittedly far worse. At a time of

counties; many of them have saved money; and all of them are well-informed and capable of treating with their landlords or their stewards upon equal terms. . . . We have no custom as that of eking out the wages from the poor-rates." In Cornwall there is said to be no distress; provisions are cheap, and rents, though high, are regularly paid (*H. O.* 42. 22).

[1] Grey to Howick, January 8, 1830 ; *Howick Papers*.

[2] *Cf.* letter of Tenterden to W. Waterman, November 16, 1830 : " The labourer says ' we will not starve, and you (the farmer) must give us 2s. 3d. a day. We know you cannot afford it, but you must refuse to pay your tythes, and we (the peasantry) will support and protect you in the refusal ' " (*H. O.* 44. 22).

expanding commerce and great increase of production, when the upper classes of society were living in luxury, the wages in many villages were little above starvation point. Certainly the dwellers in the great towns were passing through a crisis of extreme hardship, but they were at least associated, and combination was not wholly impossible ; the crowded state in which they lived made them accessible to any would-be bene-factor. But the poor of the villages were far apart and utterly disorganised ; remote from the centres of knowledge and in many cases unable to read or write, they had no means of making their grievances known, till they took the last desperate course of insurrection. If it were not for the fatal prominence to which their hopeless efforts in the autumn of 1830 raised them, and for the untiring enthusiasm with which William Cobbett devoted himself to their cause, it is likely we should know nothing of the conditions of life under which a large part of the nation suffered under Pitt and Canning and Wellington and Grey, in the days of Trafalgar and Waterloo and the great battle for Reform.

The earnings of labour in these years varied enormously. The great war acted as a system of natural protection for the farmer, and wheat prices reached an abnormal height. Wages indeed also rose, but in nothing like the same proportion, and the labourer was constantly reduced to the precarious assistance of the poor rate. In the words of Thorold Rogers, " dearth had become an institution." [1] However, the strain relaxed, and the twenty years before 1830 show in the main a rapid descent in average wholesale prices. Between 1809 and 1829 they have been almost halved. From 1820 onwards the decline is to be mainly attributed to the contraction of the currency, caused by the Bank of England's resumption of cash payments, whereas the world's output of gold did not increase. Nor was credit manufactured to meet the expansion of enterprise which followed Huskisson's reforms. [2]

---

[1] " Between 1800 and 1812 the nominal wages of agricultural labourers and artizans were considerably increased, either by actual payments or by parish allowances. Still the rise was not proportionate to the increased cost of living, for dearth had become an institution. . . . But the wages of persons employed in factories were not increased, or very partially, and many people were out of work altogether" (Thorold Rogers, *Six Centuries of Work and Wages*, ii. 410).

[2] I am much indebted for this summary to Mr. W. T. Layton's *Introduction to the Study of Prices*, particularly chap. v.

It might naturally be expected that the working classes would have shared the benefit to the consumer. This, however, was not the case. On the one hand labour had not yet recovered from the disorganisation resulting from the industrial revolution. Some of the old trades were falling out under the pressure of machinery, and the factories' demand for women and children was disastrous to adult male labour. On the other hand, as regards the working classes, the fall in wholesale prices is deceptive. The articles in which the charge was most marked were largely raw materials, manufactured produce, and luxuries, while those which most nearly touch the poor fell little in the ten years after 1820, if at all. Especially this was so in the case of bread.[1] The Corn Law of 1815, which forbade the importation of foreign wheat till the average price in England was 80s. the quarter—more than twice the figure it has reached in any of the last thirty years—remains a dark spot in the history of class legislation. The limit was lowered in 1823 to 70s., and in 1828 a sliding-scale was introduced, but in the meantime the population was increasing at the rate of nearly 200,000 a year. " The price of wheat, indeed, fell, for in many cases wages were too low to permit the people to buy bread. The demand was, however, large enough to prevent the price of wheat falling as fast as other commodities." [2]

As to the wages of agricultural labour, and their purchasing power, it is hard to generalise. Different parts of the country vary much, and allowance has to be made for harvest and other perquisites. An estimate for the whole of England gives an average of 14s. 6d. in 1810, of 12s. in 1820, and of 11s. in 1830 ; at the last period 7s. was a common weekly wage in the west, but in the north the average was higher.[3] It must be remembered that the enclosure system often deprived the labourer of extra comforts which had gone to swell his earnings in former

---

[1] The average price per imperial quarter of wheat was 95s. 3½d. for the five years 1811–15, 80s. 9½d. for 1816–20, 57s. 3½d. for 1821–25, and 61s. 7½d. for 1826–30 (*Gazette* prices). A 4-lb. loaf of bread cost 12½d. in 1805, 21½d. in 1812, 11d. in 1820, 10d. in 1822, 11d. in 1825, and 10½d. in 1830 (*Blue Book*, Cd. 2645, p. 155).

[2] Layton, p. 43. The farmers quoted in the *Letter to Sir James Graham* say that the poor would have been much worse off but for the introduction of potatoes—an interesting admission in the light of Cobbett's furious attacks on that harmless necessary vegetable.

[3] Bowley, *Wages in the United Kingdom*, p. 34.

days. "The riches that he had been promised by the champions of enclosures had faded into something less than a maintenance. The wages he received without land had a lower purchasing power than the wages he had received in the days when his wages were supplemented by common rights."[1] Unemployment too was common, as is proved by a total poor rate of nearly £7,000,000 for a population of less than fourteen millions, and often the dole allowed by the overseers seems to have been meant rather to stave off the labourer's importunity than to give him any hope of real maintenance. On the whole it would appear that the labourer of the twenties received wages of much the same purchasing power as his father's at the beginning of the war ; he would have been better off in the middle of the eighteenth century, but far worse at its close. If anything, the improvement would tend to illustrate the truth that men are most dangerous not in the extreme depths of misery but when they have enough to know how much better off they might be. Still in 1830 destitution was prevalent, and actual starvation well known. And there are things worse than sheer poverty : among these the demoralising effect of the old poor law may well be ranked. The commissioners of 1832 found their chief task in the problem of the able-bodied village pauper ; the rural population was as much the most important part of the question to poor-law reformers then as the urban population is now. And the legislation of 1834 does deserve all praise for the way in which it faced and overcame what was its most pressing difficulty. The disgrace is that legislation was delayed till the labourers were goaded into breaking the ties of their allegiance and bringing down on their heads the penalties of a barbarous code of law.

Wages in the towns were also falling from the level to which the war prices had perforce driven them, but the decline is far the most noticeable in the case of the hand-loom weavers, the worst victims of the industrial revolution.[2] Their distress seems

[1] J. and B. Hammond, *The Village Labourer*, p. 241. *Cf.* a letter of John Allwright to the Home Office : " The poor do bitterly complain at the very high price of provision, saying their wages is no more than they had fifty years ago, and provision is above double the price, and starve they never can submit to " (*H. O.* 40. 29). Often the conviction of a grievance is as potent as the fact of it.

[2] " The earnings of the hand-loom weavers diminished at an extraordinarily rapid rate between 1790 and 1840, so that whereas at the former date they were a fairly well-to-do and contented set of men, at

to have been the same in all parts of the country, and riotous attacks on machinery were the result. It is difficult to see how they supported life at all. Among factory workers in the great cotton-spinning industry wages were higher, but the figures for the cotton trade generally show at the same time a steady increase in the numbers employed and a continuous fall in wages.[1] In fact, the few years round 1830 mark the nadir reached by wages of cotton operatives in the century, and another clue is revealed in the search into the springs of the democratic movement. With this and other reservations, such as the continued high price of food, we may accept Mr. Bowley's summing up of the twenty years before 1830. Nominal wages were falling, but prices were falling faster, and real wages therefore rising slowly.[2]

Nevertheless, when Parliament met in February 1830, there was a widespread belief in the kingdom that distress was prevalent to a degree that hardly the worst years after the war had surpassed. Members came up to town from the country with their heads full of the speeches they had made and heard at county meetings, where resolutions had been passed describing the extreme misery of all engaged in agriculture. Industry and commerce were declared to be suffering no less ; politicians in the great towns found eager audiences where a few years before their diatribes had fallen unheeded. In the previous October the London Radicals had been roused by "the accumulating distress which pervades the productive classes of the community." Cobbett returned from a tour he undertook during the winter and early spring armed with local statistics and first-hand information which persuaded him that all England, from the professional to the labouring classes, was in a grievous plight, in fact on the edge of starvation. Serious statesmen spent the winter in unwonted economic inquiry. The state of things was attributed to very various causes, among which the currency, the beer and malt taxes, the corn law, "free trade," and the rotten boroughs were all popular. The High Tories made the most of this discontent as a ground of assault on the Government, declaring that matters had reached

the latter date those who remained were earning a miserable 5s. a week at the expenditure of 14 hours' daily work" (Bowley, *Wages in the United Kingdom*, p. 110).

[1] G. H. Wood, *History of Wages in the Cotton Trade*, p. 127.
[2] Quoted by Layton, *Introduction to the Study of Prices*, p. 151.

a pitch compared to which the suffering of 1816-19 was mild, though their ingenuity was taxed to discover the link between agricultural distress and Catholic Emancipation. The Whigs found a valuable cry in retrenchment and reduction of taxation. So heavy was the air with this subject that the Opposition could find no better ground for the first party division than the question of fact whether distress was general or only partial, as the King's Speech had it.

The Ministerialists, on the other hand, were convinced that the country was really flourishing, though bad harvests and the late trade depression might have caused temporary disturbance ; much of the agitation they held to be purely factitious.[1] They were supported by several authorities with no motive to defend them. The *Morning Chronicle* said the complainers could not have it both ways ; farmers might be poor because food was cheap, but cheap food could not hurt the factory hands.[2] And there was no evidence of widespread unemployment. The *Times* declared the fall in general prices should more than console landowners for their lowered rents.[3] Francis Place agreed that the distress was not general, and threw contempt on the ignorant babbling of members of Parliament, among whom Peel alone spoke with any understanding.[4]

Where contemporary opinion was so divided, it is important to form a rough idea of the true facts of the case, in view of the real and alleged connection between the condition of the country and the growth of the Reform movement in 1830. On the one side it was said that the demand for change was a morbid symptom only appearing when the country suffered from some real or imaginary distemper ; on the other that the authority of Parliament was deservedly called in question when it had failed so signally to keep the nation in prosperity.[5]

[1] Arbuthnot to Wellington, October 28, 1829 ; *Despatches*, vi. 265.

[2] *Morning Chronicle*, January 27 : " There is a prodigious deal of exaggeration of the extent of distress."

[3] *Times*, January 28.

[4] Add. MSS. 27,789, f. 133.

[5] " The distress into which the nation has been plunged by the enormous taxation has made the people everywhere wish for and petition for a reform in the House of Commons. This feeling has been gaining ground very fast, for more than three years ; and the divers exposures which have taken place, together with our own acute sufferings, have made even the farmers cry aloud for Parliamentary Reform " (Cobbett, *Twopenny Trash*, September 1830).

The average price of wheat rose 6s. per quarter in 1829, reaching a higher point than the average of any year since 1825, when all prices rose sharply before the financial crisis came to a head. The price of flour in like manner rose in 1829, and the quartern loaf cost a penny more, a most important fact.[1] Monthly prices in these years also show rapid fluctuations ; wheat rose 14s. 6d. between February and August 1830, and several times reached the price at which foreign corn was permitted.[2] Moreover wholesale prices generally show a tendency to rise for 1829-31, though their direction for the period as a whole is decidedly downward. All this is in favour of the claim that the time was one of exceptional distress. On the other hand, every reason for discontent the poor had in 1829 and 1830 they had just as much and more so in 1825. The quartern loaf had then too risen to 10½d. ; the wholesale price of wheat showed a more sudden rise, and rose higher ; also prices other than wheat stood at a level far above any reached in 1830. And there could be no comparison between the present state of things and that during the war, in 1812 for instance, when the quartern loaf cost 1s. 9½d., and meat was also dearer. So from this point of view there was no immediate cause to rouse the poor to protest and resistance in 1830 more than, say, in 1825. It is of course true that five years had aggravated their distress ; and if they could look back with thankfulness to 1812, they could also look beyond it with regret to the days before the war, when food of all kinds was cheaper. And, to take no account of modern improvements in wages, the average price of wheat in 1829 was higher than it has been in any year between now and 1856. The poor rate too tells a dismal story. Averaging close on two millions in the three years ending 1785, it had passed four millions in 1803, and now stood at nearly seven millions—the worst year since 1821.

In 1829 and 1830 industry and commerce were but slowly recovering from the depression which followed the boom of 1825.[3] In the former year both our imports and our exports

---

[1] *Bluebooks*, Cd. 2337, p. 240 ; Cd. 2645, p. 72.

[2] Tooke, *History of Prices*, ii. 199 ff.

[3] " The year 1825 closed with a financial panic and widespread commercial disaster. The four years that followed were years of contraction and distress. Thousands of workmen in all trades lost their employment, and wages were reduced all round " (*History of Trade Unionism*, p. 100).

had declined from the level of 1828, though the rise of both in the ten years after 1820 was part of a continuous and accelerating increase. Certainly the manufacturing population did not keep silence as to their distress, though their cry was not as loud and as universal as that from the land. In the hardware industry there was much discontent; at the foundation of the Birmingham Union, Attwood spoke of the exceptional distress of the town as the cause and justification of his coming forward. Lord Howick, who was at Birmingham at the beginning of 1830, found the manufacturers most despondent. Prices, profits, and wages were all low, in spite of general activity; some businesses were being practically run at a loss. This agrees with Tooke's general statement: "During the greater part of this interval (1828-32), while corn had been rising and was at a comparatively high range, the prices of most other descriptions of produce were falling. . . . The fall of prices of raw materials, and the still greater fall of the prices of manufactured articles, in consequence of the rapid improvements of machinery, had the effect of greatly extending the consumption both at home and abroad, and there was consequently a considerable extension of both the home and foreign trade, and the revenue was flourishing. But while the fall of prices was in progress, the importers and the manufacturers and the mining interests were, in some branches, suffering severely." [1]

In the industries thus depressed it is natural to find that wages felt the full effect, but it is by no means true that all workers in towns were badly off. Different places varied much. [2] In Cumberland it is said that employment was general and no class in distress except the weavers. The *Manchester Guardian* took the same line. "The distress in the cotton manufacture is *not* general: the thousands upon thousands of workpeople engaged in factories, whether mere spinning-mills or public establishments also, we believe, are as fully employed, and as well paid now, taking their money wages and the reduced price of commodities together, as they have been at any former period."

[1] *History of Prices*, pp. 209, 213.
[2] An anonymous letter to the Home Secretary from Birmingham states that 10,000 families were "*entirely* out of employment," and could get nothing better from the poor-law authorities than an occasional dole of a florin (*H.O.* 44. 19). See also the account in the *Manchester Guardian* of February 27 of a public meeting held recently at Manchester.

Except therefore in certain industries, it would appear right to accept Mr. Bowley's statement that real wages were rising slowly, and to maintain that the declaration in the King's Speech of February 1830, that distress was " partial," was more true to the facts than the amendment of the Opposition.

But though the working classes as a whole might have been nearer to destitution in the bad years of the war, the Government had failed to remove the angry feelings which had existed with more or less intensity since the persecutions of 1817 and 1819. The events of that time had fully persuaded the labouring population that their rulers were their enemies, and turned the thoughts of many towards revolution. The emancipation of collective action secured in 1824 was due to a few wire-pullers, not to the ministers, who played a far more characteristic part in its partial repeal next year. The trade depression and extensive unemployment which had intervened showed working men how precarious was their position in society ; poor law and factory conditions held up before their eyes its degradation. Even had no alternative to the present system been offered, dissatisfaction and distrust must have been great. But for many years doctrines had been in the air which taught that government by landlords and capitalists and holders of sinecures was by no means the only possibility. To say nothing for the moment of the influence of Paine and the political revolutionaries, the early English socialists had proclaimed their pregnant discovery of the workman's right to the entire produce of his labour, and denounced the iron rules of the economists and the theory that the labourer's wage must simply be the price of his maintenance. As Professor Foxwell points out, the year 1824–25 was triply important in the democratic movement.[1] " It saw the repeal of the Combination Acts, the first adoption of co-operative views by working men, and the issue of three independent socialist works." One of these was Thomas Hodgskin's *Labour Defended against the Claims of Capital*, which was perhaps rather a forerunner of Syndicalism in its advice to labour to win its own battle ; another was Gray's *Lecture on Human Happiness*, attacking the unproductive classes. Godwin, Hall, and Thompson, though differing in detail, all stood for a more equitable

[1] Introduction to Menger's *Right to the Whole Produce of Labour*, lxxxi.

distribution of wealth, and ideas of communistic and other utopias were abroad ; State Socialism, however, was yet unborn.

Important as was the work of the Ricardian socialists, it could not compare with that of William Cobbett and Robert Owen, who in their different spheres exerted an immense influence in forming working-class opinion. Of Cobbett and the wide circulation of his *Weekly Political Register* much has been already said. Understanding, as the politicians did not, the ways of life and thought of the working classes, for over twenty years he had eloquently appealed to their class consciousness and insisted that it was the taxation imposed by their luxurious and corrupt rulers which kept them poor. He was familiar with their intimate habits, complaining with genuine indignation of the disgrace of a potato diet, pouring hatred and scorn on the views of Malthus, and giving week by week little scraps of kindly advice to the cottagers, which endeared him to their hearts as a champion and friend. William Lovett, the son of a Cornish fisherman, who came up to learn cabinet-making in London shortly before this time, and who was by no means a partisan of Cobbett's, speaks of the vast influence of his " long teaching of the multitude." His gospel was one of hope and the possibility of speedy relief if Englishmen would only awake and assume the place in politics which a reasonable Reform would give them. He denied Huskisson's statement that " the present generation must be contented to submit to this state of things," and, though he had no wish for an armed revolution, believed in a revolutionary change. To say nothing of his aversion to paper money, his economics were rather dangerous, as when he suggested that " Grey's 154 " might pay off the national debt between them.[1] But in firing the minds of labourers with ideas of their true dignity his work was invaluable, and the sustained vigour of his efforts ranks him among the greatest popular leaders of all time.

Robert Owen resembled Cobbett in appealing to the imagination of his readers and hearers and in his real desire to uplift the oppressed classes, but in little else. His course of life had been completely different from Cobbett's, so full of varied incident on both sides of the Atlantic. Owen had been engaged in industry from boyhood ; throughout his life it was more real to him than politics. As soon as, and even before, he found

[1] *Twopenny Trash*, August 1830.

himself in the enjoyment of independent control at New Lanark, he devoted his remarkable business ability to improving the condition of his operatives, playing the part of benevolent despot. The experiment was highly successful from every point of view, and gave Owen unlimited confidence alike in his own powers and in the immediate responsiveness of human nature to changed circumstances. Nothing, he thought, was needed but education and wise direction to transform mankind into docile beings who would readily adapt themselves to any reorganisation of society, however fundamental, and live in peace and amity on the lines laid down for them. Owen soon won a name for himself as a successful and philanthropic administrator. In 1813 he published his views in *Essays* which were widely read in high circles ; four years later he brought out a scheme for a co-operative village, inaugurating the principle for which his name now stands. The Reforming Radicals disapproved, but in the years which followed Owen worked hard at making his project known in Britain and America.[1] His object was the universal voluntary association of the workers of the country ; he had no use for the State or for any part of the community that was not industrial. The England he desired was in many ways like that which William Morris has imagined in *News from Nowhere*. Co-operative communities were formed which aimed at being economically self-sufficing and doing away with the exploitation of labour by capital ; part of the scheme was a labour currency, in which an hour's work roughly approximated to sixpence. But apart from the fact that the members got on one another's nerves, the project failed because it aimed too high and rested on theories not supported by facts. Owen ignored the power of inheritance and custom in the lives of men ; he believed he could renew the world in a generation, making no allowance for the ill-developed organisation and social consciousness of the working people of his time. His rejection of religion as ordinarily understood damned him in respectable eyes, and his scorn for politics cut him off from the main stream of the democratic movement. Cobbett and he were both contemptuous of the House of Commons as it then existed ; but whereas Cobbett believed that by a wide extension of the franchise Parliament might be captured for labour, Owen considered all

[1] See Podmore, *Life of Owen.*

such hopes misdirected and illusory. Only educate the working classes, and politics would be unnecessary and obsolete.[1]

But though to reasoning men Owen's ideas might seem premature and too ambitious, they made a stirring appeal to the imaginations of thousands just becoming conscious of their dormant powers. William Lovett, who joined an Owenite Co-operative Association in 1828, writes of the vast attraction the idea of community of property held for working men.[2] It was yet the dawn of the new era opened by the French Revolution, and those who hailed it as the day of their emancipation refused to believe that any reconstruction of society was impracticable, which rested on the principles of liberty and equality. At the beginning of 1830 there were, we are told, three hundred co-operative societies in the United Kingdom ;[3] in the January newspapers Owen urged his cause in a series of long letters addressed to all classes, extolling his own theory of communism as the only permanent remedy for distress. Throughout these years there were frequent co-operative congresses, and the "Grand National" of 1834 was largely recruited by Owen's efforts ;[4] but the trade societies which were specially prominent in 1830 derived from other sources.

Before turning to the great revival of trade unionism, it may be well to mention the Factory Act movement, the work of philanthropists more orthodox than Owen, which also sprang to new life in this same year. The agitation begun by Richard Oastler in a Leeds newspaper in September, for limiting the hours of work of children in factories to a ten-hour day, was a protest against the spirit of the industrial revolution. It would appear to be a mistake to attribute the misery of the operatives too largely to the introduction of machinery ; often the worst cases occurred among the hand-loom weavers.[5] But the general

---

[1] "To Robert Owen, whose path was blocked on the political line by the disfranchisement of five out of six of the adult male population, open voting under intimidation, corrupt close corporations in the towns and a Whig oligarchy at the centre, the idea of relying on the constitutional instrument of the polling-booth must have appeared no less chimerical than his own programme appears to-day" (S. and B. Webb, *History of Trade Unionism*, p. 405).

[2] *Autobiography*, p. 44.

[3] Podmore, *Life of Owen*, p. 396.

[4] *History of Trade Unionism*, p. 119.

[5] See Hutchins and Harrison, *History of Factory Legislation*.

speeding up of industry wantonly sacrificed the workers' health
and comfort to increase of production, no less than it marred
the face of " England's green and pleasant land." The bar-
barity of the system was most patent in the case of children,
whose conditions of labour in mines, factories, and field gangs
in no way differed from slavery. The Reports of the various
Commissions on the subject form one of the most terrible indict-
ments that can ever have been drawn up against men in a position of power and responsibility. Ill-fed and ill-clothed children
no more than seven years old worked for anything up to eighteen
hours a day—or night—in atmospheres and in attitudes which
stunted their growth and sometimes left them cripples for life.[1]
Labouring as they did in droves, and awoken from scanty sleep
only to the unvaried round of heartbreaking toil, they saw no
joy or freedom in their grey lives, and the stream of English
manhood and womanhood was poisoned at the source.

In 1819 the efforts of Sir Robert Peel the elder led to the
passing of a bill much weakened by the absence of adequate
sanction ; in 1830 conditions were as bad as ever. The only
change was in the spirit of the grown-up workers, prepared at
last to unite for the emancipation of their children under the
leadership of men of very various opinions. Oastler, a Tory
and an Evangelical, was supported by the Vicar of Bradford, a
Wesleyan minister, and a large number of Radicals, among
whom John Doherty, secretary of the Cotton Spinners' Federation, was prominent.[2] The Factory Ten-Hour Day movement
was highly fortunate in not suffering from the obstinate refusal
of parties and religions to combine, which so sorely damaged
the cause of education in those days, and many other enterprises for the people's good. Even here it was not without
difficulty that Oastler was persuaded in the autumn of 1831
to work in concert with the operatives of Huddersfield, they
being for the most part " radicals and dissenters." [3] Union
was made necessary by the emasculation of Hobhouse's Relief
Bill by the Commons, who thought a twelve-hour day for
children more reasonable. The agitation was at first confined
to Yorkshire, Oastler's native county, where factories were very
numerous and the local interest in the slave-trade question

[1] " Alfred " (Samuel Kydd), *History of the Factory Movement*, i. 96.
[2] Hutchins and Harrison, p. 44.
[3] " Alfred," p. 124.

gave special strength to the appeal.  Yorkshiremen were quickly stirred at the thought that their county, so nobly identified with the struggle to liberate the slaves in West Indian plantations, allowed the children in its own great towns to bear a hardly less iniquitous yoke.  Thus at the time when Parliament met in November 1830 the conscience of the north was being aroused on this question of the factory children ; the air was full of protests against the callous cruelty of employers and indignant comparisons of the swollen wealth of the great capitalists with the extreme misery of the little children on whose forced labour their princely state was founded.

Far more important, however, as a manifestation of the democratic spirit was the great wave of trade unionism which passed over the country between 1829 and 1834.  It has been already stated that the repeal of the old Combination Laws in 1824 was won for the working class by no effort of their own ; the credit belongs almost solely to Francis Place and Joseph Hume.  But unionists were not slow to enter into these men's labours ; the outbursts of 1825 were violent enough to cause a reaction which enabled Parliament to limit its concession.  The new unionism was less wild and at the same time more ambitious. Though intended in the first instance merely to prevent the reduction of wages, it was highly and widely organised by men of real talent and lofty aspirations, to which the speculations of Hodgskin and Owen directly contributed.  In the words of Mr. and Mrs. Webb, " the disillusionment of the newly emancipated Trade Clubs in the collapse of 1825 left the working class organisations prepared for these wider gospels."  Henceforth the ruling class had to deal not with mere local strikes due to temporary distress or personal friction, but with the fear of a general secession of the plebs, which might be used as an engine of social revolution.[1]

The birthplace of this movement was Ramsey, in the Isle of Man, where John Doherty arranged in December 1829 a meeting of representatives of the cotton spinners of the three kingdoms. Its object, he assured the High Bailiff, was not political, but

---

[1] " It is the attempt on the part of the trade union leaders to form not only national societies of particular trades, but also to include all manual workers in one comprehensive organisation, that constitutes the New Unionism of 1829-34 " (*History of Trade Unionism*, pp. 140, 193).

industrial—to form a national union of cotton spinners.[1] But even this ambitious project was only part of a yet more gigantic scheme, first broached at Manchester in February 1830. Doherty was again the leading spirit ; his efforts now resulted in the formation of the National Association for the Protection of Labour, or United Trades General Union, as it was originally styled ; it was intended that local branches should be set up, and delegates were sent about the country to explain the nature of the plan. Its professed object was to resist the lowering of wages, not to raise them ; strike pay was fixed at eight shillings a week ; and Doherty was appointed general secretary.[2] No trade which was not organised was to be admitted to the benefits of the central body, which charged an entrance fee of one pound to each union which joined it. In March Doherty started the *United Trades Co-operative Journal*, urging all trade societies to affiliate themselves. Co-operative bodies, it said, were all very well in their way ; but workmen who did not join a trade union also were unlikely to have a penny to start co-operation with. This piece of advice is interesting as showing the feelings of the unionists to Owen's scheme, which they held could not replace, though it might be a welcome addition to, collective bargaining. Their relations to the Political Unions will appear later.

Indications were not wanting that the powers of the new Trades Union might be called into play at no distant date. Besides the acknowledged distress in the weaving trade in Norfolk, at Spitalfields, at Carlisle, and in Lancashire, and in the ribbon trade at Coventry, we hear of strike riots in March and April among the bleachers of Preston and the Bolton spinners. Already the masters were falling foul of the Trades Union.[3] At Bolton the malcontents held a meeting to petition Parliament and form a Political Union as well. In the course of the summer there was trouble in the stocking and carpet trades, as well as a strike at two Ashton cotton factories. Troops were sent to Bolton and Kidderminster, and the officer commanding the northern

---

[1] *H. O.* 41. 7.

[2] *United Trades Co-operative Journal*, No. 19.

[3] A Preston bleacher complains to the Home Office of the strike among his men. " The Union consists of two parts, one of particular trades, as printers, bleachers, spinners, and so on, the other is the Union of all these—has a share of all their subscriptions, and the directors of it command the whole " (*H. O.* 44. 19, April 20).

district strongly advised the permanent retention of a regiment at Blackburn to check the constant outbreaks of the manufacturing population.[1] As autumn came on, the spirits of the working class were excited by the amazing success of their brethren at Paris and Brussels, and the strength of the Trades Union was increased. The revolution of July was a vast encouragement even to those who took no interest in technical politics. It stood for the exaltation of their kind, and that which to us seems tame and prosaic was to them the most thrilling fact in history.[2] By the end of August the Government were seriously alarmed by the strike in progress in the Stalybridge and Ashton cotton-spinning district, where employers complained bitterly of the " piquetting " system and consulted with the magistrates as to the amount of protection that could be given to imported strike-breakers. The attitude of the Government's representatives is a study in reluctant neutrality. Their hostility to the unions was undisguised, and Peel chafed at the inadequacy of the law against " piquetters " ; he was reduced to issuing muskets and ammunition to the manufacturers to protect their property.[3]

Throughout October the alarm of the authorities increased ; a spy employed by the Manchester magistrates to watch the more prominent Radicals in the north reported that "the working class is generally infested with a spirit of Revolution." [4] Meetings were held under the tricolor to hurl defiance at the military and the borough-mongers. Complaints poured in to

---

[1] *H. O.* 40. 26.

[2] Colonel Shaw writes to the Home Office (August 26): " It will be unfortunate if the masters attempt the plan of introducing new hands at present : the excitement caused by the Revolution in France is greater than I could have anticipated ; they talk a great deal of their power of putting down the military and constables " (*H. O.* 40. 26).

[3] The leading men think " that the population is most completely under the guidance of the leaders of the Unions of Trades, so much so, that they insist not only on the masters giving them such wages as they demand, but that they regulate the whole work in the factories, in all its details, in the manner which the Union prescribes; and the men refuse to communicate with their masters, referring them for terms to the leaders of the Union " (*H. O.* 40. 26).

[4] A Birmingham pamphlet reads : " No one can ponder on the marked and loud similarity of feeling between the English and French on this ' consummation devoutly to be wished ' without feeling a moral conviction that, unless a speedy change of measures takes place here, we must have something like a revolution."—*H. O.* 52. 11.

the Home Office that trade unionism was becoming a public menace : were not the journeymen hatters dictating to their masters ? [1] Cotton and silk manufacturers told the same tale ; if only the Combination Laws had not been repealed, all would yet be well.[2] To such protests Peel lent a ready ear, and suggested that small shopkeepers should be induced to unite with the upper classes to quell the rioting which might be expected to follow the rejection of the men's demands.[3] Towards the end of the month matters were complicated by the outbreak of a serious coal strike in the Oldham district. There had been resistance on the part of the South Wales miners in the spring to truck payments and the reduction of wages, but the present affair was better organised, in that the colliers were rapidly incorporating themselves in Doherty's Trades Union, and were prepared to combine with the Ashton cotton-spinners. Baffled in his hope of assistance from the lower middle class, Peel thought of parliamentary aid to quell the union, but realised that even in an unreformed House more evidence would be demanded of the Government than it could easily produce.[4]

At Carlisle, where it was supposed that the Co-operative

---

[1] *H. O.* 40. 25, October 19 ; the hatters were refusing to work with non-unionists.

[2] *H. O.* 52. 6.

[3] Peel to Foster, October 25 ; *H. O.* 41. 7.

[4] Peel to Foster, Oct. 30 : " The whole of the operatives in the Collieries are associated for the purpose, ostensibly, of mutual protection against the masters. The Spinners and Weavers are in like manner associated, and are all bound by Oath to the Rules of their association. . . . The associated numbers in the Trades Unions, of which Doherty is the Secretary and Director, are variously stated, but amount certainly to many thousands, and their funds are very great. That of the Collieries, which is distinct, is also very powerful, but being of more recent institution is still poor in funds ; but as they are beginning to join with the General Trades Union, the Headquarters of which is, I believe, in London, and which extends to Glasgow, &c, the means of the latter will be brought to the assistance of the former, and render the Union complete, and by the Masters quite irresistible. . . . Mixed up with all this, there is a strong and rapidly increasing political feeling. They have their reading-rooms, their newspapers, and all the means of obtaining information and circulating it. . . . The recent events in France and Belgium have excited the greatest influence among them. . . . All business between Masters and Men is carried on by the Union " (Major-General Bouverie, O. C. Manchester district, to Lord Fitzroy Somerset, October 30, 1830 ; *H. O.* 40. 26). In a letter to Lord Fitzroy, dated November 6, Bouverie estimates the membership of the Trades Union in October at 80,000 and its weekly receipts at £330.

I

Society was quietly arming with a view to rising if the King's speech should prove unsatisfactory, the police found difficulty in executing warrants, and doubts were cast on the fidelity of the post office and the troops.[1] At the heart of the trouble were the ill-paid weavers both in the city and at Netherby. Hardly had the Lancashire miners begun to return victoriously to work, when riots, which extended over more than four days, broke out at Carlisle ; attempts were made to burn the King and the Prime Minister in effigy, and at night the magistrates were powerless. At the same time the cotton manufacturers of the Stalybridge and Ashton district added to the confusion by threatening a lock-out, involving 52 mills and 16,000 men, for December 4, unless their workers would accept a reduction of wages. It seemed most unlikely that the spinners would submit, for the Trades Union was rapidly increasing its numbers and absorbing many small trade societies, while according to one of its own leaders it was becoming more and more political.[2] Such was the condition of affairs in the industrial north when Peel —we can hardly believe with reluctance—transferred the burden of home government to the untried shoulders of Lord Melbourne.[3]

Most unfortunately for the incoming ministry, at the same time that organised labour was spreading terror among the upper classes in the north, there broke out in the south an insurrection far more serious. The agricultural labourers demanded a higher rate of wages, and in default of this proceeded to throw off their allegiance to the State. First in Kent and Sussex, but afterwards throughout the south and east of England, threshing machines were broken by insurgent crowds and wheat-ricks secretly burnt at the dead of night. There was little organisation among the labourers ;[4] they would band

---

[1] *H. O.* 40. 25.

[2] Betts declared at a meeting near Manchester : " Trades Unions and Political Unions were now so intimately blended together that they must be looked upon as one " (*H. O.* 40. 27).

[3] See a note (*H. O.* 40. 27) dated November 19, 1830 : " I take the liberty of recommending . . . the whole of my recent confidential communications with Mr. Foster respecting the Trades Union at Manchester to the immediate and serious consideration of my successor in the Home Department.—Robert Peel."

[4] Report of Colonel Brotherton (*H. O.* 52. 9) : " The insurrectionary movement seems to be directed by no plan or system, but merely actuated by the spontaneous feeling of the peasantry."

together village by village, often under the leadership of a Dissenting minister, who with one or two others would form a deputation to ask a rise of wages from the farmers ; twelve to fifteen shillings a week was often the living wage suggested. In Kent there had been occasional fires in June and July, but the movement did not really gather to a head till October and early November, when the labourers of Battel rose and destroyed several ricks.[1] Suspicion fell heavily on Cobbett who had lectured there a few days before, and Peel was anxious to prosecute him as instigator.[2] After the middle of November the agitation spread to the counties of Berks, Hants, and Wilts, and by the end of the month Gloucestershire, Oxfordshire, Herts, Northamptonshire, and the East Anglian counties were all infected. Panic was created over agricultural England by dark letters, signed " Swing," found about house and farm, in which rick and roof-tree were threatened unless the wages of the hungry labourers were increased. Insurance offices were even more hardly hit than the farmers, who sometimes actually scored by their loss ; placards were posted to show the labourers how ill their weapons were aimed. Often the farmers sympathised with the insurgents, and in some cases actually joined their ranks. Among the gentry such feelings were rare ; pity was sunk in fear, as they found themselves in a land of rebels and watched their ricks blazing in the winter night. They had no understanding of this strange Jacquerie.

The Government found it easier to suppress the revolt than to assign the guilt. Scarce as mounted troops were, they met with little resistance when once on the spot, and the capture of labourers armed with bludgeons was an inglorious task. When the military were not available, eager Lords Lieutenants led out the Yeomanry in counties where that force still existed, though the suppression of a labourers' revolt by a corps of farmers officered by landlords did not pass without protest.[3] Special constables were largely raised in the towns. In some cases the

[1] Their manifesto is quoted in *The Village Labourer*, chap. xi. : " Now gentlemen, this wat we intend to have for a maried man to have 2s. 3d. per Day and all over 2 children 1s. 6d. per head a week and if a Man has got any boys or girls over age for to have employ that they may live by there labour and likewise all single men to have 1s. 9d. a day per head and we intend to have the rents lowered likewise. . . ."

[2] *H. O.* 44. 22.

[3] Radnor to Melbourne, November 29 ; *H. O.* 52. 11.

middle class, who formed the staple of the force, refused to serve; at Ditcheat the inhabitants objected to being enrolled unless the incumbent would reduce his tithes from £1600 to £1000. Hunt paraphrased the oath they were asked to take as one " to uphold high rents, high tithes, and high taxes." At Holt fifty men declared their willingness to turn out to protect all property but threshing machines ; they did not wish to show " distrust to their poorer neighbours." In the Royston district no labourers would serve ; it was suggested that the men employed under Government on the roads should be forcibly sworn in. Officers were sent about the country to supervise the enrolment and generally to organise the southern counties for the preservation of order.[1]

Before the end of December the revolt was crushed ; its importance lies less in any results to which it actually led than in the light it throws on the condition of rural England and the dangers the Government's slack policy had produced. In 1760 Parliament resigned its function, inherited from Tudor days, of securing, however rudely, a standard of living for labour. The vicious system which grew up in the interval had been constantly denounced, but indolence won the day. Not till the starving poor were actually up in arms was the country's attention arrested, and then the danger was magnified to the exclusion of the need for redress.[2] There were several indeed who wrote from country halls and vicarages pleading that the landed and governing class should humbly set themselves to regain by mercy the confidence they had forfeited, and the new poor law was the honest payment of an admitted debt ; but for the moment the attitude of the ministers was more nearly summed up in the judge's words at Winchester : " We do not come here to inquire into grievances. We come here to decide law." It

[1] The Home Office thought of using the services of the Irish Revenue Police or the crews of Scotch Revenue cutters ; Government pensioners might also possibly be embodied. At Cambridge the Vice-Chancellor refused to allow the undergraduates to march against the insurgent labourers who had marched in from Shelford and Cherryhinton (*H. O. 52. 12*).

[2] Sir T. Denman, the Attorney-General, wrote on December 25 from Winchester : " The cases are much less aggravated than we supposed. The arsons end in smoke issuing from a workhouse chimney where the furniture was destroyed and burnt. The appearance of the culprits, ringleaders and all, is very forlorn " (*H. O. 40. 27*).

was not surprising if the labourer considered that the Government had first goaded him into crime and then with pitiless severity punished him for giving way.

There seems little doubt that sheer want in most cases drove the villagers to this hopeless vengeance, though it was the part of the prosperous classes to deny it.[1] Almost every possible explanation but the obvious one was sought out, to lessen the guilt of those who should have fed the poor. Men persuaded themselves that the fires were lit by foreign missionaries who crossed over from France for the purpose. It was suggested that evil-disposed men were in the habit of driving past by night and setting fire to ricks by missiles as they went. Of course the Radicals came in for their share of suspicion; it was unbelievable " that the Agricultural Labourers have of their own inventions raised these mobs or caused the fires "; though discontent might be there, it was the republicans of their own class who worked it up to the point of insurrection. Those who escaped the snares of the Radicals were " affected by the discourses of the lower order of preachers." Others put the whole trouble down to the Jesuits.[2] With less improbability Cobbett was regarded as the arch-rebel and prime mover of the revolt. Certainly his influence upon the farmers and superior labourers had been great; he had taught them that they might win their own salvation by organised effort, he inspired them with a divine discontent, and he was in the habit of declaring his belief that if the labourers were not relieved a revolution was imminent. We hear too of villages where his writings were read aloud to groups of eager workmen.[3] But apart from the fact that the vast majority of the agricultural labourers could not read, it

[1] A Marlborough parson declared (*H. O.* 40. 25): "I am not aware of an instance in which distress has been pleaded as the cause of raising or joining a mob. One of the prisoners has between two and three thousand pounds; shoemakers, blacksmiths, carpenters, were the most active of the rioters, the Agricultural Labourers, heated with beer, became very active." The information that men of various trades were prominent in the mobs is interesting; but the mass of evidence tends to show that distress was constantly pleaded as the cause of rising.

[2] *H. O.* 40. 25; 52. 9; 44. 23.

[3] Carlile declared (*Prompter*, December 18) that the *Political Register* was read everywhere in the agricultural districts. " Mr. Cobbett has the power to raise to resistance by any one week's *Register*. A serious word from him to the people would decide that point. The inflammable spirit is abroad."

is absurd to suppose Cobbett capable of such cruel folly as to urge the country people to an enterprise he knew was hopeless as well as criminal.   It is more rational to accept his own statement that there was no evidence to suggest the fires were due to anyone but the labourers of the district where they broke out.  " Conspirators " from London, he said, would soon lose their bearings, if they wandered about the countryside at night ; as to " cheap periodicals," he knew none but his own writings and Methodist tracts.[1]  Ordinary papers were beyond a working man's purse.   He entreated the Government to apply themselves to the relief of the labourers, rather than to their punishment for acts which, however wild and wicked, were the natural outcome of sullenness born of despair.   They had struck blindly at those above them, not so much with the idea of benefiting themselves as of attacking the system which had brought them so low.

Their defence was not very prudently taken up by the London Radicals.   Richard Carlile, while refusing to accept the charge of incendiarism as proved against them, justified their general attitude of hostility to constituted authority.  " Yours is a state of warfare, and your ground of quarrel is the want of the necessaries of life in the midst of an abundance."   The new ministry was, in fact, called to take office at a time when to a large extent government did not rest on the consent of the governed.   So far were they from deriving strength from their position as the established rulers of the land, that it was actually a disadvantage to them ;  they were faced at the outset with the need of winning back confidence for discredited institutions. Parliament had become a laughing-stock to many in the working classes, and revolution was discussed purely as a question of expediency.   The labourers of the south had rejected their allegiance to the constitution by force of hand ;  their fellows in the metropolis were now doing so in the sphere of thought.

From the days of Wilkes there had been a tradition of Radicalism in London ;  sound constitutionalists were afraid it might become the Paris of Great Britain.   But as the merely political Radicals became respectable, a lower stratum was formed specially connected with the working class.   The inspiration of Owen and Hodgskin blended with the influence of Paine to create an opinion far more distinctively Radical than that which had pro-

[1] *Twopenny Trash*, February 1831.

duced the demand for Reform at such meetings as took place in 1829 and the spring of the following year. The thrilling events of the summer and autumn abroad added a touch of reality to abstract thought and awoke a faith able to remove governments. From the autumn of 1830 the movement assumed a new vitality ; its appeal was wider and far more confident than ever before. At the bottom of most of the agitation in London we find a knot of really able men, possessed of considerable force of character, marred only by personal jealousies which weakened their unity. Besides Cobbett and Orator Hunt, who in spite of their endless bickerings and mutual contempt represent much the same agricultural type of massive ruggedness in person, thought, and speech, Lovett made the acquaintance of Watson, Cleave, and Hetherington, all of whom wielded great influence among the semi-Owenite crowd at the Rotunda, and were closely connected with the struggle for the freedom of the press. Cobbett's difficulties on this matter have been already mentioned ; and though the champions of the cause often stood for no very high standard of journalism, they were true martyrs for a most important principle. It was monstrous for the upper classes to despise workmen as ill-informed and uneducated on political subjects, when a daily paper cost sevenpence owing to the heavy stamp-duty.[1]

A definite " Unstamped Agitation " was set on foot in 1830 for the enlightenment of the working man. On October 1 Hetherington published the first of his *Penny Papers for the People*, followed next year by the famous *Poor Man's Guardian*, " established contrary to ' Law,' to try the power of ' Might ' against ' Right.' " It also cost a penny. For this bold defiance of authority Hetherington was boycotted in his ordinary printer's business, and a number of sentences were inflicted on him, to meet which a fund was opened. It is impossible not to admire the constancy of these obscure champions of free knowledge, who returned again and again to the charge in the face of obloquy and punishment. In November appeared the *Prompter*, issued from the Rotunda by Carlile for threepence weekly : it was

---

[1] Place puts this view forcibly in a letter to Hume, dated January 12, 1831 : " Had there been no tax on Newspapers, no duty on advertisements, no obstruction to the free use of the press, there would have been no riots, no insurrections of husbandry labourers, no burnings, no murderous hangings, no transportations . . ." (Add. MSS. 35,149, f. 10).

meant to be the organ of the new Radicalism in every line of life and to fight the battle of democracy without quarter.[1] Its attitude on the question of physical force is best given in Carlile's own terms. " All that has been said about arming and resistance at the Rotunda, may be summed up in a few words. The people of Paris and Brussels have been praised for what they have lately done, generally by all the speakers. This feeling is common to nine-tenths of the people of this island. I have said that there is much legislative tyranny existing in this country, deserving resistance ; but always holding up moral resistance as preferable to physical resistance, if the moral can be made effectual ; if not, as an ultimatum, I recommend the physical resistance, whenever there is a prospect of its success." [2] Only a few months were to pass before many of all ranks in England were resolved that the utmost bound of moral resistance had been reached, and such doctrines became matter of practical importance ; even at the end of 1830 serious men believed that any day might bring forth a violent revolution.[3]

The object of this chapter has been to show that, quite apart from the purely political agitation, culminating in the retirement of the Tories from office, there was in 1830 a definite awakening of the democratic spirit, nothing less than the birth of a new era in English history, of which the Reform Bill was only an incomplete symptom. The low level of real wages in the country's most important industries inclined the discontented to doctrines of social change, and weakened the English prejudice against innovation. In certain ways the movement was foreshadowed in 1819, when extreme distress led to violent outbursts of feeling against the Government. But the excitement then was due rather to temporary causes, and with their disappearance peace was restored. In 1830 the distress could no longer be

---

[1] " The *Prompter* summons the press to its aid, and pledges a brave and glorious struggle, and a successful war, under its tri-coloured banner, against the aristocratical or clerical despotism, corruption, and ignorance of the whole country."

[2] *Prompter*, No. 1, November 13.

[3] An anonymous letter to the Home Office ends : " Depend upon it the country is ripe for a revolution, and perhaps the greatest one that has ever happened in any country—there only wants some rich bold adventurer to start it, then good-bye to England's King and Ministers " (*H. O.* 44. 19).

directly attributed to the war ; some of the barriers in the path of organised labour had been removed; the great Tory party had played itself out ; and, above all, the French and Belgian workmen had shown that a revolution was not necessarily a unique and catastrophic event, terrible and overwhelming as in 1789, but a permanent weapon in the hands of the oppressed.

The result was that labour had come to the knowledge of its strength, though it had not yet learnt how best to use it. Among other things it had discovered that the ruling class could show no outstanding proof of their fitness to govern. The long muddle of the poor laws and the corn laws, the excessive national debt, and the scandals of the pension list, were inseparably connected with aristocratic rule, and identified it with selfishness and corruption. Parliament had lost the confidence of the middle and lower classes in its power and desire to redress their grievances, and was regarded as an ancient farce. The Rotunda is " the real House of Commons," said Carlile. Most fortunately for the Constitution, if not for the labourers, the chasm between the masters of physical and political power was bridged by the rich and strenuous middle class ; their absorption in the electorate restored the legislature to a position of stability. Otherwise the forces of privilege and brute strength must have clashed in disastrous war.

It is plain that a class rift of this nature did exist, and that the Government was entirely on one side. It stands out beyond all question in the Home Office attitude to the strikes and the agricultural rising, a grim coercive attitude more ready to punish than to prevent. It stands out in the game laws which allowed the rich man to set spring-guns to protect his coverts and transported the starving labourer who violated their sanctity. It was fully recognised by the workmen whose emotions, strained by want, were played upon by highly coloured accounts of wasteful taxation and pensions showered upon bloated bishops and peers.

Socially too, it was complained, the cleavage had widened. The old happy relationship of squire and tenant had given place to the horrors of the parish cart, while the great man, less landlord now than employer, kept his serfs in ignorance and gloom, very different from the joyous village life of merry England. The rich had ceased to mix with the poorer classes, and their disdainful ladies no longer sat in the theatre to display their beauty and magnificence to the admiring pit. " They have so completely cut the people, that is all whom they consider beneath them, that they have themselves almost gone out of the cognisance of the working people in every respect but as enemies." [1]

This sentiment of irreparable antipathy pervades the writings of Cobbett and the London Radicals. " Everything in nature is a state of prey, physical or moral. Man, like every other animal, has no rights, privileges, advantages or pleasures, but such as he can conquer or defend, or receive as a slave in the shape of a boon." [2] It must be a straight fight between democracy and the parliamentary oligarchy ; there could be no compromise. The war was waged on many fronts : by political democrats in Unions and frantic demands for Radical Reform, of a nature to express the will of the working class effectively in the Commons ; by industrial democrats in trade associations and strikes on as large a scale as their inefficient organisation allowed ; by revolutionary theorists on platforms and in the press ; and by the " dumb children " of the fields and farms, whose anguish had no means of penetrating to the ears of power, in blind revolt and sullen submission to compelling force.

As for the governing class, with untroubled conscience they believed for the most part, if they were Tories, that all must somehow turn out for the best under our matchless constitution of Church and State, if only the Land were given a chance ; if they were Whigs, that a fine time was coming, with a pure but well-connected ministry governing a grateful country on the most liberal principles of *laissez-faire*, supported by the solid worth of the middle-class. There were few who, like the young Disraeli, looked down beneath the thin crust into the boiling waves of restless energy, and sought to understand the desires of labour. The author of *Sybil* assured his readers that the pictures of the Two Nations which he painted were drawn from his own observation ; if he had not stated the whole truth, it

---

[1] Place to Hobhouse, December 5, 1830 ; Add. MSS. 35,148, f. 74. When Lady Spencer was told that the poor were rising against the rich, she said, " On the contrary, it is the rich that are rising against the poor " (*Recollections of a Long Life*, iv. 64).

[2] *Prompter*, November 13.

was because the ignorance of his contemporaries would not
believe it.  Like the mariners in the legend, they had supposed
that the ship of their luxurious civilisation was safe anchored
in the unchanging earth ; they were to learn that it was fast
bound to a monster now first stirring in its sleep and making
ready to draw them with it into unknown seas.

# CHAPTER IV

## THE WHIGS IN OFFICE

" Go pluck the jewels from the Crown,
    The colours from the mast,
  And let the Three per Cents come down—
    We can but break at last.
  If Cobbett is the first of men,
    The second is Lord Grey ;
  Oh must we not be happy, when
    The Whigs are in to-day ! "
                    W. M. PRAED, *The New Order of Things.*

IT was taken as a matter of course that Parliamentary Reform
would be officially adopted by the Duke of Wellington's successor. " We are all Reformers now " was generally admitted
by all but a small group, though many were confident that the
barest minimum would satisfy the people. Even the Duke,
still believing that any change would be a national disaster,
confessed his position was untenable ; he resigned when he did
to prevent Reform being carried with a rush, and to interpose
a time for reflection, such as the keenest Radical would not refuse
to a new administration.

As to its probable composition, and even its probable head,
speculation was hopelessly at sea. Grey, Lansdowne, Goderich,
were all suggested as Premier, or even the Duke, as head of a
ministry in which Palmerston and the Canningites should replace
Peel, Goulburn, and Murray. So long was it since Whigs had
ruled the country, that there was little certainty to go upon.
It was on Lyndhurst's advice that William's choice fell on Grey.
The royal appeal at a time of such difficulty, if not danger,
appeared more in the light of a demand on his chivalry than an
offer of coveted distinction. In any case we hear nothing of
his definite renunciation, eight months ago, of all intention to
take office again, if indeed that renunciation was anything more
than an outburst of temporary depression. It was therefore in
accordance with all expectation that Lord Grey made leave to
bring in an extensive measure of Reform a condition of his

accepting office; the events of the last fortnight had taught him that the time was at length ripe for the cherished desire of his youth. The King had been prepared for the request by his retiring ministers, and promised Grey his support for such a measure. Though even then probably preferring the Tories, he was resolved to do his duty as a constitutional king and give the new administration every chance.[1] But Grey's immediate task was to form a ministry equal to the stress of circumstances. He was, in his own words, " appalled at the difficulties "; the King himself did not see how a Cabinet could be built up without the assistance of the Ultra-Tories.[2] Though men of ability and even genius were not lacking in the ranks of the Whigs and Canningites, hardly anyone, with the exception of Palmerston, had any experience of office worth mentioning; it was felt that at a crisis of the State this was a serious loss, and Grey would willingly have exchanged much brilliancy in speculation or debate for a measure of that businesslike efficiency and familiarity with the ways of government which Peel so pre-eminently displayed.

By applying first to Lansdowne and Holland, Grey showed that his ministry was to be formed on the orthodox lines of Whiggism; if the old tradition of the party was anywhere preserved, it might be looked for in the son of Shelburne and the nephew of Fox; both had been members of the administration of All the Talents, and so served for a few months under the great leader. Holland had much of his uncle's frankness and charm. Throughout the long years of opposition he had continued his advocacy of every liberal cause; though his political life had been spent entirely in the Lords, his trust and interest in the people far surpassed the average measure of the Whigs. A Radical journalist saluted him as " the last and best of the Whigs of the old school; the long-tried friend of civil and religious liberty; the champion of toleration and of the oppressed."[3] He was endowed with that rare gift, a mind so fresh and open

---

[1] See *Memoirs of Baron Stockmar*, i. 313, for a curious document which the King handed to Sir Robert Peel in January 1835, describing his own behaviour since he came to the throne.

[2] Grey to Princess Lieven, November 16; *Lieven Correspondence*, ii. 121. Wellington to Northumberland, November 17; *Despatches*, vii. 361.

[3] *Memoirs of Albany Fonblanque.*

that the new ideas of successive generations find in it always a welcome and a home.

Lord Lansdowne, who as Lord Henry Petty had filled the post of Chancellor of the Exchequer almost as young as Pitt, had seen more recent service as Home Secretary under Canning. Of no marked abilities as a constructive statesman,[1] he was a valuable party asset owing to his mastery of detail and personal charm. He would have made an ideal Whip, though perhaps he might even more have enjoyed the post of Patronage Secretary. The master of Bowood was certainly more of a Georgian Whig than a Victorian Liberal, and in the struggles of the next few months he by no means went as far as young Tom Macaulay, whom he had brought into Parliament for his pocket borough of Calne. Grey described him in 1827 as the most moderate of Reformers, if indeed he had ever publicly avowed the cause at that time ; in the great campaign now to open, his part lay rather with the organising staff than in the firing-line. However, his chief thought him worthy of no secondary place in the Cabinet, and pressed upon him the seals of the Foreign Office. After full consideration Lansdowne declined the honour on grounds of health, preferring the Presidency of the Council with its then nominal duties.[2] The similar post of Chancellor of the Duchy was given to Holland ; the patronage it included gave congenial employment to his strong-willed and somewhat alarming lady, to an extent which recalled the palmy days of the eighteenth century.[3]

Having thus provided for the two representatives of the Whiggism of his own generation, Grey turned to the man without whose loyal help he declared his task would have been impossible, a man connected by name and lineage with older days and by intellectual and personal sympathy with the present. Of the two responsible posts he filled, Althorp was less fitted for the Exchequer than the leadership of the Commons ; for the latter he was marked out by the unofficial part he had played in the organisation of the party in the late session. His rooms

[1] Sefton put it more bluntly, writing to Creevey, January 12, 1828 : " Petty . . . is admitted by common consent to be the damnedest idiot that ever lived, not even excepting the domestic Goderich " (*Creevey Papers*, p. 486).

[2] Lansdowne to Grey, November 18, 1830 ; *Howick Papers*.

[3] *Recollections of a Long Life*, iv. 72.

*Photo: Emery Walker, Ltd.*

JOHN CHARLES, VISCOUNT ALTHORP, THIRD EARL SPENCER,
1782–1845

*From the Drawing by* CHARLES TURNER, *in the National Portrait Gallery*

at the Albany served as a Whig committee-room, where bills had been drafted and lines of policy discussed throughout the last fortnight. A Tory or a most moderate Whig at Harrow and in his early Cambridge days, he fell at Trinity into a set whose influence persuaded him to throw in his lot with the advanced wing of the Opposition, led at that time by Romilly and Whitbread. His father, though he had himself supported Pitt's Government, made no attempt to coerce his son's opinions, even when they went to the risky length of favouring the ballot and triennial parliaments. Althorp's character was admirably suited to win the confidence of the English House of Commons. He was the very opposite of the professional politician; of the dangerous cleverness of Canning or Brougham he was wholly guiltless. And if heartily to dislike one's job is a sound test of trustworthiness in a statesman, Althorp was of all men most dependable. Never really happy away from his Northamptonshire home, he came up to London for the session like a schoolboy from the holidays; if in finance he was hardly Walpole's equal, in a healthy preference of sport to politics he rivalled, if he did not surpass, the Norfolk squire. It was with the most extreme reluctance that Althorp yielded to Lord Grey's insistence on his accepting office, as he afterwards reminded him; and the darkest hours of the Reform struggle had for him this much of light, that they promised an early release from greatness.[1] In the debates of Parliament he was so obviously incapable of soaring above his hearers' intelligence that he won a well-deserved reputation for honesty. A more straightforward man never lived; this quality, together with a noble loyalty to Grey, prevented him from taking part in the compromises on which

---

[1] In a letter to Russell he writes: " I have not been able to escape and have been obliged to sacrifice myself, for to me it is an entire sacrifice, but a difficulty occurred which I did not foresee and which could only be got over by my taking office" (*Early Correspondence of Lord John Russell*, i. 312). The allusion is presumably to Brougham, who would otherwise have been the natural leader of the Whigs in the Commons. Brougham himself wrote, in an interesting memoir preserved among the Althorp Papers: " I doubt if anybody ever hated being in office as much as he did. Others I have known hate it occasionally—for instance, Lord Grey always hated it for the bulk of the session, and began to like it towards the vacation. But A. detested it equally at all times. He often said, when he got up in the morning, he wished he might be dead before night came. But he went through the duty manfully, and so as never to let anyone perceive he disliked it."

Canning's administration was built up, though he did not refuse
it his support.   It was probably his honesty quite as much
as his skill in money matters which secured him his much criticised appointment by Goderich as Chairman of the Finance
Committee.   At the Exchequer, for which a high position in the
mathematical Mays at Cambridge and the scrupulous accuracy
of his kennel accounts were his main qualifications, he was
obviously an amateur, though industrious and sensible.   His
real service to the country lay in his work as leader of the House
of Commons at a crisis when passions were fierce and open, and
when the ministry's resolve to steer a straight course between
Tory and Radical extremes exposed them to ceaseless taunts of
inconsistency and double dealing.   Here the tried temper and
stainless integrity of one man, and that the leader, were of priceless value.   His biographer, Sir Denis Le Marchant, quotes a
saying of Sir Henry Hardinge: " It was Althorp carried the
Bill.   His fine temper did it.   And in answer to a most able
and argumentative speech of Croker, he rose and merely said
that ' he had made some calculations which he considered as
entirely conclusive in refutation of the right honourable gentleman's arguments, which he had mislaid, but if the House would
be guided by his advice, they would reject the amendment,'—
which they accordingly did.   There is no standing against such
influence as this."   Though periods of stress and conflict do no
doubt act as a refining fire by which high talent and sterling
worth are brightened in the eyes of posterity, their effect is not
as a rule immediately such.   There is a good deal of soot in the
flame ;  great men are accused by little men, and even by great
men, of mean and mercenary conduct ;  it is hard to see one's
own standards clearly, and harder still to see that anyone,
especially an opponent, comes up to them.   Those characters
are rare which in time of peace have created such an impression
of perfect honour that the bitterness of war dares cast no slur
upon it.   Though Althorp's appointment made it plain that
in the duels of the two party leaders his great schoolfellow Peel
would invariably win the day as far as mere speaking went, the
arrangement was generally approved, such was Althorp's command on the respect and devotion of his friends.   Palmerston,
who had offered Grey his services as leader, was fully satisfied
with Althorp's promotion.

The inclusion of the Canningites was a necessary part of

Grey's scheme ; from his personal point of view it was made easier by the death of Huskisson in September, though Huskisson's financial ability and experience of office would have strengthened the ministry in two exceptionally weak points, and saved them from certain unfortunate mistakes which shook their credit in the business world. The Canningites had shown by their rejection of Tory offers and avowed conversion to Reform that there would be no difficulty on their side. Eventually the three Secretaryships of State were allotted to them. Palmerston, who had been a member of every administration since 1807, was given the Foreign Office at Lansdowne's suggestion, and a free hand to deal with a complicated European situation. The Home Office, least of all likely to be a bed of roses, had been meant for Palmerston if Lansdowne should become Foreign Secretary ; in the new circumstances it was after considerable hesitation assigned to Melbourne, who as Irish Secretary in Canning's administration had been Lansdowne's subordinate. The Colonies went to Goderich, and the Board of Control to Charles Grant, a Canningite and a " Saint," with a rather ill-founded reputation for eloquence. Prosperity makes strange bed-fellows, and in the heat of the Reform struggle the Canningites must sometimes have wondered how they came to be on the side of a bill so different from anything they had favoured before. Palmerston, we are told, disliked it at first sight, and he and Melbourne never showed the least enthusiasm for it. Once embarked, however, with the Whigs, they felt it their duty to see them through, though at least in the last few months their sympathies were probably much more with the Opposition. It was by an accident, dating from 1828, that they found themselves on the Whig side at all ; but such accidents must often occur in party government, which pledges men to measures they would never have dreamed of proposing. The sense of comradeship is stronger than cold reason, and without pretending to approach every question with an open mind politicians follow their colleagues in the line of least resistance.

Grey further sought to broaden the basis of his administration by including certain of the High Tory Opposition, sufficient in number to strengthen the Cabinet without too much swaying its policy. It should not be said that he refused to divide the spoil with those who had helped him to secure it. The desire for Reform now for some time avowed by a section of their

K

party made the invitation possible without a sacrifice of principle on the minister's part. It was accepted, however, by none but the Duke of Richmond, an honest country squire, in whom distrust of the late Government overpowered antipathy to Whiggism; the grant of Catholic Emancipation had indeed removed the main partition, and in October Grey had counted on his defection from the ministry should it coalesce with the extreme Cumberland party.[1] The admission of Richmond to the Cabinet showed breadth of mind and desire to conciliate on Grey's part, but it was a mistake from the point of view of party solidarity, as appeared in the hour of trial; and in the eyes of Liberals in the country it was a concession to the vicious group system, so dangerous alike to the efficiency and permanence of administrations in the last few years, and not less to belief in the sincerity of party ties.

The remaining places of importance were reserved for genuine Whigs. Sir James Graham had deserved a signal reward by his effective attacks on the late Government for maintaining a costly pension list; his speeches had caught the attention of Cobbett, by whose means they had made a wide appeal. Suggested by Lord Lansdowne for the high office of Home Secretary, he was finally appointed to the Admiralty, where his dangerous inclinations to economy would not have too abundant scope. Lord Durham was a more difficult problem. His intimacy and strong influence with Lord Grey, his undoubted talent and fiery energy, and not least his valuable connection with Radical thought in London and the provinces, assured him a place of honour, if not of power. On the other hand his defects were great and obvious: lack of balance, tactlessness, and a peevish temper which landed him in countless quarrels. Between him and Grey there was a real affection, and he was most useful in keeping his father-in-law in touch with shades of opinion that never entered the stately solitude of Howick. But in many ways he was the evil genius of his life; himself only too prone to moods of despondency, and nervous to the point of fretfulness, the old man could hardly have found a worse companion for his hours of strain and worry than this spoilt young spitfire with wild views and a thoughtless tongue.[2]

[1] *Lieven Correspondence*, ii. 102.

[2] Durham had an unpleasant way of speaking of his colleagues which comes out strongly in Lord Broughton's *Recollections, e.g.* iv. 256 ff. But

For all that, it is curious to find a man of such untiring activity selected for the dignified but hardly inspiring post of Lord Privy Seal. Durham himself complained that he had nothing to do, though in a few weeks his hands were full enough. His unstable health may have had something to do with it ; or Grey may from the beginning have wished to keep him free for the important duty which soon devolved on him ; more probably it was felt that his appointment to high administrative office would scare the moderate Whigs, and certainly his talents were better fitted for striking out general lines of policy than for the sustained effort of departmental work, where the need of co-operation with a permanent staff might have been too much for his vain and domineering nature. It is only fair to Lord Durham's character to say that the impression he left on the more congenial minds of the Radicals outside the charmed circle of Westminster was far more favourable than that formed by his colleagues. John Stuart Mill had hopes that Durham might come into office as the head of an advanced Liberal party. Albany Fonblanque, Leigh Hunt's successor as editor of the *Examiner,* wrote of him : " His firmness has no more connection with violence than the timidity of some of his contemporaries with prudence. Seeing his way clearly he walks in it fearlessly, within the fences of intelligence and property." [1] With the constitutional and conventional caution of the Whigs he was impatient and out of sympathy. In an advanced stage of democracy he would have been more at home : his unusual confidence in the good sense of the people would have borne happier fruit, and from a public platform his glowing language might have taken the national imagination. It was his misfortune to live in an age when demagogy was frowned upon, even if it had been possible for a responsible statesman in the House of Lords to establish any connection with the common people. In the society of the dignified rulers of his day all his worst points stood out, and, if in temper and impetuous heart we may liken him to Achilles, over him too might a goddess-mother have lamented that to one whose life the gods had cut so short they need not have given dishonour also.

it is fair to say that they seem to have shown little restraint in their remarks upon him.

[1] *Life and Labours of A. Fonblanque,* p. 32. Place wrote : " I had on some occasions several years before this time acted in public matters with Mr. Lambton. . . . I had seen enough of him to satisfy me that he would go through with anything he undertook " (Add. MSS. 27,792, f. 45).

But if the case of Durham was difficult, that of Brougham was thornier still. Incomparably the most effective speaker in the Opposition ranks, the member for Yorkshire was probably at the end of 1830 the greatest political personality in the country, to a great part of which the Whig party meant Henry Brougham, and Henry Brougham alone. Here was a man who might be said to have turned out the ministry single-handed; at the mere sound of his trumpet of Reform their walls had fallen flat; the fateful motion was still down for discussion, and its proposer had refused to postpone it beyond the 25th, declaring that no change of ministry could possibly affect him.[1] If he held to his vaunt, his proposals must take all the wind out of a Reform ministry's sails. Almost before the Cabinet had met, its members would be forced to pronounce on a measure which the mover's energy and the nation's enthusiasm would not allow to lapse. Brougham must obviously join the Government, but in what capacity was the vital point.[2]

In 1822 Grey had virtually proposed to him that he should lead the party in the Commons. Since then the split of 1827 had weakened their mutual confidence, and in discussing the possible formation of a Whig ministry in March 1830 Grey warned his son not to choose Brougham as leader.[3] Althorp had by this time come to the front, and Brougham's defects of temperament were an obvious disqualification for such a post.[4] But it is none the less astonishing to find Grey now in November daring to offer this mighty man, keen lawyer though he was, the subordinate post of Attorney-General. He was not even to be a member of the Cabinet. There is a story that Brougham's only answer to Grey's note was to tear it up and stamp on it, and certainly his disdain was justified. This offer, quite as much as his exclusion

[1] Bedford to Russell, November 17: " I foresee great difficulties with Brougham. You will read his declaration in the House. I found him at Holld. House last night under great excitement. Angry at having been persuaded to put off his Motion [from the 16th]—too absurd ! Lord Holland thinks he ought to resign his Reform Measures into the hands of the new Ministers. The lawyer thinks differently " (*Early Correspondence*, i. 313).

[2] Lansdowne to Grey, November 18 ; *Howick Papers*.

[3] Grey to Howick, March 9 ; *Howick Papers*.

[4] A friend of Creevey's spoke in 1817 of Brougham's " unpopularity and want of discretion " (*Creevey Papers*, p. 265 ; see *Speeches of Earl Russell*, i. 105).

in 1835, gave him a real grievance against the Whig party. Willing enough to consort with him and use him, they played their old game, and because he did not belong to their circle by birth sought to deny him the due reward of his talents.

For a couple of days it seemed as if the attempt to form a ministry would break down. Brougham's own wish was to be Master of the Rolls, with a permanent salary and a seat in the Commons. But to this Grey and his colleagues objected, knowing that Althorp could not possibly hold his own in face of the other's brilliant oratory, which they feared might compromise the Government's policy and destroy the balance in any case so hard to maintain.[1] Finally, the King's leave was obtained for the offer of the Great Seal to this dangerous ally; if anyone could outweigh his personality, it would be Grey himself; the field in the Commons would be left clear for Althorp, and much needed support given to the Whig debaters in the Lords.[2] At first Brougham refused to be muzzled; he succumbed at last to Althorp's urgent appeal to his generosity. It seems fair to give him credit for a genuine sacrifice of self-interest in the cause of Reform. For otherwise the deadlock was hopeless; and Brougham fully realised that on the day he took his seat on the Woolsack he said a long farewell to all his real greatness, and renounced his splendid position as champion of the people and foremost lance in the noblest lists in the world. Nor can the popular hero have enjoyed giving up the motion to which he was pledged, and eating his words so emphatically pronounced

---

[1] According to Le Marchant, Brougham's secretary, Grey asked Lord Althorp's opinion on the subject, when Lord Althorp simply answered: " If Brougham is left in Parliament with an irremovable office, the Ministry will not last three months, and I certainly will not belong to it ! " (*Memoir of Althorp*, p. 261). Brougham himself always believed the objection came from the King, and cites a note which he received on the 18th from a friend who had heard at second-hand that the Duke on retiring from office had warned the King not to let Brougham have the Rolls (*Brougham Memoirs*, iii. 78). Croker confirms this (*Croker Papers*, ii. 80), and it is certainly difficult to see what motive of his own the King could have had.

[2] Hobhouse wrote in November 1830 on the authority of Durham: " At the meeting of Lord Grey's friends at Lansdowne House, it was discussed who was to be Lord Chancellor—Lord Lyndhurst ? ' No.' Brougham ? ' Oh, no, no ! ' Everybody was against him ; and when he was subsequently selected, Lord Holland said, ' Then we shall never have another comfortable moment in this room ' " (*Recollections*, iv. 256). It would appear that Lord Tavistock, afterwards 7th Duke of Bedford, took Brougham's part. See *Brougham Memoirs*, iii. 83.

in the Commons but a day or two before,—an inconsistency of which the caricaturists took full advantage. Yet, after all, the Great Seal could hardly be considered a thing of no attraction to an ambitious man, and Brougham could not foresee that within four years he would quit office never to return.[1]

Among members of the administration not in the Cabinet were two leading representatives of different strains of Whig talent, charged with the seed of two great conflicting parties, but " concordes animae nunc et dum nocte prementur." Lord John Russell was young and delicate—it is said that his brother asked that he might not be given laborious office,—and Edward Stanley, though full of brilliant promise, had not yet won his spurs as the Rupert of debate. However, his energies were given ample play in the government of Ireland, possibly the severest task of all that faced the new administration.

In Scotland the idea of a Whig ministry still seemed almost a contradiction in terms. To such a degree had all the powers and arts of government been identified with the name of Dundas, that Melville's retirement on the break-up of the Liverpool Cabinet in 1827 appeared little short of an abrogation of the Scottish polity. For many years Scotland had not been ruled by a responsible minister, but, in the words of Cockburn, was " handed over as a province to some proconsul," who exercised all the patronage of office on condition of returning a compact body of Government voters to Westminster.[2] As Argyll had " managed " Scotland for Walpole, so did the Melvilles for Pitt and Liverpool ; they were independent satraps, absolute in their domain so long as the tribute of votes was duly paid. Canning, we are told, had meant to continue the system, and " to let Lord Binning *have* Scotland," but on his death the administration

---

[1] The exact details of these negotiations with Brougham are very difficult to unravel, and his own account does not make the task easier. See *Brougham Memoirs*, iii. 73-85 ; Roebuck, *History of the Whig Ministry of* 1830, i. 433-444, 470-476 ; *Creevey Papers*, p. 556 ; *Life of Campbell*, i. 489. Brougham took the title of Lord Brougham and Vaux —" vox et praeterea nihil," as the wits had it. Nevertheless he proudly continued to sign himself " H. Brougham."

[2] See Cockburn, *Life of Jeffrey*, i. 77 ff. Lord Henry Petty wrote to Creevey in 1807 : " Archd. Hamilton writes to me that Melville is more than ever minister *de facto* in Scotland, and that a year's fasting has so sharpened the appetites of his followers, that not a chaise is to be got on any of the roads which lead to Dunira, so numerous are the solicitors and expectants that attend his court " (*Creevey Papers,* p. 85).

DRAWING for TWELFTH CAKE.
A Hint to Cabinet Makers.

was vested in the Home Office, and Lansdowne, Peel, and Melbourne were in turn responsible for governing the country.[1] However there was as yet no Scotch Office, and much political, as well as legal, work fell to the Lord Advocate, whose office therefore was of far wider range than that of the English Attorney-General. For this post Grey selected Francis Jeffrey, founder and late editor of the *Edinburgh Review*, the foremost survivor of that band of lawyers who had stood up almost alone for Whig principles when to avow them meant courage and self-denial. His duty was now clear ; to quote Cockburn again, " Jeffrey was fortunate in this, that when he came upon the parliamentary stage, he was not, at first, distracted by variety or perplexity of objects. For upwards of fifty years the Whig party in Scotland had, without one moment's diversity or relaxation, been demanding Parliamentary and Burgh Reform, as the two definite things that for this country were all in all." [2]

The two Government Whips were Lord Duncannon and Edward Ellice ; the latter, " Bear Ellice," was responsible for dispensing patronage and also, it would appear, for instructing the press.[3] Early in January he and Durham engaged one Buckingham, a gentleman " of more than respectable literary attainments," [4] at a salary of £500 to arrange for a supply of Government articles to three London newspapers. The editors undertook to insert " as Editorial articles, and without alteration or delay," anything they might receive from Buckingham, and at the same time to adopt a general tone friendly to the administration. In return they were to have " early information of any news or intended changes, in the power of the Government to give." Buckingham's articles were to be revised by Durham.[5] This scheme would appear not to have been entirely satisfactory,

---

[1] See Cockburn, *Memorials of His Time*, p. 447.

[2] *Life of Jeffrey*, i. 310.

[3] In 1829 Croker had suggested that a member of the Wellington Cabinet should regularly instruct the press : " The times are gone by when statesmen might safely despise the journals, or only treat them as inferior engines, which might be left to themselves, or be committed to the guidance of persons wholly unacquainted with the views of the Ministry " (*Croker Papers*, ii. 23).

[4] *Random Recollections of the House of Commons*, p. 336, where Buckingham comes under the head of " literary members."

[5] J. S. Buckingham to Durham, January 7 ; *Lambton Papers*.

for we find Buckingham a little later making another suggestion to Durham.   " I may perhaps be permitted to say this, that if there could be found for me any appointment in the Treasury, Board of Control, Board of Trade, Colonial Office, Admiralty, State Paper Office, British Museum, House of Lords or Commons, or elsewhere, with a salary attached of £1000 a year, for the duties of which I should be considered competent, I would very willingly appropriate the whole sum of £1000 a year to the bare management of an Evening Paper for the year required, or longer if necessary, and live upon the £500 to be allowed for the superintendence or labour afforded now." Unfortunately the answer to this very handsome and catholic offer is not preserved, but the fact that in May Buckingham was standing for the borough of Woodstock suggests that it was unsuccessful.   Eventually he sat for Sheffield in the reformed Parliament, where it is regrettable to learn that " there was a strong prejudice against him, owing in a great measure to the general impression that he was a political adventurer." [1]   We hear no more of any attempt by the Government to work the press.

Lord Grey might well take pride in reviewing his forces. They included six men who rose to be Prime Minister of England, while two more, Althorp and Lansdowne, might have had the honour had they cared.  It must have been satisfactory to the chief personally to count among them, besides his son-in-law in the Cabinet, a son at the Colonial Office, a cousin in charge of the Woods and Forests, and a brother-in-law at the Treasury as Patronage Secretary.  The ancient spirit of the party was potent yet, and, had a strict Whig of the old school objected that of His Majesty's confidential servants two were neither peers nor the heirs to peerages, Grey could reply that his Cabinet at least boasted between them a greater acreage of land than any that had preceded them.[2]  So far at least the ministry gave little menace of revolutionary change ; the names of Spencer, Russell, Richmond, Stanley, Ponsonby, gave a fine flavour of family government, and Grey might have looked Newcastle and Rockingham in the face without a blush.

On the whole the composition of the ministry gave satisfaction.  The admitted need for Reform, confirmed by the petitions now pouring into both Houses from all parts of the

[1] *Random Recollections*, p. 337.    [2] Parker, *Life of Graham*, i. 90.

United Kingdom, predisposed the moderates to acquiesce, and the troubled condition of the country rallied support to the Government. The majority of Whigs looked forward to a golden age, and believed Lord Grey would do just enough to keep in favour with public opinion, without yielding to dangerous tendencies. The *Edinburgh* complacently surveyed the non-committal attitude taken up by the party when in opposition, urging that they had never pledged themselves to violent change. They must be careful not to do more than was necessary ; " the staff of the people will be with them and will comfort them." [1] The *Edinburgh* discovered later that the people also had a rod, which was far from at all times comforting the ministers. Above all it naively pressed them to resist the " culpable indifference to office " by which the party had lost so many opportunities in the past.

On the Tory side feeling was remarkably friendly ; the Government believed that no opposition would have to be faced before Christmas.[2] The approval of Richmond's followers was only tempered by the thought that all the Cabinet were not like Grey ; they realised, however, that moderate Reform was the best barrier to Radicalism, and declared that Catholic Relief had obliterated the main differences between Whig and Tory. Only the Cumberland section stood aloof and regretted that Richmond had touched the accursed thing. Among the party of the late ministry, still dazed by the unparalleled swift-ness and severity of their defeat, there was little heart, except in some of the rank and file, for immediate renewal of the contest. Wellington refused to take any action with a view to an immediate recovery of power, and betook himself with characteristic sense of duty and good temper to serve the Crown in Hampshire, where the disturbances were at their height. Realising to some degree the intensity of the popular feeling, and the im-possibility of his forming a government while the Ultra-Tories were still hostile, he preferred to wait for the storm to pass.[3] Peel, too, was not sorry for a respite from what had for some

[1] *Edinburgh*, January 1831.

[2] Howick to Charles Grey, December 7 ; *Howick Papers*.

[3] " The Government is scarcely yet at an end, and the gentlemen to whom its dissolution is to be attributed in a great degree, propose that I should think of forming another upon a broader basis. . . . I will not now join a scheme for getting together another administration " (To the Duke of Buckingham, November 21 ; *Courts and Cabinets*, i. 144).

time been a losing battle, and indeed spoke of retiring from public life.[1] The Duke's view must have appealed to anyone not blinded by party spirit. No honest opposition could be raised on the question of Reform, to some measure of which most of the party had professed themselves converted.[2] No one but a factious meddler would wish to embarrass matters at the Foreign Office, and, as to the state of things at home, the sympathies of the upper classes were everywhere the same.[3] And quite apart from the split on the Catholic question, there were many Tories who believed that their disasters were entirely due to the false consistency of the Duke of Wellington; they considered he had made a fatal mistake in excluding Lord Grey on the King's death and so forcing him into active opposition. As late as January Lord Hertford would have liked the two leaders to toss up for the Premiership, with Palmerston or Vesey Fitzgerald to lead the Commons; failing that, it were well to come to terms with Grey on the basis of his aristocratic sympathies. Lord Londonderry hoped the violence of the " Liberals " might induce Grey to join a constitutional party embracing Peel and the Ultra-Tories.[4] Such suggestions tend to explain the amazement of the Tories in March, when the Reform Bill appeared, and the growth of that bitterness of hatred which is reserved for traitors only. They had expected something so very much milder from that high-born Cabinet; Whigs were all very fine as orators, they supposed, but in action were generally accounted weak-kneed and unbusinesslike. The lack of keen hostility to the new administration was largely due to contempt.

This opinion was shared by men on the other side, intimate with the political situation. Tavistock and Hobhouse com-

---

[1] Croker to Hertford, November 18; *Croker Papers*, ii. 77.

[2] " Absolute resistance, *in limine*, to any Reform is manifestly no longer practicable" (Grenville to Buckingham, November 21; *Courts and Cabinets*, i. 146).

[3] Jeffrey to Empson, January 31, 1830 : " The only party that can now turn us out must be mad or worse, to risk the experiment in the present temper of the country and state of the times. The real battle that is soon to be fought, and the only one now worth providing for, is not between Whigs and Tories, Liberals and Illiberals, and such gentlemanlike denominations, but betweeen property and no property—Swing and the law " (*Life of Jeffrey*, ii. 233).

[4] Hertford to Sir Robert Wilson, December 24, January 11, May 23; Add. MSS. 30,112, ff. 131, 140b, 156. Londonderry to Buckingham, January 5; *Courts and Cabinets*, i. 190.

plained that efficient Reformers were few in the Cabinet, and needed all the encouragement they could get. Francis Place had been sceptical as to the value of a Whig ministry at all, considering the material available. In Grey and Lansdowne he saw no force of character or perseverance ; Holland was a relic of a bygone age. The Canningites might be Tories for all the sympathy they had with democracy ; Lord John Russell had never gone beyond the most milk-and-water resolutions for Reform ; only in Durham, and to a less degree in Brougham, was any real confidence to be put. Of Durham, Place wrote : " They who understood his character relied on him much more than on any other member of the Cabinet, and, except Brougham, on all the rest of his colleagues taken together." [1]

Such Radicals as Burdett, however, were highly pleased with Lord Grey's professions, and Place himself was forced to admit that a better Cabinet could not in the circumstances have been chosen. But the people must exert continued pressure to keep the Government up to the mark, and as often as possible bring their sincerity to the test. He was disgusted at Burdett's refusal to join his agitation for a county meeting, on the ground that the ministry should be given a chance first. Such an attitude was to court deception ; it was just in this way that the Reformers had been duped the last time the Whigs were in office.[2] His hope was that the sustained enthusiasm of the people, strung to an unprecedented pitch by the exciting events of the summer, might prevail on the ministry to carry out their general declarations in a more liberal sense than was usual. This, he claimed, was what actually happened. " No sooner was the declaration of Lord Grey made than it was considered as the declaration of ministers, and there was a simultaneous movement not only of the political associations but of the Reformers all over the kingdom, as if there had been mutual communication among them. . . . Meetings of almost every description of persons were held—in cities, towns, and parishes, by journeymen and tradesmen in their clubs, and by common workmen who had no trade clubs nor associations of any kind.[3] Alexander Somerville describes how one November day he and his mates were quarrying on the Lothian coast, when a small boy came waving

[1] Add. MSS. 27,789, f. 192, 259.
[2] Place to Hume, November 22 ; Add. MSS. 35,148, f. 73.
[3] Add. MSS. 27,789, ff. 204, 252.

a paper: "'The Tories driven from power at last! Glorious triumph of the people!'... Those of us who knew least of politics knew enough to understand the importance of this announcement. We took off our hats and caps, and loud above the north wind, and the roaring sea, shouted 'Henry Brougham for ever.' At that time we knew little of Earl Grey." Sydney Smith also bears witness to "the liberality which is bursting out in every part of Scotland." The English political unions were not backward in expressing their delight. On December 13 that of Birmingham, which a month before had petitioned for the dismissal of the Tories, now held a meeting in support of the ministers, praying them to introduce vote by ballot, triennial parliaments, and payment of members. About the same time Attwood's brother Charles founded the Northern Political Union at Newcastle, with Cobbett's strong approval. In January the Birmingham Union celebrated its first anniversary; Attwood gave its numbers as now amounting to 9000; he was ready, he proudly said, to produce as a National Guard for the King, in case of danger, "two armies, each of them as numerous and as brave as that which conquered at Waterloo."

The attitude of the London Radicals to the Government was less polite. They cared more for the expulsion of the Tories than for the accession of the Whigs, who as aristocrats were no less the born enemies of the working-class.[1] Men who refused to look at any Reform short of manhood suffrage and the ballot could hardly expect anything of that sort from Lord Grey. "The Duke did not deceive us," said Carlile at the Rotunda; "the Earl must, if he preserve his double pledge, to stand by his order and to reform." The general feeling of all but the fiercest revolutionaries is best summed up in the *Prompter*:[2] "Of the Whigs, let us say that we will thank them for all the changes they may make, but not promise to be satisfied with anything they have yet promised to do." More serious to the Government than the distrust of the cheap press was the actual defeat of Stanley, at Preston, by Orator Hunt, whose tumultuous advocacy of the ballot and Radical Reform for once overpowered the strong Derby interest. Had the result been otherwise, serious rioting was apprehended; Stanley wisely decided not to provoke it by insisting on a scrutiny. Hunt's triumph was a new departure in working-class

[1] *Penny Paper*, November 23.     [2] November 27.

politics.[1]  A small Somersetshire landowner, he had been
prominent among the less respectable Reformers even before
the time of Peterloo ; he had travelled widely about the
country, with the combined object of preaching Radical doctrine
and advertising a patent dye of his own invention for colouring
cheese.  With a little more tact he might have played a valuable
part in Parliament, and as it was he courageously called attention
on countless occasions to a point of view not usually expressed
in the august assembly.  But the offensive tone of the long
speeches he was constantly making, and his total lack of the
sweet reasonableness essential to one in a minority, destroyed
any impression the novelty of his opinions might have made.
He was deservedly regarded as an unpleasant bore, and proved
his own worst enemy.  His strained relations with Cobbett
were notorious, and he had shortly before this quarrelled with
the Rotunda set, who complained of his arrogance and selfishness.   There was something fine, however, in his persevering
efforts, amid ceaseless obloquy and frequent persecution, to
secure the good of the poorer classes, to which he did not by
station belong.

His administration formed, it was Lord Grey's chief duty,
after taking measures for the restoration of peace at home and
completing the arrangements necessary at the opening of a
reign, to approach what he himself called " the perilous question " of Reform.  He concurred with the bulk of conservative
opinion that ideally the occasion was most unsuitable for so
important a step.  He would have preferred that the rebuilding
of the Constitution should take place in an atmosphere of
cloistered calm, in which due weight might be given to all the
considerations that political philosophy might suggest.  Hating
to be hustled, he would gladly have postponed the question ;
only cruel necessity compelled its discussion in the heat and glare
of popular excitement.  Here, of course, he was utterly at
variance with the Radicals, whose one hope was that the pressure
of the moment would squeeze out of the Whigs something far
more drastic than they would naturally have produced.

It would be interesting to know at what point Grey first
resolved to produce a measure of anything like the scope of the

[1] See Trevelyan, *Life of John Bright*, p. 18, for the delight caused at
Rochdale by this victory.

actual bill. "The first disposition of his mind," he said in Parliament, "was undoubtedly to limit the Reform within a much narrower compass; but after full consideration and discussing the matter with his colleagues, he was convinced that nothing short of the present measure would tend to the desired result of satisfying the country." We cannot tell what influence his intercourse with Durham and Ellice at Howick in the summer may have had; certainly, in selecting his Radical son-in-law as chairman of the sub-committee to draft the bill, Grey must have known what he must expect, and we are told that his instructions recommended a wide and comprehensive scheme. In his appeal to the Duke at the beginning of November he had repeated his disavowal of all theories based on natural right; his attitude was the same when he faced Parliament after the arrangement of his ministry, though he and Lansdowne both denied that they merely intended to enfranchise the large towns. From the first he never aimed at satisfying the Radicals, who formed no part of the "rational public" it was his duty to conciliate. Grey was frankly an opportunist; but his dread of attempting to legislate ahead of public opinion was tempered by the Whig determination that improvement should be imposed on the people from above. It might be wise, therefore, to offer a measure wider than was absolutely required by imperious need, if such generosity would induce the grateful country to drop further agitation and leave its future to the Government. Heartily afraid of the people let loose, he desired above all things a "permanent solution"; his statesmanship told him that a really extensive measure would in the circumstances best preserve the ideals he believed in.

Even granted that he held this view in theory, it showed remarkable courage and farsightedness to follow it out so liberally in practice, and by itself puts Grey in a high place for political wisdom and capacity of rising to an occasion. Whether or not he was right in believing that his projected measure would only strengthen aristocracy as the ruling force, he completely falsified the prophecies of most Tories, who expected some petty proposal that would not even attempt to satisfy anyone.[1] Twenty years later Sir James Graham declared as

[1] Hertford to Wilson, [October] 17: "They tell me Lord Grey is to resume command of the Reformers, so probably some of the uninhabited Burgage boroughs will be bought up as in Ireland either by public money

his considered opinion "that the Reform Act embodied what his [Grey's] heart and conscience entirely approved." [1] Lord Grey's heart and conscience, however, were most fortunately adaptable to circumstances ; it is unlikely that a few months earlier they would have sanctioned anything so revolutionary. On the other side he was resolved, in the face of criticism, that the measure must be something which Parliament could swallow ; he would not force upon it, under threat of dissolution, a bill of which he knew it must disapprove, and play solely to the electorate. The imputation that he had done so he vehemently denied. How finely he gauged the Commons' capacities appeared on the division on the second reading. Apart from this fundamental question, whether the sentiment of Parliament was to be respected or not, opinion was most keenly divided on the ballot. Though certain of the Cabinet were known to favour it, it was hardly thought possible that it could be officially sanctioned. And as regards the people's acceptance of the measure, this might prove the crucial point.[2] The more optimistic Reformers, however, were content to wait and trust the influence of the growing popular demand. "Every move is in favour of the people," wrote Parkes of Birmingham. "I think the Whigs *must* and therefore will do something real ; and when the wand of Reform once touches the body of corruption she will soon vanish." [3]

For a few weeks Lord Grey was able to transfer the burden of thought to other minds ; we have it that he casually asked his son-in-law, coming down the steps of the House of Lords, if he would take charge of the first drafting of the Reform Bill, with Lord John Russell as his collaborator ; [4] Sir James Graham

---

or by the populous towns themselves to whom the Elections will be transferred " (Add. MSS. 30,112, f. 111).

[1] Parker, *Life of Graham*, i. 119.

[2] Place said that Althorp, on being asked whether anyone in office would be allowed to advocate the ballot, replied " Certainly not." Seeing that Althorp himself favoured the ballot, was believed to have induced Graham to vote for it in the Committee of Four, and could not have known the Government's intentions so early, the story, if true, can only give his individual opinion (Add. MSS. 35,148, f. 73). On February 7 Drummond, a banker, wrote to Place : " Even if the ministers be not beat, I doubt their giving the ballot, and without that the people will not be content " (Add. MSS. 27,789, f. 254).

[3] Add. MSS. 35,148, f. 77.

[4] *Recollections of a Long Life*, iv. 178.

and Lord Duncannon were added to form the famous committee, which proceeded to sit at Lord Durham's house.

Meanwhile the Cabinet was engaged with matters more pressing than even the state of the representation. In Ireland, where Daniel O'Connell was starting the agitation for Repeal of the Union, agrarian and industrial discontent belied the promises of those who had declared that Catholic Relief would put all to rights. The Clare election had first shown English statesmen the potential political power of the Irish electorate ; and though the disfranchisement of the forty shilling freeholders had blocked one outlet, we read that elections could still be manipulated by men of " revolutionary " temper, at least in the three southern provinces.[1] And for many months henceforward the trouble arising partly from tithe agitation and partly from sheer hunger was to complicate affairs in England and weaken the Cabinet's solidarity. But in Great Britain no less the Whigs had come into a most undesirable inheritance ; north and south troops were scouring the country, and householders trembled for their lives and property.

The main responsibility for restoring order fell to a man who was chiefly known as a fashionable dilettante with philosophical leanings, and except for a few months had never been in office at all. Melbourne was not originally thought of for the Home Office ; Palmerston and Graham had both been suggested, and the final selection of such an untried man to succeed Peel was a general surprise. For one called upon to face a social upheaval hardly equalled since the days of Wat Tyler, Melbourne's record was not encouraging to democrats. As William Lamb, he had moved in the luxurious society of Carlton House, where his father was an intimate guest ; by birth and upbringing a Foxite Whig of the aristocratic cast, he fell early under the glamour of Canning's intellect, to which for one of his fastidious taste there was at that time no rival in the sphere of public life. Sir James Graham described to Roebuck in 1851 how repulsive the sordid politics of the Westminster Rump appeared in Regency days to the *jeunesse dorée* who met at Brooks's to discuss the glittering themes of high statesmanship alone worthy of men of family and fashion. Lamb was near the heart of the brilliant circle, and it is not altogether surprising that the

[1] M. Fitzgerald to Wellington, January 28, 1831 ; *Despatches*, vii. 401.

violence of Hunt and the Radicals in 1819 persuaded him to vote for the Six Acts of the "Savage Parliament." Henceforward he was a professed Canningite, and in 1827 he accepted from his master the post of Chief Secretary for Ireland. So little of a Whig had he become, that he consented to join the Wellington administration ; he resigned from it with the rest of his party. On the question of Reform he, like so many other clever young men, had followed the lead of Canning, on the ground that a popularly elected house would lead to the tyranny of the collective will ;[1] he believed that private interest in action was alike more prudent and more effective. When others were for staving off the evil day by small concessions, his philosophic mind held aloof. Best to leave well alone ; but if a change was necessary, let it be a broad and generous measure on which a firm stand might be made for the future.[2] Convinced in 1830 that the time had come, he had no hesitation in joining the Reform ministry.

This attitude was of a piece with his whole nature, which concealed energy beneath a languid surface. The death of his elder brother had released him, unfortunately as some friends thought, from the drudgery of the Bar ; he devoted his new leisure to wide reading beyond the ordinary limits of men of his class, and to following up the philosophical training he had received at Edinburgh from Dugald Stewart ; he only dabbled in politics. His naturally *fainéant* disposition was tinged with melancholy by family troubles, of which the chief were his wife's foolish infatuation for Byron and his son's feeble growth. The result was a detached and slightly contemptuous habit of mind, inclining him to doubt whether things were worth doing. Men who admired his talents said he only lacked a spur to exertion, which the status of a younger son might have provided.[3] But where prompt action was obviously demanded, he could take a firm and definite line, as he showed in his new duties at the Home Office.

[1] *Melbourne Papers*, p. 100.
[2] He wrote on November 7, 1838 : " My opinion was then against reform altogether, and chiefly because I thought that it could not be moderate or limited. The adoption of any of the partial measures proposed seemed to me certain to hasten and advance its progress " (*Melbourne Papers*, p. 118).
[3] *E.g.* Albany Fonblanque, *Memoirs*, p. 88. *Manchester Guardian*, November 27 : " It will be an agreeable surprise to us if [Melbourne] should make an industrious or efficient public officer."

L

Holding strong views of his own on the faults of the poor law in certain particulars, he was genuinely anxious to discover the true facts of the situation which faced him, and with this object did not disdain to enter into communication with " Tailor Place," through his brother and his brother's secretary.[1] He wished to use no unnecessary violence in repression, as is shown by his repeated instructions that the military should be as little used as possible ; spies, too, he would not stoop to employ, though Peel had on occasions actually suggested their use. But the kindliness which charmed society, and a few years later enabled him to help the young queen in a way for which the Empire must be lastingly grateful, did not reach below his own class. The feeble strivings of organised labour in the north filled him with scornful indignation ; the magistrates, landed gentry, and manufacturers of Lancashire should have united to crush this democratic tyranny.[2] The insurgent labourers were punished with a severity utterly out of proportion to the wrongs committed and the need of an example, seeing that at the time no further danger was apprehended. Petitions for mercy were curtly pencilled, " Merely acknowledge receipt." The same hardness and lack of sympathy with working class aspirations appears in his treatment of the cheap press and of the many deputations which applied to him from time to time. A little tact would have smoothed his path considerably in dealing with the working men of London. Early in December, for instance, it was understood that the King was to receive a deputation from 40,000 " artisans " and manufacturers of London. Their cold reception caused great disappointment and considerable ill-feeling.[3] Melbourne was not a cruel man, and the condition of the country required that strong measures should be taken to keep the King's peace. But the ignorance and misunderstanding which made panic possible are inexcusable, and the Home Secretary cannot be acquitted of a callous disregard for the happiness of the poor, for whose good

---

[1] George Lamb made a fruitless attempt to induce Place to issue an appeal with the object of pacifying the insurgents. Apart from disinclination to do the Government's dirty work, Place thought the occasion unpropitious, though as a matter of fact he had no hope of any real improvement in the labourers' lot while they continued to breed at an excessive rate (Torrens, *Memoirs of Lord Melbourne*, i. 352, 367).

[2] Melbourne to Lord Derby, January 11, 1831 ; *Melbourne Papers*, p. 122.

[3] *H. O.* 44. 23

government he stood reponsible, not less than for their obedience to the law.

The disorder in the south occupied the first meeting of the new Cabinet, which resulted in a proclamation expressing the Government's intention to repress outrage, and in circulars sent to encourage Lords-Lieutenants and magistrates in their duty. These were followed on December 8 by another circular, again sanctioned by the Cabinet, warning magistrates against weak concessions. In certain cases bodies of magistrates had issued recommendations to the occupiers of land to raise their labourers' wages as the simplest method of restoring quiet. Melbourne was strongly against any such action which might seem to bear an official stamp, as likely to disappoint and embitter labourers if the advice was not complied with.[1] Peel before him had cautioned landowners against yielding to intimidation. When the rising first broke out, there were only four cavalry regiments in the south of England, but in time these were reinforced as well by regular as irregular troops. In various counties the Yeomanry were assembled, and steps were taken to embody the militia; in districts where the Yeomanry had been disbanded, associations of gentlemen and farmers were formed with Melbourne's approval; sabres, but not firearms, were allowed them from the Ordnance Department; in one case a party of gentlemen coming back from hunting dispersed the rioters. The Home Office correspondence shows how completely in the country districts the administration was identified with the landowning class. The Lord-Lieutenant was alike the chief magistrate, the military commander, and the leading territorial magnate and receiver of rents. It would be surprising if this union of functions in one order and one person did not intensify the bitter class feeling which lay under the labourers' revolt. It was possible that the great man might also be in the Cabinet, and so prove the unity of spirit which animated central and local government alike. For villagers who came up for trial before Lord Lansdowne at Salisbury it must have been difficult to distinguish the judge from the landlord or the statesman. The

---

[1] Melbourne to Hon. J. Wodehouse, December 17; *H.O.* 41. 9. To a Norfolk gentleman who wrote describing the immediate good effects of a lowering of rents and tithes in his neighbourhood, and suggesting that the example might be more widely followed, Melbourne's reply was " Nil " (*H. O.* 52. 9).

same set of men, as it seemed to them, pocketed the rents which helped to keep their wages low, owned the pheasants they poached, passed the statutes which punished them for poaching, imprisoned them when they demanded food, and tried them when they fell into the meshes of the law.

The means by which the insurrection was suppressed showed how unsatisfactory were the existing arrangements for keeping the peace. In the absence of any local police there was no alternative to the use of the military, including Yeomanry corps, and the clumsy expedient of raising special constables. No effective force was present on the spot to nip a disturbance in the bud. The charge against the Duke of Wellington of aiming at a military government was inconsistent with the attacks on Peel's new police. Without them the intervention of soldiers was the natural thing ; all through the period covered by the Reform agitation troops were moving about the country, to an extent which suggests the coercive occupation of a conquered land. The constant use of the military, and the more constant preparations for using them, however deplorable as likely to create ill-feeling, can hardly be blamed in the absence of any adequate alternative.

By the middle of December the officers sent out to organise the civil force and enrol special constables reported that the country was generally quiet ; at the same time the Kent winter assizes gave an earnest of the temper of the Special Commissions that were to follow. Mr. Justice Bosanquet's charge to the Grand Jury expounded the cruel law of those days, which made almost any act of a member of a riotous assembly felony. For instance, to obtain meat and drink by intimidation was robbery punishable with death. All present and concurring were equally guilty with those who made the actual demand. To send a threatening letter might incur transportation for life.[1] These penalties were not the obsolete relics of a bygone age ; many of them were but two or three years old. One section of an Act of 1827 made the destruction of a threshing-machine punishable with seven years' transportation ; another affixed the death penalty to the firing of a rick. The judge made it plain that he was unlikely to soften the rigour of the law. " The distress exists, I believe, but I believe also it has been much exaggerated." One man was condemned to death for stealing a piece of meat

[1] H. O. 52. 8.

valued at four shillings ; another to transportation for fourteen years for the theft of a five-shilling hat.[1] Three men guilty of arson were appointed for execution in a week's time. Melbourne approved on the ground that the example would be the more striking.[2] This was on December 18, when the serious part of the revolt was well over.

So much for Kent. The counties of Hants, Wilts, Dorset, Berks, and Bucks were visited by Special Commissions, on which lawyers and laymen sat together to try the shoals of labourers brought up before them. Where the numbers were so great, the Government might well have rested satisfied with the prosecution of ringleaders, and considered the case one for discretion rather than strict law. The circumstances were obviously exceptional, arising from an admitted distemper in the body politic, which called for the physician rather than the hangman. Campbell, the future Lord Chancellor, wrote : " In my opinion none of the poor devils should be put to death, for, after all, machine-breaking was their object, and the taking of money, which is called robbery, is merely incidental. No personal violence was offered or seriously intended." [3] But the authorities were resolved on the uttermost farthing. The Attorney-General was sent down in the full pomp of office ; and the reports of Maule, the Solicitor to the Treasury, show a keen professional desire for convictions on the part of the Crown lawyers. The following sentences at Winchester alone, where no case of homicide or wounding was proved, testify to the wholesale nature of the proceeding. To be executed, six ; to be transported for life, ninety-five ; to be transported for lesser periods—often amounting to life, since the Government did not pay the ex-convict's return fare from Australia—thirty-six ; to imprisonment with hard labour, sixty-five. Sixty-seven were acquitted.[4] It would be monstrously unfair not to add that not all these sentences were carried out ; eventually in the whole of England, though the only life lost had been at the hands of the Yeomanry, three men were executed, and 457 transported for various terms.

[1] *H. O.* 52. 13.    [2] *H. O.* 41. 9.
[3] *Life of Campbell*, i. 498.
[4] For these details I am indebted to Mr. and Mrs. Hammond's *Village Labourer*, where a thrilling account is given of the methods and proceedings of the Special Commissions, from the labourers' point of view.

It would be false to say that the national conscience was touched; for the " Swing " letters had caused widespread fears not in one order of society only, and many men accustomed to the barbarous code of law then in vogue saw in the punishment only a necessary deterrent to future crime. The Commons rejected the proposal for a general pardon by an enormous majority. Melbourne's attitude was approved by the opinion of his class. But a deep moral indignation awoke in many whose position did not incline them to the stricter view. Petitions were presented begging for mercy for the misguided men whose provocation was so great. The Government should have shown signs of a conciliatory spirit before, not after, their severity had crushed the joy and hope from the life of many villages. The circular of December 8 was justifiable only if the Cabinet set to work at once to provide the poor with the necessaries of life. " Hunger will not be appeased by Special Commissions to hang and transport a few hundred men." [1] Cobbett exerted the fulness of his powers to plead the labourers' cause. A little kindness shown in earlier times would have meant so much; now, after the revolt had broken out, the Government's policy of stark repression was futile.[2] Terrorisation might prevent riots and the breaking of machinery, but it could never stop the firing of ricks under cloak of night. Those who took this line were amply borne out by the renewed incendiarism which marked the autumn of 1831 to a hardly less degree than the year before; attention to the labourers' plight died down with the danger, and little was heard of the schemes of redress the crisis had produced.[3] The villagers were left to nurse a sullen grievance against society, which they vented from time to time by wild and secret acts of vengeance.

Not unconnected with the suppression of the agricultural

[1] *Prompter*, December 4.

[2] Cobbett says that one of the labourers who was afterwards transported took a Reform petition from North Hants to Brighton in the autumn. " If the King had not been advised not to receive it, but to receive it graciously, there never would have been a riot in those little hard parishes" (*Twopenny Trash*, April 1831).

[3] Grey, however, wrote to Brougham, December 30, 1830: " I wish you would think of some plan for furnishing employment for the labourers who are in want of work, by subscriptions, which might be assisted by a grant of money, after the meeting of Parliament " (*Brougham Memoirs*, iii. 90).

insurrection was the attack on the cheap press, by which Melbourne infuriated the Londoners interested in politics. William Lovett gives in his autobiography a list of the punishments inflicted during those weeks on the martyrs of the Unstamped Agitation. Time and again Hetherington and his friends were sent to prison or fined for their resolute insistence on the right to issue cheap knowledge to the working classes. Lovett himself also fell foul of authority over his refusal to serve in the militia while deprived of the parliamentary vote—thus setting to other disfranchised classes a precedent for withdrawal of allegiance. The ensuing distraint of his goods was carried out with peculiar offensiveness. Another editor indicted in the month of December was Richard Carlile, the charge being that certain sentences in the *Prompter* addressed to the insurgent labourers were seditious ; with furious abuse he turned on the ministry, retracting any good he had ever said of them ; eventually, when the case came up, Carlile was sentenced to a fine of £200 and two years' imprisonment. Later on Cobbett himself was called upon to answer a similar accusation ; it could not be said that the Government confined its attentions to the weak and misguided. The effect of all this campaign was to exasperate the Radicals with the ministry, and prejudice them strongly against the embryo Reform Bill. The Tories might be tyrants, but they were at least honest ones ; it was just like the hypocritical Whigs to profess liberal principles, and then to set on foot a persecution recalling the worst days of Castlereagh.[1]

The Government were unwise from every point of view in prosecuting papers which represented an extreme form of opinion, and which can have had little circulation outside those whose ideas they reflected. Even where the law is plain, such prosecutions cause bitterness and spread the feeling that legislation is behind the advance of public thought. In Cobbett's case the law was not plain, and the Government were condemned by results. All along we find the ministers submitting points to the Law-Officers, and seemingly anxious for opportunities

---

[1] *Prompter*, December 18 : " I am summoned to a new war by the Whigs, the liberal reforming Whigs ! the men who have taken office to graduate a revolution. . . . Are you sure they'll do it ? I am not. Do you think they wish to do it ? I have my doubt on that point." *Prompter*, January 1, 1831 : " There is nothing more evident, at the close of this year, than that the Whigs intend a reign of terror."

to prosecute. Such an attitude is surprising in an administration which necessarily depended more than most on popular support. Probably Grey considered the King's confidence worth all such risks ; and William hated nothing more than Radical agitators.

In the north the ministry were confronted by equal difficulties, but of another kind. The labourers' revolt had not penetrated to the northern counties where agricultural wages were higher. Special constables were enrolled in large numbers in case of danger, but nothing occurred in the rural districts more serious than an occasional threatening letter and here and there a fire, which as likely as not was due to private malice. The industrial centres on the other hand, and especially the Manchester district, were feeling the full effects of the new labour movement. The most important feature at the time of Melbourne's accession was the situation at Ashton, Stalybridge, and Dukinfield, where fifty-two masters had threatened to shut their mills unless the operatives accepted a reduced rate of wages to come into force on December 11.[1] Low as their funds were known to be, it was not expected that the men would comply, and troops were drafted into the district after the usual custom of the time when industrial disputes were apprehended. From the beginning of December it became usual for crowds of operatives to parade the neighbourhood in procession, waving tricolor flags and firing pistols. On the 6th a gathering of several thousands was addressed by Doherty, at this time very active in propaganda, and Betts, the local secretary to the Union ; work was forcibly stopped at several mills, and windows were broken ; hitherto, however, the strike only involved small numbers, though it was expected that some 20,000 would be thrown out of work on the 11th. Already the civil power was overawed ; the magistrates were anxious to arrest Doherty and Betts, but doubted if the letter of the law justified them in doing so.

The matter loomed large in the minds of the Cabinet, and General Bouverie's reports were regularly submitted to the King. Bouverie himself thought the men had no wish to use violence if they could attain their ends peaceably, but feared that in time lack of money would lead to riots. He was himself inclined to blame the masters, whose aim, in some cases admitted, was to crush the unions. On the other side the processions of

[1] *H. O.* 40. 26 ; the lockout was originally threatened for December 4.

strikers continued, and picketing carried on by mobs of five to seven thousand created general alarm. Melbourne, who was inclined to judge any combination to raise wages a conspiracy punishable at common law, declared the behaviour of the strikers to be "manifestly most illegal."[1] He was disgusted by the attitude of some of the masters, which suggested collusion of a very questionable sort ; moreover, difficulties were caused by the refusal of the middle classes to serve as constables against the workmen, whether from fear or sympathy. At the same time the excitement was increased by the Preston election, where troops were wanted to keep in check Huntite mobs marching in procession with banners inscribed " Bread or blood."

Hitherto the cotton strike had been sectional ; on December 17, however, the delegates of the General Body of Operative Spinners, assembled at Manchester, proclaimed a national strike of all spinners, to begin on December 27 unless the Union rates were granted. But this ambitious project was more than the rude organisation would stand ; not only the Scotch and Irish delegates, but several important English districts, protested against a national strike when funds were so low.[2] The affair ended in a fiasco and a loss of prestige to unionism, but it showed what might in the future be expected when the forces of labour were more highly developed.[3]

The failure of the general turn-out did not directly affect the local one already in progress. Towards the end of the month the processions had stopped by order of the committee of the union, but picketing was still going on, and had in some instances been punished. However, the strikers had lost spirit, and, when on the 28th the union allowance was lowered from ten to five shillings, it was expected that many men would go back to work on the first day of the new year.[4] In Cheshire about the same

---

[1] " A number of persons proceeding armed with bludgeons or other unusual formidable weapons and going to a place where a meeting for some purpose such as advancing wages, for instance, had been publicly announced " are clearly acting illegally. They are " illegal assemblies of a most dangerous description " (*H. O.* 41. 9).

[2] *H. O.* 40. 25.

[3] On December 21 Melbourne wrote to Foster : " The strength of the Union is incompatible with the trade and security of the district ; " he assured him that the Government would not fail to bring the question before Parliament (*H. O.* 40. 26).

[4] *H. O.* 40. 26.

time the weekly pay sank to two shillings and sixpence. The back of the strike was broken, though interest had been aroused by visits of Hunt to Manchester and Oldham. Foster, the local magistrate, in his anxiety not to be made a party in the dispute, had refused to intervene in any way ; but early in January 199 shopkeepers and publicans of the Ashton district petitioned Lord Derby, the Lord-Lieutenant, to act as mediator and put an end to an intolerable situation, which was not due, they said, to political or revolutionary motives on the part of the men. Lord Derby consulted with the Home Secretary, but refused to take any step, and before long the men returned to work on the masters' conditions, though in some cases mill-owners had been already induced to grant the union scale of wages.[1]

Strikes also took place among the cotton-spinners of Glossop-dale, and in the north-western coalfield generally. Unionism in this industry was spreading south from Lancashire and Cheshire, where it was very strong, to Derby, Shropshire, and Stafford.[2] The Trades Union was chiefly recruited from printers, spinners, and colliers, and there are traces of combined action between the two last industries.[3] But in spite of Doherty's efforts, which included the foundation in January of the *Voice of the People,* a paper with an estimated circulation of 30,000, the National Association for the Protection of Labour was seen to have failed. For three years more the movement continued, and at no time during the Reform struggle did strikes and other signs of labour unrest entirely cease ; [4] but the new organisations had outgrown their strength ; the workmen's class-consciousness was not sufficiently developed; and by the end of 1834 the splendid bubble was pricked. In the eloquent words of Mr. and Mrs.

---

[1] *H. O.* 40. 27.

[2] It was asserted that the men's action could not be due to distress, as wages were high in the coal-trade, averaging 5s. 4d. per day in Cheshire and 3s. 6d. to 4s. in Stafford (*H. O.* 52. 6). In places, it is said, the men were prevented by the unions from earning more than 6s. a day, in order to reduce the amount of coal got.

[3] Coal was refused to mill-owners who rejected Union terms, and on December 27, the day of the proposed general cotton strike, the Stafford-shire colliers were expected to down tools.

[4] About this time the Potters' Union and Leeds Clothiers' Union were formed ; the important Builders' Union started later. The coal strike on the Tyne and Wear will be mentioned in its place.

Webb, " the records of the rise and fall of the ' New Unionism ' of 1830-4 leave us conscious of a vast enlargement in the ideas of the workers, without any corresponding alteration in their tactics in the field. In council they are idealists, dreaming of a new heaven and a new earth, humanitarians, educationalists, socialists, moralists : in battle they are still the struggling half-emancipated serfs of 1825 . . . always oppressed and miserably poor." [1] But to the " respectable " classes the essential weakness of the new movement was not apparent ; they could not tell that society was not threatened by a giant conspiracy against its very existence. Dark stories were told of the strange rites and oaths by which members were admitted to the unions ; the outward effects were visible and fearful, in the shape of picketing mobs, closed mills, and banners with alarming devices As the south had shortly before trembled at the threats of a desperate peasantry, so the north was now thoroughly cowed by the awakening of labour, and that sensation of general unrest set in which marks a society that feels the ground is crumbling beneath its feet.

During the anxious winter of 1830, Lord Durham's committee was busy with its important task of drafting the Reform Bill. Of its formation and proceedings accounts are extant from three original sources, whence a synoptic narrative can be constructed. Sir James Graham wrote down what he remembered in 1851 for the historian Roebuck's benefit, and Russell's contribution forms part of the New Edition of his *Essay on the English Government*, published in 1865. We have, however, information much more nearly contemporary, owing to the lucky chance of Durham's quarrel with Brougham in 1834. A fiery speech by Durham at the Edinburgh Reform festival had incensed Brougham, who retorted in the October *Edinburgh* by accusing Durham of having favoured a policy of " clipping and compromise " with regard to the Reform Bill. Durham wrote angrily to Lord John Russell for confirmation of his own version, and was with difficulty prevented by Grey from publishing the whole story without any respect for the tradition of Cabinet secrecy.[2] The correspondence of the two protagonists,

---

[1] *History of Trade Unionism*, p. 138.

[2] Grey to Durham, October 19, 1834 : " You may easily imagine how much and how deeply I regret the sort of controversy which has arisen

Durham and Russell, makes it possible to learn the chief facts as to the birth of the great measure.

As has been already said, Durham was asked to lend his assistance by Lord Grey in the House of Lords "shortly after the formation of the Government"; he gladly consented to work with Lord John Russell, the recognised Whig leader in the Commons on the subject of Reform.[1] These two were both sons of original "Friends of the People"; both had proposed measures of Reform in the past, and both were free from serious departmental work; Durham's intimacy with Lord Grey ensured that the Prime Minister's own views would be known to the Committee. The only other minister who could have the same claim to be selected was Brougham; and he, apart from his duties as Lord Chancellor, might possibly be considered bound by the measure he had outlined in November, while his strong personality would also tell against his choice for such a purpose.[2] Durham and Russell, with Grey's approval, proceeded to co-opt Sir James Graham, stamped as a keen Whig by his retrenchment

between you and the Chancellor, and I should not deal fairly with you, if I did not say that I think there are faults on both sides. . . . I consider all statements of what may have passed in the Cabinet, without the express permission of the King, as positive breaches of duty." Durham made certain statements in a speech at Gateshead, which do not seem to have wholly satisfied Russell, who wrote to him, October 22, 1834: "I am far from thinking that what you stated at Gateshead was not in accordance with the fact, and the whole fact, as far as you went. But it struck me at the time that your going into the statement you did, and going no farther, would give rise to an inference that I was not justly entitled to any peculiar merit in the formation of the Reform Bill" (*Lambton Papers*).

[1] Durham to Russell, October 22, 1834; *Howick Papers*. Russell says it was "in the latter end of November or beginning of December" (*Early Correspondence*, ii. 52).

[2] Mr. S. J. Reid states in his *Life of Lord Durham* (i. 352) that "Brougham never forgave the passing over his claims in favour of Sir James Graham when the Committee of Four, charged with the preparation of the Reform Bill, was constituted. . . . Brougham's exclusion from the Committee of Four—he seems to have persuaded himself that it was at the instance of Durham—was evidently rankling in his mind all through 1833." No evidence, however, is quoted. If this was Brougham's feeling at the time, it certainly does not appear in the account of the arrangement given in his *Memoirs* (iii. 93), which runs as follows: "After many preliminary discussions, we agreed that the whole subject should be referred to a committee, consisting of Graham, Durham, Duncannon, and John Russell. . . ." Of course pride may have kept Brougham silent, but it is unlike him to give no hint of a grievance, if such existed.

JOHN GEORGE, FIRST EARL OF DURHAM

*From the Painting by* Sir THOMAS LAWRENCE, P.R.A., *at Lambton Castle*

speeches in the late Parliament.[1] Lord Duncannon, Grey's connexion by marriage, was marked out for a fourth place by his favour in the King's sight and his knowledge of Irish borough history ; as one of the two Government Whips he was likely to know what the party might be trusted to approve Graham had no such special qualification ; he is described by one authority as a " pocket-vote of Lambton's " ; by another as constantly consulting Althorp and taking from him views more advanced than his own. The personal friendship of the members promised a smooth course to the Committee, and this was no small thing where Durham was involved. So far the arrangement was natural enough ; but it is surprising to be told that Durham was only dissuaded by Russell from adding the Duke of Richmond.[2] Russell's statement that the Duke had never been a Reformer is not strictly accurate, but certainly it was strange that " Radical Jack," of all people, should choose the one Tory from a Whig administration for a service of such importance. It can only be suggested that Durham was still swayed by the opinions which made him wish to effect a union between the Whigs and Tories after the passing of the Catholic Relief Bill.[3]

The Committee being thus formed, Durham asked Russell, as the member last in charge of the subject, to prepare a skeleton with the principal heads of a possible bill. He was to be guided by Lord Grey's instructions " that the outline of a measure should be prepared, large enough to satisfy public opinion and

[1] Graham replied to Durham's invitation : " I shall have the greatest pleasure in obeying your summons for 12.30 to-day ; and no honor, which Lord Grey could have conferred on me, would have gratified me more than being chosen by him as an associate with such colleagues in so noble an undertaking " (*Lambton Papers*).

[2] *Speeches of Earl Russell*, i. 52.

[3] Brougham's *Memoirs*, iii. 507. This incident, perplexing in any case, is complicated by the fact that Creevey, writing from Bessborough in 1833 (*Papers*, p. 606), gives a completely different account of it. He declares that towards the end of the Committee's sittings Grey added to it the Duke of Richmond, and that this " gave great umbrage to Durham. From that day forth he and the Duke fought like cat and dog." This version sounds more intrinsically probable, but it cannot stand against Lord John Russell's explicit statement that it was he who thwarted Durham's wish for the Duke's inclusion. I have found no independent confirmation of either tradition. In April 1832 Grey wrote to Durham of Richmond : " He certainly was, like some others, not originally very friendly to reform " (*Lambton Papers*).

to afford sure ground of resistance to further innovation," but maintaining the essential character of the Constitution.[1]

The representation of Great Britain, as Russell found it, was the same, with the solitary exception of the transference of Grampound's two members to Yorkshire in 1821, and the merging of a few boroughs in their surrounding hundreds, as it had stood since the Union with Scotland.[2] The 513 English members were apportioned as follows : counties, 82 ; universities, 4 ; cities, boroughs, and Cinque ports, 403 ; Wales enjoyed twelve county and twelve borough members. In the English counties the franchise had for four centuries been confined to the forty-shilling freeholders. Of the 203 English boroughs, in fifty-nine the franchise was of the scot and lot order, roughly including all rate-payers ; however, in some of the boroughs of this type the electors were all the " potwallopers," that is to say, practically all heads of families. In thirty-nine boroughs only burgage-holders might vote ; in forty-three the Corporation ; and in sixty-two the Freemen. But a more practical division was into close and open boroughs. The notorious Gatton, for instance, had a scot and lot franchise, but its inhabitants were so few that its members were in fact nominated by the patron ; in other cases the town itself might be populous enough, but the parliamentary borough was only a small area within it. Corporation boroughs were practically always close. Burgages, too, could be easily bought up by a wealthy man, and distributed among his dependents for each occasion ; Lord Lonsdale " settled at Haslemere a colony of Cumberland miners, whose only business was to occupy the burgage houses, and obey Lonsdale's behests at the elections." At Old Sarum the seven votes which returned its two members were attached to bare ploughed fields.[3] In some towns, such as Cambridge, Freemen could be treated at will by the municipal oligarchy, and no condition of residence was imposed. However, no hard and fast rule can be laid down. Different boroughs varied greatly in tradition ; we have seen how in the 1830 election several close boroughs made efforts to open themselves, while even in pocket boroughs, as Sir Manasseh Lopez learnt to his cost, the voteless multitude could make their voices heard

[1] Parker, *Life of Graham*, i. 120.
[2] For the following account of the state of the representation I am indebted to *The Unreformed House of Commons*, by E. and A. Porritt.
[3] Porritt, i. 34, 35.

and their fists felt. Closest of the close were the nomination boroughs, which simply registered the patron's decision—whether or not in return for favours promised or received. At the other end of the scale stood such constituencies as Westminster and Preston, where practically every adult male inhabitant enjoyed the vote, and where men like Hobhouse and even Hunt stood a chance of election.

It is not possible to state accurately how many borough elections might, and how many might not, be fairly described as open. The Friends of the People in 1793 declared confidently that 306 members were returned by 162 individuals, including the Treasury; in 1827, after the Union with Ireland had added 100 seats, Croker estimated that 276 members were returned by patrons, and that of these the Tories appointed 203.[1] This gives colour to Disraeli's assertion that during the war the borough nominations were rearranged in the Tory interest. Of the Irish boroughs seventeen were said to be controlled by patrons in 1831.[2] The Scotch representation provided practically no outlet for the voice of the people; the fifteen burgh members were chosen at second-hand by close corporations, which filled up vacancies in their own ranks. The inhabitants of the Royal Burgh of Dundee, in petitioning Peel for an alteration of their constitution or " sett," declared that the town's affairs lay completely at the mercy of the magistrates and Town Council. " In that body likewise is vested the exercise of the political privileges of the Burgh. . . . Since 1818 the Town Council have consisted of twenty-one members—eighteen self-elected; two returned by the suffrages of the guildry and one by the nine incorporated trades." [3] The constituency of Edinburgh, which alone among the burghs returned a member of its own, amounted to thirty-three. The electors in the counties were not even necessarily the landowners, but the possibly non-resident holders of certain feudal rights, known as " superiorities," roughly corresponding to the lordship of a manor in England. Throughout their history the forty-five Scotch members had the reputation of being constant supporters of the Government.

To compare with this number, it is well known that Cornwall returned forty-four members, of whom eighteen came from the area of twenty-eight by twelve square miles surrounding Lis-

---

[1] *Croker Papers*, i. 372.    [2] Porritt, i. 310.    [3] *H. O.* 102. 40.

keard.[1] Cornwall is a flagrant case, but the south of England generally was far more heavily represented than the now populous north, whose great industrial centres, such as Leeds, Birmingham, Manchester, Sheffield, returned no members at all.

Thus the main anomalies of the system were three: many insignificant places returned members, while many important towns did not ; even in large towns the members were often elected by a tiny fraction of the population, to say nothing of out-voters ; counties and parliamentary boroughs in England, regardless of their relative importance, returned all alike two members.[2]

The corruption ingrained in the old *régime* was extensive and manifold. The Government bribed the patron or member or both by means of distinctions and offices or by actual cash. The patron and member bribed the electors in the same way. Often there was no question of bribery, simply of barter, and seats were advertised for sale in the daily press. In 1830, £6000 seems to have been an average price for a seat during the life of a Parliament, or £1500 to £1800 a year. The excess of these figures over those mentioned as usual in the eighteenth century justifies the complaints, so common at the time, that prices had greatly risen.[3] Even keen Reformers like Burdett and Ricardo bought seats, and so conscientious a man as Romilly preferred this method of entering Parliament to the alternative of accepting a seat from the Prince of Wales. " I formed to myself," he wrote, " the unalterable resolution never, unless I held a public office, to come into Parliament but by a popular election, or by paying the common price for my seat." [4] Such scruples were most exceptional. The member did not, as a rule, receive his instructions regularly from his patron ; more usually he was left to follow his own judgment on the condition, expressed or implied, that he should retire in the case of his own views and his patron's coming into conflict. Scarlett, for

[1] Porritt, i. 92.

[2] As a matter of fact there were five single-member borough constituencies, and after 1821 Yorkshire had returned four representatives. The City of London also had four members.

[3] In 1734 the price for a seat is mentioned as £2000, in 1768 as £4000. Rosebery, *Chatham*, p. 76 ; Winstanley, *Lord Chatham and the Whig Opposition*, p. 212.

[4] Romilly to Creevey, September 23, 1805 ; *Creevey Papers*, p. 41. Denman likewise in 1826 declined a seat offered him by the Duke of Norfolk.

instance, Wellington's Attorney-General, resigned his seat for Lord Fitzwilliam's borough of Malton after speaking against the Reform Bill, and was succeeded by Jeffrey, the Whig Lord Advocate.[1]

It is not easy to say in what light this trafficking was looked upon by society in general. The middle and working classes, of course, detested it, and strictly, after 1809, the sale of seats was illegal, though winked at by custom. County seats were still considered the most honourable, and nearly everyone, but for the question of expense, would rather have sat for a large town than for a rotten borough. Peel, however, when invited in October 1830 to stand for Liverpool, chose not to surrender his pocket seat at Westbury. After mentioning the heavy work the honour would entail, " I may also add," he continues, " that I think that a Minister of the Crown has an advantage in being free from the double, occasionally perhaps the conflicting, obligations which are imposed by high responsible office and by such a trust as the representation of Liverpool." [2] The case of ministers was regarded as exceptional, but on the whole it may perhaps be said that in the abstract all sides would have admitted that abuses had grown up and that the state of affairs was unsatisfactory, but that no blame attached to the individual, except perhaps in some scandalous case of direct bribery, for falling in with the accepted fashion.[3]

[1] Porritt, i. 322. Cf. *Creevey Papers*, p. 414. Lord Kensington offers to return to Canning the seat of his son, who has voted with Burdett.

[2] *Peel Papers*, ii. 162. He gives his rejection on seeking re-election at Oxford as a case in point.

[3] We may perhaps compare the general attitude nowadays towards modern electioneering methods. Reformers hoped, though vainly, that their bill would kill bribery. Lord Howick writes to his brother in August 1832 : " I declared my intention not to spend a shilling [in the election], a determination to which no Reformer has a right to object, since if I were as rich as Crœsus upon principle I should equally refuse to spend money in any such manner. Under the new law every man who wishes to do so can give his vote without any serious trouble or inconvenience, and if the electors choose to be influenced by beer, Reform is of no use. Men who pay for their seats will expect their seats to pay them somehow or other " (*Howick Papers*).

The whole subject of the relations of members of the unreformed Parliament to their patrons, their constituents, the Government, and one another, is treated exhaustively and in detail by Mr. Porritt, who has collected a vast mass of individual cases. It is from the study of these alone that a fair picture of the state of things can be obtained.

M

Such was the strange medley of rights and interests which
Lord Durham's Committee was charged to adapt to the demands
of the new England which had grown up since the days of Walpole
and Newcastle and Pitt.   They did not suffer from lack of suggestions.   The chairman, at Grey's request, received the deputations and memorials from numbers of public bodies about the
country, and represented to some degree the views of the Reformers in the great towns.[1]   Lord Tavistock urged that not
less than a hundred seats should be remodelled.[2]   A pamphlet
with almost prophetic grasp of the possible called for the abolition of rotten boroughs, a £10 rent franchise in the towns, and
county districts in which copy and leaseholders should be added
to the electorate.[3]   Radicals declared that nothing short of
household suffrage and ballot would satisfy them ; others im-
patiently pressed the ministers to take up Brougham's still-born
project of November, the general principles of which were the
enfranchisement of the great towns, virtual household suffrage
for resident borough voters, and the removal of one member
from a sufficient number of insignificant places to allow for the
new boroughs ; in five cases only were both representatives to
be taken away.   Now, however, after the events and discussions
of the last two months, in which the rotten boroughs had come
in for the chief abuse, general opinion demanded more drastic
treatment of the offenders.

Lord John Russell has described how, in drawing up his
scheme, he determined to follow the principles of Burke and of
Grey's speech of 1810—that speech which, in Place's view,
marked the Friend of the People's apostasy from progressive
ideas,[4]—namely, to preserve the essential form of the Constitution and trust the magical properties of the old lamp.   But in
December 1830 he put on these principles a construction very
different from that which he had proposed in December 1819,
the days of the reign of terror.   Althorp, whom he consulted,
was delighted to find that his friend went further than himself,

---

[1] The Radical Colonel Jones forwarded him letters in December from
London shopkeepers praying for a full Reform, and Charles Tennyson
commended to him his bill of 1828 to enfranchise Birmingham (*Lambton
Papers*).

[2] *Recollections of a Long Life*, iv. 75.

[3] *First Epistle to Viscount Althorp*, by " Paulus Apollos."

[4] Add. MSS. 27,789, f. 262.

and even then suggested a scheme which came short of that adopted. "The plan I now state," he wrote from Downing Street, " is, I think, my lowest, that is, I should not think Government ought to propose anything below it. Procure a hundred seats by disfranchisement, give forty-two of them to large towns and manufacturing districts. Let the right of voting in the new towns be householders rated at £10, in the districts persons qualified to serve on juries. Disqualify out-voters. The towns to be disqualified to be selected according to their population. . . . Give Scotland a representative Government. I think this will do. . . . I suppose for the present I must give up Ballot; I am no bigot, I do not consider nothing gained unless all is. With the Reform I will have if I have any, the people shall have the power of taking what more they want and this is sufficient." [1]

The object Russell set before him was, in his own words, to give the vote " to the greatest number of independent men," free from the tyranny of ignorance and, if possible, of corruption ; they were to represent " the public opinion of the time," though this principle was not to bar the inclusion of a few men of intellect more likely to find support from a rich patron than from the multitude. The fruit of Lord John's meditations appeared in the shape of a document in ten clauses, which together with the alterations originally in Durham's handwriting is printed in the *Essay on the English Government and Constitution.* [2] The clauses marked " approved " proposed that the fifty least populous boroughs should be totally disfranchised ; that fifty more should send only one member ; [3] that eighteen large towns should send two members ; [4] that four or six members should be added to the metropolis ; that twenty counties should send two more members each ; that copyholders and leaseholders with twenty-one years' interest should vote in counties. These recommendations, with certain extensions, were embodied in the Committee's report ; as to the right of voting in the new boroughs, Russell was inclined to make the jury qualification serve, adding

[1] Althorp to Russell ; *Lambton Papers.*

[2] Pp. 238–250.

[3] Durham's marginal notes observe this would embrace boroughs of under 1400 and 3000 inhabitants respectively. It was discovered later that 2000 and 4000 would be truer estimates; these figures appeared in the bill.

[4] Raised by the Committee to " about thirty," *i.e.*, all with 10,000 inhabitants.

a £10 restricted householder suffrage for the old borough constituencies, with the exception of London, Westminster, Southwark, which were to remain as before. As an alternative to jurymen in the new boroughs, he suggested householders rated at ten or fifteen pounds. The Committee, however, preferred a uniform right of voting for the old and new boroughs, which they fixed at £10, reserving their life-interest to those enjoying " the multifarious and inconvenient rights of voting now in existence." Other changes suggested were the enforcement of residence, a system of registration, and the limiting of polling to two days.

Two further recommendations were made, both of which have now passed into law, but which at the same time were considered vital parts of the Radical programme and were eventually dropped by the Whig Cabinet. Russell's draft had made no allusion to the shortening of the duration of parliaments or to voting by ballot. Annual elections had been demanded by the more advanced pre-Revolution Reformers, on the mistaken analogy of medieval times, and, in spite of obvious practical inconvenience, were sanctioned by Bentham in his crusades against corruption ; they were now supported by all the extreme Radicals, as one of their three points, but by them only. Durham proposed triennial parliaments, which most certainly the House of Commons could never willingly have swallowed ; on Russell's motion, five years was fixed as a compromise.[1] But the real struggle occurred on the question of the ballot, at the time the chief distinguishing mark of an advanced Reformer ; it had been sacrificed by the Birmingham Union not without regret in many quarters, and its advocates considered it the one remedy against illicit influence.[2] Right at the end of the Committee's sittings this disturbing proposal was introduced by the Chairman, and it says much for his influence and Althorp's that the Committee adopted it.[3] Graham is supposed to have voted for it on Althorp's

[1] Durham to Russell, October 22, 1834 ; *Howick Papers*.

[2] Parkes to Place, December 5 ; Add. MSS. 35,148, f. 77.

[3] It is interesting to find among Lord Durham's papers of this date a letter from Colonel Jones inclosing the answers to questions addressed by him to several prominent Londoners. The first question is : " Would a high qualification of franchise, with the Ballot, give more satisfaction than a lower and more general extended right of suffrage without the Ballot ? " The answers are nearly all " Yes." " I think the Ballot is now quite essential," writes one ; " The people look upon the Ballot as their

advice, and with the idea of using it as a lever in the Cabinet.[1]
Lord John Russell was rootedly opposed to it, but bowed to the
decision of the majority.[2]   As a concession, however, the borough
qualification was raised from £10 to £20.[3]

It is remarkable that the great feature of Pitt's last Reform
proposals, which Lord John Russell himself accepted in 1823—
the principle of compensation—does not seem to have been so
much as mentioned.   It was probably felt that the hard-taxed
people would not stand so great an expenditure as would have
been necessary, even were it in itself defensible.   The precedent
of the Union with Ireland was not encouraging.

The Committee's duties were now over ; on January 14 they
signed a report addressed to Grey and drawn up by Durham,
who all along had sat pen in hand keeping the minutes.   They
had naturally talked over the matter with the Prime Minister
and kept him apprised of their progress,[4] but the original scheme

only security," says another.   "These," comments Jones, " I consider
quite enough to persuade you and even Lord G. that the Ballot is generally
considered as the panacea for parliamentary corruption—do therefore
urge it to be adopted as part of the plan of reform.   The Ballot will secure
your government the support of all the staunch reformers in the Country,
and will not alienate from it the moderate and the timid" (*Lambton
Papers*).   It would seem, however, from the dates that this appeal came
too late to have suggested to Durham the step he took.

[1] Le Marchant, *Memoir of Althorp*, p. 292 ; *Essay on the English
Government*, p. 251 ; *Life of Graham*, i. 120 ; *Life of Durham*, i. 237.

[2] In contradiction of Lord John's assertion that he was the one of the
four who opposed the ballot, we read in the fragments of Lord Lyndhurst's
*Recollections* given by Mr. Monypenny in his *Life of Disraeli* (i. 387) that
Duncannon was the objector ; this is given as secret history, and it is
further said that Graham was in the habit of insinuating that it was he who
protested.   If this is so, we have three claimants.   There is no hint in
Graham's own account that he was in the minority ; Russell explicitly
states that he himself was : " finding the other members of the Committee
against me, I consented."   Lyndhurst's authority is not given.   Again
I believe Lord John Russell's account.

[3] Durham was furious with the allegation (attributed to Brougham)
in the *Edinburgh* of October 1834 that he and the rest of the Committee
fixed on £20—" which would have destroyed a hundred rotten boroughs
and created about twice the number," but that the Cabinet changed it
to £10.   " My recommendation of the Jury or £20 qualification was dependent on the adoption of Ballot " (Durham to Grey, October 18, 1834 ;
*Howick Papers*).

[4] Grey to Lady Grey, January 2, 1831 : " My whole morning has been
occupied with . . . a long discussion on the proposed plan of Reform
with Lambton and Lord John Russell " (*Howick Papers*).

was mainly the work of the four men who met to discuss it in Cleveland Row, and especially of Durham and Russell, guided, of course, by Grey's preliminary instructions. An unprofitable controversy has been waged over the proportion of credit assignable to each of the two main collaborators ; it is enough to say that the first draft, which the report followed in essentials, was Russell's work, while the bold additions bear the tokens of the Chairman's courage and strong will. But where four men, of the calibre of these four, have sat round a table discussing a measure for weeks, it is impossible to resolve into their separate shares the fused product of their united minds.

If Roebuck, versed as he was by long study in the politics of a former generation, and by personal experience in those of his own, was as much at a loss in 1851 to account for the breadth and boldness of the Whig Reform Bill as contemporaries were taken aback by it, it may be worth while to stop to look at it with his eyes and prepare ourselves to share his wonder. For we need go no further ; by the middle of January the essential form of the great Act was fixed. Even from Brougham's proposed bill it is a wide leap ; from the old half-hearted ventures of the Whigs, a whole heaven. Sir James Graham, attempting in reply to the historian to explain the change, laid stress on the joint effect of the passing of Catholic Relief and of the Duke's attitude to Reform, as shown in March 1828 and November 1830, in waking the spirit of the Whigs. " All the passions and all the hopes of an angry and disappointed Opposition, notwithstanding different shades of wishes and of opinion, were concentrated in a combined effort to carry Parliamentary Reform." [1] Guided by this hint, we realise that even apart from the spur of public expectation party zeal was worked up to the point where sheer reason is superseded ; where individual judgment might have hesitated, corporate feeling urged a fighting policy and carried the day. And among fighting men no Whig surpassed Radical Jack, whose strong influence over his father-in-law, if to Grey and the party alike it often brought vexation, on this occasion at least played no small part in the production of a winning strategy. Though we may not believe Lord Grey's reported boast that he never read the newspapers,[2] it is yet true that

[1] *Life of Graham*, i. 118.

[2] Martineau, *History of England*, ii. 45 ; contrast *Lieven Correspondence*, ii. 61.

he came little into touch with popular feeling. " Neither Lord John Russell nor Althorp," says Sir Denis Le Marchant, " had any connection with the Radical Leaders." [1]  Graham was very doubtfully disposed to the democratic movement.  Durham and Brougham alone may be said to have really understood the middle-class point of view by sympathy and connection, and both were in constant correspondence with Lord Grey ; it is probable that they were the main channels by which he became aware of the rising enthusiasm of the people.  Brougham, however, had not gauged the force of the hatred for the nomination boroughs, though he afterwards generously admitted that it was Schedule A which carried the bill.[2]  Nothing made such a good cry in the country, except the pension list, as the iniquities of the borough-mongers, and the fact that most of these were Tories made it easy for the Whigs to take the popular side.

It would appear then that Lord Grey's statesmanlike conviction of the need and advantage of an extensive measure was the prime source of the Reform Bill ; that the wisdom of Russell and the will of Durham embodied this conviction in a bold and simple form ; and that, as regards the moderates in the Cabinet and the party generally, it was proved once again that a keen and determined minority will by their very momentum overbear a comparatively indifferent and undecided majority.  But the conversion of the King, the Cabinet, and the Commons must be treated in its place.

---

[1] *Memoir of Althorp*, p. 308.     [2] *Memoirs*, iii. 92.

# CHAPTER V

## THE FIRST REFORM BILL

"It was not a good bill, though it was a great bill when it passed."

JOHN BRIGHT.

WHEN the report of the Committee of Four had been drawn up and signed, Grey at length had a definite basis to work on. Though office was always to him an anxious and toilsome burden,[1] his talents now had a more congenial field than the vague discussions of policy to which they had been largely confined in Opposition. He lost no time in forwarding the completed report to Lord Lansdowne, already identifying himself with it, but declaring his objection to the ballot.[2] In the course of the next fortnight the proposals were laid before the Cabinet; here discussion centred mainly on three points—the ballot, the amount of the borough qualification, and the rotten boroughs. The ballot could not face the opposition of Grey, Lansdowne, Brougham and others, and was accordingly struck out, in Durham's absence.[3] The qualification, for all that, was left at £20 till after the King had seen the report, though such a moderate as Melbourne urged the lower figure, content where he yielded to yield handsomely.[4] The sweeping abolition of nomination boroughs was carried in spite of the Chancellor's strong objections, which at one time had alarmed Grey seriously.[5] Otherwise the draft was

[1] Grey to Lady Grey, January 1, 1831, from Panshanger: "A happy new year to you. I am afraid I must look neither for happiness nor peace during its continuance, if my possession of office should continue so long" (*Howick Papers*).

[2] Grey to Lansdowne, January 15, 1831: "I object to the Ballot, and would rather be forced to yield to it than introduce it in the bill" (*Howick Papers*).

[3] *Correspondence of Earl Grey with King William IV and Sir Herbert Taylor* (henceforward called *Correspondence*), i. 114. Durham to Russell, October 22, 1834; *Howick Papers*.

[4] *Memoir of Althorp*, p. 294. Graham to Durham, January 27; *Lambton Papers*.

[5] Grey to Durham, January 24; *Correspondence*, i. 81. Graham to Durham, January 25: "*The measure* on the whole was well received, Brougham alone dissentient and disposed to carp by raising little points

approved with remarkable unanimity, and the minister felt that he had a compact Cabinet behind him when he set off with Althorp to submit the report to the King at Brighton on January 30.

Some time previously Grey had sounded the King on the momentous question, possibly at the advice of Durham, who felt that the sovereign's preliminary sanction would be useful in the Cabinet ;[1] but these communications had been vague, and merely served to show that while William acquiesced in the need for a considerable Reform he was extremely nervous of anything that could possibly be described as revolutionary. So far his conduct had been exemplary from the ministers' point of view; he had heartily approved their measures for quieting the country, he had offered them his royal assistance in bringing Stanley in for Windsor on his defeat at Preston, and he shared to the full their dislike of the Radicals. Fear of the Radicals was in fact William's dominant motive at this time ; nor is it surprising, seeing that some English journalists were wildly republican, and that on the Continent insurrections had actually broken out, or were just about to break out, in France, in Belgium, in Spain, in Italy, and in Poland. His sentiments were heartily shared by Queen Adelaide, whose childhood had been spent in war-ridden Germany, and was unlikely to offer any too pleasing memories of republican methods. She made no secret of her personal preference for the Tories, and, sweet-tempered as she ordinarily was, seems to have shown little civility to Lady Grey at Windsor.[2] The King's secretary, however, Sir Herbert Taylor, denied that she made any attempt to influence the King, or indeed discussed politics with him. The false rumours on this head, which did so much afterwards to disturb her peace of mind, were not yet rife, but it is as well to understand at the outset that such conduct was most uncharacteristic of her and was believed by no one who had any means of knowing.

The free and easy habits of the Court did, however, give colour to the reports which soon arose that the King was not as discreet as he might be, and that news reached the Tories

when he could found no real objections and very much inclined to defend the Nomination Boroughs " (*Lambton Papers*). We owe these two interesting notes to the fact that Durham was unwell and therefore unable to attend the Cabinet.

[1] Durham to Grey (undated) ; S. J. Reid, *Life of Durham*, i. 242.

[2] Greenwood, *The Hanoverian Queens of England*, ii. 359, 399 ; *Creevey Papers*, p. 604.

from quarters where there should have been no leak. The general tendency of the Court was to Tory views, and Sir Herbert Taylor thought it well to assure Grey at the outset that " there never was any Court from which and of which so little could be told, which every servant in the house . . . might not tell. Their Majesties are accessible at all hours ; the apartments are open to everyone ; there is no seclusion, no mystery, nothing to conceal. The King sees numbers of persons in the course of the day and converses freely with them upon subjects on which they may give him information ; but I am confident that, although he may listen to them, he never converses upon any matter which may be the subject of communication with his Government, or respecting ministerial or official arrangements in contemplation." [1] Yet, though in January Grey expressed himself as satisfied with the King's desire to have his personal friends around him irrespective of their politics, later events caused some unpleasantness. Sir Herbert Taylor himself was above all suspicion, and played a most difficult part with extraordinary tact and honesty. A Tory by conviction, he was the channel of the most intimate political correspondence between the King and his Whig minister, to both of whom he was of invaluable assistance. He had to interpret his master's secret wishes for the Government's information and to remove misunderstandings on both sides. All this he did with unquestioned impartiality and unwearying diligence. In the published correspondence of William IV and Lord Grey, the letters to and from Taylor are frequently even more important than the direct communications of the King and his minister, as expressing tendencies forming in the mind of one or other party which they were unwilling to state formally, as must have been the case in the official letters. The completeness and intimate nature of the correspondence make it the main source of material for the history of the Reform Bill, so far as the intentions and difficulties of the Cabinet are concerned.

The first hints Grey obtained of William's attitude to Reform were not altogether encouraging. The King, he gathered, had been anxiously brooding over this " perilous question " for some time ; though eager to efface his " early prejudices " against Reform, and confident in Grey's desire to preserve the Constitution with as little change as possible, he looked forward

[1] *Correspondence*, i. 61.

to the introduction of the measure at such a time with unfeigned reluctance, and indeed declared his belief that the country's feeling on the matter was much exaggerated.[1] His natural fears of any change in the democratic direction were heightened by what he considered the late intolerable encroachments of the Commons in the region of finance. He had gathered from Lord Holland that his rights as Duke of Lancaster were threatened, and in December notice was given of a motion on this subject. This the Government agreed strenuously to oppose, and the King was appeased.[2] For the rest Grey could do nothing but harp on the acknowledged need for Reform and the terrible consequences of its refusal, while promising that everything possible should be done to meet the King's wishes ; with this end in view he avowed his readiness to maintain the existing duration of Parliament.[3]

The personal will of the sovereign at the beginning of last century was by no means a negligible factor. It was of great importance as well in the control of policy, as in the formation of a Government. It was thought possible in 1829 that George IV might refuse the royal assent to the Catholic Relief Bill, but Wellington's real struggle was to secure his previous acquiescence. It seems to have been held that this was a necessary preliminary to the introduction of an important bill ; the opportunity for the royal veto had merely been transferred from the last to the first stage. It is not surprising, therefore, that Grey was nervous as to the result of his visit to Brighton ; with King and Cabinet behind him, he felt secure that he could eventually carry the measure, bold as it was ; but if the King should refuse his assent to the principle of the proposed bill, there was no telling how the country would take it ; nor was it easy to see what alternative Government was available.

It was therefore with supreme relief that Grey wrote to his wife next day to assure her that all was well.[4] The King had

---

[1] *Correspondence*, i. 54.

[2] " Earl Grey cannot be surprised that the King should view with jealousy any idea of Parliamentary interference with the only remaining pittance of an independent possession which has been enjoyed by his ancestors during many centuries, as their *private* and *independent* estate, and has now, as such, lawfully devolved upon him in right of succession " (*Correspondence*, i. 11).

[3] *Correspondence*, i. 71.

[4] Grey to Lady Grey, Brougham, and Durham, January 31 ; *Howick Papers; Brougham Memoirs*, iii. 93 ; *Correspondence*, i. 91.

had the whole measure explained to him, and had given it his general approval. He reserved his criticisms, however, for a detailed communication by letter. If the document sent by the King in fulfilment of this promise had not expressly sanctioned the scheme submitted in all essential particulars, Lord Grey could hardly have guessed from its preamble that such was its intention.[1] After declaring that nothing could have induced him to permit the proposal of the ballot or universal suffrage, William gave a broad summary of his views on the question, which were those of a regular anti-Reform Tory. He doubted whether the danger of altering a Constitution which "worked" well in practice was not greater than the advantage ; whether the respectable part of the country desired Reform ; whether the preponderant representation of property was not reasonable ; and whether the further popularisation of the House of Commons might not lead to " a democracy in its worst form." One cannot but admire the King's honesty in thus stating his opinions ; but it is a shock to find him proceeding to give his consent to Durham's report, which, save for the omission of the ballot, had passed the Cabinet practically unaltered. He hoped its broad lines would "remove at once and for ever all rational grounds of complaint," and oppose an " effectual check " to " that restless spirit of innovation, which aims in secret at nothing less than the overthrow of all our institutions, and even the Throne itself." On one point the King had misunderstood the provisions of the bill ; he had gathered with pleasure that the forty-shilling freehold qualification in the counties was to be raised to £10 in future. However, Grey's assurance that the old franchise would "operate rather favourably than otherwise for the landed interest " quieted him. He acquiesced in the lowering of the borough qualification, if necessary, from £20 to £10, and in the suggested innovation of quinquennial parliaments. His recommendation to use the new census was not adopted till the introduction of the third Reform Bill.

Straightforward as the King was and desirous to support his ministers to the extreme limit of his conscience, it was a cruel irony that he did not foresee what must be the result of so bold a scheme. His real wish, as may be gathered more fully from a letter of Taylor to Brougham,[2] dated January 19, was that the Cabinet should introduce and pass such a measure as should

[1] *Correspondence*, i. 94.    [2] *Brougham Memoirs*, iii. 98.

avoid any serious opposition in either House. Alarmed by the state of affairs at home and abroad, beyond all things he dreaded the excitement in the country which a general election or a struggle with the Lords must provoke.[1] From this he looked to his confidential advisers to save him, and trusting their discretion he consented to a bill the full meaning of which he cannot have realised. As things turned out, he saw his ministers deliberately, as it seemed, steering for the very rocks he had wished to avoid. For all the charges and countercharges that have been made, there was really no deception or treachery on either side—simply misunderstanding. The King, who had not seen the inevitable consequences of the bill, might not unreasonably fancy that the Cabinet had taken advantage of his good nature to drag him far further than he had meant to go. The ministers, who had built on the fact of the King's acquiescence in their plan, might no less reasonably consider themselves left in the lurch when they discovered to their cost his real feelings. The agreement was made without a full understanding of its terms or of the actual mind of the contracting parties. To make matters worse, Reformers in the country received a yet more erroneous impression ; it was inexpressibly annoying to the King to find the bill, to which he reluctantly consented from a sense of duty, held up as his own darling project, while his lips were sealed by constitutional decorum.

It must already stand clear that William claimed and exercised a far wider control over his ministers' policy than could a modern constitutional king. He by no means held it his duty to endorse anything his ministers might propose. He declared outright that he could never have sanctioned the ballot or universal suffrage ; "nothing should ever induce him to yield."[2] This is the more remarkable in that the ballot was recommended in the report of the Committee of Four, and the King knew this. Beyond doubt he would have had the courage of his opinions and dismissed the ministry rather than agree to either of the measures mentioned. In the last resort of course his choice must have lain between compliance and going to Hanover, supposing the Government had held to such a proposal and been supported by the Commons and the country. But the royal prestige was very great, and the King's known objection to a measure would have gone far to wreck it ; as matters stood, Grey

[1] *Correspondence*, i. 96.      [2] *Ibid.*

expressed his submission in terms his Radical supporters would not at all have approved. "On the question of the Ballot," he wrote to the King, "the strong and decided opinion expressed by your Majesty must operate as a command which Earl Grey feels himself bound to obey." [1]    The King's approval was indeed of extreme importance, and justified the high spirits of ministers. "If the King be with us, the battle is won," rejoiced Graham, and Holland wrote off from Brighton to tell Russell that his child was "Royally and nobly adopted." [2]

Thus encouraged, the ministers might proceed with full confidence to face the business of the session, now beginning. Althorp announced that on March 1 Lord John Russell would introduce the Reform Bill on which the Cabinet were agreed. Russell's old connection with Reform marked him out, against the wish of Brougham, for this signal honour, an earnest of Cabinet rank.[3]  It was no doubt also felt that, great as were Althorp's merits as leader of the House and his power to turn away wrath by a conciliatory speech, he could not rise to eloquence such as so great an occasion demanded. Russell accordingly proceeded to master the details of the measure ; he was soon struck by the extreme narrowness of the £20 householder franchise, and, little more than a fortnight before the day, wrote to Durham begging him to call Lord Grey's attention to the matter. His own conviction was that nothing above £10 would be satisfactory, and this figure was finally fixed in the bill.[4]

It had been agreed that the bill should be sprung upon a

[1] *Correspondence*, i. 106.

[2] Graham to Durham ; *Lambton Papers*.  Holland to Russell, January 31 ; *Early Correspondence*, ii. 13.

[3] Holland to Russell, May 3, 1831 ; *Early Correspondence*, ii. 22.

[4] Russell to Durham, February 13 : "When we agreed to make Ballot a part of the plan to be proposed to Lord Grey, we did so on the ground that such a concession to popular feeling would enable us to vest the elective franchise in a body above corruption and deeply concerned, by reason of their property, in preserving our mixed constitution. That proposal has been since rejected, and the £20 franchise now stands alone, a mark for all the noisy and turbulent advocates of popular rights. . . . (In some of the boroughs to be preserved, the number of £20 householders is very few indeed.  I mention some, as Wilton 14, Westbury 3, Wenlock 6, St. Germains 1, &c. . . .)    I fear the constituency would be very small indeed, and we should be accused of creating new close or corrupt boroughs. . . . From these returns, taken together, I arrive at the conclusions—First, that the franchise must be lowered, nor do I well see how we can stop till we reach £10 " (*Lambton Papers*).

surprised House as the best chance of success for so bold a measure. Its nature was therefore jealously kept secret, and nothing was known outside the circle of ministers and the few, such as Burdett, whose criticism they thought it wise to forestall.[1] Among the initiated, opinions varied. Lord Howick, representing the most optimistic view, expected that the approval of the country would frighten the Opposition into accepting the measure as the alternative to revolution.[2] But in the Cabinet there was certainly an undercurrent of mistrust. Palmerston, we are told, was " much dissatisfied " with the bill,[3] and Grey was strongly pressed by his conservative supporters to compromise and come to a preliminary understanding with the Tories. He was especially warned to keep his hands off the rotten boroughs, unless he wished to be left alone with the Radicals. Nor was it too late to strengthen the Cabinet ; even Peel was suggested as a possibility. Grey, however, though not averse to the last surprising suggestion, except on the ground that there was no place available, answered staunchly that he had " passed the Rubicon and must go on." [4] Hesitating and variable as he had been for many years in opposition, from henceforward we find in him no looking back from the essential parts of the bill. His honour was pledged, and, in spite of misrepresentation and attacks from both sides, he kept a straight course.

At the very opening of the session difficulties had arisen over the Civil List ; the ministers found themselves in an awkward pass between the need to fulfil their pledges of retrenchment and their desire to keep in good odour with the King. They had wished to grant a sum for an outfit for the Queen, but were compelled to drop the idea by the opposition of Grant, who actually threatened to resign, and so, to his colleagues' disgust, " for a mere trifle, was about to risk the fate of a Government and of a Kingdom." [5] The King and Queen agreed to abandon their claim with admirable good temper, and Grey was con-

---

[1] *Brougham Memoirs*, iii. 103.

[2] Howick to Charles Grey, January 31 ; *Howick Papers*.

[3] Stanley to Graham, February 27 ; *Life of Graham*, i. 104.

[4] *Lieven Correspondence*, ii. 170–176.

[5] Graham to Durham (undated) ; *Lambton Papers*. Grey to Brougham January 31 ; *Brougham Memoirs*, iii. 94. These letters supply the name of the recalcitrant minister, which is discreetly suppressed in *Correspondence*, i. 91 ff.

firmed in his resolve to maintain all existing pensions. Sir Herbert Taylor was instructed by the King to assure Lord Grey " that he considers that you are embarked in the same boat with him, and that he may rely upon your principles, and he hopes also upon the influence of your character, for support in his endeavours to maintain the Monarchy and the Aristocracy of the country, in that position which the Constitution has assigned to them, and to protect both against the encroachments which are daily attempted." [1] The King wrote more than once during the financial discussions to protest against " the systematic determination they betray to reduce the influence of the Crown, and to lower the dignity of the Monarchy."

The anxieties of the Government were increased by the reception of Althorp's budget ; in fact one of its chief points, the tax on transfers of property, was almost immediately abandoned in deference to the cry of bad faith raised in Parliament. A resignation of the Cabinet was considered, but Althorp's sense of the duty of introducing Reform forbade him to seize the welcome opportunity.[2]   In Ireland, too, O'Connell's withdrawal of his plea of Not Guilty to an indictment for seditious conduct, and the pleasure this gave the King, were a poor triumph to set against the fact that an indictment of one so influential had been thought necessary.[3]   Yet more serious was the odium incurred by the prosecution of Cobbett for inciting to incendiarism—a step well calculated, if such reminder was needed, to keep alive the memory of the Special Commissions.  And on this occasion the ministers reaped the odium without the fruits ; Cobbett welcomed the attack, and prepared to carry the war into the enemy's country.  At his triumphal trial in the summer he declared that the Whigs had started more political prosecutions in seven months than the Tories had done in as many years.[4]  The Special Commissions and attacks on the press alienated the Radicals, whose hopes of any Reform worth the name from such tyrants were sinking fast ; [5] fundholders were alarmed by

[1] *Correspondence*, i. 117.
[2] Althorp to Grey, February 14 ; *Althorp Papers*.
[3] *Correspondence*, i. 129.
[4] *Annual Register*, July 7.
[5] Cf. *Prompter*, February 19 : " The Civil List won't do ! The Budget won't do.  The Whigs won't do, unless they carry a good householder suffrage as a reform of the House of Commons.  This will be a charity and a cloak for their many sins. . . . The secret is, Lord Althorp, we want

the budget ; Tories, if not yet actively hostile, were contemptuous of the show the Whigs made in Parliament.[1] In fact the Government were overdrawn on their original account of popularity, and were now living solely on the credit of their promised Reform. The King was at length converted to the wisdom of introducing it soon, and those in the secret who had faith could have wished the date earlier still.[2]

At this critical period Lord Grey and his friends were much disgusted by a series of attacks on him in the *Times*, which at the same time extolled the Chancellor to the skies.[3] The editor of the *Times* was Thomas Barnes, but the paper was believed to be inspired by Brougham, and his brother was known to write for it. Durham, who allowed no one to worry Grey but himself, seems to have lashed out at Brougham with his usual recklessness. Brougham wrote an indignant protest to Grey : " I *have not the most remote* influence in the quarter referred to, and as soon as I heard of the thing, I asked my brother to see the person supposed to be concerned and express how annoyed I was at such a way of praising me at the expense of those I most loved and respected. . . . I had intended to reserve this with my more general complaints (which I dare say you have been expecting for some time) pointed at the same quarter, meaning to say nothing till the Reform motion was over. But having seen my brother to-day and knowing Lambton is not apt to be very *quiescent* when he has got a thing in his head (or rather a ruffle in his temper) I could not tell how far he might be influencing

---

a revolution ; we want that cheap and good government which nothing but revolution will bring us." Hobhouse wrote (February 23) : " The Finance schemes of Ministers are universally decried, and were it not for Brougham's Chancery Reform and the expected Parliamentary Reform, would turn them out " (*Recollections*, iv. 86).

[1] Cf. *Greville Memoirs*, ii. 116 : " The government, strong in the House of Lords . . . is weak in the House of Commons to a degree which is contemptible and ridiculous. . . . Palmerston does nothing, Grant does worse, Graham does no good, Althorp a good deal of harm : Stanley alone has distinguished himself."

[2] *Brougham Memoirs*, iii. 101.

[3] E.g., *Times*, February 26 : " Lord Grey knows—he must know—what the public opinion is with respect to the number of his connexions associated with him in place. . . . There is one person in particular, unfavourably known in the City for his connexion with the celebrated Greek loan." For other such personalities in the *Times*, see the issues of February 28, March 15, and May 23.

you. . . ." [1] " That you have somewhere a very injudicious friend," Grey replied, " and I a most unprovoked and malicious enemy, is quite clear." Grey declared that he did not suspect his Chancellor, and was perhaps sincere ; but the general opinion, both on this and on other occasions, branded Brougham as untrustworthy and dishonest.[2]

As the great day approached, and indeed throughout the month of February, the table of the Commons was laden with petitions for Reform from all parts of Great Britain ; many of these asked specifically for the ballot and universal suffrage. On the 26th the House met for the presentation of petitions only. Lord Althorp was in charge of " about a hundred," including one from Manchester boasting 12,245 signatures, and another from Edinburgh with nearly 22,000 names. On the morning of March 1 the House was packed with members anxious to reserve seats for so unique an occasion. It was, of course, the old House of Commons, now nearing the end of its long life, a chamber at all times more august than comfortable, but on a crowded night " in some degree a second edition of the Black Hole of Calcutta." [3] Lord John Russell rose at six o'clock to introduce the bill. The effect of his speech on an audience tense with excitement was highly dramatic. On all sides the chief emotion was amazement at the largeness of the plan, in which the total disfranchisement of sixty boroughs stood out by its superb insolence. The climax came when Russell read out the lists of condemned boroughs. It was a ludicrous spectacle to see members lying back in disgust, not knowing whether to be amused or enraged, while " a little fellow, not weighing above eight stone," solemnly pronounced the doom of the ancient boroughs for which they sat. As each venerable name was read, a long shout of ironical laughter rang from the benches opposite. " More yet," smiled Russell unperturbed, at the end

[1] *Howick Papers.* This letter, like most of Brougham's, is insufficiently dated (Saturday), but the incident related in the *Creevey Papers*, p. 561, of Sefton's rebuking Brougham for an attack on Grey in the *Times*, would seem to fix it.

[2] He is habitually spoken of in Creevey's correspondence as " Beelzebub " or " the Arch-Fiend."

[3] *Random Recollections of the Houses of Commons* (J. Grant), 1836, p. 2 : " It was dark, gloomy, and badly ventilated, and so small that not more than four hundred out of the six hundred and fifty-eight members could be accommodated in it with any measure of comfort."

of the fateful roll, and turned to the second schedule of forty-seven boroughs, from each of which one member was to be taken. Advanced Reformers cheered lustily as he took his seat, but the general opinion was that the Government were mad, if indeed in their already discredited state they were not themselves riding for a fall.[1] A couple of nights before, a Whig lawyer expected by many to succeed Lyndhurst as Chancellor had said that the disfranchisement of fifteen boroughs would be as good as a republic ;[2] Brougham himself, Reformer of Reformers, had dared go no further than five. Indignation was only tempered by amusement for the majority of the Tories, though for men of insight by deep misgiving.[3]

It is well known that Peel was regretfully blamed for not having risen at once to move the rejection of the bill, as proposing not Reform but Revolution. But so well had the secret been kept that the Opposition could infer the probable contents of the bill from nothing but their own low estimate of the Whigs and the composition of the Cabinet. Moderate Reformers as many of them were by now in theory, they had resolved not to oppose the first reading ; and, rightly or wrongly, Peel did not change his tactics at the last moment.[4] There is a tradition that in this he yielded against his better judgment to the advice of Lord Granville Somerset.[5] Brougham had feared that he would not only divide the House, but divide it at once, declining to debate so wild a measure. As it was, Sir Robert Inglis was allowed to follow Russell in a longish speech, and the ministers seated in breathless suspense round Brougham's dinner table learnt from his secretary's report that Peel had missed what they believed to be the one chance of the Tories.[6] This opinion

---

[1] *Recollections of a Long Life*, iv. 87. The list of boroughs to lose both members formed Schedule A of the Bill ; those to lose one member made up Schedule B. Sir Denis Le Marchant, also an eye-witness, says that Russell sat down *in a profound silence*. But he may have left the House before the cheering began (*Memoir of Althorp*, pp. 298, 310).

[2] *Lieven Correspondence*, ii. 174.

[3] The *Standard* (March 1) described the measure as " overdone even for Westminster or Preston." " The Bedlam scheme can never be put into execution."

[4] Croker to Hertford, February 21 ; *Croker Papers*, ii. 108. Wellington to Croker, May 1, 1832 ; *Despatches*, viii. 293.

[5] Croker to Hertford, March 15 ; *Croker Papers*, ii. 110. Monypenny, *Life of Disraeli*, i. 387.

[6] *Brougham Memoirs*, iii. 104–6.

was largely shared by men on both sides ; it was thought that
the momentary effect of surprise would have been conservative,
and that timidity would have carried the day before the people's
voice was heard.[1]  Some believed that Peel would still have won,
had not the unforeseen length and vigour of the debate given
time for favourable opinion to be created outside Parliament.
Probably this view was correct.  Many moderate Reformers
were converted to the bill when they had recovered from the
first shock ; and the difference of a single vote would have
thrown the bill out.  But it would not have killed Reform.
For us, who know both how the popular demand had waxed up
till then, and how it flared up afterwards, it is hard to be persuaded that the middle classes would have dutifully borne so
vast a disappointment, when they had once caught sight of
their desire.  The one night of March 1 would not have been
forgotten, and the Tories—on the assumption that Grey would
have demanded a dissolution and resigned on its refusal—would
have found immense difficulties in passing a moderate Reform
Bill with their schisms half-healed and their principles in chaos.
Still it is important to remember the Tory tradition that, but
for Peel's mistake, " the question would have been finished " ;
it was useful as an argument that the Whigs had engineered the
demand they claimed to be spontaneous.

Supporters of the Government were at first divided, and
wanted time to find out what other people thought before committing themselves.  Lord Howick wrote to his father from the
House to say that the party on the whole were favourable, though
much astonished.[2]  Hobhouse and " the Mountain " had cheered
long and loud, but rather in admiration of a gallant feat than from
much hope of its success.[3]  Greatly delighted as they were, the
members for Westminster feared that Grey had fallen between
two stools ; he would not pass his bill, and if he did he could
not convert their own constituents to the £10 qualification.
They were rejoiced to find general approval.[4]  " You have been
good boys," wrote the old Radical Colonel to Durham.  " I

---

[1] *Greville Memoirs*, ii. 126.

[2] *Lieven Correspondence*, ii. 178.

[3] *Recollections*, iv. 87.  "The Mountain" were the advanced wing of
the Reformers in Parliament.

[4] The reforming press was fully satisfied, though the *Morning Chronicle*
would have liked electoral districts.

congratulate you. You have given the death-blow to the borough-mongering faction, and we will give them sepulture." [1] But it was not to please such as Colonel Jones that the Reform Bill had been framed. However, as the week went on, party loyalty asserted itself, and even moderate Whigs were emboldened by the raptures of the country to throw in their lot with the bill ; Hobhouse found a change of tone in the House as early as the second evening. [2] A series of letters from the future Lord Campbell has an interest as showing the gradual conversion of his cautious mind. [3] On February 27 he wrote : " Anything which amounts to the formation of a new Constitution I shall oppose, as I hold the formation of a new Constitution to be an impossibility, and there has as yet been no instance of it in the world." On March 2 : " We are quite appalled. There is not the remotest chance of such a bill being carried by this or any other House of Commons. . . . It is unquestionably a new Constitution." On March 3 : " The general belief is that the Bill must be thrown out on the second reading. . . . I feel inclined as a choice of evils to support, and even to speak in favour of the Bill." On March 4 : " The sensation in the public mind is great beyond anything in my time. . . . With the shop-keepers and farmers it will be very popular. Not so with the populace." On March 5 : " The measure takes very much with the country." On March 10 : " Ministers certainly have the country with them." And finally, to anticipate, on March 24 : " Ministers, notwithstanding all their blunders, are now secure. Reform has been a grand *coup d'état* for them. . . . Budget and all is forgotten."

Even in those heroic days of speech-making, a seven nights' debate was something out of the common, and though it was known that a division would not be challenged the champions of either side came down night after night with well-conned orations to answer the best speech of the evening before, bent on showing their full powers in a sport still held high in honour both in

---

[1] Jones to Durham, March 2. Another friend of Durham's wrote of the bill as " the greatest triumph of just principles since the signing of Magna Charta" (*Lambton Papers*).

[2] *Recollections*, iv. 89 : " It is curious to see the change of opinion as to the passing of this Bill. The other day nobody would hear of the possibility of it, now everybody is beginning to think it will be carried" (*Greville Memoirs*, ii. 126, March 11).

[3] *Life of Campbell*, i. 503 ff.

Parliament and in the country.    Unfortunately the efforts which then had the greatest effect do not thrill a modern reader ; and often the few speeches which even to-day lend something of fire to the dreary columns of Hansard were damned by the ear as academic and essayish.    Very rare are they which stand both tests, but among them is young Macaulay's wonderful peroration on the second night.    Had the Opposition learnt nothing, he asked, from the strange history of Catholic Relief ?    How long would they wait before yielding to this other inevitable reform ?    " Do they wait for associations more formidable than that of the Corn Exchange, for contributions larger than the Rent, for agitators more violent than those who, three years ago, divided with the King and the Parliament the sovereignty of Ireland ?    Do they wait for that last and most dreadful paroxysm of popular rage, for that last and most cruel test of military fidelity ?    Let them wait, if their past experience shall induce them to think that any high honour or any exquisite pleasure is to be obtained by a policy like this.    Let them wait, if this strange and fearful infatuation be indeed upon them, that they should not see with their eyes, or hear with their ears, or understand with their heart.    But let us know our interest and our duty better.    Turn where we may, within, around, the voice of great events is proclaiming to us, Reform, that you may preserve.    Now, therefore, while everything at home and abroad forebodes ruin to those who persist in a hopeless struggle against the spirit of the age, now, while the crash of the proudest throne of the Continent is still resounding in our ears, now, while the roof of a British palace affords an ignominious shelter to the exiled heir of forty kings, now, while we see on every side ancient institutions subverted, and great societies dissolved, now, while the heart of England is still sound, now, while old feelings and old associations retain a power and a charm which may too soon pass away, now, in this your accepted time, now, in this your day of salvation, take counsel, not of prejudice, not of party spirit, not of the ignominious pride of a fatal consistency, but of history, of reason, of the ages which are past, of the signs of this most portentous time.    Pronounce in a manner worthy of the expectation with which this great debate has been anticipated, and of the long remembrance which it will leave behind.    Renew the youth of the State.    Save property, divided against itself.    Save the multitude, endangered by its own ungovernable passions. Save the aristocracy, endangered by its own unpopular power. Save the greatest, and fairest, and most highly civilised community that ever existed, from calamities which may in a few days sweep away all the rich heritage of so many ages of wisdom and glory. The danger is terrible. The time is short. If this bill should be rejected, I pray to God that none of those who concur in rejecting it may ever remember their votes with unavailing remorse, amidst the wreck of laws, the confusion of ranks, the spoliation of property, and the dissolution of social order."

The next night brought up Peel, whose rising had been eagerly awaited. Great as Peel was in office, it seems to have been his fortune to command even greater attention and respect when just out of it ; 1830, 1835, and the years after 1846 are cases in point ; and if at this time some of his party found him unstable and unsatisfactory, they could not get on without him nor cease to admire his unrivalled parliamentary talent.[1] Althorp had said that the ministers' " desire was to place the representation in the hands of the majority of the middle classes." Peel held the bill's great defect to be that in doing so it disfranchised all below that order. " I think it a fatal objection that every link between the representative and the constituent body should be separated, so far as regards the lower classes. It is an immense advantage that there is at present no class of people, however humble, which is not entitled to a voice in the election of representatives." Not opposed to all Reform on principle, he refused to concur in a " reconstruction " of the House of Commons. " Let us never be tempted," he ended, " to resign the well-tempered freedom which we enjoy, in the ridiculous pursuit of the wild liberty which France has established. What avails that liberty which has neither justice nor wisdom for its companions—which brings neither peace nor prosperity in its train ? It was the duty of the King's Government to abstain from agitating this question at such a period as the present—to abstain from the excitement throughout this land of that conflict—(God grant it may be only a moral conflict !)—which must arise between the possessors of existing privileges, and those

---

[1] " What everybody enquires is, what line Peel will take, and though each party is confident of success in this question, it is thought to depend mainly upon the course he adopts and the sentiments he expresses " (*Greville Memoirs*, ii. 122). See *Croker Papers*, ii. 99 (Hertford to Croker), 108, 112.

to whom they are to be transferred. It was the duty of the Government to calm, not to stimulate, the fever of popular excitement. They have adopted a different course—they have sent through the land the firebrand of agitation, and no one can now recall it. Let us hope that there are limits to their powers of mischief. They have, like the giant enemy of the Philistines, lighted three hundred brands, and scattered through the country discord and dismay ; but God forbid that they should, like him, have the power to concentrate in death all the energies that belong to life, and to signalise their own destruction by bowing to the earth the pillars of that sacred edifice, which contains within its walls, according even to their own admission, ' the noblest society of freemen in the world.' "

The Lord Advocate followed on March 4, calling attention, as a Scot well might, to the change in the spirit of the people in the last five and twenty years. Referring to Peel he said : " To represent the franchise of a few bands of pot-wallopers, in certain towns, scattered thinly over the face of the country, as the vital link by which the great body of the labouring classes are connected with the Constitution, does appear to me, I confess, a very notable extravagance." He was answered by Croker, who already was acquiring that intimate knowledge of details which made him the most dangerous critic of the bill's anomalies. Manchester was to have no more members than Tavistock, he pointed out, and Bolton, with its 22,000 inhabitants, only half as many as Lord Lansdowne's pocket borough of Calne. He had telling statistics, too, to support his claim that ministers had themselves manufactured the demand for Reform. " I find that, in the year 1821, 19 petitions only were presented in favour of Reform. In the year 1822 the number was reduced to 12. In the year 1823 the number was 29. In the year 1824 there was no petition at all. In the year 1825, no petition ; in the year 1826, no petition ; in the year 1827, no petition ; in the year 1828, no petition ; in the year 1829, no petition ; and even in the session 1830, only 14 petitions presented in favour of Reform." Then came the dissolution ; the Whigs organised a clamour in the country : " 650 petitions have been the result of that appeal."

When at last Russell rose to reply, it seemed to weary listeners that every conceivable argument on either side of the question had been exhausted. " Nothing talked of, thought of, dreamt of, but Reform," wrote Greville.[1]  But in the meantime, while night after night the House of Commons echoed to the tones of a stately rhetoric too soon to pass away, and lynx-eyed Whips strove to neutralise its effect on doubtful votes, in the country all went beyond hope for the Reformers.  Petitions poured in no longer for the ballot but for the bill, the Common Council of the City taking the lead.  Probably political excitement had never been so universal before.[2]  Near Edinburgh, labourers were clubbing together to take in the *Caledonian Mercury*, two days late, for half-price, to the scanting of their porridge, and poring over the long debates.[3]  At Manchester, where a great Reform meeting had been held at the end of January, the *Guardian*, once the supporter of Peel and Wellington, was enthusiastic.  "All parties," it said of the bill, "seem pleased with it to a degree we could hardly have conceived possible."[4] At Westminster, where Place, though himself delighted with the bill, urged a meeting at the "Crown and Anchor" to demand the ballot and so prevent the ministry going back on their word, Hobhouse carried a simple vote of confidence.  "Never before," he exulted, "were the Whigs bold nor the Reformers prudent."[5] Even Richard Carlile in his cell was willing to forgive his perse- cutors for this great gift to the people.[6]  He could not drop the ballot, but sooner than endanger the bill he would consent to postpone it.  Even Hunt and O'Connell, though with ominous reservations, spoke in its favour, and Cobbett accepted the gift with gratitude.

Lord Grey himself was triumphant at his first success in

---

[1] *Memoirs*, ii. 124.

[2] "Never had a Government measure so large and active a body of supporters.  The new police were forgotten, and the punishments in- flicted on the agricultural rioters ignored" (*Courts and Cabinets*, i. 226).

[3] *Autobiography of a Working Man*, p. 152.

[4] *Manchester Guardian*, March 5.  "All parties" can hardly include the Tory *Manchester Courier*, which called the bill not Reform but Revolution, and declared that in Manchester and other large towns the £10 franchise would be equivalent to universal suffrage.

[5] *Recollections*, iv. 92 ; Wallas, *Life of Place*, p. 259.

[6] *Prompter*, March 5: "If the King and his present Ministers will persevere in carrying their proposed Reform of the House of Commons, I, Richard Carlile, will become what is commonly termed a ministerial man. . . . I will no longer quarrel with them as Whigs. . . . I am satisfied, and no reasonable man can, as I opine, be dissatisfied with this minis- terial measure."

winning the people's confidence. "All this would be delight-
ful," he said, "if I were only twenty years younger; but I have
still strength enough for this fight, and with the support of the
King and people, I cannot but think I have a good chance of
victory."[1]   In justifying the bill to Lord Wellesley he declared
its first effect had been to set aside the clamour for Radical
Reform.  Still his own colleagues were not unanimous; in
Duncannon's words, "Necessity joined him to many whose
opinions differed much from his own, and who had a great
*gulp* to make before they could agree to such a measure as
the Reform Bill."[2]   From a letter of Grey to Lansdowne, dated
March 4, it would appear that the Lord President was not free
from qualms arising from the bill's reception in the House.  Grey
pressed him to state his views to the Cabinet, declaring that for
himself personally he felt committed "without the possibility of
retreat."[3]   Wynn, the Secretary at War, found the bill altogether
too strong for his stomach, and resigned; his place was given to
Sir Henry Parnell, whose motion on the Civil List in November
had led the Duke to abandon office.

The interval before the second reading gave the opposition time
to rally.  No official union as yet took place between the Ultra-
Tories and late Ministerialists—"Peel and Wetherell[4] do not *yet*
speak," Grant told Greville,—but overtures of peace were made,
and both sections vied in opposing the bill.[5]  The Duke, still seeing
no necessity to give members to Birmingham or take them from
Old Sarum, refused to yield to public opinion, and comforted his
supporters with rumours that the Cabinet were regretting their
rashness.  Lord Grey, it was thought, could only have consented
to the bill in a fit of bad temper; the Whigs were apparently

---

[1] *Lieven Correspondence*, ii. 180.

[2] Duncannon to Durham, undated; *Lambton Papers*.

[3] *Howick Papers*.

[4] Sir Charles Wetherell (1770–1846) left the Wellington administration,
in which he had been Attorney-General, on the subject of Catholic Relief.
His attacks on his old chief, and later on the Whigs, were a curious
mixture of fierceness and humour.  He was also famous for his ill-fitting
clothes, and particularly for the "lucid interval" between his waistcoat
and his breeches.

[5] On February 22 Princess Lieven wrote to Grey: "The Ultras and
the Tories are agreed to give their support to Ministers, provided the plan
of Reform be moderate, but to fight you if you go too deeply into the
great question of the Rotten boroughs" (*Lieven Correspondence*, ii. 170;
*Greville Memoirs*, ii. 124; *Despatches*, vii. 408).

running amok ; incapable of government themselves, they had determined to make it impossible for anyone else.[1] On the advice of Wellington and Peel it was decided to meet the bill on second reading with a direct refusal, rather than with an amendment of moderate Reform—"moderate gunpowder," as Croker called it.[2]

King and Commons between them gave the ministers an anxious fortnight. On March 18 the Government were defeated on a proposed alteration in the timber duties by a majority of forty-six ; considering the triviality of this matter of detail, it is hard to acquit the Opposition of having taken this opportunity, assisted by vested interests in the timber trade, of a flank attack on the Reform Bill. Certainly all Reformers took it so, knowing the fury of the Tories with their alleged treachery. The Cabinet determined to ignore the result of a division on a side issue, but it was inevitable that they should think yet more seriously of the course to be taken, if they should fail on the second reading, or, more likely, be beaten in Committee.[3] Grey proceeded immediately to sound the King on his readiness to dissolve, should need arise, thus early forcing upon his consideration one of the two events he was most anxious to avoid. The possibility of a dissolution had, of course, been all along at the back of Ministerialists' minds ; advanced Reformers had counselled it before Christmas.[4] They believed that in spite of the influence of the days of July the Parliament of 1830 had in it too much of the old Adam to accept any but nominal Reform, and that in the circumstances it was sheer waste of time to present to it a measure it was bound to reject. However, the ministers had no wish to face so awkward a problem before they must ; only Sir James Graham, while in temporary leadership of the House, had rather indiscreetly hinted that the Cabinet would not shrink from an appeal to the country.[5]

---

[1] Hertford to Wilson, May 23 ; Add. MSS. 30,112, f. 156. Eldon to Lady F. J. Bankes ; *Life of Eldon*, iii. 123.

[2] Wellington to Buckingham, March 14 ; *Despatches*, vii. 409 (dated March 19, *Courts and Cabinets*, i. 249). Peel to Chandos, March 14 ; *Peel Papers*, ii. 179.

[3] *Correspondence*, i. 155, 162.

[4] *E.g.*, Ellice and Hobhouse ; *Recollections*, iv. 78.

[5] *Recollections*, iv. 79 : "Sir George Clerk sagely observed that, 'Perhaps the present Ministers might not have it in their power to do so, as there were two words to that bargain.'" The King himself was annoyed (*Correspondence*, i. 158, 166).

But now that the question had actually to be mooted, Grey was confronted by the King's positive refusal to dissolve in the present state of the country.[1] Hitherto William had given his ministers every support ;[2] their action as to Ireland and Foreign Affairs had won his confidence, and even now he was eager on every ground that they should continue in office. But as to a dissolution, his sense, already expressed, of the risk of a general election remained unaltered ; unprecedented political excitement might be expected to combine with the general unrest to the danger of throne and altar. The probable effect on the wild condition of Ireland caused him particular alarm. He therefore limited his support to hoping for a favourable division on the second reading. Intent, however, as Grey was to secure a majority, he continued on the 21st and 22nd, the actual days of the debate, to put the case for a dissolution before the King as strongly as possible, respectfully claiming the unfettered right to propose it if the Cabinet should so decide ; the Lord-Lieutenant would answer for the tranquillity of Ireland. But the fight was hopeless ; on the 21st Taylor had avowed his belief that the King's objections were "final and conclusive." The same day the King gave his reasons at length, amounting, as he said, to a "sacred duty" not to dissolve—an ominous declaration from a son of George III. Pointing to Duncannon's late election for Kilkenny, to the need of troops in the County Clare, and not less to the domination of the trade unions—which he persisted in regarding as formed for illegal purposes—in the north and west of England, he calculated on disastrous results if an election should take place in every constituency in the three kingdoms. Even if actual outrage were avoided, the appeal to an excited populace on a definite issue would mean the return of candidates pledged to "democratic and revolutionary" measures. And

---

[1] As a matter of fact Grey had not consulted the King officially, but had written to Sir Herbert Taylor to find out the King's opinion. Taylor showed Grey's letter to the King, who expressed his sentiments direct to Grey. But premature as the definite statement was, it was all to the good that the Prime Minister should know the true position (*Correspondence*, i. 154 ff.).

[2] At the time of the introduction of the bill, William gave Grey *carte blanche* to fill up an appointment in the Household, as a special mark of confidence. He was reported to have said in March, "I shall give these men fair play. If they can succeed, well and good ; but if they cannot, I know my resource" (Arbuthnot to Peel, March 9 ; *Peel Papers*, ii. 178).

suppose such a House elected and willing to support the Government; could it fail to come into violent conflict with the Lords —the second great evil which he was resolved to avoid? To the last objection there was indeed no answer that the King was likely to accept.

Lord Grey's next move was to forward to Sir Herbert Taylor a letter he had received from his impetuous son-in-law, in comment on the foregoing correspondence which had been circulated among the Cabinet.[1] Durham laid vehement stress on two points; first, the final rejection of the bill threatened far worse dangers than a general election, which would focus excitement on support of the ministry. "Is there an instance," he asked, "of any excitement at elections, producing occurrences unconnected with the electioneering objects of the moment?" Secondly, a new administration had a right to work with a Parliament elected under its own auspices, to use a charitable word. If the King refused the Whigs this fair demand, the country would believe him to be no sincere Reformer. In a second letter, dated March 23, Durham urged that the constant rumours of the King's refusal to dissolve were actually inclining members to oppose the Reform Bill, and so increasing the likelihood of the distasteful request being made.[2] These two powerful letters were submitted to the King the day after the division. No further result, however, ensued beyond expressions of confidence, and William's assurance—in reply to a remark of Lord Grey's—that he was in no way personally offended by Durham.

At this juncture, therefore, the ministers were faced by the King's absolute refusal to dissolve. For the first, but by no means the last time, it stood manifest that the King had not bargained in February for all that was expected of him by the Cabinet. He had shared the belief, held also by Lord Grey and others, as Taylor pointed out, that the Commons' approval of the bill might be fairly counted upon.[3] No suggestion of a dissolution

[1] Durham to Grey, 12 noon, March 22; *Correspondence*, i. 193.

[2] *Life of Durham*, i. 250. *The Standard* was remarkably well informed. On March 21 it said: "The King will not permit a dissolution. . . . He will not convulse the country for [the ministers'] convenience." And on March 23: "At so late an hour as 11 last night the King was firm in his determination not to permit a dissolution. This we can assert upon authority which has never deceived us."

[3] Grey wrote to Taylor on January 13: "If what we shall have to propose shall obtain His Majesty's sanction, I should have little fear of

had been made.  Grey seems to have been unaware throughout that his own class would take his bill for the revolutionary measure which in fact it was.  It would appear that he was as much disappointed by its reception in Parliament, as the approval it won in the country exceeded his hopes.  If in a way Grey was wise in not suggesting difficulties to the King before they were actually imminent, the policy had grave disadvantages also. At no point in his navigation could he see any long stretch of clear water ahead ;  each step of progress meant its own effort, and, still more, its own anxiety.  What Grey wanted, and at times almost seems to have thought he had secured, was *carte blanche* to carry the Reform Bill.  This a constitutional king and a son of George III would not and could not give.  Nor indeed was any alternative to this hand-to-mouth procedure open to Lord Grey.  Consummate parliamentarian as he was, he could not gauge beforehand all the possibilities of a situation which was constantly shifting according to psychological issues ranged over a field of an extent previously unknown.  Hard enough to foretell the feelings of peers and boroughmongers ; how was he to allow for the ocean waves of popular opinion now first bursting into the land-locked sea of politics ?  To terrify the nervous King with imaginary difficulties was alike inconsiderate and imprudent.

While these protracted negotiations were going on behind the scenes, the second reading of the Reform Bill had been carried in the Commons by one vote.  It is hardly possible to dispute the opinion of the third Earl Grey (the Lord Howick of 1831) that a difference of a single vote would have led to a Tory administration.[1]  The members who thronged the House on the night of March 22 did not know this ;[2] but if they had, the excitement could have been no greater.  To the last the betting was practically even.  On both sides fear was probably the dominant motive—fear of the people triumphant or enraged ; but many other considerations, noble or ignoble, had full weight.

carrying it through Parliament."  As late as February 28 he wrote to Princess Lieven : " Our calculations give us a majority of about seventy." This  last estimate is surprisingly wide of the mark (*Correspondence*, i. 52 ; *Lieven Correspondence*, ii. 176).

[1] *Correspondence*, i. 183.

[2] Duncannon told Hobhouse on March 19, rather on Sir James Graham's model, that the Cabinet was resolved, in case of necessity, to dissolve Parliament (*Recollections*, iv. 95).

Men were fighting for property which lawyers told them was theirs by chartered right ; for a princely inheritance of power ; for the old institutions of England. Their opponents believed they stood for the dawn of a new era superseding the night of corruption ; in other words for the dethronement of the Tories. Party spirit and the joy of battle had worked these feelings to a fever of enthusiasm, when at three o'clock in the morning the Speaker put the question to the fullest House ever gathered for a division at Westminster.[1] The scene which followed has been painted once for all by Macaulay. " It was like seeing Cæsar stabbed in the Senate House, or seeing Oliver taking the mace from the table ; a sight to be seen only once, and never to be forgotten." According to the practice of the old House of Commons, the Ayes, in this case the Tories, marched into the lobby, while the Noes remained in the House and were told first. The Ayes were then counted as they filed in, and as the House gradually filled it was seen how perilously close the numbers must be. At length the counting finished, but still the result was doubtful. " The tellers scarcely got through the crowd ; for the House was thronged up to the table, and all the floor was fluctuating with heads like the pit of a theatre. But you might have heard a pin drop as Duncannon read the numbers. Then again the shouts broke out, and many of us shed tears. I could scarcely refrain. And the jaw of Peel fell ; and the face of Twiss was as the face of a damned soul ; and Herries looked like Judas taking his necktie off for the last operation. We shook hands, and clapped each other on the back, and went out laughing, crying, and huzzaing into the lobby. And no sooner were the outer doors opened than another shout answered that within the House. All the passages, and the stairs into the waiting-rooms, were thronged by people who had waited till four in the morning to know the issue. We passed through a narrow lane between two thick masses of them ; and all the way down they were shouting and waving their hats, till we got into the open air."[2]

It is an interesting fact, particularly in view of later history, that the bill was carried on this its first and supreme trial in the

---

[1] The most urgent whips had been issued, at least on the Ministerialist side. That sent to Hobhouse is bound up in Add. MSS. 36,466.

[2] Macaulay to Ellis ; Sir George Trevelyan's *Life and Letters of Lord Macaulay*, Popular Edition, p. 147.

Commons by the votes of the Irish members. England and Scotland were against it, though in England the close boroughs only just outweighed the open boroughs and the counties.[1] But the one vote was all-important.[2] It gave Grey a respite, and the King an opportunity to change his mind should circumstances alter. The ministers' plan could no longer be scoffed at as visionary and absurd, when it had received the sanction of a full House of Commons. And it was plain, as Durham observed, that only the possession of the usual Government influence was needed, to secure a working majority for the bill.[3] For the moment, however, Parliament had done its work. After a Lords' debate on the 28th, which gave Durham and other Whig peers an opportunity of supporting the Reform Bill, and Wellington one of repeating his objection to all Reform, both Houses adjourned till after Easter, when the Commons would go into Committee.

In the country the news of the second reading of the bill crowned the enthusiasm which had never waned since its introduction. Edinburgh, Glasgow, Birmingham, and other large towns were illuminated ; at Glasgow the novel magnificence of gas lights was immensely admired ; sometimes, as at Newark, the rejoicings took the form of burning the anti-Reform member in effigy. At Dundee a riot was caused by the magistrates' order to put out the Reformers' bonfire.[4] Public demonstrations in favour of the bill, which had been common on its first appearance, now became general. Twenty-two county meetings at least were held and passed resolutions in the ministers' support.[5] An enterprise of more practical promise was the formation, a

---

[1] The amendment was lost by 301 votes to 302 : England, 241 to 238 (Counties, 27 to 53 ; Close boroughs, 168 to 83 ; Open boroughs, 42 to 93) ; Scotland, 26 to 13 ; Ireland, 36 to 53 (Counties, 21 to 40).

[2] " A dreadful Race," wrote Graham to Durham, " won by an accident at last" (*Lambton Papers*). The accident was Calcraft's (or Sir Andrew Agnew's) going over at the last moment (see *Memoir of Althorp*, p. 303).

[3] Durham to Grey, March 23 ; *Life of Durham*, i. 249.

[4] Airlie to Melbourne, March 31 : " Very bad and damnable doctrines have been set forth among the people as to *their rights*, and it is now strongly impressed on them that, as they have no voice in the Election of a member of Parliament, it is improper that they should be called on to serve in the militia " (*H. O.* 102. 41).

[5] *Bury and Norwich Post*, April 13.

week before the second reading debate, of the Parliamentary Candidates Society.[1] This association, of which Place was the moving spirit, while it enjoyed the patronage of such men as Bentham and Hume, was intended to provide a bureau for supplying constituencies with suitable candidates, and to make public the conduct of sitting members. It was an idea after Bentham's own heart, though utterly opposed to the old theory of the dignity of representatives.[2] The society never came to much ; Place attributed its failure to the incapacity of the gentlemanly amateurs he was forced to work with. It was in any case too far removed from the conditions under which elections were actually carried on, and demanded more organisation over the country than the Radicals of the day possessed ; but it is interesting as an early attempt to introduce the central caucus into English politics.

The Radical press continued to urge its readers to do all they could to support the Government in carrying its instalment of Reform ; it was outside influence which had extorted the present measure, and by outside influence it must be secured and improved on. Cobbett, more optimistic than most, believed that, now the long frost had broken, the swollen waters would sweep on unchecked, with all good things borne gradually nearer on the tide. " Lord Grey," he said, ". . . who is the real and sole author of this Reform, has never had any hand in any of those measures which have caused our sufferings." [3] Even at the Rotunda a meeting of five hundred assembled in welcome to the bill, and terrible threats were held out to the boroughmongers if they should delay it for as much as three months.[4] Woe betide the Queen if, as report now had it, she was using her influence against the people.[5] The *Westminster*

[1] Add. MSS. 27,789, f. 330.

[2] The *Standard* commented on its Address : " Nine-tenths of the £10 householders are instinctively Benthamites and Jonesites, though few of them have perhaps heard the name of the sage or the Radical colonel. All that they want is a point of union, and a common leader ; this the Parliamentary Candidate Office will supply" (Quoted, Add. MSS. 27,789, f. 347).

[3] *Twopenny Trash*, April.

[4] *Prompter*, March 26.

[5] *Morning Herald*, April 6. We learn from letters of Lord Grey that the Queen was much hurt by these unfounded rumours now beginning. " I believe implicitly," he wrote, " what Taylor says, as to her not wishing to interfere, and that the King, if she were so inclined, would not let her.

O

*Review*, representing more respectable thought, confessed that
the Whigs had gone as far as was possible without provoking
the aristocracy to civil war, and stood deservedly high in the
people's favour. "There is no doubt that the estrangement
which had long been growing between the Whigs and the community at large, has, by one energetic step . . . been removed.
The Whigs are now as they were in 1688, the acknowledged
leaders of the community against the common enemy."[1] They
might look forward to as long continuance in office as they liked,
with a constitutional opposition of ultra-liberals. There were
others, however, who prophesied that the Whigs would drop
out, as a result of their own bill, leaving the Tories and Radicals
to dispute the field.[2]

Nevertheless, with the exception of those few who knew
how short-lived their success promised to be unless the King
changed his fixed opinions, the Whigs were fully satisfied with
their position. It was largely rumoured that the Tories meant
to make no fight in Committee; while, if they did, the Cabinet
was supposed to have full permission to dissolve at pleasure.[3]
The City was by no means entirely with them, but an influential
meeting of merchants and bankers had pronounced for the bill
in the Egyptian Hall, and on April 4 the ministers were entertained at a Guildhall banquet. As a good omen of old feuds
forgiven, Thomas Hardy, the veteran Reformer, declared himself "now for the first time a ministerial man," and a supporter
of the Government which was behaving in the very way which
Pitt and Dundas had called treasonable in the black days of 1794.[4]
Grey himself had good reason to be pleased with the King's
loyalty, as shown by his immediate dismissal from the Household
of two members who had voted against the second reading.
He also had occasion to remark on the Queen's gracious manner

But these annoyances may ultimately irritate, and do considerable mischief" (To Durham and Lady Grey, April 7; *Lambton* and *Howick
Papers*).

[1] *Westminster*, April 1831.

[2] *Greville Memoirs*, ii. 127.

[3] Howick to Charles Grey, April 4: "I really do begin to think there
is a chance of our carrying a Reform bill through, even without a dissolution; at first I thought that with so small a majority on the second reading, it would be impossible to get through Committee, but our enemies are
beginning to see that it is absolutely impossible to prevent its being carried
at last" (*Howick Papers ; Morning Herald, e.g.* March 24, 29).

[4] Hardy to Hobhouse, April 2 ; Add. MSS. 36,466.

towards him.[1] His correspondence with the King during these weeks was mainly taken up with foreign affairs ; it appeared that Palmerston's long efforts to keep out of an embroilment with France over Belgium were likely at length to prove successful. The universal concord seemed only marred by the disgust of the boroughmongers and a few workmen in the north for whom Hunt claimed to speak. And on the Continent the insurgent Poles were enjoying the one short spell of success which rewarded their hopeless valour.

The Tories had been disappointed by their defeat, but were not despondent. Even should things go wrong in the Commons, the King they believed, and the Lords they knew to be safe.[2] But, after all, a majority of one vote could hardly carry the bill through Committee, and it might be actually an advantage, in view of popular feeling, to have defeated it on a point of detail, not of principle. Peel was anxious for an early victory, and hoped to secure it on the Government's proposal to lower the number of English members, while increasing those from Scotland and Ireland.[3] Here the party would be on strong ground, especially after their implied approval of Vyvyan's moderate Reform scheme. Even Eldon wrote to his brother : " All the petitioners, or many of them, whose petitions I presented against the Catholic Relief Bill, are petitioners for the Reform Bill ; for, say they, a House of Commons which could vote for that Emancipation Bill, cannot be such a House of Commons as ought any longer to exist." [4] But the Duke of Wellington still held out ; he refused to see the necessity of any Reform, declaring that he at least would never sit in Parliament again if the bill should pass.[5] On the question of reunion, too, he was not encouraging. It might well seem natural that the two wings of the Tories should shake hands in the presence of the enemy ; and the influence of the Dukes of Cumberland and Buckingham was at work to unite Wellington and Eldon.[6] But the Duke believed that both sections would work better at the prime object

[1] Grey to Lady Grey, April 7 ; *Howick Papers.*
[2] *Standard*, March 23.
[3] Peel to Croker, April 15 ; *Croker Papers*, ii. 114.
[4] *Life of Eldon*, iii. 126.
[5] Wellington to Buckingham, March 24 ; *Courts and Cabinets*, i. 261.
[6] Cumberland to Buckingham, March 31, April 8 ; *Courts and Cabinets*, i. 272, 279.

of defeating the Reform Bill, if their hands were unfettered by any permanent entente ; he therefore refused to make any advances, though regretting the existence of the breach.[1] Croker regretted that Peel also made little effort to heal the schism, and from other sources there were complaints of his cold unsatisfactory aloofness.[2]

On April 18 Lord John Russell explained the changes the Government proposed to introduce in the bill.   Several boroughs from Schedules A and B were reprieved, certain new towns were enfranchised, and eight counties received an extra member— making the total of the House 627 instead of 596.   He did not fail to point out that of the members representing those counties and towns, which Peel had chosen in 1829 as typical of public opinion, sixty-eight had voted for the second reading of the Reform Bill, and only fifteen against.   The battle in Committee was fought on General Gascoyne's motion that the number of members for England and Wales should not be diminished ; this would mean that, if additions were to be made, as the bill pro-posed, to Scotland and Ireland, the number of the entire house must be raised—a step awkward in itself and contrary to the King's wish expressed in January.   It was believed that the motion was a deliberate attack by the Opposition on the prin-ciple of the bill, and the Cabinet, apparently against the advice of Brougham and Russell, had resolved to stake its fortunes on the issue.[3]

Grey had prepared the King for such an event, and received the reply that nothing had altered the old objections to a dissolution.[4]   The defeat of the Government by eight votes on the night of the 19th pointed therefore to their immediate resignation.   Brougham actually wrote out a memorandum for his successor in the Court of Chancery.[5]   In the morning the Cabinet met and drew up a formal minute advising a dissolution,

---

[1] Wellington to Lord Falmouth, April 3 ; *Despatches*, vii. 426.

[2] Croker to Hertford, April 19 ; *Croker Papers*, ii. 115.   *Greville Memoirs*, ii. 134.

[3] " He [Gascoyne] afterwards confessed to me," wrote Hobhouse (*Recollections*, iv. 101), " that his motion had been agreed upon as the best way of defeating the Reform Bill ; yet this was denied by him, and by others, in the course of the debate." *Life of Graham*, i. 109.

[4] *Correspondence*, i. 219.

[5] *Memoirs*, iii. 110.

and this Grey submitted to the King.[1]  William asked a day to think over it.  Next morning a lengthy document, " verbosa et grandis epistola," came from St. James's ; the King declared that his objections to the proposal had not been removed by the assurances of his ministers.  He had to balance the rival disadvantages of a change of Government in the disturbed state of Europe, and a general election in the disturbed state of the United Kingdom, particularly of Ireland, where Lord Anglesey's pledge that the peace could be kept seemed hard to reconcile with his wish for coercive legislation.  Notwithstanding, swayed by the importance from the diplomatic point of view of a continuity of administration, and by the unlikelihood of any other stable government being formed, he had decided to acquiesce in a dissolution as the least of two evils.  Lastly, he urged that the bill to be introduced next session should be if anything more moderate than the defunct one.[2]

Though the deadlock of May next year was longer, more dramatic, and fraught with greater momentary issues to the country at large, Miss Martineau is probably right in saying that the real crisis of the Reform struggle was in April 1831.[3] The fate of the ministry and of the bill, which had not yet attained the place in the nation's enthusiasm which it held a year later, hung for twenty-four hours on the decision of a man whose natural common-sense was warped by an ignorant and irrational fear of the working classes.  He had not been in Ireland, yet he set up his own judgment as to the probability of riots there against the assertions of those on the spot.[4]  Lord Grey now had borne in upon him the bitter truth of the words Fox wrote to him thirty years before.  " The Court, without any invidious consideration of particular characters, is a miserable foundation to build a system of Liberty and Reform upon." [5] If William had sent for the Tories, they would of course have introduced a measure of moderate Reform ; even so, both in

---

[1] *Correspondence*, i. 225.

[2] *Ibid.*, i. 214, 227–232.

[3] On January 21, 1832, Wellington wrote to Lord Howe : " From the moment that the King dissolved the late Parliament in April last, I have considered His Majesty as exactly in the position in which King Charles I stood when he consented to the bill to deprive himself of the power of dissolving " (*Despatches*, viii. 169).

[4] *Correspondence*, i. 229.

[5] *Memoirs and Correspondence*, iii. 341, quoted in Mr. Hammond's *Fox*.

the House and out, they would have had a strong opposition to face, but there would hardly have been anything of the nature of organised revolt at the time, though probably events would soon have produced one. Certainly the next Reform Bill would have come considerably before 1867. The third Lord Grey wrote of the "altered circumstances" in which the King eventually assented to the dissolution.[1] At first sight it appears that very little change had taken place. It is possible that the delicate state of relations with Belgium may have played some part ; but the deciding factor seems to have been the Government's majority on the second reading division, which made it probable that a new administration would have a thorny path. This was the only important consideration not present before the division of March 22. It was William's duty as a constitutional king to keep the country supplied with a government, alike for the sake of home and foreign affairs. In the present case the difficulty of forming an adequate new one supported the maxim that a change is as such undesirable.[2]

What, however, must strike a modern reader as strangest is the fact that the King for some time refused to allow his ministers to appeal to the country, while admitting that they had "the feeling of the people avowedly and manifestly in their favour."[3] This is only another proof that William's views of what was constitutional differed widely from those that would be accepted to-day. He did not admit the doctrine of the people's sovereignty in any sense, nor was he at all prepared to be a mere puppet in the hands of his servants. On one occasion he embarrassed such a good Whig as Lord Grey by quoting with approval a sentiment from the *Patriot King* : "As every new modification in a scheme of government and of national policy is of great importance, and requires more and deeper consideration than the warmth and hurry and rashness of party conduct admit, the duty of a Prince seems to require that he should render by his influence the proceedings more orderly and more deliberate, even when he approves the end to which they are directed."[4] In short, it was impossible for William IV

---

[1] *Correspondence*, i. 183.

[2] For the King's defence of his action see *Memoirs of Baron Stockmar*, i. 317.

[3] *Correspondence*, i. 164.

[4] *Ibid.*, i. 382.

to hand over his political conscience altogether to his ministers ;
he was certainly not encouraged to do so by the appeals addressed
to him by Opposition peers who should have known better. He
did hold himself morally responsible for the government of the
country ; here lies the chief point of difference between his and
the modern idea of kingship.

Even from the modern point of view, William had a case
for refusing to dissolve. Grey himself was extremely apologetic in urging it. The Parliament the King was expected to
dismiss had hardly been in existence for six months ; if it were
argued that the popular enthusiasm which had changed all, and
on which Grey relied, had only arisen since the introduction of
the bill, the King might reply that a reaction such as the Tories
expected could easily set in in as short a time. The fact was
that there was hardly any precedent for so sudden an outburst ; in 1831 it took the place of that party feeling which is
now kept alive by elaborate organisation. but it was no ordinary
feature of the time, even at a general election.

The dissolution was hastened by the events of the night of
the 21st. The news of the King's conversion had got about
in the course of the day, and in both Houses the angry Opposition resolved to make a final desperate stand. In the Upper
House Lord Wharncliffe, a Canningite who professed moderate
Reform but had vehemently opposed the ministerial measure,
gave notice of an address praying the Crown not to dissolve.
In the Commons, with the same object, a division was carried
against the ministers, postponing the report of the Ordnance
estimates already voted. Althorp thereupon sent Lord Howick
and Charles Wood, the Prime Minister's Secretary, from the
House to Cleveland Row, where Grey and others of the Cabinet
were dining with Durham ; they were to say that in his opinion
the dissolution should no longer be delayed. On receiving
Althorp's message Grey wrote on the spot to the King, urging
that the prorogation should take place next day. The King
agreed, in a note written the same night, and fixed noon for a
meeting of the Council, so that orders might be made out for
proroguing Parliament by Commission ; at 11.30 he would
receive Lord Grey in audience.[1]

---

[1] *Correspondence*, i. 234. Much valuable information is given here in
a note by the 3rd Earl Grey (the Lord Howick of 1831), who states that his
recollections were confirmed by Wood, his fellow messenger.

But circumstances caused yet another change of plan.  Lord
Wharncliffe's motion for an address to the Crown against a
dissolution was now down for the next day in the Lords ; and
ministers had learnt from an official of the House that the peers
were likely, in accordance with their privilege in such case, to
carry Wharncliffe's motion before admitting the Lords Commissioners.[1]  Such an address would not of course affect the Crown's
right to dissolve ; but the breach between the Houses, so much
dreaded by the King, would be a fact long before there was any
need for it, and the new House of Commons would be faced by
the certainty of a conflict.  Brougham thought the altered circumstances would have induced the King to revoke his consent
to dissolve.  The only hope was to persuade him to prorogue
Parliament in person, as the Lords could not keep their sovereign
waiting at the door.  Consequently a Cabinet was summoned to
meet early on the 22nd ; the objections of the timid to the
change of tactics were finally quashed, Brougham tells us, when
he " appealed to the Duke of Richmond, and asked him if he had
ever seen a council of war held on the field just before going
into action ; he said, ' By God ! never ; neither I nor anyone
else.' "[2]  Grey and the Chancellor then went in to the King.[3]

Of this interview many stories are told.  The ministers were
most apologetic, but as soon as William heard of the Lords'
proposed interference with his prerogative, he consented at
once to go.  There were difficulties, however, about making
the correct arrangements, as the House was to meet at two
o'clock.  Peers had to be found to carry the Sword and Cap of
Maintenance, the Crown had to be fetched from the Tower, and
an escort of cavalry was wanted.  The Life Guards at Knights-
bridge not arriving in time, Brougham took it on himself to
order up the troop on duty at the Horse Guards.[4]  When Lord

[1] Brougham says he was told by William Courtenay, Clerk of the
Parliaments in the House of Lords (*Memoirs*, iii. 113).

[2] *Memoirs*, iii. 114.  Though in a matter tending to his own glorifica-
tion Brougham's word is not wholly to be trusted, we can at least take
from him the fact that this Cabinet was held.

[3] Mr. S. J. Reid (*Life of Durham*, i. 257) says that Durham was also
present ; but there seems to be no authority for this, and it is probable
that Mr. Reid, whose account here is rather confused, fails to distinguish
between the private audience and the Cabinet and Council, at which
Durham was no doubt present.

[4] Brougham's account is confirmed by Lord Howick on the authority
of an officer in the regiment (*Correspondence*, i. 236).

Albemarle, snatched from his breakfast by Durham, declared there was no time to plait the cream-coloured ponies' manes, the King vowed that if needed he would go in a hackney coach. Though we have not first-hand evidence for this famous remark, Creevey says it was told him by Grey himself and it was certainly current the next day.[1]  A speech from the Throne was hurriedly prepared, and circulars were sent from the Treasury informing peers that the King would come to the House soon after three to prorogue Parliament.[2]

The events of the afternoon should be surprising to any who may cherish the illusion that the aristocratic unreformed Parliament was a temple of stately calm and decorum.  In the Commons the Speaker took his seat in full robes at 2.30 ; within a few minutes the House was in an uproar.  After Sir Richard Vyvyan had made a fiery speech interrupted by calls to order, derisive cheers, and finally the guns from the Tower announcing the King's approach, Burdett and Peel, scarlet with excitement, struggled for a hearing.  The Speaker, equally furious, and the leader of the House also attempted to speak ; half the members present rose to their feet and surged across the floor, while the whole House shouted in a turmoil of confusion.  At length the unruly scene was interrupted by Black Rod summoning the House to the Lords.  Here party feeling ran no less high : the peers had assembled, some in robes, some not, at two o'clock, but the Chancellor did not arrive till twenty minutes to three, when prayers were read.  For half an hour there was an exhibition of violent temper and excitement, the Whigs striving to prevent the infuriated Opposition from carrying Wharncliffe's address before the arrival of Majesty.  A noble marquis shook his fist at a noble duke ; the Lord Chancellor was hooted by the Tories ; lovely peeresses trembled for their lives.  If, as Disraeli tells us, " there is scarcely a less dignified entity than a patrician in a panic," a patrician in a passion cannot be far behind.  Brougham, who had left what he describes as a " bear-garden exhibition " to await the King, added to the hubbub by suddenly " skipping in " and shouting out that the Commons

---

[1] *Creevey Papers*, p. 571 ; *Correspondence*, i. 236 ; *Recollections*, iv. 108, where Hobhouse adds that William replied to Grey's apologies in appropriately nautical metaphor : " Never mind that, I am always at single anchor."

[2] *Standard*, April 24.

had refused supplies. Order was only restored by the actual appearance of the King, with his crown awry, attended by the Officers of State. His speech prorogued Parliament with a view to its immediate dissolution.[1]

The dissolution of April 1831 aroused fiercer extremes of political excitement than can often have attended the act of a constitutional monarch. The Tories saw in it the sudden shattering of their power in the Commons, and, worse, a precedent of most pernicious force.[2] Forbidden by the law of their being to blame the sovereign personally, they turned with bitter indignation on the ministers, whom they might fairly accuse of having appealed from Philip sober to Philip drunk. They had committed a measure of deepest importance, affecting the very fabric of the Constitution and requiring the subtlest criticism of statesman and publicist, to the crude judgment of potwallopers and ragamuffins, whose god was their belly or their pocket. The new members would be delegates indeed, returned by the influence of brickbats and bludgeons to swallow a bill they could not digest.[3] The words of the King's speech left no doubt as to the issue on which the elections would be fought. " I have been induced to resort to this measure for the purpose of ascertaining the sense of my people, in the way in which it can be most constitutionally and authentically expressed, on the expediency of making such changes in the representation as circumstances may appear to require." Out of their own mouths Tories condemned the recreant ministers, whose language on the dissolution of 1807 was exactly applicable to the present case. " Why then," Grey had asked of the ministers of the day, " did they take this step ? In order that an appeal should be made to the people, as it was stated in His Majesty's speech, while recent events were fresh in their recollection—in other words, during the prevalence of that base cry, which it was hoped

---

[1] See *Recollections*, iv. 105; *Greville Memoirs*, ii. 135; *Brougham Memoirs*, iii. 117; Martineau, *History of England*, ii. 35.

[2] The Duke discouraged the idea of a meeting of Peers to protest against the dissolution. " We have been dissolved by the King as a House of Parliament. Our character of Peers continues, and we shall meet in that character without his authority, and contrary to his inclination, to discuss his last act in relation to ourselves. This will not look or sound well." The rest of the letter is a fine example of the Duke's loyalty and nobility of temper (Wellington to Wharncliffe, April 23 ; *Despatches*, vii. 432).

[3] See *Courts and Cabinets*, i. 294.

would have an influence on the Elections." " Is it not clear,"
Holland had demanded on the same occasion, " that that was a
most improper period for a dissolution of Parliament, when,
instead of a cool and dispassionate appeal to the people, it could
only be an appeal to their inflamed prejudices and passions ? " [1]
The ministers' behaviour in the late crisis did not tend to inspire
confidence ; Richmond had insulted the dignity of the peers by
vexatious obstruction, and Brougham was accused of having
openly lied, in asserting that the Commons had stopped supplies,
when they had merely prevented the vote on the Ordnance estimates from being reported on a certain night.[2] The Tories
faced what they considered a sham general election with sullen
resentment ; the necessity of union was becoming more and
more patent.

In the country generally the dissolution was received with
unbounded delight ; since the division of April 19 it had been
hoped for, and Reformers were urged to petition in its favour.[3]
For once a general election would have interest for ordinary
men. Those of the last thirty years had been dull and formal
affairs, fought as a rule on vague unmeaning issues, and appealing little to any passions but those of greed and local rivalry.
Election after election, the same men had sat for the same constituencies, which perhaps they never visited, and as often as
not without a contest ; now things would be very different, and
the wildest excitement was let loose. The alarms of the timid,
however, were unfounded, and the Funds remained steady.[4]
London was brilliantly illuminated, with the usual danger to un-
sympathetic windows ; those of Apsley House were not spared.
The King himself won enormous popularity on both sides
of the Tweed ; he was given credit for being an enthusiastic
Reformer, and the bill was almost considered his own handi-
work, so closely was he identified with it.[5] The Opposition
were exasperated by this general persuasion, which they said
had been intentionally, and most unconstitutionally, created or
at least encouraged by ministers. But in truth passion ran so

[1] *Parl. Debates*, ix. 620 ; quoted by Lord Wynford, October 7, 1831.
[2] Brougham maintained that he had not exaggerated the effect of the
manœuvre (*Memoirs*, iii. 117).
[3] *Times*, April 21.          [4] *Morning Herald*, April 23.
[5] The common election cry on the Whig side was : " Vote for the two
Bills."

high that whatever course William had taken would have been represented as a party act. For this both parties were responsible, but even more so the tradition of partisan kingship bequeathed by the two last monarchs. The politics of the seventy years just passed had been so much influenced by the personal opinions of the prince, that enormous weight was given to the least indications of William's own sentiments. The dramatic prorogation confirmed the existing desire to idolise him on the part of the masses ; having once assumed the character of the keen Reformer, he had to pay the price of his popularity by being henceforth judged by an entirely fictitious standard. Between the two parties trying to give a political sense to everything he did, William was in a most awkward position. Strict impartiality was demanded in theory, but in practice so many matters, great and small, from a dissolution to a riband, were left to the King's personal choice that it was extremely hard for him to satisfy all parties. Even in Queen Victoria's reign some acts of the sovereign were hotly canvassed, but the modern exalted ideal of the Crown's superiority to party must be attributed to her splendid example. In 1831 the imperfect development of ministerial responsibility forced the Crown into prominence, and all William's conscientious desire to do his duty did not save him from criticism. He was naturally no less disgusted by the panegyrics of the Radicals ; [1] as though to prove their falsehood, he wrote to Lord Grey two days after the dissolution, pressing him to modify the Reform Bill with a view to conciliating its opponents as far as possible, now that the victory had been won. He repeated his fears of a spirit in the country hostile to property and the class system, fostered " by the poisonous influence of a licentious and unobstructed press." [2] The King was also much annoyed at the riotous scenes on the night of the illumination, for which the Lord Mayor was generally though wrongly held responsible. Lord Grey's answer to the letter was cautious and non-committal ; he was at this time rather perturbed at the King's attitude towards him and to the Reform question, which he was inclined to attribute to the

---

[1] " I revoke and recall everything that I have published, or that may be in the course of publication, to the disadvantage of this king. I think he has done all that a good man in his situation could do " (*Prompter,* April 30).

[2] *Correspondence,* i. 239 ff.

## JOHN GILPIN!!!

Away went Gilpin, neck or naught;
Away went hat and wig;
He little dream'd when he set out
Of running such a rig.

unrealised influence of the Princesses and others of the Court.[1] The fact was that both Grey and the King were suffering from the strain of the last few weeks, nor is it surprising if they had got slightly on one another's nerves. There is evidence that neither of them was very well; the tension had been more or less continuous since the middle of January, and the political atmosphere was one of constant excitement.

But there was little rest in parliamentary circles. Both sides prepared themselves, as never before, for what might be the last electoral campaign under the old rules; they made the most of the fact, and enormous sums were spent. The London press exhorted the provincial papers to do their utmost. The Reformers, who had started early, made ready to contest seats hitherto unchallenged. Cobbett urged his readers to sink all personal feelings of hostility to the ministers in their determination to return none but Reformers, thus disappointing those who hoped the Radicals would follow Hunt in disapproving of the bill.[2] The Whig borough owners sacrificed personal to party interest, and returned members pledged to Schedule A; wealthy men contributed largely in cash and enabled Edward Ellice, the Patronage Secretary to the Treasury and broker-general in boroughs, to buy up a handsome number of votes.[3] £15,000 had already been subscribed from Brooks's, when a finance committee, of which Hobhouse was a member, met at the "Crown and Anchor" to organise the so-called Loyal and Patriotic Fund, to which Brougham, Durham, and Palmerston among others contributed for the expenses of the election.[4] On the Tory side, it was estimated, over £400,000 was spent: the Duke of Northumberland alone was believed to have promised £100,000 to support his county candidate.[5]

[1] Grey to Taylor, May 8 (*Correspondence* i. 259); to Holland, April 26: "I am not without suspicion that the opponents of the Government contrive, unsuspected by him, to convey to him their notion through the numerous channels which his constant entourage opens to them" (*Howick Papers*).

[2] Add. MSS. 27,789, f. 296.

[3] Porritt, i. 322; Le Marchant, *Memoir of Althorp*, p. 319. An instance may be taken from Greville (ii. 140): Lord Yarborough sold the four Holmes boroughs in the Isle of Wight to the Government for £4000. Lord Cleveland subscribed £10,000.

[4] Add. MSS. 36,466; *Recollections*, iv. 109.

[5] Add. MSS. 27,789, ff. 390–394. Grey to Charles Grey, May 2; *Howick Papers*.

The sinews of war thus provided, Reformers threw themselves eagerly into the contest. The cities of London and Westminster led off by returning six bill-men; Burdett hurried off to Leicester for work on the hustings. The Radical colonel Evans had been promised £1000 towards contesting Preston; but finding on his arrival there that he had appeared too late for any chance of success, he galloped down with relays of coaches and four to Kent, where he and John Nicholson managed to win Dover and "that sink of corruption, Maidstone." [1] At Bury St. Edmunds, where thirty electors voted, a real fight took place for the first time in living memory, resulting in the defeat of one anti-Reformer. [2] The excitement enabled the notorious freemen of Sudbury to raise their figure to £10 a head, and the neighbouring villages were illuminated as Reform triumphed. Western pocket boroughs, in some cases, gave their patrons no little trouble. At Cricklade a Reformer was returned in the teeth of the boroughmongers of the district and the High Church and Evangelical clergy; at Malmesbury near by, the two successful nominees of the patron refrained from entering the town, where they were burnt in effigy; a candidate was also run by certain of the Stroud Political Union, but the thirteen electors, of whom six were illiterate, earned their yearly payments of fifty or thirty pounds, as the case might be, by voting straight. In Pembrokeshire, where the inhabitants could not read English papers, it was felt that the Tory, who was also Lord-Lieutenant, might pride himself on having a nomination county. [3]

---

[1] Add. MSS. 36,466.

[2] *Bury and Norwich Post*, May 4.

[3] Add. MSS. 36,466. A side-light is thrown on rotten borough politics by the following letter of J. A. Roebuck, the historian, to " Father Place," dated May 2, 1832 : " The inhabitants [of Christchurch, Hants] are all stout Reformers. Why ? Because they hate Sir G. Rose. . . . But they by no means desire to be represented in the hope of being well governed. What they desire is to be well paid by the candidates, and for this reason they dislike the ballot. Their short-sightedness is wonderful; they hope to pass from the hands of Sir G. Rose into those of Sir G. Papps, who is the greatest landowner here " (Add. MSS. 35,149, f. 139). Excellent descriptions of elections in the last years of the unreformed parliament are given in Mr. Stanley Weyman's *Chippinge*, and of course *Pickwick*. Jeffrey gives a good account of his election for Malton, Lord Fitzwilliam's borough, in April of this year in a letter to Cockburn (*Life of Jeffrey*, ii. 234).

In the English county elections the anti-Reformers were smitten hip and thigh. Yorkshire returned a squad of four ministerialists, Lord Lonsdale lost one of the Westmorland seats, and in Northumberland, where even the working people had offered to subscribe out of their wages, Lord Howick won a blood-less victory.[1] Durham had shortly before returned a Reformer, in spite of the Londonderry interest, the non-resident freemen strangely enough voting Whig. In the eastern counties, too, Reform was doing famously, with or without funds, by the efforts of itinerant organisers. Tavistock wrote of the " most glorious day I ever saw," from Bedfordshire, where the freeholders were running a second Reform candidate themselves. " You have raised a noble spirit in the old country," another brother con-gratulated Lord John Russell, " far beyond anything I could have imagined. I know no sight so grand, as a People roused from their apathy, determined to assert their rights and free-dom." [2] Lord Strathavon was rejected in Huntingdonshire, though a Reformer, because he would not pledge himself to the bill ; his opponent was the first independent candidate who had been elected after a contest since 1688, and that in face of coercion applied to his rival's tenants. Russell himself was invited to stand for at least three counties, and was eventu-ally returned for Devonshire.[3] Finally, out of eighty-two knights of the shire elected, seventy-six supported the bill.

The cause was even more fiercely favoured in Scotland, if with less success.[4] What would in England be called the uneducated classes have generally shown in Scotland a more intelligent interest in abstract political questions, as southern candidates for Scottish seats discover to their cost on the platform.[5] So,

[1] Howick to Lady Grey, May 2 ; *Howick Papers*.

[2] *Early Correspondence*, ii. 19.

[3] Sydney Smith wrote to Lady Holland : " I met John Russell at Exeter. The people along the road were very much disappointed by his smallness. I told them he was much larger before the Bill was thrown out, but was reduced by excessive anxiety about the people. This brought tears to their eyes " (*Memoirs of Sydney Smith*, ii. 322).

[4] The votes of the Scottish members were almost equally divided on the third reading of the bill in the new Parliament. The *Scotsman* had hoped for a majority for the bill of 24 to 21 (*Manchester Guardian*, May 23).

[5] Alexander Somerville, who joined the Scots Greys in 1831, observes that, whereas few privates in an English or Irish regiment could write, nearly every man in a Scottish corps was a writer or accountant (*Auto-biography*, p. 188).

in the Reform struggle, a disproportionate amount of petitions
came from north of the border, and feeling was marked by
a passionate intensity which often broke out in violence.[1]
The south-west was especially turbulent, and anxious Lords-
Lieutenants warned Melbourne of the likelihood of riots and
worse at the elections. Lord Queensberry asked for troops to
be sent to Dumfries " in consequence of the very great excitement among the middle and lower classes composing the
boroughs of this county." The Sheriff of Lanarkshire found
it " difficult to describe the degree of political excitement which
exists in the mind of a large portion " of the west of Scotland.
It was the same in the counties of Stirling, Dumbarton, and Ayr,
where the mob sacked a house before the Dragoons could dis-
perse them.[2] At Glasgow a great Reform procession of 50,000
paraded the city. On the Border the unruly behaviour of
Jedburgh and Selkirk cast a shadow over the last days of Sir
Walter Scott, who, in spite of growing weakness of body and
mind, had in the winter written vigorously against Reform, and
had more recently been hooted for his opinions on a Jedburgh
platform. He suffered the same discourtesy at the Roxburgh-
shire election, which he insisted on attending. " We found the
town in a most tempestuous state," wrote Lockhart ; " in fact,
it was almost wholly in the hands of a disciplined rabble, chiefly
weavers from Hawick, who marched up and down with drums
and banners, and then, after filling the Court-hall, lined the
streets, grossly insulting everyone who did not wear the reforming colours. Sir Walter's carriage, as it advanced towards the
house of the Shortreed family, was pelted with stones." For
all this display, the anti-Reformer was returned by forty votes
to nineteen. In Scott's own words, " The day passed with
much clamour and no mischief. Henry Scott was re-elected—
for the last time, I suppose. *Troja fuit*—I left the borough in
the midst of abuse, and the gentle hint of *Burk Sir Walter*.
Much obliged to the brave lads of Jeddart."[3]    It was no shallow

---

[1] On September 23 the Lord Advocate said in the Commons : " Scotland had little better than 2 millions of inhabitants, England and Ireland
had 22 or 23, yet the petitions from Scotland in favour of Reform were
more numerous than those received from all the rest of the Empire put
together " (*Hansard*, 3rd series, vii. 535).

[2] See letters and reports in *H. O.* 102. 41.

[3] Lockhart, *Life of Scott*, 1st edition, vii. 286.

emotion that in his own country could so rudely drown the affection felt for the Wizard of the North.

On the east coast riots in Haddington were held to prove "that the people have adopted Reform with an intensity that will not brook disappointment."[1] At Edinburgh an attempt was made to break the long spell of oligarchic rule and bring in Francis Jeffrey, the Lord Advocate. In spite of petitions from "almost all the public bodies" and a large open meeting, the thirty-one town-councillors elected a Dundas.[2] A night of rioting followed, which, taken with the other Scottish outbreaks, suggests that the long proscription of public meetings merely resulted in greater violence when the privilege was restored.

In Ireland the alleged official interference of the Castle caused deep indignation among the Tories when Parliament met. It was asserted that half-pay officers had been most unfairly influenced, and that proceedings in Dublin especially had been very corrupt.[3] This was denied by Stanley, but a committee of the Commons reported on August 8 that " it appeared to the Committee that certain persons holding high official situations, or considered to be connected with the Irish Government, did use undue influence to promote the return of the two members." One great effect of the bill in Ireland had been almost to stifle the demand for Repeal of the Union, as King William was forced to admit ; at no time, however, was the state of affairs across the water at all satisfactory during the Grey administration. Indeed the Whigs did not profess to have any real policy to heal the country, after representation of a sort had been granted to her Catholic inhabitants.

Over the United Kingdom therefore generally the Government had swept the elections by the end of May. In practically every open constituency the bill was regarded as the talisman promising a new era of light and freedom ; it embodied the political and social aspirations of all who wished to escape from the slough of the last few decades and to claim their proper position in the body politic. The old bogey of revolution, so useful a dozen years ago, was duly trotted out, but ceased to

---

[1] Rt. Hon. J. Abercrombie to Chancellor, May 29 ; *H. O.* 102. 41.

[2] Cockburn, *Life of Jeffrey*, i. 318 ; *Autobiography of a Working Man*, p. 155.

[3] *Hansard* (3rd series), iv. 128, 217 ; *Despatches*, vii. 437.

P

terrify.[1] In Cambridge University alone had the Government suffered a serious reverse, Palmerston being rejected for the coveted honour he had held for twenty years; his defeat was put down to the clergy, who had raised the cry of the Church in danger.[2] A striking light is thrown on the keenness of the political temper of the day by the fact that Hobhouse was prepared, after voting for Palmerston, to leave Cambridge for Dover, where Sir Robert Peel might be waiting for him with pistols.[3]

Great, however, as was the universal excitement, and though the elections did not pass without riots at various places, there was no such unusual disturbance as to justify the forebodings of the King and the Tories.[4] At one town only was there a really serious riot, and there the civil force was disgracefully inadequate, consisting of two magistrates and two policemen. During the election at Wigan a mob took possession of the town, doing grievous harm to the persons and property of the voters, whom they completely intimidated. Houses were gutted, and the disorder was eventually quelled by the military.[5] No notice of this scandalous occurrence was given or taken by the authorities for nearly three weeks. Otherwise the riots, such as they were, gave little trouble, though the Duke of Wellington complained that the elections were conducted under sheer terrorism. This is the more remarkable, seeing that in April and May of this year the majority of the colliers on the Tyne and Wear went out on strike.[6] Although several pits were worked under protection of the troops, most of the owners came

---

[1] Cf. Morley's *Life of Gladstone* (i. 72), where some amusing scenes from the Oxfordshire election are given. The young Canningite bade a labourer he was canvassing take warning from the revolutions in foreign countries. " Damn all foreign countries," the man answered, " what has old England to do with foreign countries ? "

[2] Palmerston was provided with a Government seat for Blechingley. Grey to Stanley, May 27 ; *Howick Papers.*

[3] Hobhouse describes the circumstances in his *Recollections*, iv. 111.

[4] Add. MSS. 27,789, f. 396.

[5] H. O. 52. 13.

[6] Durham, who was a coalowner on a large scale, wrote to Melbourne on April 19 : " As soon as the infantry are stationed . . . I shall get on one or two pits to work—others will do the same, and that step will tend more than any other measure to put down ' the Union.' Because a great part of the men, I sincerely believe, are anxious to go to work, and will do so when they perceive that we can effectively protect them. And secondly this measure will defeat their grand plan of starving the country " H. O. 52. 12).

to terms by the end of May, and the strike succeeded.[1] No
political feeling, however, seems to have come in.

It is of course unwise to attribute definite political purpose
to the action of a mob, which must depend so much on mere un-
thinking impulse; the forces which sway the strange personality
we call a crowd have not yet been fully analysed. But it is at
least probable that the mildness of the spring disturbances compared with those of October was due to the general sense of satisfaction and triumph at the earlier time, whereas the autumn
was shadowed by defeat. It is suggested in Somerville's *Autobiography* that the reason why the riots did not delay the cause
of Reform by frightening the middle classes was that the national
opinion was already formed, so that the Reformers were in no
need of proselytising. Certainly it would appear that violent
tactics are likely to have a different effect according as they
are used by a majority or a minority, and in this case it was
the respectable shopkeepers and superior artisans who were most
warmly attached to the Whig Reform Bill.

There is always a danger in speaking as if the opinion of
" the country " or " the people " was ever exclusively on one
side, and particularly so in dealing with a question which was
hotly debated for at least eighteen months. One must be a very
convinced democrat to claim that in such a case the determination of the majority has a right to be hailed as the general will in
anything but a technical sense. Some attempt will be made in
the next chapter to estimate the position of the various parties
with regard to Reform ; only a Whig partisan could maintain
that the population of England in 1831 with the anti-Reformers
eliminated may fairly be called the people. It is, however,
allowable to use the word " people " in the special sense of the
middle and lower classes with political intelligence, or perhaps
rather with political will. In this sense, as Place said, the main
body of the people was distinctly on the side of Reform. It
included roughly Nonconformists, the professional classes,
merchants and manufacturers, tradesmen and artisans in towns,
and the traditional Whig aristocracy. Against them were the
Church, the Law, the Universities, the Services, many great
bankers, and most farmers and country gentlemen. Working-
class opinion was in general divided between those who supported
the bill and those who thought it a feeble half-measure. Hunt,

[1] *H. O.* 40. 29.

indeed, maintained in Parliament that the Stafford and Warwickshire workmen left out of the franchise by the bill would rather see members chosen by the gentry than by the class immediately above themselves. But when he claimed to oppose the bill in the name of factory workers generally, he was disowned by a public meeting of the " Spinners, Weavers, Mechanics and other working-men in Manchester." [1] In Yorkshire factories interest in Reform was eclipsed by local zeal for the Ten Hour Bill, but there is hardly enough evidence to support Samuel Kydd's contention that most operatives engaged in that movement believed the bill would only put more power into the hands of the employers.[2] As a matter of fact the working-class does not really come into prominence till after the rejection of the bill by the Lords in October. The rank and file of the Political Unions hitherto formed were recruited mainly from clerks and small shopkeepers and their assistants, in fact from what might nowadays be called the collared class. The manual labourers who were in any way organised were chiefly occupied with industrial matters, and their associations rather took the form of trade unions, whether confined to one industry or not. In the course of the summer, however, the working-men of London formed a political society on a larger scale than heretofore, and this example was largely imitated throughout the country, in a way the Government by no means welcomed.

For the moment, however, the Whigs had profited by the popular excitement to the full ; the elections were safely over, assuring them an invincible majority when the new Parliament met in June. Grey's position was in fact unique in the constitutional history of his time, and ranks him as in a sense the earliest of modern Prime Ministers. He was not the King's choice, like Pitt, whose triumph at the polls in 1784 the late election recalled, nor was he that of Parliament, on Bagehot's principle ; [3] he stood henceforth directly on the support of the people, who had returned him to power as representing the Reform Bill.

[1] Add. MSS. 27,789, f. 296.

[2] " Alfred," *History of the Factory Movement*, i. 331. They said : " Experience has taught us that manufacturing capitalists, with some exceptions, are our opponents : the Reform Bill will increase the influence of that body as a power in the State, and therefore prove injurious to our interests."

[3] " The House of Commons is an electoral chamber ; it is the assembly which chooses our president " (*English Constitution*, chap. v.).

This is a characteristic feature of British government to-day. The constituencies return members pledged to support one or other party leader, who thus enjoys a commanding position, and is able as a rule to exact strict obedience. But before and for long after the dissolution of 1831 party discipline was loose, and the numbers on divisions doubtful and fluctuating. In this, as in so many points, the struggle for the Reform Bill looks forward not to the decades which immediately followed its passing, but to the more democratic system of the twentieth century. But eighty years ago the organisation and exploitation of popular feeling were strange and exceptional, whereas now they are the permanent basis of party politics. Lord Grey accepted them reluctantly enough, but they raised him for the moment to a pinnacle no minister had reached since the days of Pitt, and which it is doubtful if Peel, or Palmerston, or even Gladstone ever attained after him.

Thus strong in the people's support, the friends of the bill were emboldened to resist any " clipping " of its wings in the Cabinet, or at the King's suggestion. " I will attend to your advice," wrote Althorp to Durham, " and pledge myself as deeply as I can to the three main points to which you allude. I entirely agree with you, and am quite of the same mind as to the £10 franchise. I cannot consent to any alteration in it." A fortnight later he gave an account of a recent Cabinet : " Lord Grey spoke very decisively against making any alteration in the Franchise, but I observed he used the words ' raising its nominal value ' always, however his expressions were so strong that they silenced Palmerston, and Lansdowne admitted that it was too late to make any change. I should say that with the exception of Palmerston all present agreed that a very probable consequence of attempting to conciliate the House of Lords by concession would be to lose the House of Commons, and Lansdowne expressly said that this would be absurd to the highest degree." [1]

Grey was equally firm with the King, who besought him to modify the bill so as to avoid a collision with the other House, and declared his anxiety " not to detach himself from the great body of the Aristocracy, and not to be reduced to the alternative of seeking, under difficulties which may arise, the precarious support of a democracy." To this Grey truly answered that " no concessions that could be made, short of a total destruction

[1] Althorp to Durham, May 14, 29 ; *Lambton Papers.*

of all the beneficial effects of the bill, would satisfy those by whom it has hitherto been most violently opposed." [1]   But any doubts for the future arising from the hinted uneasiness of the sovereign were outweighed by the signal honour of the Garter conferred on Grey at a critical period by the King's spontaneous act. [2]   There loomed indeed grimly in the distance the threatening ramparts of the Lords, but in the foreground lay a broad plain on which the Whig battalions might go out the second time with good hope to wage the battle of Reform.

[1] *Correspondence*, i. 275, 279.

[2] Howick to Charles Grey, May 28 : " My father's getting the Garter in the manner he did  has annoyed them [the Tories] almost more than anything else, as it puts an end to their lies about the King . . . it certainly has had a good effect, the King of his own accord having done what he has" (*Howick Papers*).   Wellington called it "a gross impropriety" (*Despatches*, vii. 449).

# CHAPTER VI

## OPINIONS AND IDEAS

" The earth, restive, confronts a new era, perhaps a general divine war."
WALT WHITMAN.

THE position of the unreformed House of Commons during its last years was in many ways unique. While it retained the prestige and power which the Revolution had secured it, its proceedings interested and influenced a far wider circle in the country than ever before. It was still the centre of the nation's political life in a sense unreal to later generations. Nowadays, when a statesman wishes to inaugurate a new movement or generally to submit his point of view to his countrymen, he addresses a mass meeting in the Albert Hall or the Free Trade Hall, or some other such popular gathering. Then it would have been inconceivable for him to choose any other audience but the House of Commons. Even the Tamworth Manifesto would have been out of place before the Reform Act. Those who most derided the system of election to the House respected as a rule its venerable antiquity and glorious past. August as the Roman Senate, it could claim no small share in repelling an invader more fearful than Hannibal himself. Within its walls tradition held an absolute sway. Mr. Burke, Mr. Fox, Mr. Pitt were accepted as models and standards for all time ; the same halo was beginning to encircle the memory of Canning. If his death seemed for the moment to have ended the flow of " that large utterance of the early gods," men trained in the same school were still in the front of public life, and it might well appear that the impending crisis would unlock their lips to no less majestic eloquence.

On the other hand the recent growth of the provincial press had given the middle classes of the towns access to its debates. To us it is a marvel how Chatham's oratory stirred the country to the extent it did, when we remember the inadequate reporting and elementary journalism of his day. Even in his son's time newspapers were few and scrappy. But in the thirties, besides a keen competition among the London dailies, every provincial town of any importance had its weekly paper, while Birmingham enterprise went to press three times a week. And this was found profitable although the Government fourpenny stamp kept the price of each copy up to sevenpence. A glance at a newspaper of the time shows the interest which its readers took in parliamentary politics. It consisted, as a rule, of four pages, of which three and a half or more were not unusually taken up with the debates of the Lords and Commons. Allowance must of course be made for the lack of other news owing to the slow and laborious system of communication, but the mere fact that readers tolerated such an arrangement bears striking witness to the firm hold of Parliament on the interest of the country. When the Houses were not sitting, the space would be largely filled up with reports of county meetings or other political matter, such as letters from " Briton " or " Protestant," or proceedings in the French Chamber. Advertisements, Society news, and curious or sensational incidents, held a subordinate place.

This attention paid to Parliament is the more remarkable in view of its extremely aristocratic nature. Its atmosphere had changed in some degree since the days of Fox, but a seat in the Commons was still the usual perquisite of the son of a noble house. The election of such members as Ricardo, Hume, Macaulay, had not altered the prevailing temper. Even the Radicals Burdett and Cochrane were men of birth and station. The House was a club where town and country members might spend part of the season in attending a glorified Quarter Sessions —if indeed they did attend it, for a seat was by no means incompatible with a post in a foreign embassy or even with the accomplishment of the Grand Tour. It was calculated that a quarter of the 1900 House of Commons had been educated at Eton or Harrow ; in 1830 the proportion must have been enormously greater. Two Etonians led their respective parties in the Lords, two Harrovians in the Commons ; of the twelve prime ministers who ruled England after the death of Portland, Eton and Harrow could each claim five. It was the golden age of the public schools, and of that education with which they have been hitherto identified. Their system aimed at the training of statesmen, at a time when statesmanship consisted largely in winning and retaining the confidence of an assembly of some six hundred gentlemen. Special attention was therefore paid to oratory, and oratory of a particular type—large, dignified, lofty, appealing to the sense of honour and responsibility of a privileged class. Such was the object of the speech-days so much in vogue, not less than of the specialised study of the Classics as the model of language and taste. Parliamentary eloquence was founded on the pure and lordly speech of the ancient poets and orators, who were freely quoted in the ordinary conversation of gentlemen ; Shakespeare was their only rival, but he was known with a thoroughness that would be rare to-day. Similarity of education combined with similarity of social position to produce a close society favourable to high spirit and intensity of life rather than to breadth of sympathy. For effective debate it is necessary that speakers and audience should share a common fund of experience and a common " hinterland " of thought. If new ideas are presented, it must be against a familiar background. But for political progress the interchange of widely different points of view is essential. The old parliamentary system tended not to a creative clash of ideas, but to uniformity. This was certainly a more comfortable state of things for unimaginative country gentlemen, and even for brilliant politicians anxious for change on orthodox gentlemanly lines. The discordant complaints of such an outsider as Hunt spoilt the gallant sport entirely ; the only thing was to ignore him.

Superficial, however, as were ordinary political differences, there were some events which divided men's opinions so sharply that the rent appeared even in the daily intercourse of social life. Opposite views on the French Revolution led to the breaking up of friendships, and reached to the sphere of impulse and imagination which lies behind mere intellectual reasoning. That crisis tested the real quality of men's minds, subjecting them to a fiery trial of which they never lost the scar. The Whig minority in those years were not Tories out of office ; to the Government they were traitors and revolutionaries, men outside the pale of the Constitution. For nearly a generation the feeling of implacable antipathy continued ; it was softened at length by lapse of time and the aggression of Napoleon, which united both parties in resistance. To the rancour of the years of mortal stress succeeded the normal opposition of rival parties. The Tories still maintained their hatred and dread of Jacobinism, but by the time the storm which followed the peace had been safely weathered, the edge of their feelings was dulled.  The Whigs who had defended France in revolution lost their old reckless ardour ;  Grey and Mackintosh retreated some way from the position of the Friends of the People and of *Vindiciae Gallicae*.  And beside the veterans on both sides there was growing up in the decade after Peterloo a younger generation of politicians, to whom the French Revolution might mean much as the dawn of a new era, but never quite the same as it had meant to those on whom its first awful shock had burst. Young men like Lord John Russell and Macaulay accepted it as one fact among many, and sought to give it its proper place in history.

Fifteen years of Tory government had now passed since the peace ; Canning, Huskisson, and Peel had brought about innovations to which both parties might give their approval. The eyes of Englishmen turned from foreign dangers to industrial and scientific advance at home.  Commerce and manufactures had made great strides, new roads were knitting the country together, and the use of steam for locomotion opened up a boundless prospect.  But the voice of distress was heard, and the condition of Ireland forced on a measure which aroused bitter hostility.  There followed a year of tension and excitement, culminating in the Revolution of July, thrilling enough to stir the blood but not provocative of general panic.  It was felt that something must happen.  Lord John Russell speaks of a " vague desire " in the minds of men ; Lord Holland smelt the battle afar off, and took up his disused pen, for memoirs might once more be worth writing.  " Agnosco veteris vestigia flammae," he finely wrote, a true nephew of Charles Fox.[1]  For weeks the air was charged with rumours of impending revolution ;  there were more than rumours of an insurgent peasantry in the southern counties, and of strange secret combinations of desperate men in the north.  In startling succession came the Duke of Wellington's declaration against Reform, his refusal from fear of riot to allow the King to visit the City, and the fall of his Government.  Then again a period of waiting, and finally the Reform Bill.  Within a few days it

[1] *Further Memoirs*, p. 211.

was manifest that this would be no mere parliamentary struggle over the details of a complicated measure, but a battle-royal which would range all England in hostile camps. Once again political differences would invade ordinary social life, and men to whom the usual course of parliamentary affairs made no appeal would find themselves drawn to take a side in this momentous conflict. Many indeed, in the disillusionment which followed the passing of the Act, asked themselves what difference it had all made, and why they had been so excited. But at the moment those who held haughtily aloof were few, for the enthusiasts on both sides contrived so to exaggerate the extent of the issues involved, that nearly all interests seemed to come within their scope.

From the time when Tories first realised the full meaning of the bill, and Reformers the certainty of strenuous opposition, an intensity of passion was kindled which smouldered sullenly throughout the long debates and burst into flame at such moments as the dissolution, the rejection by the Lords, and the demand for a creation of peers.[1] The circumstances in the King's closet, in the Cabinet, and in the country, attending the course of the second and third Reform Bills will be noticed in later chapters; to follow the progress of the several discussions in the two Houses would seem unprofitable, even if the ground were untrodden. Probably no measure has been so thoroughly debated in Parliament before or since. Presented thrice to the Lower House and twice to the Upper, it spent forty days in the summer, and twenty-two in the winter, in the Committee of the Commons, and this at a time when the closure was unknown. It is not surprising that after no long period the speeches were more remarkable for earnestness than originality, and their value lies less in the arguments used than in the point of view they express. This is especially true on the Tory side. Suddenly called upon to clothe in logical dress sentiments which formed part of their unspoken theory of life and almost of their religion, the opponents of the bill often seem worsted in argument by its supporters, whose case was alike stronger on paper and lent itself more easily to rhetorical exposition.

[1] " The rage of faction at the present moment exceeds anything that has been known in our day. . . . Lord Mahon said to me yesterday that friendships of long standing were everywhere giving way " (Macaulay to Hannah Macaulay; Trevelyan, *Life and Letters of Lord Macaulay*, p. 169).

Certainly at first sight the position of the Reformers looks impregnable to modern eyes. Though we grant many anomalies and imperfections in the Reform Bill itself, it seems difficult to explain the Tory opposition to any Reform whatever, except on the theory, attractive perhaps to a light-hearted Liberal, of a " double dose of original sin," or original stupidity, in the Conservative temperament. Holding the modern view of representation, which is largely the result of the historical success of Lord John Russell's bill, we smile in a superior way over the story of Old Sarum with its bare fields and two members, contrasted with unrepresented Manchester's rising population of 180,000. Birmingham, Leeds, Sheffield, Wolverhampton, Huddersfield, Gateshead, were also voteless, while eight members sat for the whole of London. The twenty-three northern counties of England included only seventy-four of the two hundred and three parliamentary boroughs in the country, in spite of the fact that the centre of gravity had been rapidly shifting northwards since the industrial revolution. The south coast, on the other hand, was dotted with boroughs, while Cornwall alone returned forty-four members, one less than the whole of Scotland. And, in view of the patron's influence, acquired, as the case might be, by money or hereditary connection, only a portion of the enfranchised boroughs could be said to return the members that sat for them. Such anomalies were glaring and invited attack, as ever since they have invited ridicule. But their condemnation at the bar of posterity does not do away with the need of trying to understand why educated men defended them eighty years ago. Burke, Canning, and even Peel were neither knaves nor fools, and they all with no hesitating voice declared against the Reformers of their day.

The Whig plan, as introduced on March 1, 1831, and subsequently modified, was to disfranchise totally fifty-five boroughs and to take one member from thirty more ; to give two members to twenty-two towns, and a single member to twenty others ; to establish in all these boroughs a uniform £10 householder qualification ; also to add members to certain counties and to extend the county franchise beyond the forty shilling freeholders. The proposals for the counties raised comparatively little criticism. The battle raged fiercest round the disfranchisement clauses and the single £10 qualification.

The indignation this measure aroused, as soon as the Tories saw it was no jest, was such as is reserved for traitors. At a time of almost unparalleled popular excitement the Ultra-Tories had helped in ejecting the Wellington ministry and so raised the Whigs to power. Remembering Lord Grey's promise to stand by his order, both sections of the new Opposition had acquiesced in the veteran Reformer's insistence on a change in the representation. Judging by the leader's character, by the former ventures in that line already tried by the Whigs, and by the composition of this motley Cabinet, Tories and Radicals had alike expected that Grey would produce some moderate inconclusive measure which, while staving off the popular demand for more, would leave things very much as they were. The bill actually proposed left no single constituency in the United Kingdom unaltered, except the universities, and confessedly transferred the prevailing power to the middle class. In all good faith the Tories believed that a deadly blow was being levelled at the Constitution.

Representing as they did the great established interests— the Aristocracy, the Church, the Land—they saw in the new popular movement simply a manifestation of the spirit of hostility to all law and authority, the spirit of the French Revolution, testing all institutions by the touchstone of pure reason. This they held to be an utterly pernicious attitude. The weight of the past made it impossible, even were it desirable, to start with a clean slate. There were some principles, some institutions, which must be taken for granted. As human intellect had not created them it must not question them ; its proper task lay in the application of its skill to their successful working and the improvement of details. Among these heaven-born entities to be accepted but not criticised they ranked the British Constitution. The origin of this cult of our political system as such can hardly be definitely dated ; it would appear to be a product of the Roman-minded eighteenth century, when the civil liberty of Englishmen under the Revolution settlement offered a vivid contrast to the insecurity of the subjects of Louis XIV and his great-grandson. Blackstone, of course, was its high priest, and Burke a devoted worshipper ; nor did the perversities of George III seem in any way to weaken the theory. The course of history since Burke's day confirmed his judgment in the eyes of many. The stability of our institutions and the sanctity of our shores had been preserved when the governments of most European nations had been shattered by convulsions from within or without.   While the capitals of Italy, Germany, Spain, and Russia had been stages in the triumphal progress of the universal tyrant, England had stood single-handed against the Continent, and after Waterloo towered among the nations in prestige no less than in real power.   Englishmen were firmly convinced of their infinite superiority in all respects to less fortunate peoples.   The same spirit in which Coningsby speaks of "the degraded patricians of the Continent" was mighty in our fleets and armies, creating a full assurance of victory against any odds.   But without disparaging the merit of our captains by land and sea, it might fairly be claimed that it was the unique vitality of our Constitution, as personified by Pitt at home and abroad, which enabled us to keep up the unequal fight.

> " Sic fortis Etruria crevit,
> Scilicet et facta est rerum pulcherrima Roma."

Foreign nations had recognised the fact.   To say nothing of Hamilton and Montesquieu, the French system of 1815 was avowedly modelled on our own.   In the eyes of all Europe the English Constitution was the Constitution *par excellence*.   In the years since the Congress of Vienna we have seen the rise of many new polities in all quarters of the world, and the fall of no small number also.   In 1830 it was not so ; there was little precedent for Constitution-building, and what precedent there was was not auspicious for monarchists.   It is not surprising that many rallied to the cry of the Constitution in danger.

The answer of the Reformers was of course that the Tories were confounding the substance with the accidents of the Constitution.   It was absurd to call the disfranchisement of Old Sarum revolution ; if every trifling abuse, trifling in theory but grave in practice, had been thus shielded from attack, the Constitution would never have attained the very fair level of practical utility it was allowed to possess.   Their efforts were in fact aimed at the restoration of the old principles of the Constitution, and they claimed that they were more truly in harmony with its essential spirit than the literal conservatism of the Tories.   This reply was met by the dilemma stated by Canning ; the Whigs either were or were not restoring a state of things which had formerly existed ; if they were, he challenged them to point to any definite time when the representation was as they proposed to make it ; if they were not, they must be evolving a new system of their own ; and personally he trusted the wisdom of six centuries rather than that of Lord John Russell and Henry Hunt. The dilemma was unfair, and could be evaded; but it carried conviction largely at the time. Gladstone has told us how he and many of his contemporaries followed the lead of Canning, attracted alike by his personal brilliance and his intellectual descent from Burke and Pitt. Such was the attitude of men who opposed Parliamentary Reform on principle. There were others who, while holding the same views, differed on the question of tactics, believing that the enfranchisement of a few large towns, though really unnecessary and in itself undesirable, might be useful as a sop to the popular demand; of such men was Huskisson. Others again held, not only as a matter of policy, that some such moderate Reform was wise and just, and regretted the obstinacy of their leaders in not complying ; but the Whig Reform Bill was a very different thing.

At this point it is well to consider what were the principles of our matchless Constitution, as understood and worshipped by the Tories. They may perhaps be divided into three : the theory of checks and balances, variety of representation, and property the basis of political power. With the first and third of these principles all moderate Reformers agreed ; the difference lay solely in the construction put upon them. The second they did not accept to the same degree, though they maintained that in practice their plan would be found to square with it.

The theoretical perfection of our polity was held to lie in the successful fusion of the monarchical, the aristocratic, and the popular elements, in proportions which forbade the preponderance of any one. Thomson's *Liberty* was constantly quoted in praise of

> "The full, the perfect plan
> Of Britain's matchless Constitution, mixt
> Of mutual checking and supporting powers,
> Kings, Lords, and Commons."

" So long as England is England," wrote the author of *Order against Anarchy*, " the institutions themselves must remain " ; and the corollary was added that if they were to remain they must preserve the same relative power; else the unstable equilibrium would collapse, and old-time objections to a mixed form of government be justified.  But it had become clear that with the obsolescence of the royal veto, and the gradual but unquestioned subordination of the Upper to the Lower House, the balance was no longer maintained in the manner belauded by political philosophers.  George III, however, and the great families of the eighteenth century, had discovered a means of preserving their power, quite as effective but much less invidious. By the simple expedient of Treasury and nomination boroughs the influence of the Crown and the nobility remained potent in the Constitution.  The King's personal power in the Commons did not survive the reign of George III, but that of the ministry and the aristocracy did, and by the time of the Reform Bill the practice had acquired enough prescriptive sanction to find apologists.  The Theory of Checks was now construed to mean that King, Lords, and People must each be duly represented in the House of Commons, if stability was to be maintained. Or, as Reformers put it, the people's share in the Constitution was now to be one-ninth, while the other two elements acquired the same amount in addition to their original thirds.

The Tories proceeded to argue that on their theory the people was amply represented already.  If other evidence were lacking, the results of the two last dissolutions proved it beyond debate. And apart from the growing numbers of popular members in the Commons, and the increased sensitiveness of the House to voices outside, there had sprung up of late among the people a mighty institution which might fairly be said to outweigh the influence of King and three Estates together.  No complaints could be made of the under-representation of the people while the press exerted its present monstrous power.  The least further concession on this point would infallibly lead to Democracy.  The word Democracy occupied in 1831 the position which the word Socialism holds to-day in a similar connection. It was understood to mean something vaguely terrible which might " come " and would " come " if the respectable classes did not stand together.  The change from a word of political to one of primarily economic application is significant of a shifting of outlook, but the meaning was the same to conservatives. Democracy, like Socialism to-day, or possibly Syndicalism, which seems a yet more up-to-date bogey, was regarded not so much as a complicated theory of political reorganisation but as

an impending era of evil, affecting the whole course of private
life, something cataclysmic and all-pervading. If Democracy
came, King and Lords would disappear, and old landmarks of
every description would be swept away. Nothing could resist
the flood of popular domination if the dykes of patronage and
boroughmongering were once removed. "The people" were
pictured as a horde of ragamuffins howling for the ballot and
the blood of the aristocracy.

To this the obvious answer was that if the people's desire
was really for a republic, it was vain to hope to stay them by
means of nomination boroughs; Fox had gone further and
said that, if the Crown and the Peerage were in truth institutions at variance with the national will, it was not only impolitic
but unjustifiable to buttress them with artificial props. The
Tory counter was that, whereas the sober and deep-lying feeling
of the people was strongly attached to their ancient institutions,
temporary and superficial disloyalty might be, and frequently
was, stirred up by agitators, and that the restless energy of the
anarchical section overbore the contented quiet of the sound-
hearted majority. The danger of a House of Commons too
faithfully mirroring the people was that it would also reflect
their prejudices and moods of transitory passion. Such, it
was claimed, was the true explanation of the election of
1831, at which, contrary to sound constitutional precedent,
pledges to vote for the Reform Bill had been extorted from
many candidates. The lesson of the French Revolution must
not be forgotten. The States-General had not the faintest intention when they met of guillotining or discrowning the King;
yet so it fell out. On the principle that power uncontrolled is
power abused, Tories argued that it was unreasonable to expect
an undiluted popular assembly to submit to any restraint; it
must shortly degenerate into mere mob-tyranny, from which
the step to the abolition of the monarchy would be easy and
rapid.[1] Lord John Russell's bill was, on the face of it, no final

---

[1] Peel said on July 6: "Without imputing disaffection to the people,
or a deliberate intention on their part to undermine the Monarchy, or
destroy the Peerage, my belief is that neither the Monarchy nor the Peerage can resist with effect the decrees of a House of Commons that is
immediately obedient to every popular impulse, and that professes to
speak the popular will; and that all the tendencies of such an assembly
are towards the increase of its own power, and the intolerance of any
extrinsic control."

measure. Prescription once disregarded, there was no reason but mere accident why the franchise should not go below the £10 householder ; bad as the actual proposal was, it was merely a stepping-stone to universal suffrage.[1]

The principle of variety of representation might be called one of the happy accidents which testified to the superhuman excellence of the Constitution. Not only had the knights of the shire always been distinct from the citizens and burgesses—at one time almost to the extent of forming another Estate of the realm,—but different boroughs had evolved different modes of election, roughly divisible into four groups—Scot and lot, Burgage, Freeman, Corporation. Besides, some boroughs were close and some open, so that various constituencies represented very diverse interests. It was the Tory contention that by this haphazard means all interests in the country were able to make their voice heard in Parliament. The county members stood for the land ; the open boroughs returned men who might be expected to express the town point of view. Wide constituencies like Westminster, Liverpool, and Preston admitted the representatives of the shopkeeping and artisan classes. Finance, Commerce, Manufacturing were represented by men whose wealth enabled them to buy a seat for some rotten borough. Even India and the Colonies were represented in the same way by retired experts, as were the Services and the Law. Intellect not blessed with riches might enter Parliament by way of the university seats, or in more cases by the favour of some enlightened patron. It was thus that by far the greater number of the distinguished statesmen of the last few decades had been enabled to adapt themselves to parliamentary life in early youth, without the expense of an appeal to popular constituencies which might not appreciate their promise of genius. The

---

[1] One cannot help feeling that the theory of Checks so often mentioned was even then obsolete. The Crown had ceased since the early years of George III to play anything like a coequal part with the Estates of the realm. The Cabinet were already a committee of the House of Commons, and no longer the King's servants. So much for the monarchical element ; the democratic was also a sham, for the Commons were practically as aristocratic as the Lords. It would have been much truer to say that the Prime Minister was now the monarch, assisted by a council of colleagues ; the two Houses of Parliament together made up the aristocratic element in the State ; while the electorate supplied the democratic. In this sense there was a real system of Checks and Balances.

abolition of this private entrance into the House for young men of talent by no means won the approval of Brougham, himself for some time a member for a pocket borough.

Lord John Russell admitted that he had intentionally left some such nomination seats untouched, partly as a method to secure the inclusion of intellect and partly to provide safe berths for ministers. It was seriously urged by men who had grown up under the old methods that the new system would make it impossible to carry on the King's government at all. A reserve of seats at the unfettered disposal of government was considered absolutely necessary. Even apart from the vexatious rule which then, as now, forced members who had accepted certain offices under the Crown to seek re-election, it might often happen that a minister was rejected by a popular constituency. Nowadays this means a clumsy process by which a member for a safe seat retires, to enable the minister to re-enter the House. Before 1830 nothing was easier than to return him without dust and heat for a pocket borough which he need not even visit. So Peel was returned for Westbury when Oxford rejected him in 1829, and Palmerston two years later, on his defeat at the sister university. So conscious was Russell of this serious inconvenience, that more than once he declared his willingness to accept a bill enabling ministers *ex officio* to speak and propose measures in either House.

But more important than such objections, however reasonable, was the abandonment once for all of the harmony in diversity of the old Constitution ; the new system transferred the franchise in all English boroughs to the £10 householders, which meant the small shopkeepers and superior artisans. How far it was desirable for this class to obtain the vote was fit matter for discussion. But it was surely unnecessary to give them the predominance in every contested election in the country. In this point the Whigs had utterly and wantonly violated the old just principles of distribution. Their object was not far to seek. Not more fiercely did Conservatives attack the Manhood Suffrage Bill of 1912 as an attempt to keep a Liberal Government permanently in power, than did the Tories of 1831 accuse their rivals of adjusting the franchise to secure for themselves a constant majority. Disraeli declared that the Reformers had aimed at and contrived to obtain " a dissenting and low Whig constituency " in the country. Politically speaking, for the future England would indeed be a " nation of shopkeepers." Until the next instalment of Reform produced a yet more pernicious uniformity, every borough in England would utter the mind of one class only, and that the men whom Place, with the bittter experience of a lifetime's wire-pulling among them, described as "among the most despicable people in the nation in a public point of view." [1]

Reformers always answered that the uniformity they established in theory would not work out as such in practice. The local circumstances of particular places would give the £10 qualification different values about the country. In the new metropolitan boroughs, for instance, it would practically amount to household suffrage, whereas the places which just escaped one or other of the Schedules would still preserve a close constituency. But to plead such accidents was not to repel the charge of having by coarse generalisation sacrificed a subtle system with great possibilities. It was much easier to point out that the old plan of variety failed in reality to afford the advantages attributed to it. A patron might, it was true, use his carefully acquired boroughs to return a young genius from the university; he was much more likely to secure a member who would vote straight for his master's interests. Rich financiers and merchants could buy seats; but it was not necessary that their individual interests should coincide with those of their class. To assert that factory owners and rich nabobs represented their operatives and the population of India was like saying a wolf was a fit person to represent the lambs with whom he was so intimately acquainted. Nor was it hard to show that the alleged benefits were obtained at the cost of much corruption, and, in any case, most indirectly; in the absence, too, of all responsibility to constituents, there was no guarantee against the victory of "sinister" motives. Above all, granted that all interests were represented, there was no reason whatever to suppose that they were represented in correct proportions. A vote without the hope of ever making it prevail was little use. Working-class opinion, it was said, found due expression in the voice of the members for Preston and one or two other popular constituencies. But in face of the vast preponderance of the

---

[1] Wallas, *Life of Place*, p. 261. "The real fact is, that, under the present system, all places are not represented, but all classes are; and that, in the new system, every place will be represented, but only one class" (Lord Mahon, December 16; *Hansard* (3rd series), ix. 370).

landed interest that voice might as well, or better, be silent; as Hunt found to his cost. The agricultural labourer was not represented at all, except through his landlord; nor was the factory operative; nor the farmer who was not a freeholder. The whole system was absolutely haphazard, and depended for justice on the hope that an assembly of rich men would be able and willing to sympathise with interests generally supposed to be exactly opposite to their own.

Whether it was possible to secure, by any such reconstruction of the Third Estate as Disraeli suggested, a representation of interests favourable to liberty, is an interesting but hardly a practical question. The scheme rests on the historical theory of the Commons being the House not of the people but of a privileged class. It was urged that the admission of another class, such as for instance the capitalist or manufacturing interest, on the lines of that innovation by which the burgesses joined the knights of the shire in the thirteenth century, would have provided an intelligible basis for Toryism and a logical barrier to further concession. The £10 qualification " virtually conceded the principle of Universal Suffrage." [1]  Certainly Lord John Russell never considered the matter from Disraeli's point of view, though in his first draft laid before the Committee of Four there are traces of a desire to preserve some variations of franchise.[2]  To sweep away all anomalies as alien to the spirit of the age was a far simpler, but possibly not a more statesman-like proposal; it effaced the ruins out of which a system of minority representation might conceivably have been built. Would Fox and his little band, it was asked, have found seats during the war with France, if they had been forced to apply for the suffrages of £10 householders ?  It was argued that the swamping of the electorate by one vast class must mean the disfranchisement of every interest but that of the proletariat, a prospect dangerous to freedom.  The Whig Reform Bill made no contribution towards solving the problem of modern states-manship, how to secure the control of the people by the people for the people.

If constitutionalists believed no longer in the divine right of kings, they held most firmly to the divine right of property. Both political parties maintained that any other basis for

[1] *Coningsby*, ch. vii.
[2] *Essay on the English Government* (new edition), p. 248.

representation was dangerous and Jacobinical. The "stake in the country" argument was at the height of its power, and was accepted by all but the most pernicious Radicals. The Tories carried it further ; though weight should be given to all property, it stood to reason that property in land had especial claims to rule the State. For a moneyed man might invest his capital abroad, and indeed all personal wealth might be shipped across the Channel in case of danger at home. The landed class alone were tied to the country for good or ill. However great the risk, they could not carry off their acres with them. Thus their stake in the nation was greater than all other, and logically entitled them to a supreme share in the guidance of its destinies. Besides the immobility of their property, it was the most important to the life of the people. Especially during the war it had been agreed that England must as far as possible produce her own food, and of course in the eighteenth century and before it she was mainly an agricultural country. In 1821 it was calculated that a third of the population was engaged on the land. But the proportion was rapidly sinking. The demand which the industrial revolution made for factory hands drew families from the country districts, and from the beginning of the century commerce and manufacturing began to challenge the predominance of agriculture. In fact Capital's desire to break down the Land's monopoly of political power gave the Reform movement after 1820 much of its driving force and most of its respectability. The £10 constituency was well suited for the return of moneyed magnates of the middle class, such men as Thomas Attwood in real life or Oswald Millbank in fiction.

The Whig chiefs, most of them owners of large estates, were indeed unlikely to depreciate the claims of their order. The Reform Bill provided for a great increase of county members, and the interests of the territorial aristocracy were further safeguarded by the Government's reluctant acceptance of the so-called Chandos clause, which a majority of the Commons passed against the ministers.[1] This, however, could not atone for the overwhelming majority which the towns would command in

[1] The Chandos clause extended the vote in counties to tenants paying a yearly rent of £50 and upwards. It was opposed by the Government, and generally by all far-sighted Reformers in the country, on the ground that the landlords would thus acquire an indefinite number of faggot votes.

future. A £10 qualification, working out at a weekly rent of three shillings and tenpence, was an insult to the rights of property, and little better than a mere potwalloper franchise. Such men could have no sense of responsibility; their stake in the country was insignificant, and would not deter them from supporting anarchy and confiscation. Their hopes from a revolution would outweigh their fears. Once give the poor the opportunity to despoil the rich, and by the law of their being they must take it.[1] This principle was admitted by both Tories and Whigs; but the Whigs thought the influence of the ten-pounders would act the other way.

But anti-Reformers did not only anticipate spoliation as the result of the bill; they discovered it actually embedded in every line of it, naked and unashamed. The abolition of the small boroughs without compensation and without proof of corruption or even abuse, was robbery; so was the disfranchisement of future freemen and potwallopers.[2] It was argued by Tory lawyers that electoral rights were property in the strictest sense; rights in many cases conferred by charter, invariably sanctioned by long prescription. To us, who have seen several Reform Bills and are accustomed to drastic interference by the State on the plea of public good, the case seems absurdly feeble. But the measure of 1831 was a new departure in various directions, and the precedent of Pitt's Reform motions was for compensation; his final proposals in 1785 had actually made disfranchisement optional. But the Whigs had alike more recent and more telling authority in the Catholic Relief Bill, by which the Tories had at one stroke deprived the Irish forty shilling freeholders of their votes. And they had no lack of legal talent to maintain that the franchise was a trust, not property. The dispute was one episode in the eternal frontier warfare of State and individual rights; in this case the Tories had chosen a weak position, and their most desperate efforts failed to win them sympathy or success.

It had indeed been truly said that the strength of the Constitution was unequal to the weight of odium attaching to the nomination boroughs. It was hard to convince an unprejudiced

---

[1] "I hold it as a maxim that every Government which tends to separate property from constitutional power, must be liable to perpetual revolutions; for power will always seek property and find it" (Sir J. Scarlett's *Letter to Lord Viscount Milton*).

[2] The Reform Bill preserved existing life-interests.

man that the wisdom of our ancestors really found its highest expression in the system by which a ruined mound returned two members to the great council of the nation, and that the Constitution was indeed bound up with the rights of the patron of Gatton. A Tory would have retorted that such sneers were cheap but irrelevant. Queer as it might look to a doctrinaire Reformer or a foreigner first studying it, those who knew the Constitution in being found that it worked remarkably well. A democrat might ask, " Is the People properly represented ? " For himself he put the question in this form : " Does the country enjoy an efficient government ? " There had been, no doubt, an enlightened Tory would admit, much blundering and obscurantism in the past, but the same could not be said of the years since 1822. For the first time England had formed a definite colonial and commercial policy, under Huskisson's guidance. Canning's and Peel's administration abroad and at home had been liberal in the best sense. Freedom had been granted to Nonconformists and Catholics. The party was not merely reactionary. The Whigs had chosen the beginning of a new *Aufklärung* to pronounce that the whole machine was out of order. Just when the Continent was in turmoil, just at the time when of all others a patriot would have supported the established order, they had inflamed, for their own party advantage, the already dangerous desires of the mob, and were introducing a revolution under the pretext of preventing one. On the fall of the Duke, they had abused an unparalleled opportunity of restoring quiet by a grant of moderate Reform.[1] Mere wreckers, without a single constructive idea, they were thoughtlessly demolishing the subtle product of ages of political wisdom, or rather of unplanned organic growth.

" I say nothing about the revolutionary Reform," Croker wrote to Scott, " but I think of nothing else. If it be carried, England, no doubt, may be still great and happy ; but it will be under a *different* form of Constitution and administration from that which has raised her to her present greatness and happiness. No King, no Lords, no inequalities in the social

---

[1] See Lord Harrowby's speech on the second reading on October 4 : " The Ministers have done what no Minister ought ever to do—they have brought forward a measure which it may be almost equally dangerous to adopt or to reject. [Lord Grey] might have stood, as it were, between the living and the dead, and in my conscience I believe he might have stayed the plague " (*Hansard* (3rd series), vii. 1168).

system ; all will be levelled to the plane of the petty shopkeepers and small farmers ; this, perhaps, not without bloodshed, but certainly by confiscations and persecutions. 'Tis inevitable, and this is to be perpetrated by a set of men like Lambton and Johnny Russell, whom a club in Regent Street would not trust with the management of their concerns."[1] The excellent political verse of Mackworth Praed is steeped through and through in conservative contempt for these incompetent iconoclasts.[2] Like true Radicals, instead of making the best of institutions which, though possibly in need of superficial renovation, were sound at the core, they were smashing the entire fabric ; the new Constitution could only claim the support of chill reason, not the stronger sanction of immemorial ancestral reverence. " Unhappy for England," wrote Scarlett, " will be the time when the foundations of these institutions, lying in the habits and affections of the people, shall be so far shaken by the powers of ridicule, declamation, and sophistry, as to rest upon the cold influence of reason, which excites no passion and gives no impulse to action." Disraeli spoke from the heart of Toryism when he said, " The rights and liberties of a nation can only be preserved by institutions. It is not the spread of knowledge or the march of intellect that will be found sufficient sureties for the public welfare in the crisis of a country's freedom."[3] In this unholy work the Government were not ashamed of the co-operation of men whose shallow rationalism scoffed at all institutions, human and divine. They had looked for the approval not of the respectable classes whose lofty birth marked them as the guardians of the country's welfare, but of the illiterate mobs of the hustings. The First Minister of the Crown had stooped to correspond with the chairman of an association only not illegal, encouraging the dregs of a provincial town to usurp the high functions of Parliament.[4]

The feeling against the ministers in conservative circles was more than merely political. It aroused something like the antagonism which the upper classes as a whole have shown to

---

[1] *Croker Papers*, ii. 113.

[2] See *The Political and Occasional Poems of Winthrop Mackworth Praed*, edited by Sir George Young, 1888.

[3] Monypenny, *Life of Disraeli*, i. 324.

[4] Lord Grey had written to Thomas Attwood explaining the Government's intentions with regard to the £10 franchise.

the fiscal policy of Mr. Lloyd-George, a belief that the Government was striking at the roots of the established social order to please the proletariat. Then, as now, there were keen supporters of both parties in every rank of life; but, speaking generally, Society considered Grey a traitor to his class, and few could reconcile the introduction of the bill with his promise to stand or fall with his order. Disraeli described " the coroneted Necker, the worn-out Machiavel, wringing his helpless hands over his hearth in remorseless despair, and looking up with a sigh at his scowling ancestors." Whiggery had hitherto been the most aristocratic of creeds; it seemed to have been at length captured by Radicalism. The minister's action in forcing a dissolution on the King raised furious criticism; the monarchy was being used as the engine of its own overthrow. This indignation reached a higher pitch when the question whether peers would be created to pass the bill was being discussed in every village in the country.

The purely secular hostility to the Reform Bill was strongly reinforced by religious motives. The Church of England, which in those days as often as not was understood to mean the clergy, was with conspicuous exceptions against the bill. It was the eve of the Oxford Movement, and in this connection it might truly be said that the darkest hour preceded the dawn. Almost everywhere a deadly lethargy enwrapped the land, and of the two parties in the Church which showed any vitality both were hostile to the Reformers. High Church fervour manifested itself in intolerance of Protestant Dissenters on the one hand and Roman Catholics on the other. Both the repeal of the Test and Corporation Acts and Catholic Relief were strongly supported by the Whigs, and against the latter bill a vehement Church agitation had been worked up in the country. The efforts of the parsons had ejected Peel from his seat for Oxford, which with Cambridge was a stronghold of bigotry and reactionary Toryism. Newman, not yet of note in the country, spoke with disgust of " the two-bottle orthodox " who controlled the politics of the university.[1] There, however, the first-fruits of a sincerer worship had lately appeared in the publication of the *Christian Year*. There was life too in the Evangelicals, among whom the members of the Clapham Sect held a prominent place. In private and public life they stood for a higher standard

---

[1] *Apologia pro vita sua*, p. 72.

of morals than that generally prevalent, and the abolition of the slave-trade is inseparably connected with the names of William Wilberforce, Zachary Macaulay, and Sir Fowell Buxton. Simeon, whose influence at Cambridge was so great and so lasting, was of the same school. In politics the Clapham Sect had been supporters of Pitt; Perceval, a noted Evangelical, succeeded him as Prime Minister. Indeed most of the best known philanthropists of the time were Tories, such as Sadler, Oastler, and Ashley. Brougham of course is notable on the other side, and there were two " Saints " at least, namely Charles and Robert Grant, in the Whig administration. But the Evangelicals as a whole tended to Toryism; a complaint of their anti-Reform zeal in the 1831 election has been already mentioned; they could hardly support a Government which on occasion had forced the House to sit on into Sunday morning discussing their godless measure.[1]

If keen High and Low Churchmen at the universities and other intellectual centres were against the bill, the episcopal bench and country clergy were no less so. That the bishops were Tories is hardly surprising, seeing there had been only one year of Whig government since 1783; the pity was, for their own sakes, that they mostly represented the reactionary or Eldonian type of Toryism, with an instinctive dread of any change, especially in the popular direction. It is most unfortunate that at this crisis in her fortunes the leaders of the National Church were wholly out of sympathy with the reforming spirit of the times, and their unpopularity was a serious handicap to the institution it might have been their privilege to bring into touch with the people. As it was, they were simply regarded as haughty aristocrats, and their large, and no doubt exaggerated, incomes did much to stir up that class jealousy which was expected by many to issue in a revolution and overthrow established Church and State together. The country parsons in many instances were equally unpopular and out of sympathy with their flocks. Accustomed to preach little but the duty of submission to the cruel will of a God who seemed inexorably identified with the upper classes, they were called invidiously Black Dragoons or Black Recruiting Sergeants. Some idea of the sense they entertained of their sacred calling may be gathered from Miss Austen's gallery of clerical portraits. It is a shock to

[1] See the Duke of Newcastle's *Address to the People.*

realise how many of her young men are in Holy Orders ; certainly their parishes, if they have such encumbrances, do not waste much of their time.   Possibly the lists of advowsons for sale which often fill the first column of an 1830 newspaper should prepare us to expect no very high ideal of service from their incumbents.

When the Church was so inefficient and unspiritual, it was unlikely that either her discipline or her doctrine should escape censure.   In her walls already breached by the Test Repeal and Catholic Relief Acts other obvious points invited attack. To say nothing of tithes, so hated in country parishes, Non-conformists had a manifest grievance in the Church-rate, a grievance often embittered by the manner of the exaction. Dissenters were thus bound to the Reformers alike by gratitude and hope.[1]   From the Church point of view the bill promised political power to just those sections of the people who were held likely to use it against the establishment.   It was impossible but that 250,000 newly-enfranchised Dissenters should, if true to their opinions, attempt to carry them out in action.

Moreover the democratic movement generally was hostile to the Establishment, largely because the reluctance of narrow-minded Churchmen to impart any but religious instruction to the working classes drove seekers for knowledge into the arms of opponents of the Church.   Hence the education of the masses became widely identified with secularism.[2]   Many of the extreme Radicals were proselytising agnostics.   Carlile wrote, " I always smile at the idea of a Christian Reformer or a Christian Radical." He had a great admiration for a certain Taylor, an unfrocked clergyman who in lectures at the Rotunda rationalised, or rather astronomised, Christianity.   Carlile himself accused the orthodox of attempting to pay off the account of their vices by religion, " a sort of paper currency payable in heaven "—an ingenious theory which seems to anticipate the Musical Banks of Erewhon.[3] Thus the Whigs, besides the suspicion they incurred as the

---

[1] " The Dissenters with scarcely an exception supported the Liberal party " (Skeat's *History of English Nonconformity*, p. 585).   " The Romanists, with, I believe, only one or at most a very few honourable exceptions, have been found in the foremost ranks of Reform " (*An Address, &c.*, by the Duke of Newcastle).

[2] " Mechanics' institutes became the debating societies for radicals, republicans, and anarchists of various species ; for atheists, and for dissenters of every description " (*An Address, &c.*, by the Duke of Newcastle).

[3] *Prompter*, June 4.

party of Dissenters and Catholics, were tainted in the minds of the orthodox with the stain of rationalism and agnosticism. Had not their Chancellor founded the University of London " on the avowed basis of infidelity " ? [1]

Minds less subtle than Newman's connected the decay of reverence for the Constitution with disloyalty to tradition in higher spheres. To them Liberalism was the enemy, the spirit whose logical workings were most clearly manifested on the Continent in dislike of the Catholic Church and Christianity in general, opposing and exalting itself " above all that is called God, or that is worshipped." " The hostility to the Church establishment I look upon as the chief source of all the evil of the present hour ; no moral principle can be said to sway the public mind ; indifference, bordering on infidelity, on the one hand, puritanical fanaticism on the other, these two extremes meet in order to effect one great work of destruction." [1]

But if the faces of most of the clergy were firmly set against the ministry and the bill, the support of Thomas Arnold and Sydney Smith compensated for much opposition. To both these great men the main danger of the Church seemed to lie in resistance to Reform. Arnold, overrating as he himself admitted in later life the strength of the disestablishers, believed that the pressure of outraged Nonconformity might be enough to turn the scale ; a few years' delay, he feared, might give to democracy a momentum that would overthrow the social and political order. Less engaged in secular affairs than the other, who for five and twenty years had contributed to the *Edinburgh Review*, Arnold probably felt more active hatred of the " Movement " party, seeing in Utilitarian principles a godless spirit fatal to religion and to his grand conception of a Christian State. He always shrank from co-operation with social Reformers except on the definite basis of Christianity, though he welcomed the help of Nonconformists and Roman Catholics. In both men, however, a keen intellectual contempt for reactionary Toryism united with deep moral indignation at the oppression that system sanctioned. Sydney Smith wrote of " the cruel laws of Perceval, Eldon, and Castlereagh," Arnold of the " wickedness of that spirit which maintains the game laws," " profaning the holiest names by the lowest principles," and of " selfish lords and squires and clergy,

[1] *Tory Union our only Safeguard*, 1830.
[2] *Letter to the Duke of Rutland*, by the Hon. A. Trevor, M.P., 1831.

who would irritate the people to madness." [1]  He protested
against the suggestion that the clergy should urge the duty of
submission on their flocks.  Looking with compassion and
alarm on the spectacle of the Two Nations long separated by a
system of bad government, which continued the lawlessness of
the feudal ages, he augured a happier era from the bill that
Sydney Smith described as " a magnificent measure, as wise as
it is bold."  Both men, however, paid the penalty of their Liberalism in the reprobation and distrust of their clerical brethren.

Thus secure of the devoted support of the Church, the
Universities, and Society as a whole, the Tories maintained that
all the established oracles of wisdom and authority were united
against the bill ; to the solemn warning of Burke, Pitt, and
Canning, the ministers could only oppose the alleged voice of
the people.  To this they replied that if the people had declared
for anything, it was for the ballot and universal suffrage.  Did
the Whigs propose to oblige them ?  But as a matter of fact an
election conducted amid falsehood, intimidation, and violence
was no index of the nation's sober judgment.  Already there
were signs of reaction from the " rash fierce blaze of riot " which
had disgraced England ever since the revolution of July.  The
excitement for Reform was purely factitious, not a national
movement at all.  There had been no trace of it till the French
set the example, and then the Whigs had fanned the feeble flame
for the purposes of the 1830 election.  The whole of the recent
unrest had arisen from the agitation of a traitorous faction.
The English people had never clamoured for Parliamentary
Reform except when either distress at home or revolution abroad
had momentarily thrown their minds off their balance.  And
even were there a real popular demand for Reform, the
British Empire was governed not by a sovereign people but by
the King in Parliament.  The Constitution acknowledged the
force of no plebiscite ; the ideal of aristocracy was government
for the ignorant many by the wise few, and it was a high crime
in any member of Parliament to waive his own judgment in
deference to the mob. [2]

[1] G. W. E. Russell, *Sydney Smith* (English Men of Letters series), p. 140 ;
Stanley, *Life of Arnold*, p. 243.

[2] " We are here to consult the interests, not to obey the will of the
people, if we honestly believe that that will conflicts with those interests "
(Peel, September 21 ; *Hansard* (3rd series), vii. 436).

The attitude of the High Whigs differed from that of the Tories less in their theory of politics than in their view of the strategical necessities of the moment. Their minds were essentially parliamentary, and as such partisan. Pride and sense of loyalty gave them a natural bias to support the party measure, perilous though they might consider it to be. They no less than the Tories believed in the sanctity of established institutions ; they clung if anything more fondly to the ideal of aristocratic government. It has always been the Tory custom to submit to the leadership of men of humble origin ; Canning, Peel, Disraeli, are obvious instances. Their rivals seem to have made a point of preferring birth to brains. Fox himself yielded precedence to Portland and Grenville. Rockingham was no great statesman, but he was England's only marquis. A party with these traditions was not likely to consist of mere levellers. But their reading of the history of the last few years taught them that the surest way of preserving their order was to concede with grace what would otherwise be wrested from them perforce. It was far better to pass a Reform Bill of their own drafting than to leave it to the clumsy brains of the people— a most dangerous precedent. If the measure to be granted were framed skilfully and passed promptly, the actual difference it made need be very small, and the aristocracy might still continue to rule. Though constituencies might change, the class of member returned would not. The rotten boroughs must certainly go ; in their case the scandal was too glaring ; but it was a consoling and an important consideration that most of them belonged to the Tories. Otherwise all that was necessary was to open the gates of the Constitution wide enough to admit a manageable number of the besieging force, and then to close them again firmly. Added to the existing garrison, the new electors would avail to hold the citadel of privilege as long as at any rate their generation need look forward, while the rabble without, bereft of their leaders, would soon melt away into silence. Care must of course be taken to retain the balance of power on the right side.

Such was in fact Lord Grey's idea of the probable working of his Reform Bill. " I am indeed convinced," he wrote in September 1831, " that the more the bill is considered, the less it will be found to prejudice the real interests of the aristocracy." [1]

[1] Grey to Lord Somers, September 26, 1831 ; *Howick Papers.*

Even the abolition of the nomination boroughs he was prepared
to defend on these lines.   Their retention might preserve power
in the hands of certain individuals of rank and property, but
the nobility as a whole gained nothing by Lord Lonsdale's
nine pocket members.   There was nothing to prevent seats
being bought up by the most *bourgeois* capitalists, or even by
Papists—a consideration actually used as a serious argument
for Reform.   The bill would set up many boroughs and divisions
of counties in which the influence of great landowners would
remain supreme over that of mere wealth, though methods
might require to be slightly altered.[1]   Its operation, Grey fully
hoped, would give the whole body of the aristocracy " a general
influence more congenial to their true character, and more
effectual for securing to them the weight which they ought to
possess."   He added that nothing but an extensive measure
would give " a fair prospect of a permanent settlement of the
question."

It is rather difficult to know what exactly many of the Whigs
meant in describing the Reform Bill as a " permanent " or
" final measure."   Both at the time and later the phrase caused
amusement, not to say ridicule.   Macaulay, one of the forward
wing, said he thought the bill would last till the days of its
framers' grandchildren, but he admitted in Parliament that it
was absurd to attempt to legislate for posterity.   Sydney Smith
prophesied most accurately that the question, or any dangerous
agitation of it, would rest for thirty or forty years ;  " and this
is an eternity in politics."   The sanguine Whigs would probably
have given their settlement considerably longer than this, but
they can hardly have hoped that it could be permanent in the
sense in which the system broken up in 1832 had been permanent.
And yet many Reformers believed that the enfranchisement of
three great towns would have been ample to satisfy the people.
To such men the changes embodied in Russell's plan seemed so
vast, that their imaginations may have refused to contemplate
anything beyond.   If they did so refuse, it was not from lack
of warning.   Croker and others riddled the bill without mercy

---

[1] Lord Monmouth " had early resolved to appropriate to himself a
division of the county in which his chief seat was situate ; but what most
interested him, because it was most difficult, was the acquisition of the
new borough that was in his vicinity, and in which he possessed considerable property " (*Coningsby*, bk. iv. ch. v.).

in debate, holding up its thousand anomalies, and showing that it led directly to the Radical programme. Place wrote in 1836 : " It was anticipated that the Whigs in power would soon be convinced that the Reform Acts would neither remain in the state in which they would become Acts of Parliament, nor the relative condition of the two Houses be what it had hitherto been. . . . No such knowledge was possessed by Lord Grey and his colleagues, it was evident that they supposed the Reform of Parliament to the extent they proposed to carry it was compatible with the maintenance of the power and privileges of the House of Lords and that of the Established Church. They had in some inconceivable way persuaded themselves that the Reform of the Commons' House could be, and as they framed it, would be ' a final measure ' ; had it been possible for them to foresee the consequences it could not fail to produce, they would have abandoned it. It seems remarkably strange that Lord Grey, whose intention it always was to stand by his order, should have persisted in carrying out a Reform of the House of Commons, the inevitable result of which could not fail to be the total destruction of that order, and of every other privileged order and person." [1] Were Place and Croker right, or was Grey ? In a way it is yet too early to judge, unless we decide that a statesman is only bound to forecast the immediate results of his actions. By this criterion Grey was right ; certainly Place was wrong.

The Reform Act put an end to the most vigorous popular agitation ever known in the country ; Chartism was a pitiful fiasco ; the Church was not disestablished, at least in England ; Queen Victoria succeeded to the throne, and reigned till the end of her life ; the House of Lords was not abolished ; the Army and Navy were not disbanded ; men of property, landed or otherwise, preserved an enormous influence in the political and social life of the nation. So soon as 1837 Arnold saw that his fears had been ungrounded. " In 1831 when I wrote for the *Sheffield Courant*, I shared the common opinion as to the danger which threatened all our institutions from the force of an ultra-popular party. But the last six years have taught me . . . that when an aristocracy is not thoroughly corrupted, its strength is incalculable ; and it acts through the relations of private life, which are permanent, whereas the political excite-

[1] Add. MSS. 27,790, f. 214.

R

ment which opposes it must always be short-lived." This domination of the landed gentry endured in its fulness till the Repeal of the Corn Laws.   It needed all the personal influence of Peel, and all the external pressure applied by Cobden and Bright as champions of the enfranchised and unenfranchised middle class, to force that measure through a House of landlords. Even so, the complexion of the Commons remained overwhelmingly aristocratic for twenty years, and much more than twenty years.   The Church-rate was not abolished till 1868, for all the Dissenters' hopes ; and though eighty years have now passed since the Reform Act, plural voting and a restricted franchise still prevail.   Nothing, in fact, could have been more unlike the anarchic pandemonium pictured by alarmists than the solid respectability of the Victorian age.

But if we survey a wider field, we may admit, without passing judgment on Grey's practical prudence at the time, that the prophecies of his opponents are being realised, though only to the extent that political prophets are usually successful—that is to say, in broad outline, and in the fulness of years.   If our polity is as yet a most incomplete democracy, all the advance in that direction was only made possible by the 1832 Reform Act and its logical extensions.   The House of Lords still exists, but it has been legally subdued to the Commons, and is a very different institution from the body which rejected the Reform Bill.   The patronage exercised by and for the aristocracy has been largely curtailed.   Little as the people has to say in the selection of its representatives, it can at least exact from them a high standard of work and attention to the business of Parliament.   The demands of labour and the condition of the working classes occupy the legislature to an extent which would have shocked the pig-tailed beaux who adorned the old House of Commons.   But while they would have hailed such changes as a dire fulfilment of their forebodings, they must surely have been also surprised at the essential sameness of English politics and the acquiescence of the people in the alternate rule of the old aristocratic parties.   They had not foreseen the development of the Caucus, the inevitable parasite which feeds on democracy and saps its strength.   They had underrated the intellectual apathy of the average Englishman, which makes organisation necessary if his weight is to tell in politics.   But it was Lord Grey's Reform Bill which provided the machinery for giving effect to his will when once aroused ; and in so far as this machinery has on the whole transferred to the working people far more political power than they possessed before, and so altered the whole orientation of our public life, we must agree that the Tory prognostications were right.

Whether any alternative measure could have had a more permanently conservative effect is another matter. Certainly the Reform Bill as passed could not afford a permanent solution in any real sense. How far it was expected to afford one by the politicians of its day was really a matter of temperament, according as a man held a static or a progressive theory of the State and its institutions. Tories and High Whigs took the former view. They subscribed to the maxim of Sir Egerton Brydges quoted and endorsed by the *Quarterly :* " There are many principles, rules, and doctrines which ought not to be admitted to be brought into debate." They held that England without the trinity of King, Lords, and Commons would be England no longer. To them an aristocratic polity was good because it produces least changes in the laws ; Governments should administer, not legislate ; the presumption was that institutions suitable for one generation would also suit the next ; antiquity as such was a virtue. But the younger Whigs, soon to be called Liberals, worshipped Progress. Their theory of the State was dynamic. King, Lords, and Commons might be the best Constitution for England now ; they need not necessarily be so always. If they ceased to be so, it would not be treasonable to try a new arrangement. The position is typically stated by Arnold : " There is nothing so revolutionary, because there is nothing so unnatural and so convulsive to society, as the strain to keep things fixed, when all the world is by the law of its creation in eternal progress." This doctrine was not far from the as yet undiscovered theory of Evolution. Those who held it could look upon no political measure as final, except in a very limited sense.

The Liberals were mostly young men, inheriting lightly convictions which had cost their fathers hard and courageous thought. " Between 1828 and 1830 a new race came to influence public affairs, who did not remember the horrors of the French Revolution, and who had been teased to death by hearing their parents talk about them. The harsh and cruel spirit which those horrors

had awakened in their contemporaries became itself, by the
natural law of reaction, an object of disgust and almost of horror
to the next generation." [1]   Some of them had fallen under the
spell of Canning and his enlightened colleagues, but all were
disgusted at the welter in which they saw the country's institutions—the poor law, the game laws, the penal code, the state
of Chancery.   Everything was antiquated, decayed, and above
all corrupt.   Corruption was the foul ogre against whom they
whetted their maiden blades.   They had rejoiced at the two
recent measures of religious toleration, though the glory was
not theirs ; in the July Revolution they had heard the trumpet-
call of liberty, whose sound was gone out into all lands.   The
events of the autumn were a series of delicious excitements,
culminating in the fall of the long tyranny.   A golden age of
light was now beginning—

> " Bliss was it in that dawn to be alive,
> But to be young was very heaven."

An infinite enlargement of human power seemed to have
been made possible by the invention of machinery ; man had
added a new kingdom of subject spirits to his empire ; strange
monsters of iron were to run his errands with a strength and
swiftness before unknown.   A ride in a train was as novel and
exciting as a ride in an aeroplane to-day.   " I was looking only
yesterday at an old memorandum book," said John Bright long
after, " and I saw a note in it that on a certain day I had walked
from my house up to the railway station to see the train come
in from Manchester with its passengers.   It was a new thing
the wonder of which to me has never ceased, and I think the
power, the speed, and the grandeur of these great locomotive
engines can never grow old, and that we can never regard them
without wonder and without admiration." [2]   Nothing seemed
too high for the soaring intellect of man.   And at length political
improvement was to keep pace with the advances made in
science, in commerce, and in industry.   " The Schoolmaster
was abroad " ; and the paltry plea that the Constitution had
worked well was out of date.

[1] Walter Bagehot, *Biographical Studies*, p. 322.

[2] Speech at Rochdale, September 25, 1877; *Public Addresses by John
Bright*, p. 414.   The aristocratic Whigs by no means shared this feeling.
Lord Sefton got Creevey to oppose an early Railway Bill in the Commons
(*Creevey Papers*, p. 430).

The Reform Bill exactly met the desires of the new generation, and fastened them, if not already set there, on the Whig
party. Of the earlier middle-class magnates many, like the first
Sir Robert Peel, had been Tories. Canning had been supported
at Liverpool by Gladstone's father ; Macaulay himself was intended for a Tory. And we have seen that the *Manchester
Guardian*, hot against the Corn Laws, yet favoured Wellington
till the day of his mad pronouncement. But from the night
of March 1, 1831, the bulk of the middle class was sworn to
" the Bill, the whole Bill, and nothing but the Bill." Their
alliance with the Whig aristocracy was signed. Macaulay did
not misrepresent his order when he declared nine years later
that he " was at that time only one of those . . . millions of
Englishmen, who were deeply impressed with the conviction
that the Reform Bill was one of the best laws that ever had been
framed." [1] In their eyes, it struck the extreme point boldness
could reach without danger to the social system ; the political
balance was just on the side of property. True children of the
industrial revolution, they held Property in superstitious veneration as " the nourisher of mankind, the incentive of industry,
the cement of human society." [2]

It so happened that Property generally went hand in hand with
Education ; this pointed to the middle classes as the proper repository of political power.[3] Unfortunately the March of Intellect had
not yet penetrated to the working people, who would therefore be
likely to use the vote against their own best interests, possibly to
the destruction of sacred property. Liberals, and not Liberals
only, were strongly convinced of the need and duty of supplying
education ; they favoured, according to their views, the schemes
of Lancaster or Brougham's Useful Knowledge Society.[4] But, said

[1] Speech of January 29, 1840 ; *Speeches of Lord Macaulay*, p. 92.

[2] Sir J. Mackintosh, *Hansard* (3rd series), ix. 678.

[3] " Our fervent wish, and, we will add, our sanguine hope, is that we
may see such a reform of the House of Commons as may render its votes
the express image of the opinion of the middle orders of Britain. A pecuniary qualification we think absolutely necessary; and in settling its amount,
our object would be to draw the line in such a manner, that every decent
farmer and shopkeeper might possess the elective franchise " (*Edinburgh
Review*, October 1829).

[4] " If there are no barbarians to break in upon us, like the Picts and
Scots of old, we have let the great body of the people grow up like barbarians in the midst of our civilisation. Neglecting almost all means of
instilling into them betimes a dutiful veneration for the institutions of

Macaulay, " it is not necessary now to inquire whether, with universal education, we could safely have universal suffrage. What we are asked to do is to give universal suffrage before there is universal education." [1]    To this and the other demands of labour his answer was No. Much better to entrust the franchise to that class, small enough to have a corporate wisdom of its own, yet too large to be exclusive, whose width of interest and progressive spirit entitled it to speak for the future as well as the present. " The higher and middling orders," wrote Macaulay with glorious audacity, " are the natural representatives of the human race. Their interest may be opposed, in some things, to that of their poorer contemporaries, but it is identical with that of the innumerable generations which are to follow." [2]    Surely a superb theoretical basis for any structure of class tyranny. By such opinions Macaulay deserved and won his proud position as the representative of the £10 householders of Leeds in the first Reformed Parliament. The *bourgeoisie* of the provinces were naturally delighted with the bill ; it appealed to their practical good sense and did not outrage their sentimental reverence for the Constitution. Most of all they rejoiced in the abolition of boroughmongering, that insult to property and intelligence alike, to which they attributed all the legislative errors of the last few years. The future they were content to leave to the guidance of that Divine Providence which in war and peace had shown itself the especial guardian of the British race.

The cramping effect of middle-class domination on the national life in several spheres during the Victorian era has perhaps created a prejudice against that order and their eminently respectable views. But in the reign of William IV a glamour attached to them as stormers of the hard-won citadel of power and founders of a new civilisation. It was they who

their forefathers . . . we have allowed the flagitious part of the press to act . . . &c. " (*Quarterly Review*, January 1831).

[1] Speech of May 3, 1842 ; *Speeches*, p. 126.

[2] *Edinburgh Review*, March 1829. Cf. *Manchester Guardian*, December 4, 1830 : " As the mass of the middle classes never can have any interests adverse to the happiness and prosperity of those below them in society, the rights of the humblest order would be quite safe from violation under the protection of representatives chosen by a constituency, in which that mass had a preponderance." " Property and knowledge are the great instruments of civilisation."

had enabled Pitt to hold the Continent at arm's length, and by their enterprise they were about to raise England yet higher above the rival nations. Drawing their inspiration from such different sources as Bentham, Arnold, Macaulay, they provided the driving power of common sense and humanity which cleared the land of many relics of the cruelty and folly of the past. But they were richer in enthusiasms than in ideas, and their work and principles were essentially non-constructive. Their dominant notion was that of Progress—a world gradually improved by successive onslaughts of the liberal spirit. " The History of England is emphatically the history of progress," wrote Macaulay ; [1] the Reform Bill was to him part of a golden chain of which the Great Charter, the Reformation, and the Revolution were other links, if not the invention of gunpowder and of steam-engines.

The Liberals, however, do not appear to have had any very definite idea what goal they were progressing towards ; one gathers it was a kind of permanent international exhibition, a Crystal Palace in which the middle classes might worship the three gracious forms of Peace, Plenty, and Property. In politics their danger lay in a certain doctrinaire self-sufficiency and lack of imagination. The writer of an article in the *Edinburgh* on " Signs of the Times," complaining in something of the Carlyle spirit that the age was essentially one of machinery and materialism, found support for his views in the state of politics. " Men are grown mechanical in head and heart, as well as in hand. They have lost faith in individual endeavour, and in natural force of any kind. We might note the mighty interest taken in *mere political arrangements*, as itself the sign of a mechanical age. There is a science of *Dynamics*," he protested, " in man's fortunes and nature, as well as of *Mechanics*. The French Revolution itself had something higher in it than cheap bread and a Habeas Corpus Act. Here, too, was an Idea : a Dynamic, and not a Mechanic, force." Philosophy had yielded to physical science ; intellect now meant mere logical power ; wonder and worship were dead. " Worship, indeed, in any sense, is not recognised among us, or is mechanically explained into fear of pain or hope of pleasure. Our true Deity is Mechanism." [2]

[1] *Essay on Sir James Mackintosh.*
[2] *Edinburgh Review*, June 1829.

The Liberals were of course rigid individualists and advocates of *laissez faire ;* modern minds will probably find something grim in Macaulay's attitude on the factory bills ; he will not think of interfering with adult labour : " The freeman cannot be forced to work to the ruin of his health. If he works over hours, it is because it is his own choice to do so. The law ought not to protect him, for he can protect himself." [1] Detesting the political conclusions of the Radical philosophers, the young Whigs were more agreed with them on economic matters. They deeply distrusted the intervention of the State at all in commerce and industry, and clung to the doctrine of the Wages Fund. It was therefore not only fear of the violence of the uneducated masses, and contempt for their folly and inefficiency, but also a firm belief in the futility of collective bargaining as a means of permanently improving the workman's welfare which led them to condemn the labour movement of the time.[2] The Liberal Arnold, inclined to sympathise fully with the poor and not afraid to denounce their oppressors, spoke of " the Trades Unions " as " a fearful engine of mischief, ready to riot or assassinate, with all the wickedness that has in all ages and in all countries characterised associations not recognised by the law." [3] This was the general opinion of educated men, and explains the rooted hostility shown even by friends of labour to trade unionism and the Chartism which followed its decline. Only lately converted themselves to Ricardian orthodoxy, they ascribed the struggles of the poor for freedom simply to ignorance of the cardinal rules which govern society, an ignorance which, however innocent, should of necessity preclude them from power. " The inequality with which wealth is distributed forces itself on everybody's notice," said Macaulay. " The reasons which irrefra-

[1] " Alfred," *History of the Factory Movement,* i. 149. However, in 1846 Macaulay voted and spoke strongly in favour of the Ten Hour Bill limiting the work of " young persons " in factories (*Speeches*, p. 207).

[2] Lord Melbourne wrote on October 24, 1831 : " These Unions may and probably will produce much mischief to the country and much loss and distress to those who engage in them. . . . They have proposed to themselves, in the settling and securing a better rate of wages and a sure supply of employment, objects which it is impossible by any means whatever, whether violent or otherwise, to obtain " (*H. O.* 41. 10). " Nothing is more certain than that turn-outs never did and never can produce any permanent advance in the rate of wages " (*Manchester Guardian*, December 18, 1830).

[3] *Life*, p. 338.

gably prove this inequality to be necessary to the well-being of all classes are not equally obvious." [1] Economic or social, or indeed political, equality was not the doctrine of any respectable party, certainly not of the Whigs. If they, the established champions of freedom during Pitt's Government, stood for equality at all, it was for that of all men before the law, not in making the law; nor did the Reform Bill mark much advance as regards equality, seeing that plural voting and practically close constituencies were retained. Equality, political and social, was sought respectively by the two divisions of the Radicals, between whom quite as fierce opposition raged as between either and the parties in Parliament.

These last were at one in accepting the settlement of 1688 as the essence of the Constitution.[2] On the border-line between them and those who did not, between the disciples of Burke and Paine, were encamped the philosophic Radicals of Bentham's school, at this crisis playing the part of opportunists. In the abstract, so far as anything can be abstract in politics, they despised kingship and the aristocracy of birth as quaint but costly survivals of barbarism; all men's interests were equally at the mercy of Parliament, and therefore every man should have a vote for its members. Ballot and annual elections they believed to be also necessary to prevent corruption. But the Utilitarians fully realised that their complete programme was impracticable so far as regarded constitutional methods. And alike on financial, political, and ethical grounds they had no wish for a revolution by physical force. It remained to organise pressure upon Parliament and the ministry from without, and, by demanding more than they could expect to receive, to hope for some part of it. In this campaign Grote, the historian and banker, was of use in stirring up opinion for the bill in the City, while Francis Place set himself to maintain a connecting service between the Government and the working classes of London. Hobhouse and Burdett kept him informed of opinion in the lobbies and at critical periods carried messages to and fro. Lord Durham, for instance, in his speech in favour of enfran-

[1] *Speeches*, p. 126.
[2] The Whig attitude, as shown in a toast at a Newcastle dinner in 1821, was: " May the memory of one Revolution ever prevent the necessity of another" (Lambton to Wilson, September 28, 1821). The Radical toast was: " To the next revolution, and the nearer home the better."

chising the new metropolitan boroughs, depended largely on statistics furnished by Place. Durham, as has been shown, was more respected by the Radicals than were most of his party ; Macaulay especially made himself unpopular by his easy manner of disposing of all below the middle classes. Nor in truth were Place and his friends under any illusion regarding the Whigs, though they agreed to give them an only too strenuous support while the bill was in passing. They detected in its provisions the loopholes for aristocratic ascendency, and never pretended that it could be more than an instalment. Especially after the inclusion of the Chandos clause, they favoured it rather as a means of breaking up the old prescriptive system than for any intrinsic value of its own.[1]

And yet the representation set up by the bill worked out in a manner to which the Utilitarians had little right to object. " There can be no doubt," wrote James Mill, " that the middle rank, which gives to science, to art, and to legislation itself, their most distinguished ornaments, and is the chief source of all that has exalted and refined human nature, is that portion of the community, of which, if the basis of representation were ever so far extended, the opinion would ultimately decide." [2]   Mill's confidence that the enfranchisement of the working-class would only strengthen his own order exactly corresponds to Lord Grey's belief that the middle-class vote would not disturb the aristocracy, and shows that classes may no more succeed than individuals in viewing themselves from the outside. Unfortunately for the chances of a business government, the philosophers never became kings in the practical sphere, and they were forced to rest content with the incomplete application of their principles by Whig legislators, till the Benthamite theory of government gave place to one based more on experience and less on abstract views of human nature.

[1] " The experiment now to be tried was believed by the people to be that of a House of Commons uninfluenced in the choice of its members by the Lords and chosen freely by the people. . . . Apprehensions that the county representation would be wholly divided between the Whig and Tory factions, and that the boroughs would become contests of the rich and powerful alone . . . were entertained by very few. . . . Yet so it was, and Lord John Russell has since openly avowed in his place in Parliament that from the first it was intended that it should be so " (Add. MSS. 27,789, f. 230).

[2] *Essay on Government.*

So far there has been no doubt of the efficacy of political methods ; Parliament has been accepted without question as the Great Council of the nation, on which its hopes depend. Nowadays we are more sceptical, and nothing is more characteristic of our political thought than the depreciation of Parliament. It needs a very keen politician to read through the debates in the morning paper. But in 1831 they were the most interesting part of it. The long confinement of seats in the Commons to the aristocracy had filled the middle and lower classes with pathetic hopes of what might be done when the charmed circle was open to their own representatives. The apple just out of reach looks sweetest ; and Parliament was never held to be so powerful as in the days of the Reform struggle. The benefits promised were so great, that the whole nation had become astonishingly political.

It was not till November 1831 that the Westminster politicians came into actual conflict with the organised ranks of the workmen they claimed to speak for. Benthamism was essentially bureaucratic ; its devotees were benevolent despots in miniature and had learnt by experience that the British artisan needed to have freedom forced down his throat, as in the case of the Combination Laws. But the London Radical working men, under their able leaders, were far from anxious to be dragooned into supporting a plan of Reform from which they saw no advantage to themselves. This is not the place to recount the various political and semi-political societies which grew up and in some cases collapsed during these agitated months. But it may be well to mention the main lines on which their thoughts ran.

The critical question touching the working-class movement of the time was whether democratic aspirations were to be directed primarily to political or social change. The two sides had much in common—the sense of degradation, the conviction of the inadequate payment of labour, and the consciousness of potential power. But while the political Radicals showed no constructive ideas by which society might be remodelled to their liking, the opposite wing were animated by revolutionary theories of pregnant force. There was, however, much overlapping in the case of individuals, and the balance wavered between the two sides, first one and then the other attracting most adherents.

Many of the political agitators were simple enough to believe that their grievances could be redressed by a change in temporary financial policy. They called for the lightening of taxes on articles which a poor man buys, for the abolition of pensions and sinecures, and for at least the partial disendowment of the Church. In matters other than fiscal, they wanted reform of the criminal code, especially as regards the game laws, and other administrative improvements. Chiefly to secure these ends, they were anxious to capture the machine of government for their own class, and to do so adopted the points of the Radical programme. But there is little suggestion of a policy beyond this removal of restrictions. Hetherington indeed called for " a heavy property tax upon all inordinate wealth," but there is no hint that his thoughts turned to social reform ; the aims of government were still negative.[1]

After this there are divisions ; the Free Press enthusiasts believed in raising the position of their class by education, though they regarded Brougham's efforts to promote working-class education by Mechanics' Institutes and Useful Knowledge tracts with deep suspicion and contempt, as baits flung by their oppressors.[2] " The political and critical writings of Locke, Hume, Paine, and Franklin, of Voltaire, Mirabaud and Volney," said the *Prompter*, " with a hundred other brilliant authors who have arisen within a century, as the offspring of the three revolutions of England, America, and France, have presented a new system of education, in relation to the present and immediate importance of which the smooth verses of Horace and Virgil, of Homer and Hesiod, are but trash." Paine would appear to have been the single author of most influence, and it was the study of him which led the National Union of the Working Classes to issue a Declaration of the Rights of Man, though with momentous additions from another source. " The Rights of Man in Society are Liberty, Equality before the Laws, Security of his person, and the full enjoyment of the produce of his labour " ; one of the expressed objects of the Union is to support organised

---

[1] *Poor Man's Guardian*, August 20, 1831.

[2] " I acknowledge but two distinctions in men, the cultivated and the uncultivated ; I believe that individual happiness is the only collective happiness. That mental power being imparted only to a few, has caused the misery of many. That mental and political power are the same thing " (*Creed of a Liberal*).

labour against reduction of wages by "the combination and tyranny of masters and manufacturers." It is the last two items which show another influence than Paine's. The declaration did not go unchallenged even by those who sympathised with its framers' hopes. Carlile set upon the theory of rights —harmless enough surely if construed as a list of objects desired ; he held inequality of status to be necessary and desirable. He denied also that a wage-earner could claim the whole produce of his labour.[1]

Cobbett cared even less for abstract right ; he did not disapprove of the class system nor of inequality in incomes ; a labourer wanted food, clothes, fuel, and lodging, not political standing as such, nor even a literary education. Essentially conservative, he put the social emancipation of the rural labourer in the first place : theory was always dangerous, and might lead to the heresies of the paper-currency men or to the despotic and anti-social doctrines of Malthus, which he hated equally.[2] The social order should be preserved until the original compact of primitive men was dissolved by the reduction of the majority of the people to a worse condition than that of the anarchic Law of Nature.[3] Then reconstruction became necessary—as in the present case, which demanded Parliamentary Reform as the first step. Here Cobbett, in his acceptance of the Whig bill, differed from many of the Radicals, who feared that the reconciling of the middle classes to the gentry would involve their own perpetual exclusion from power. It was simply a matter of tactics ; there was no belief on either part in any Reforming zeal on the part of the Whigs ; Cobbett said they had been led to church in a halter. Opinion in these circles was really revolutionary. Inspired by the Three Days of July, Englishmen were keen to show their mettle at grips with the aristocracy, pictured as grabbers of public land, money and power. Some took a

[1] *Prompter*, June 4.

[2] " Cobbett is an anti-advance man to the backbone ; he is sometimes Jacobin, sometimes Conservative, but never Liberal " (Stanley's *Life of Arnold*, p. 350).

[3] *Twopenny Trash*, November 1831. Here we have the influence of Paine, and of a greater than Paine. " The individuals themselves, each in his own personal and sovereign right, entered into a Government : and this is the only mode in which Governments have a right to arise, and the only principle on which they have a right to exist " (*Rights of Man*, Part I. p. 42 (1819 edition)).

childish pleasure in speaking of " Mr. and Mrs. Guelph," and ignoring the Reform discussions in Parliament.[1]  But, granted a revolution, it is difficult to see what government these demagogues would have substituted, or how they would have liked it to proceed.

From the disciples of Paine we cross to the disciples of Owen and Hodgskin ;  after the Labour party, Syndicalism.  Owen himself took no interest in the Reform struggle ;  his paper, the *Crisis*, founded in April 1832, ignores the thrilling condition of politics altogether.  The principles of the British Association for Promoting Co-operative Knowledge, of which five hundred branches were said to exist in the United Kingdom, were defined as Charity, Benevolence, and Industry ;  they were to be embodied in a universal voluntary association taking the place of the coercive State, and based on the growth of knowledge. Owen was encouraged by his belief that convictions and feelings are not dependent on the will, but purely on environment. By attention to the laws of human nature, a reign of universal charity could be founded in one generation, to supersede the system of competition resulting in monopolies.  Compared with the wealth thus absorbed, " the whole taxation of the country is but as a feather in the scale " ;  the Radical Reformers were on the wrong tack.  Even if taxation could be reduced, the difference would probably be taken out of wages, and the working man would gain nothing.  They, on the other hand, replied, like the trade unionists, that the capture of the political machine was essential for the setting up of Co-operation ;[2] they had no hope of effective help from the aristocracy's conversion to Owen's views.  Others challenged the theory that human nature could be radically changed by education within a single lifetime ; others the economic soundness of Socialism.

But the Co-operative societies produced an atmosphere fit for the growth of more fertile ideas.  " It was these Owenite institutions," writes Professor Foxwell, " and their periodical literature, that served to propagate the doctrines of the Ricardian Socialists."[3]  Godwin, Thompson, Gray, Hodgskin all produced theories of property which struck at the root of the established

---

[1] *Poor Man's Guardian*, No. 1.

[2] *Ibid.*, January 14, 1832.

[3] Introduction to Anton Menger's *Right to the Whole Produce of Labour*, p. lxxxii.

order, though the idea of ownership by a controlling State is not fully developed ; collectivism has not taken the place of communism. Godwin, the husband of Mary Wollstonecraft and father-in-law of Shelley, had brought out his *Political Justice* in 1793. It was the English firstfruits of the French Revolution in other than purely political fields.[1] Protesting against the inequitable distribution of power and wealth, he argued on entirely *a priori* grounds for a system of anarchic individualism. He declared that want is the only title to property, but want must be supplied by neighbourly love ; he could admit no rights whether on the part of single men or of society.[2] Co-operation and constraint are alike cramping to individuality, and must be reduced to the narrowest possible limits ; even concerts, and the performance of music by others than the composer, are rather dangerous. Though Godwin was thus anything but a Socialist, that part of his teaching which survived the transient popularity of his two quarto volumes was the challenge to private property. " My neighbour has just as much right," he said, " to put an end to my existence with dagger or poison, as to deny me that pecuniary assistance without which I must starve." [3]

Charles Hall, a doctor deeply impressed by the misery of the poor, had urged the same doctrine of the tyranny of wealth, and notably of wealth in land, in 1805.[4] Twenty years later Thompson, taking Ricardo's dogmas as " ascertained truths," was converted to communism by his sense of the unjust remuneration of labour. Gray's *Lecture on Human Happiness*, published in 1825, covers the same ground in attacking rent, interest and profit, and individual competition generally ; Gray claims all wealth for " the productive classes, excepting only the persons *absolutely* required in unproductive occupations." [5] Lastly, Thomas Hodgskin aroused the antagonism of Place,

---

[1] For the decline and fall of the enthusiasm for Godwin see the article on him in Hazlitt's *Spirit of the Age*, written in 1825. " Truth, moral truth, it was supposed, had here taken up its abode ; and these were the oracles of thought. ' Throw aside your books of chemistry,' said Wordsworth to a young man, a student in the Temple, ' and read Godwin on Necessity.' "

[2] *Political Justice*, i. 114, 1st ed.

[3] *Ibid.*, i. 112.

[4] *The Effects of Civilisation on the People in European States ;* Foxwell, p. xxxii.

[5] Foxwell, pp. xxxviii–liv.

Mill, and Brougham by his denial of the outstanding importance of accumulated capital. The workman is entitled, as against capital, to the whole produce of his labour ; the conflicting claims of individuals can then be settled by the " higgling of the market." As things were, he said, " it is a heinous crime in the eyes of a legislature composed exclusively of capitalists and landlords, and representing no other interests than their own, for us to try, by any means, to obtain for ourselves, and for the comfortable subsistence of our families, a larger share of our own produce than these our masters choose to allow us. . . . To put down combination they have departed from principles held sacred for upwards of 200 years." But let them beware. " On the side of the labourers there is physical strength, for they are more numerous than their opponents. They are also fast losing that reverence for their opponents which was and is the source of their power, and they are daily acquiring a moral strength which results from a common interest and a close and intimate union." [1]  The doctrine of the workman's right to the whole produce of his labour need not imply an organising state, but it does imply the supremacy of the producing class. This was the faith which inspired the whole movement, whether the machinery chosen to realise it were legislation, co-operation, or the strike.[2] All along, the divisions were not hard and fast ; the same men were to be found taking the lead in various enterprises, and some trade unions actually contributed out of their funds to the Reform cause, and allowed their banners to march in its processions.[3] Doherty himself did not confine his restless energies to unionism, and there was always a strong connection between the Rotunda Radicals and the co-operative movement.

It is no doubt unsafe to generalise from the eager few to the apathetic and inarticulate many ; large as was the sale of Hodgskinite and other pamphlets, the Reforming societies were never joined by half the numbers their founders hoped for, and the unorganised workers were the vast majority of their class. Still it is the strenuous who count, and Place was probably right in claiming that, in case of fighting, many more would have

[1] *Labour defended against the Claims of Capital*, i. 4, 25, 32.
[2] At the height of the political struggle the working men of London were constantly invited by William Benbow to down tools simultaneously and go off for a month's holiday.
[3] *History of Trade Unionism*, p. 159.

turned out on the popular side than were willing to pay subscriptions and attend meetings. Deeply as he disapproved of
the communistic revolt against economic orthodoxy, he admitted
that the heretics had stimulated thought to a prodigious extent
and so far done real good to the workers.[1] They had suggested
remedies in answer to the discontent around them, and called up
dazzling visions of what might be. For the moment it seemed
that the eyes which had seen light would never turn back to
the darkness of the cave, and that practical effects of deep importance must follow the fermentation of thought. " Some great
change," wrote Owen, " in the condition of man, either for good
or for evil, is about to take place. The old civilised world is
out of joint." [2] He, for one, believed that the hour and the
man had come to set it right. As Tories declared that all that
made life glorious would perish with the old order, Radicals
hoped that now for the first time freedom and joy would reign.
Thomas Arnold, equally remote from the extremes of reaction
and revolution, saw in the signs of the times a state of things
parallel to the condition of France before the Revolution, herald-
ing the birth of a new æon in the world's history and the sweeping
away of ancient landmarks.[3] By some the strange tongues of
the Irvingites were taken as a sign that the end of the world was
at hand. Many felt that " upon this time the ends of the ages
are met." Men's imaginations were touched by events abroad,
bringing home to them the fact that life was not as prosaic as it
seemed. It was not eight years since Byron had died at Mis-
solonghi, crowning his services to freedom ; and now a not less
heroic struggle had been fought and lost for the same cause in
Poland. The glorious failure had touched the romantic side of

[1] " The present mischief these two men [Owen and Hodgskin] have in
some respects done is incalculable. They have, however, set thousands
thinking, and difficult as it is and will for a long time be to eradicate the
false notions they have inculcated, yet the thinking portion of the working
people having been led by them to believe themselves of some importance
in the State, will never cease to think so, and the time will come when
they will think correctly on all which concerns their real condition in
society " (Add. MSS. 27,791, f. 270).

[2] *Crisis*, April 14, May 19.

[3] " All in the moral and physical world appears so exactly to announce
the coming of the ' great day of the Lord,' *i.e.*, a period of fearful visitation to terminate the existing state of things, whether to terminate the
whole existence of the human race, neither man nor angel knows " (*Life*,
p. 267).

S

the English nature, and in some cases its conscience ; for the misery of the Irish was hardly less than that of the Poles, and it was the same spirit of nationalism moving alike in O'Connell's demand for repeal of the Union, and, in a form adapted to the genteeler atmosphere of Whig drawing-rooms, in the sensuous cadences of Moore. The *Irish Melodies* had profited by the interest in small nations aroused by Walter Scott's stories of his own country in verse and prose.

For it was the prime of the romantic movement in art, and Scott, the high priest of romance, was beyond question the central figure of literature.[1] The last of the Waverley novels were indeed but a faint afterglow of the glory that had been, but their great predecessors had quickened countless minds with a new sense of sympathy with the past, and of adventure for the future. Keats and Shelley had hardly yet come to their own, but Byronism was still strong, with its two veins of satire and romance. On the other side in politics, but the same in poetry, were Coleridge, Southey, and Wordsworth. Nor was this warm spirit of adventure chilled by the critical and patronising tone made popular by the *Edinburgh* and *Quarterly* reviewers. Even they had enthusiasms of their own, and often did not spare to give themselves away by betraying them, till at length the dry pages of the *Edinburgh* blossomed with the splendid rhetoric of one who, while himself the most brilliant of reviewers, was carried away by the full tide of romantic feeling for history and life. So too the plays and operas that Society went to were brimful of romantic melodrama. The same spirit seems to have invaded the political stage ; we trace it in Cobbett's translation of Paine's bones from America, in the famous vow of Attwood and his men, and even on the floor of Parliament in Brougham's appeal to their Lordships delivered on his bended knees. Many of the proceedings in the Reform struggle were drenched in sentiment—the black-edged newspapers, the souvenir mugs of the Birmingham Union, the burning of the bishops' effigies, and the manifestoes of the Radical societies.

All this made easier the work of organising the expression of opinion in favour of the Reform Bill. It is only when we pierce behind the scenes that we realise how infinite were the

[1] See Hazlitt's *Spirit of the Age*, p. 245 : " Sir Walter Scott is un-doubtedly the most popular writer of the age—the ' lord of the ascendant ' for the time being."

wires the tired agitators had to pull to keep the people up to the mark ; how anxious were their fears lest in some period of waiting the demand, which in the distance looked so spontaneous, should collapse, and so afford to the lukewarm an excuse for dropping their support. In Birmingham the commanding position of Attwood and the corporate feeling of a rising town made co-operation less arduous. But in London, where varied interests might excuse temporary slackness, and the constant presence of politicians would make it noticeable, we may well believe that Place was busy enough. Time and time again a dying dog had to be whipped into new life to refute the assertion that it was dead ; the timid had to be soothed, and besides the attacks of conservatives there was an open cross-fire from the ultra-Radicals. And yet to argue that the Reform Bill excitement was in the main artificial would be untrue. We know to-day how transitory are the enthusiasms of public opinion ; eighty years ago there was no provincial daily press, no nursing of constituencies, no popular local government. For all that, during a period of twenty-two months the country was more political than ever before or since. Of course there were agitators and agents, as there must be for any concerted democratic movement ; but it may be fairly claimed that from April, and still more from October, 1831, the movement was national and represented the real desire of the enormous majority of the people.

This is no denial of the fact that many of its ardent supporters had the haziest notion of the bill's contents ; in the clamour for it were concentrated the hopes and hatreds of thousands, hopes of a sweeter and easier life and hatred of the old parliamentary system. The sullen disappointment resulting from the world's going on much as before swelled into the stream of discontent which caused the Chartist disturbances ten years later. There were some evils in our social state which called for deeper wisdom and more sympathetic understanding than the Whigs possessed ; in fact, the heartless philosophy they obeyed hardly encouraged the attempt to heal them. But for those who looked they were there ; even in the frivolous Greville we come on these lines in more serious strain, written after the cholera scare had given some hint of the appalling condition of the poor.[1] " It certainly need not be that the majority of the

[1] *Memoirs*, ii. 280.

population should be in great difficulty, struggling to keep themselves afloat, and, what is worse, in uncertainty and in doubt whether they can earn subsistence for themselves and their families.    Such is the case at present, and I believe a general uncertainty pervades every class of society, from the highest to the lowest ; nobody looks upon any institution as secure, or any interest as safe, and it is only because those universal feelings of alarm which are equally diffused throughout the mass but slightly affect each individual atom of it, that we see the world go on as usual, eating, drinking, laughing and dancing, and not insensible to the danger, though apparently indifferent about it.''

# CHAPTER VII

## THE LORDS REJECT THE BILL

" Good Lord, put down aristocrats,
Let borough-mongers be abhorred,
And from all tithes and shovel-hats
Forthwith deliver us, Good Lord."

*Poor Man's Guardian*

LATE in September the second Reform Bill finally passed the Commons, after a struggle unprecedented in parliamentary history. The House had sat without a break from June onwards, and on one occasion the debate had been prolonged till nearly eight in the morning by an Opposition anxious to exhaust every form of constitutional protest against a revolutionary bill. Divisions were forced wherever possible, and one victory was won against the ministers. The Whig landlords combined with the Tories and extreme Radicals to carry Lord Chandos' clause enfranchising yearly tenants at a rent of £50 ; the best the Governments could do was to make the clause apply to other tenements as well as farms. The opening thus made for faggot-votes was naturally held in the country to detract much from the merits of the bill. As the interminable discussions dragged on, boredom and heat proved fatal to many tempers, to say nothing of the fierceness of party spirit. Croker's scornful dissection of the bill's anomalies, and the fanatical tirades of Sir Charles Wetherell, gave ministers little peace. Althorp alone, on whom, with Lord John Russell, now of Cabinet rank, the main burden of the battle fell, remained through all the stormy scenes calm, polite, and reasonable, winning from both sides confidence in his honesty and praise for his perfect temper. " His ability was never so remarkably shown," wrote Brougham, " as on the Reform Bill. He had a knowledge of its whole details, and of all the numberless matters connected with it, which was almost supernatural. The others knew it so ill, and got into such scrapes when opposed to the most formidable opposition of Croker chiefly (who had something like his mastery of the subject), that it became quite necessary to prevent them from speaking—or what was then called ' to put on the muzzle '—and A. really did the whole." [1]   Russell, however, proved an admirable lieutenant, and the two supported one another with a harmony that was wonderful in so complicated a work.   " We are going," Macaulay told his sister, " as soon as the bill is through the Commons, to give a grand dinner to Lord Althorp and Lord John Russell, as a mark of our respect.   Some people wished to have the other Cabinet ministers included ; but Grant and Palmerston are not in sufficiently high esteem among the Whigs to be honoured with such a compliment." [2]

The Opposition, now at last a united body, were less satisfied with their leader, whose reserve was again complained of, at a time when every effort was needed to rally the party for the hopeless war against a majority, in Peel's words, " now became unassailable by reason." [3]   The Tories were indeed fighting a delaying action, to give time for the Reform fever in the country to cool before the Lords should reject the bill ; any advantage they might secure in the meantime was so much to the good. " When the Peers call to mind the circumstances," wrote an anonymous admirer to the Duke, " under which the present House of Commons was elected, no decision of that House ought to have any weight with the Lords ; not even if the Reform Bill passed by a majority of 300." [4]   As it was, the majority on the second reading showed a ministerial gain of 135 votes since March ; and, in spite of differences in Committee and declining zeal as the autumn advanced, the last stage of the bill was passed by 109.

In the country it would have been unreasonable to expect the " first fine careless rapture " of the spring to be maintained throughout the dreary weeks in Committee.   No one had bargained for so long a delay ; enthusiasm gave place to impatience, and impatience at whiles to apathy.   Ministers were blamed for their meekness by partisans in the House, and those outside could not understand how if their hearts were true they

[1] *Althorp Papers*.

[2] Macaulay to Hannah Macaulay, August 29 ; Trevelyan, p. 176. Macaulay said that Althorp combined " the temper of Lord North with the principles of Romilly."

[3] *Greville Memoirs*, ii. 153, 160, 162 ;   *Peel Papers*, ii. 188.

[4] *Despatches*, vii. 505.

could tolerate the obstruction. Petitions, not always respect-
ful, urged the Honourable House not to dawdle.[1]  On the whole
the country was quiet.  Disturbances had broken out, however,
in the west earlier in the summer, especially in the coal trade.
Riots at Merthyr at the beginning of June resulted in an attack
on the military, who fired back on the mob, killing several.[2]
Cries for Reform were heard at the beginning of the outrages,
and men who had voted Tory at the election ran considerable
risks.  But though cheap literature was admitted to have caused
some political feeling, the riot was mainly assigned to a fall in
earnings and the unpopularity of the local Court of Requests.
There were lesser disturbances in the same trade in the Forest
of Dean, as well as in Lancashire, partly attributed to the Trades
Union, and in places the incendiarism of last winter broke out
again.  All through August political unions about the country
were said to be doing " infinite mischief," though Melbourne
himself, while admitting their growth, saw no danger from their
threats to pay no taxes, unless indeed numbers of the middle
class should join them.  Nor had he serious fears of the trade
unions, whose strength he believed to have declined since the
winter, owing to the workers' own conviction of the futility of
strikes in the present condition of labour.[3]  Still there was
always the possibility of violence if the Lords should reject the
Reform Bill.

This event, which had been constantly in the thoughts of
politicians since the dissolution, was now becoming the one
topic of interest.  It will be remembered that the King, as early
as February, had regarded it as a hazard at all costs to be
avoided ; he had reaffirmed his conviction after the dissolution,
and had besought his ministers to spare no pains to arrive at a
compromise with the Lords ; in fact, he refused to contemplate
the deadlock which would result from the bill's rejection.  Grey,
no less eager to escape a conflict, had a clearer idea of the situa-

----

[1] Althorp himself wrote to Durham : " I should not mind a public
meeting at all, even if it abused me for not taking stronger measures "
(*Lambton Papers*).

[2] " We are met here to have our wages raised, but the masters have
brought the soldiers against us ; now, boys, if you are of the same mind as I,
let us fall upon them and disarm them " (*H. O.* 52. 16).   Carlile spoke
of the incident as " the first crude attempt to fight, on the part of the
British people, against the soldiers " (*Prompter*, June 18).

[3] *Melbourne Papers*, p. 129 ff.

tion than his master. If he never understood the people, he could gauge the feelings of his own order with extreme accuracy, and he realised very soon that the Lords were unlikely to bow to the majority of the Commons, however great. To the King's frequent appeals that he would so far modify the bill, without impairing its principle, as to conciliate the reasonable among the peers, he replied that no modification of the measure, short of mutilation, would appease those whose influence was likely to be decisive. It would be ruinous to forfeit the people's support and confidence, and then fail after all. The King agreed, but continued to cry for the impossible, urging the past sacrifice of his own prejudices as an example to his ministers. The whole question turned on what the principle of the bill was, and Grey soon made it clear that it was everything which any peer was likely to object to.

His colleagues were equally gloomy as to the result, and the less enterprising spirits prepared themselves for retirement from office.[1] But the forward party, believing that such desertion of the popular cause in the hour of danger would be fatal not only to the Whigs, but to the country, insisted that the bill must be reintroduced after a short prorogation, assuming, that is, that there were hopes of carrying it.[2] They were much handicapped at this time by the loss of Durham, utterly prostrated by the death of his adored son, the " Master Lambton " of Lawrence's picture, which kept him out of politics for the remainder of the session. Brougham, however, took the bold line, and as early as the beginning of September suggested to Grey that peers must be specially created if the bill was to pass. The coronation, to the necessity of which the prosaic King had reluctantly assented, gave an opportunity for several creations, but hardly as many as the strength of the Opposition Lords seemed to demand. Now therefore began the first serious contemplation of the measure which was to be so furiously canvassed for the next nine months, and to cost the Prime Minister so many sleepless nights. By tacit consent neither the King nor he had mentioned it, but, like the dissolution, it had been long at the back of their minds, and its shadow lay visibly across the path of a fearless Reformer. At first Grey

---

[1] *e.g.* Lansdowne and, at first, Althorp. See *Macaulay's Life*, p. 178 ; *Memoir of Althorp*, p. 340.

[2] Howick to Charles Grey, October 4 ; *Howick Papers*.

thought of following up the coronation batch of new peers by a second creation, should it appear desirable, before the division in the Lords ; but this plan, to which the King would never have consented, was soon given up, and the question was post-poned.[1] In any case it was likely to try the feelings of orthodox Whigs to the uttermost, and might lose as many noble votes as it won. The Opposition had foreseen the possibility, and trusted rather to dissensions within the Whig ranks than to the scruples of the ministers or of the King. For the moment, however, all hung on the action of the Lords, and anxiety was great.[2]

On the afternoon of September 22 the bill was brought up to the bar of the other House by Lord John Russell ; a meeting of Opposition peers had decided to let it be read a first time without challenge, and October 3 was fixed for the second reading. In the interval, and not less after the opening of the discussion, petitions poured in asking that the bill might be passed. There was one from the corporation of London, and one with 36,000 signatures from Edinburgh ; on the first night of the debate Brougham alone presented no less than eighty, and Grey more than forty.

That morning a vast open-air meeting was held at Birming-ham under Attwood's auspices to petition the Lords and, with more hope, to encourage the ministry to remain at their posts in case of defeat. It was the first of those great assemblies on Newhall-hill which held up to England the spectacle of the people organised and articulate, and in his humble Rochdale home inspired a mightier than Attwood with the zeal that, a generation later, was to carry a second and wider Reform of Parliament. For John Bright in after years told a Birming-ham audience how at this time of excitement his family, content hitherto with the weekly *Manchester Guardian*, was moved to take in the *Evening Mail*, whose glowing articles appeared thrice a week. " They were very stirring articles," he said. " They gave me much information, and I date some

---

[1] Grey to Brougham, September 2, 3 ; *Brougham Memoirs*, iii. 125-7.

[2] Wellington to Buckingham, August 15 ; *Courts and Cabinets*, i. 341. Grey entreated Brougham not to go up to Westmorland at so critical a time. He might come back to find a state of things which would allow him as much holiday as he liked (Grey to Brougham, September 23 ; *Howick Papers*).

portion of my political activity to the influence of that paper in those days. And I read there of your great meeting, and all the country read of it, and all the country was stirred to its very heart by what you did at that time." [1] The numbers of the meeting were put at many thousands, and spectators took pride in its order and discipline, which they too justly feared would not be emulated all over England. [2]

The speakers at a great Manchester meeting declared that the results of rejection would be appalling. They desired Reform from the economic point of view. " The immense load of taxation, and the immense debt by which it has been accumulated, is chiefly, if not entirely, to be placed to the account of the aristocracy." " I speak," said Richard Potter, the Attwood of Manchester, " in the hearing of many gentlemen who have had occasion to go up to the House of Commons on business, and who have found that its great fault is that there are no men of business there." The cause of Reform was the cause of Free Trade. [3] Even the Radicals at the Rotunda petitioned for the bill as a stepping-stone to universal suffrage, though declaring that they cared little for it otherwise. [4] Hetherington and Carlile more logically prayed that it might be rejected, as a " delusive and dangerous measure," blocking the way to real Reform ; the resulting confusion might give the working classes a chance of attaining their own desires. [5] By such ironical petitions the extreme Radicals gave the anti-Reformers much assistance in debate, but they cannot be considered to have had any practical effect.

Grey himself did not disdain to canvass his own order for their support of what he sincerely believed to be an aristocratic measure. [6] The Duke of Wellington, who had all along resolved that the bill must be thrown out, was doing the same thing, and the meeting of peers which decided to grant it a first reading decided also to let it go no further. [7] The Duke himself

[1] *Public Addresses by John Bright*, June 1, 1877, p. 353.

[2] Parkes to Grote, October 4 ; Add. MSS. 35,149, f. 77. Reformers put the numbers at 100,000 ; an anonymous correspondent of the Duke said 20,000 at the outside (*Despatches*, vii. 558).

[3] *Manchester Guardian*, September 24.

[4] Add. MSS. 27,791, f. 302.

[5] *Poor Man's Guardian*, October 1 ; *Prompter*, October 8.

[6] Grey to Somers, September 26 ; *Howick Papers*.

[7] Wellington to Bath, Sept. 22 ; to Northumberland and Bishop of Exeter, September 23 ; to Somers and Buckingham, September 24 ; to Dorset, September 26 ; *Despatches*, vii. 531–7. *Greville Memoirs*, ii. 198.

firmly believed that the country was against the bill, except for the towns where political unions were established, and held that, even if it were not, it was the Lords' duty to save it from so disastrous and revolutionary a measure. The prophecies of a violent outbreak of the people he refused to take seriously.[1]

The debate, which lasted five nights, was held at the time to have excelled all the displays in the Commons. It was in many ways a memorable occasion, well worth a journey from Oxford for the ardent young anti-Reformer who, alone of all the brilliant audience, was likely to surpass the eloquence of the speakers.[2] He witnessed an aristocracy on its defence ; a senate not less powerful in its individual than in its corporate character, claiming for the last time to override without appeal the judgment of the representatives of the people. On the one side many felt that, if the bill should pass, their place in the Constitution would be for ever gone, along with the Crown, the Church, and all for which England stood to them ; while the other side feared that one imprudent act would deliver the country beyond hope into the hands of a disloyal rabble. The Tories were mistaken in supposing that the bill would lead directly to the destruction of the Upper House. But their instinct was a true one ; it swept away to a great extent those outworks of privilege in the Commons which enabled the Lords to withstand the broken impact of popular feeling. There was little need in the old days for the Lords to oppose a bill sent up to them ; if they disliked it, their influence was strong enough to destroy it in its earlier stages.[3] But in 1831 a House of Commons was for once returned not amenable to their authority ; they were forced to fight within their own borders, with the knowledge that if they lost now they could seldom win again. The Lords thus revived a claim it had been unnecessary for them to assert ; at least since the Revolution they had been in practice the inferior House, though in theory coequal. Yet this had meant no loss of power to individual magnates. At length this power was threatened, and to preserve it the Lords risked their corporate prestige. Whether they were justified by the Constitution in doing so seems doubtful. There was no pre-cedent of at all the same importance. Certainly they were

[1] *Despatches*, vii. 530 ; *Manchester Courier*, October 1.
[2] Morley, *Life of Gladstone*, i. 75.
[3] See Bagehot, *English Constitution*, ch. iv.

unwise, as the event showed.  But in the absence of any clearly marked line of duty, it needed a wiser statesman than Wellington to lead them right.

The debate was opened by Grey in a speech which recalled how over forty years ago he had championed in his youth the same cause in far other circumstances ; he justified the proposal of so large a measure by the need of a final settlement.  To the bishops in particular he appealed to " set their houses in order," and not frustrate the desire of the people.  His own course was clear.   " By this measure I am prepared to stand or fall. If it should be rejected, the question of my continuance in office, even for another hour, must depend upon my seeing any reasonable prospect of being able to effect a measure to which I am pledged, as I think, by every tie of private honour, by every obligation of public duty to my sovereign and to my country." [1]

Grey was supported by the moderate members of the Cabinet, who admitted that their early prejudices had yielded to stress of events ; but the great defence of the bill came from the Chancellor, in a wonderful declamation that owed something of its force and fire to a bottle of mulled port.   He insisted that the question was that of Representation, and spoke in eloquent terms of the great middle class, the guardians of wealth and knowledge. Opponents had protested against yielding to the clamour of the mob.  " If there is the mob," said Brougham, " there is the people also.  I speak now of the middle classes—of those hundreds of thousands of respectable persons—the most numerous and by far the most wealthy order in the community, for if all your Lordship's castles, manors, rights of warren and rights of chase, with all your broad acres, were brought to the hammer, and sold at fifty years' purchase, the price would fly up and kick the beam when counterpoised by the vast and solid riches of those middle classes, who are also the genuine depositaries of sober, rational, intelligent, and honest English feeling.  Unable though they be to round a period, or point an epigram, they are solid right-judging men, and, above all, not given to change. If they have a fault, it is that error on the right side, a suspicion of State quacks—a dogged love of existing institutions—a perfect contempt of all political nostrums.  They will neither be led astray by false reasoning, nor deluded by impudent flattery ; but so neither will they be scared by classical quotations, or

[1] *Hansard* (3rd series), vii. 968.

brow-beaten by fine sentences ; and as for an epigram, they care as little for it as they do for a cannon-ball. Grave, intelligent, rational, fond of thinking for themselves, they consider a subject long before they make up their minds on it ; and the opinions they are thus slow to form, they are not swift to abandon. It is an egregious folly to fancy that the popular clamour for Reform, or whatever name you please to give it, could have been silenced by a mere change of Ministry. The body of the people, such as I have distinguished and described them, had weighed the matter well, and they looked to the Government and to the Parliament for an effectual Reform. Rouse not, I beseech you," he cried with dramatic gesture, " a peace-loving, but a resolute people ; alienate not from your body the affections of a whole empire. As your friend, as the friend of my order, as the friend of my country, as the faithful servant of my sovereign, I counsel you to assist with your uttermost efforts in preserving the peace, and upholding and perpetuating the Constitution. Therefore, I pray and I exhort you not to reject this measure. By all you hold most dear—by all the ties that bind everyone of us to our common order and our common country, I solemnly adjure you—I warn you—I implore you—yea, on my bended knees, I supplicate you—Reject not this Bill ! "

The main argument on the other side was that the British Constitution had worked well in the past, whereas the new system would make government itself unworkable. The House of Commons would become a democratic assembly straining to lay sacrilegious hands on property, religion, and the Crown itself. " The Ministers," said Lord Harrowby, " have done what no Ministers ever ought to do—they have brought forward a measure which it may be almost equally dangerous to adopt or to reject." On the other hand the need of some Reform was generally admitted, except by the Duke, who, in a soldier's unwary language, expressed " the greatest contempt " for the Birmingham meeting and its threats to refuse taxes. He and Lyndhurst laid stress on the Whigs' complicity in exciting the country, which, if the bill were rejected, would soon regain its normal composure. Lord Grey in reply repeated his pledge to stand by the bill or a measure no less extensive.

At length at six o'clock on the morning of Saturday, October 8, the House divided. The ministers were beaten by forty-one votes ; it was seen that, if the twenty-one bishops who voted in the majority had listened to Grey's solemn appeal, the result would have been different.[1]  We owe to Durham's continued absence an interesting letter from Brougham, written at this crisis in the fortunes of his colleague's " favourite measure."  " I have done my endeavour," he says, " indeed I never exerted myself more, and am very much knocked up.  Lord Grey exceeded himself—*I never heard anything like his reply* (his opening speech having been first rate too).  The Bishops have done for themselves, and that they begin to feel already.  They will not vote on many more bills."[2]

One would be glad to know more of Grey's oratory, which made a deep impression on men of both parties by its dignified and manly flow, befitting so typical a *grand seigneur*.  The Duke of Wellington said that his manner and speaking as leader of the Commons had been " quite perfect " ; he was wasted in the Lords.  " Nobody cares a damn for the House of Lords," the Duke complained ; " the House of Commons is everything in England, and the House of Lords nothing."  But when on an occasion like Queen Caroline's trial the Lords did catch the public eye, Grey's friends were delighted with him ; Creevey affectionately vowed, " there is nothing approaching this damned fellow in the kingdom, when he mounts his best horse."[3]  The less partial Greville wrote in December 1830 :  " His tall, commanding, and dignified appearance, his flow of language, graceful action, well-rounded periods, and an exhibition of classical taste united with legal knowledge, render him the most finished orator of his day."[4]  On this, the great dramatic occasion of his life, Grey was at his best ; it was no small feat for a man of sixty-six to win the praises of a weary House for a long speech delivered in the small hours of the morning after five nights of excited debate.[5]

---

[1] It was calculated that of the 112 holders of peerages created before 1790, no less than 108 voted for the bill ; this confirms the claim of the Whigs that the wholesale creations of Pitt and his successors had left them a long arrears to work off (Kent's *English Radicals*, p. 95).

[2] *Life of Durham*, i. 265.

[3] *Creevey Papers*, pp. 286, 336.

[4] *Greville Memoirs*, ii. 88.  Greville declared that Grey's eloquence caused his actual talents to be much overrated.  Cf. *Brougham Memoirs*, iii. 419.

[5] *Greville Memoirs*, ii. 203 ; The *Manchester Guardian* of June 18 quotes from a contemporary on Grey's speaking : " His action is not graceful, for he has acquired the practice of hiding one hand beneath

The betting had been against the bill getting through, but forty-one was a much heavier majority than Reformers had expected. It seemed to make a creation of peers almost unthinkable. " No Minister can make sixty Peers, which Lord Grey must do to carry this Bill," wrote Greville ; " it would be to create another House of Lords." Althorp, who a day or two before had agreed with Brougham that the number of creations must depend only on the amount required, now wrote to his father despairing of popular support should fifty peers be made ; he proposed that the ministers should resign and leave Reform to be carried by its enemies, as having no " reasonable prospect of carrying the bill." [1] Grey's opinion was the same on the point of creating peers. He was in fact told definitely by the King on the day of the division that no such suggestion could be received. At the same time William hoped that ministers would continue in office at so critical a time. Grey agreed at once that the amount of the majority made any idea of peer-making out of the question. " Indeed," he wrote to Taylor, " I should not have been willing, under any circumstances, to resort to such a measure, and certainly not unless a very small addition would have been effectual for the purpose."

The Cabinet met at once on the Saturday, and decided not to resign, but begged their master for a few days to consider their position before sending him a formal answer.[2] On the Tuesday this was sent ; the Cabinet would remain in office, on condition of having the King's full support for a new bill " of equal efficacy," to be introduced at the beginning of the next session.[3] Unanimity

his coat-skirt, as if standing near the fire, which is very unbecoming, but at times he extends his arms to their full length, and then his attitude is manly and imposing. He frequently, throughout his speech, advances from his seat towards the table, and retires again ; but with him this is an easy movement, unlike the awkward motions of Sir Robert Peel, who paces at regular intervals, and with invariable sameness, between the table and the bench, poising one leg upon his toe, lifting up his hand and laying it down again with the regularity of a pendulum. The tones of Lord Grey's voice are clear, but not varied or harmonious, and his utterance is distinct and firm."

[1] *Greville Memoirs*, ii. 202 ; *Brougham Memoirs*, iii. 129 ; *Memoir of Althorp*, p. 354. Grote to Parkes, October 8 ; *Reminiscences of the Events of 1831-2*, by a contemporary ; *Manchester Guardian*, October 15.

[2] *Correspondence*, i. 363-6. Jeffrey to Cockburn, October 9 : " We will not resign " (*Life of Jeffrey*, ii. 239). Brougham to Durham, Monday ; *Lambton Papers*.

[3] Cabinet minute, *Correspondence*, i. 373.

on this point had not been secured without a hitch. Palmerston wrote to Grey on the 9th complaining that Althorp had used words prematurely pledging his colleagues to the course afterwards decided on by the Cabinet. Althorp denied that he had bound anyone but himself ; and the Prime Minister, knocked up by the debate as he was, had to write to pacify Palmerston and at the same time explain that he had understood the Cabinet to be already agreed on the point.[1]

On Monday, Grey went to Windsor to discuss the situation with the King. He was forced to ask for the dismissal of Earl Howe, the Queen's Lord Chamberlain, who had voted against the Government in the Lords. Howe's position had long been precarious. As early as May 8 Grey had hinted in a letter to Taylor at the disadvantage under which the Government suffered by the conduct and opinions of persons favoured by the Court.[2] On May 14 Taylor wrote back expressing a hope that it would not be found necessary to insist on Howe's resignation, considering the regard both King and Queen felt for him. Soon after this it would appear that the King himself wrote to censure Howe for having signed an anti-Reform declaration ; on May 22 Grey was informed of the fact. Naturally, therefore, Howe was furious when the *Times* announced next morning that " a certain Earl, connected with the Royal Household, has received a severe rebuke from the King on account of his continued meddling and incessant chatter against the Reform Bill." [3] By the King's advice he wrote to ask the Duke of Wellington's opinion as to whether he ought to resign. In a second letter he apologised for writing so freely : " but really to find my sovereign weeping with me over the state of affairs, and lamenting the wonderful imprudence of his confidential servants, and actually advising his private friend to consult the political enemy of these ministers, was so new a situation for a quiet country gentleman, that I hardly knew what I did from shame and vexation." On the Duke's recommendation he did not resign : " I have the King's leave to *vote* as I like," he added ; " my opinions are firmly but temperately declared, and

---

[1] *Correspondence*, i. 375. Althorp to Grey, October 9 ; *Althorp Papers*. The name of the minister is suppressed in the published *Correspondence*, but Althorp's letter shows that it was Palmerston.

[2] *Correspondence*, i. 260.

[3] *Times*, May 23.

my Lord Brougham may yet find me a thorn in his side more
annoying than he is now aware of." [1]  To compare with this
outspoken statement we have the King's reply to a further hint
from Grey ;  William declared that, while " he had not hesitated
to discard from his household any individual, whether holding
a superior or an inferior situation, who, being a member of either
House, had withheld or stated his intention of withholding his
support from the Government upon the question of Reform,"
yet he could not believe that it was his duty to break off long-
standing intimacies with men of both parties.[2]  It was now
understood that members of the King's household must support
the Government or resign, and Lord Waldegrave gave up his
situation in the Bedchamber immediately before the Lords'
debate.  But Lord Howe continued to serve his mistress, in
spite of protest from Reformers, till Grey actually demanded
his dismissal.[3]  The King consented, but Queen Adelaide was
loth to lose her devoted servant, and her antipathy to the Whigs
was embittered.[4]  The whole affair was an anticipation of the
Bedchamber question of 1839, which cost Peel two years of
power.  But there was a difference in the eyes of the country
between a young and popular English queen, and an elderly
and unpopular German consort.

Grateful as the ministers were for the King's compliance on
this point, and anxious to soothe his fears of disturbance in the
country, yet, when William proposed to deprive two Whig
officers of their commissions for violent language used at public
meetings, they felt bound to intervene against so intolerant
a use of the prerogative.[5]  One of themselves, in fact, was in
the same condemnation.  Lord John Russell, in replying to
the thanks of the Birmingham Union, had incautiously referred
to the opinions of the majority in the Lords as " the whisper

[1] Howe to Wellington, May 23, 25 ; *Despatches*, vii. 443–6.  It would
seem that Grey mentioned the secret to Brougham, and that Brougham
must have divulged it, but direct evidence is lacking.  Cf. *Melbourne
Papers*, p. 226, for a similar indiscretion in 1834.

[2] *Correspondence*, i. 291.

[3] *Globe*, October 1.  Brougham to Durham, October 10 ; *Life of
Durham*, i. 265.

[4] Greenwood, *Hanoverian Queens of England*, ii. 383 ff.

[5] Colonel Torrens had said the Lords ought to be put in Schedule A,
while Colonel W. Napier, the historian of the Peninsular War, had
harangued a meeting at Devizes (*Correspondence*, i. 352, 368).

T

of a faction." The King was much annoyed, and Russell apologised, though, as he said, he had just heard from Birmingham " that the letters written by Lord Althorp and himself contributed in a great degree to prevent acts of violence against persons and property." [1] Grey, Althorp, and Brougham had more soberly protested against the non-payment of taxes, and done all they could to keep the country tranquil. Jeffrey wrote to Scotland entreating his countrymen to remain quiet till the bill was revived, and to express their feelings only in lawful ways.[2] But the King was worried by the excitement around him, and again besought his servants to do all they decently could to commend the bill to the Lords.

It is arguable that Lord Grey took up a weak position in continuing in office with no guarantee, or indeed ground for presumption, that he would be able to carry the Reform Bill ; that his only reasonable alternatives were to resign or to insist on permission to create peers when necessary. As it was, the crisis was merely postponed for seven months, to the disorganisation of the political and industrial life of the country. However, the King's attitude made a creation of peers impossible, and indeed it is inconceivable that the Cabinet would have agreed to propose so large a number. They would merely have given place to a Tory administration, and for this neither side was anxious, having regard to the temper of the country ; it was strongly felt that the one hope of order was in the people's confidence that the ministers were on their side. " The only thing that keeps the peace," wrote Brougham to Durham, " is *our remaining in.* All country letters to-day show this feeling to be quite universal." [3] In this matter Grey's pledge to the nation to introduce no less effective measure was of great service. And in any case the new bill had to pass all its stages in the Commons before the question of peers could become practical ; Reformers would surely prefer a Reforming Government in the interval to one which would obviously try to concede the least possible. At this time, as opposed to May

[1] *Early Correspondence*, ii. 25.

[2] *Life of Jeffrey*, ii. 239.

[3] *Life of Durham* i. 265. Lord Grey wrote : " I am persuaded that nothing can preserve the public peace but the continuance of the present administration in office, with the confidence of the people in the sincerity of their resolution to prosecute to a successful issue the cause which they have undertaken " (*Correspondence*, i. 376).

next year, the Tories might probably have offered considerably less than the rejected bill; but the unpopularity they would have incurred must have been dangerous to peace. The Whigs had, moreover, the King's definite request that they would not leave his service, and this might be taken as a half-promise of his support in time of need, if it did not suggest to the Lords that they must bow to a united King and Commons.

But the decisive factor was the vote of confidence passed in the Lower House the night before the Cabinet met. The course of a violent debate, in which one Reformer went so far as to say that the ministers' resignation would be treason to the people, showed how little sympathy there could be between a Tory administration and the majority of the House. " I do not expect open, armed insurrection," said Macaulay in a speech which infuriated the Opposition. " What I apprehend is this— that the people may engage in a silent, but extensive and persevering war against the law. . . . I know only two ways in which societies can permanently be governed—by public opinion, and by the sword. . . . If we are afraid of Political Unions and Reform Associations, let the House of Commons become the chief point of political union ; let the House of Commons be the great Reform Association." Colonel Evans vowed that if any government tried to coerce the people by the sword, he would be the first to draw the sword against it.[1] In the light of the Commons' encouragement, the ministers were justified in holding on at present, deep as their anxiety must be till they could feel certain of a majority in the other House.

The Reforming press, though prepared for the defeat of the bill, burst out in passionate denunciation. The *Morning Chronicle*, the advanced Liberal paper, appeared with black edges. The *Times*, which had reluctantly assented before the debate to the postponement of peer-making, now demanded an immediate creation of at least sixty. A short prorogation and peers at once was the demand of the forward section ; the more timid were for some modification of the bill, and no creation unless absolutely necessary. But all were at one in pressing the ministers to stay in office ; and when they did so, it was

---

[1] *Hansard* (3rd series), viii. 393, 450.

assumed from their previous declaration that they had the King's leave to make peers.[1]

The news of the bill's rejection was received in London as a national calamity. A letter of the time describes its effect on a body of middle-class passengers starting for Gravesend by the early boat. "When the paper with a black border was seen in my hand, the passengers rushed towards me, I was instantly mounted on a chair and compelled to read the debate through from beginning to end. The excitement, the disapprobation, the approbation of the several speakers were as energetic as they could have been had they been the actual spectators of the scene which the report described. The denunciation against the Bishops was fearful." [2] The division took place in the small hours of Saturday morning, and that day shops were shut and a vast meeting assembled in Regent's Park, threatening refusal of taxes to a Tory government. There was a rumour that Lord Grey had resigned, and the gloominess of the October day matched the crowd's feelings. In the City consols fell nearly a point, a run for gold was made on the Bank, and forty-four of the bankers and wealthy merchants of London, who as a body had hitherto held back from the Reform movement, now signed a petition requesting the Lord Mayor to call a meeting at which they might express "their grief, surprise, and dismay" at the rejection of the bill.[3] The same night the Common Council met at the Guildhall, and all the Reform Associations of London prepared to play their part.

For the next few days Melbourne received constant reports from the police. On Monday a large crowd collected round the Rotunda, but no damage was done except to the Duke of Newcastle's windows. Next day disorderly meetings were held in the parks, resulting in affrays with the police; a crowd of some thousands gathered in Palace Yard to pelt the Duke of Wellington and smash the panes of Northumberland House. Threats were

[1] Add. MSS. 27,789, f. 428. Campbell wrote on October 11 : "Grey was at Windsor yesterday, and received a *carte blanche*" (*Life of Campbell*, i. 528).

[2] Add. MSS. 27,790, f. 39.

[3] *Globe*, October 8 ; *Morning Herald*, October 10. See also a very able pamphlet called *Retrospect of Events of* 1831-2, *by a contemporary Witness*, published in 1878. The author, who speaks in a detached way, quotes letters from George Grote, and writes with the original copy of the Merchants', Bankers', and Traders' requisition to the Lord Mayor before him.

heard that night in a coffee-house against the lives of the Duke
of Cumberland and Lord Wharncliffe. A large body of men
from the Rotunda was prevented by the police from marching
on St. Stephen's.[1]

The enthusiasm culminated on Wednesday in a monster
procession of the metropolitan parishes, arranged for the purpose of carrying an address to the King. It was organised
by two young Radicals, who spent the interval in attending
local political centres and persuading all they could to join
the projected demonstration.[2] It eventually numbered 70,000,
the parish associations falling in successively as the procession
moved southward to St. James's, where Melbourne received
the petition. All shops were shut, and a vast crowd of spectators assembled in the streets, much to the alarm of the respectable ; the white scarves of the Rotunda unionists caused
especial dismay, though, according to Place, none of the leaders
deigned to take part. The procession, which consisted mainly
of " shopkeepers and superior artisans," behaved in an orderly
way ; an assault on Lord Londonderry, who had spoken against
the bill, was the work of loafers. There is no doubt that the
demonstration made a great impression ; it was the first of its
kind in London, and showed that sober men who did not
ordinarily bestir themselves in political affairs were willing to
take some personal trouble on behalf of this bill, thus threatening
an uneasy time for an anti-Reform administration. The discussions in the Commons that evening turned largely upon the
events of the day, the Opposition accusing the Treasury bench of
taking the part of rioters against the law, and denouncing Althorp
and Russell for corresponding with the Birmingham Union. Many
believed that these combinations were actually illegal, and nearly
all the upper classes thought them horribly dangerous. "This
is not the way," said Vyvyan, " in which the King's ministers
have been accustomed to govern the country." [3]

Late the same night Lord Grey was surprised by a deputation of seventeen delegates from several of the London parishes,

---

[1] *H. O.* 52. 14 ; *Prompter*, October 15.

[2] Powell to Place ; Add. MSS. 27,790, f. 39.

[3] *Hansard* (3rd series), viii. 605. Eldon to Lady F. J. Bankes, October
13 : " Our day here yesterday was tremendously alarming . . . immense
mob of reformers (hardly a decent-looking man among them)" (*Life of
Eldon*, iii. 153).

including Francis Place, who may safely be presumed to have been the moving spirit. He had shared the belief prevalent among his friends that the rejection of the bill would be followed by an instant prorogation of a few days, and a batch of new peers.[1] He had approved heartily of Lord Grey's declaration as far as it went, but held that the uncertainty in which he left the people as to his power to make peers was unjustifiable. He would have Grey say definitely whether he had the power, yes or no.[2] But, as we now know, such a course was impossible in the delicate state of relations between King and Cabinet. Grey had not got the power, but he still hoped he might have it ; and it would have been most unconstitutional, as well as tactless, to let the cat out of the bag and expose his master to obloquy. Pharaoh's heart would certainly have been hardened. But Place knew less of Courts than of committee rooms ; and as days passed without any hint reaching the anxious people of what the ministers meant to do, he became impatient, fearing a financial panic and the unemployment which would result ; the news from the provinces might well seem to justify his alarm. Then came the monster procession, with its suggestion of popular excitement. A meeting was held that evening at the " Crown and Anchor " ; it determined to approach Grey personally, and press him not to prorogue for a longer time than seven days. The delegates returned little wiser than before ; Grey refused to commit himself, but contrived to give the impression, in Place's words, " (1) that Parliament would be prorogued till after Christmas, (2) that a more conciliatory bill would be introduced, (3) that no new peers would be made, (4) that if the public made riots, they would be bayonetted, shot, and hanged." He said, in fact, Hobhouse tells us, that if he were driven from office it would be by such things as the deputation's memorial. Hobhouse himself disapproved of the venture, and said the delegates were so ill-favoured a crew that a friend of his got in front of one of the least attractive-looking to hide him from Grey.[3]

To understand why the prospect looked as black as it did to Place, it is needful to turn to the effect of the Lords' action

[1] Add. MSS. 27,789, f. 432.
[2] Place to Hobhouse, October 11 ; Add. MSS. 35,149, f. 83.
[3] Place to Parkes, October 13 ; Add. MSS., 35,149, f. 90. *Recollections*, iv. 148.

in the country. The very night which followed the division, it was suggested that delegates from every important town should be summoned to London to organise united support of ministers.[1] County meetings were held over England from Cumberland to Cornwall. A Manchester gathering of 10,000, including a mass of workmen forcibly turned out of the mills by enthusiastic Reformers, was eventually flooded by Radicals. Resolutions pledging the meeting to universal suffrage were tumultuously carried, and excitement is reported to have been very great. The men of Liverpool met in equal numbers, and Rochdale, Bury, Oldham, Leeds, Middleton, Bolton, Preston, followed their example. The miners of the Tyne and Wear gathered in force, and a great meeting was held at Edinburgh. Threats to pay no taxes were frequent.[2] At Birmingham a manifesto by Attwood did much to restore confidence, but at Darlington, where stones had been piled in the streets ready to throw at the first Tory peer who should pass through, Lord Tankerville and his daughter barely escaped, in a battered coach, from the violence of the mob.[3]

It is not of course to be supposed that condemnation of the Lords was universal ; at Norwich the Eldon Conservative Club was founded by working men to celebrate the bill's rejection, presenting a rather ludicrous comparison with another Conservative Club, formed at another great crisis in the fortunes of the Upper House, though not indeed by working men, and called after another veteran ex-Chancellor. So, too, Birmingham and Manchester had their Tory papers, which denounced the incompetent revolutionaries in office as lustily as the *Standard* or *Morning Post ;* but in the main the provincial press burst out in furious tirades against those who had destroyed the cherished hopes of the bourgeoisie. " The rejection of the Reform Bill by the House of Lords is a refusal of justice to the people, and fatal evidence of the utter indifference of the higher classes to the wants and claims of the millions." " The oligarchy and the democracy are now at open war with each other." [4] The feeling

[1] Letter of Grote, October 8, quoted in *Retrospect of Events, &c.*

[2] *H. O.* 40. 29 ; 52. 13. A Manchester official wrote : " The intention of refusing the payment of rates and taxes appears to be more generally diffused, and should the example be set in other parts of the country, it may probably be adopted in this neighbourhood to a considerable extent."

[3] Malmesbury, *Memoirs of an Ex-Minister,* i. 37.

[4] *Hull Portfolio,* October 12 ; *Liverpool Albion,* October 13.

among the middle class, who had lately been swelling with pride at the prospect of the franchise, was one of fierce indignation at the arrogance of these two hundred peers ; the natural admirers of the aristocracy turned against it as a privileged political body. The little politicians of the bar and counter snapped their fingers at the ermined tyrants, and vowed that they could stand this no longer. In solemn tones they bade the nobility beware of the outraged majesty of the £10 householders. Much was said in letters, at meetings, and in conversation, of the will of the people. The nation had willed the bill with the voice of twenty-two millions, and the peers, reclining in splendid state, had chosen to flout it.[1] As a matter of fact, any body of country gentlemen chosen at random would have done the same, if left to their unfettered opinion, but the fact that the actual rejectors were lords made the affair vastly more dramatic. Considerable force was lent to the clamour by the recent abolition of the French hereditary peerage by the Casimir Périer ministry, which gave huge delight to the republicans.[2] Indeed half the prayer of the revolutionary Radicals had been granted ; " Mr. Guelph," however, was still supposed to be on the popular side.

But if the hostility to the lay peers was bitter and almost personal, it was nothing to that against the Bishops. " *The Bishops have done it,*" said Carlile ; " it is the work of the Holy Ghost." " Pay no more tithes, no more Church rates without compulsion," ran a Coventry placard, " but in God's name don't withhold payment of the taxes ; rather contribute an extra mite if necessary, to support the King and his minister in this fearful emergency. Remember, it was the Bishops who caused the bill to be rejected." [3] The concentrated hatred of the Englishman for privileged parsondom burst on the heads of the devoted twenty-one. They were attacked with extraordinary venom ; a preacher who attempted to defend them saw his congregation file out of church.[4] The Bishop of Durham wrote pathetically that he dared not show his face in his palatinate ; Bishop Phillpotts of Exeter was advised to postpone

---

[1] " Shall a small but very corrupt faction of Pensioners, Boroughmongers, and Bishops resist a nation's will ? " (Placard of the Chard Political Union ; *H. O.* 52. 12.)

[2] *Poor Man's Guardian*, October 22.

*Prompter*, October 15 ; *H. O.* 52. 15.

'At Ashton-under-Lyne ; *Prompter*, October 22.

consecrations ;[1] at Worcester, " Judas Iscariot, Bishop of Worcester," was chalked up on the cathedral walls.[2] On November 5 Guy Fawkes was almost invariably superseded by a mitred figure as the centre of illumination. The bishops' exclusion from the House of Lords was loudly called for, and it was thought by many that their order could never recover from its unpopularity in England until the Church was disestablished.[3] The bishops' letters of the time show real fears that the Establishment would have to go, and it is sometimes suggested that it was the spiritual awakening assisted by the Oxford Movement which preserved it. The correct answer would seem to be that disestablishment was impossible without a revolution. No responsible statesman wished it, and the Whigs as a party would certainly never have introduced it ; the mildest of motions against the Church revenues broke up their Cabinet in 1834. The passing of the Reform Act turned men's thoughts in calmer channels.

However, the angry feelings in the country took more serious forms than mere demonstration and abuse. Riots occurred in the west at Blandford, Sherborne, and Yeovil, and large numbers of special constables were enrolled. But worst of all were the events at Derby and Nottingham. At Derby the news of the division arrived in the evening of the Saturday ; immediately crowds met and attacked the houses of known anti-Reformers. They proceeded to force the Borough Gaol, and were not re-

---

[1] Exeter Placard, November 5 : " Woe to the Bloody Set, on Saturday the common enemy will be burnt," *i.e.*, the Bishop. The Bishop wrote to Wellington : " There are strong indications of an expectation, if not of an actual plan, of insurrection against property among the lowest orders. This detestable Reform Bill has raised their hopes to the utmost " (*Despatches*, viii. 35).

[2] *The Radical*, October 21.

[3] " Let the clergy," wrote the dissenting editor of the *Manchester Guardian*, " bear all the blame which they deserve, for their too general resistance to the progress of political improvement." The following poem occurs in the *Prompter* :—

> " I hear the people raise the cry—
> Nor can I see the reason why
> The bigot Bishops should not die !
>     I do not mean as men !
> But as a body corporate,
> A large excrescence of the state—
> An awkward clog, a great dead-weight—
>     A useless bloated wen."

pulsed from the County Gaol till three of their number had been wounded to death. On Sunday night troops arrived from Nottingham, and next day the streets were cleared, and order restored.[1]

At Nottingham the general feeling of disappointment was increased by local dislike of the Duke of Newcastle, patron of Newark, who had defended his action in evicting his Reforming tenants by the immortal " May I not do what I will with mine own ? " Anti-Reformers' windows were broken on Sunday evening, but a troop of the 15th Hussars was equal to keeping order, and next day a Reform meeting was held without disturbance. But the working people were in a state of great excitement, and on Monday night, while the eighty troopers were defending the House of Correction against the mob in the awkward streets from which the gas had been cut off, the mass of the crowd attacked Nottingham Castle, the property of the Duke, and set it on fire before the soldiers could save it. Other houses and mills in the neighbourhood were assaulted and burnt, and, though the town was soon quieted, the state of the manufacturing country districts round alarmed the authorities. The Duke himself complained that he could not show his face for fear of causing a riot, and begged Melbourne to send a Special Commission, of which he himself wished to be Chairman, to try the violators of his property. After this it is not surprising to find a petition from the town asking for the Duke's removal from his Lord-Lieutenancy. A Commission was sent in January, though to Newcastle's disgust his name was not included, and eventually nine men were condemned to death for the riots in October ; three of these nine were executed, despite petitions for the transmutation of their sentences.[2] Arson was then a capital offence, and the conduct of the men was as bad as it could be ; but there can be no excuse for the attitude of the authorities as shown in the following letter from the Home Office. The writer reminds his correspondent from Nottingham " that, it being contrary to the etiquette of the Bar for any gentleman to take a brief as counsel without a special retaining fee, the prisoners for trial under the Special Commission about to be held at Nottingham cannot have the aid of counsel for want of pecuniary means, and you therefore requested to know whether His Majesty's Government will appoint and retain some Counsel of eminence to undertake their defence. In reply

[1] *H. O.* 52. 12.　　　　[2] *H. O.* 52. 15, 19.

I am to inform you that His Majesty's Government must decline to give any directions to appoint and retain Counsel to undertake the defence of the Prisoners." [1] It is not stated that the prisoners went undefended ; but the etiquette of the barristers, the refusal of the Home Office to take any steps, and the behaviour of the Duke of Newcastle, give one some idea of the grounds on which the working classes mistrusted the machine of government.

The outrages at Derby and Nottingham were eclipsed three weeks later by the far more terrible riots at Bristol, but the question of physical force now began to harass people's minds. The exact relation of these acts of violence to the popular desire for Reform is somewhat complicated. It is not to be supposed that Reformers decided in cold blood that such outbursts would help on the cause, and the fiercest Tories did not accuse ministers of wishing to create them. On the other hand it is a mistake in most cases to hold that they were not political at all. " It does not seem to me possible," wrote Place, " to convey by words the peculiar state the country was in, nor the determination there was among an immense number of people to have the bill or a great change in the government, come what might. The disposition of the working classes to show that they could fight still remained in full vigour, but the notion that they like the Parisians ought to spare the lives and property of the aristocracy had subsided, and contrary notions were very generally entertained. . . . The especial notion that the aristocracy, under which term they included all who were rich and not engaged in some profession, in trade or commerce, were the cause of their low wages, of all their real and imagined grievances, generally prevailed among them, and the rejection of the bill by the Lords was to them conclusive evidence that they, the " unproductive " class, were resolved . . . to continue their oppression and robbery of the working classes." [2]

It was claimed by the supporters of Attwood that by the foundation of political unions he had saved the country from universal riot, and that in the places where there were strong unions no outrages occurred. [3] There was much truth in this.

[1] *H. O.* 41. 11.

[2] Add. MSS. 27,791, f. 19.

[3] Attwood to his wife, October 13 : " You know I always told you there would be no disturbances in places where our Unions exist. Un-

Beyond all doubt the country had become very political, whether party or class feeling predominated, and the arrival of news from Westminster was awaited by eager crowds. In the crisis of the struggle the inhabitants of provincial towns used to go out along the roads to meet the London coach. An event like the rejection of the bill naturally caused intense excitement, and an excited crowd generally wants to do something. Sydney Smith indeed did much to turn the public indignation into the healthier channel of laughter by his famous speech at Taunton, comparing the resistance of the Lords to Mrs. Partington's efforts to sweep back the Atlantic, in the great storm of 1824. " The Atlantic was roused. Mrs. Partington's spirit was up ; but I need not tell you that the contest was unequal. The Atlantic ocean beat Mrs. Partington. She was excellent at a slop, or a puddle, but she should not have meddled with a tempest. Gentlemen, be at your ease—be quiet and steady. You will beat Mrs. Parting-ton." [1] But unfortunately Sydney Smiths have always been rare. Where unions existed, a point of assembly was prepared, and the fervour could pass off in highly spiced oratory ; where there were none, the crowd was left to its own impulse, and a mere hint would be enough to produce a riot, though probably not a quarter of the mob had any active wish for it. At Bristol local antipathies embittered feelings, but even at Bristol there was more accident than design.

The ministers were much perturbed by the outrages, which their opponents attributed to the temper their bill had excited in the people ; the nervous King was quite as likely to take this view as to consider the excitement a reason for passing the bill. Brougham and Russell appealed to the country not to alienate respectable minds from Reform by violent methods, but the Tories had them in a dilemma. If riots took place, this was used as an argument against giving power to such hooligans ; if not, it was said that there was a reaction, and that the people cared nothing for the bill. For this reason Lord Ebrington's motion on the 10th was considered good policy on the Whig part, as the vote of confidence might be used as an excuse for the country's tranquillity.[2] What with the press, the threats to

happily they have not got them at Derby and Nottingham " (C. M. Wakefield, *Life of Attwood*).

    [1] Russell, *Sydney Smith*, p. 148.
    [2] Scarlett to Wilson, [October] 18 ; Add. MSS. 30,115, f. 51.

DAME PARTINGTON and the OCEAN (OF REFORM)

Published by Thoˢ McLean, 26 Haymarket, Octʳ 26ᵗʰ 1831

refuse taxes, the riots, and the midnight deputation, the Government were most awkwardly placed ; it was constantly asserted in the House that they were truckling to the mob, if they were not " legally participators in treasonable misdemeanours." [1] It was no doubt a relief when on October 20 the King prorogued Parliament, commending to members of both Houses " the preservation of tranquillity in your respective counties."

Eager Reformers about this time felt that matters were by no means satisfactory. No peers had been created, an indefinite prorogation faced them, and they had nothing tangible to go upon but the pledge of the Government to introduce a bill not less efficient than the last. Nevertheless Grey had given no encouragement to his midnight interviewers, and was known to have said the bill must be " improved " to tempt over moderate Reformers.[2] There were rumours too that Brougham was playing false, and might join a coalition Cabinet. In spite of this the more constitutional of the Radicals, such as Burdett, Grote, and Mill, were willing to trust Grey ; they believed him to be an honest man, and he alone could realise the full difficulties of the situation.[3] On the other hand, in London anyhow, the enthusiasm of the people had cooled since the great procession of the parishes ; this was noticeable on the occasion of the prorogation ceremony. It seemed only too likely, especially if the recess should be prolonged, that men would sink into an apathy of disgust at the shuffling and procrastination of the Whigs, and not rise again except perhaps with revolutionary violence. All pointed to the belief that with characteristic incapacity the ministers had lost an opportunity that might never recur.[4]

In the circumstances the only thing to do was to form unions, if

---

[1] Speech of Wetherell ; *Hansard* (3rd series), viii. 709.

[2] Grote to Place, October 20 ; Add. MSS. 35,149, f. 109.

[3] Add. MSS. 35,149, ff. 103, 105, 117.

[4] Place to Grote, October 16, to Burdett, October 19 ; Add. MSS. 35,149, ff. 93, 101. " It will be very difficult indeed to induce [the people] again to show so much zeal in so quiet a way. To keep as much as we can the people from retrograding is now our duty." Cf. *Prompter*, October 22, 29 : " There will be no Reform of Parliament made by Parliament." " Lord Grey will make a few more despicable shuffles and contradictions, and then be kicked out of office, amidst the hootings of every man of every party in England. The nation will then cry : ' No more Whigs—no more middlemen—no more constitutional reformers. Let us have a fair battle with the Tories.' "

possible including both the middle and the working classes, to rally and keep up to the mark the undirected Reforming desires of the people, alike in the interests of the bill and of peace itself, and, so far as it could be done, to maintain the alliance with the parliamentary Whigs.[1]  " Three men in my lifetime," wrote Parkes of Birmingham, " by mental power and peculiar circumstances, have held in their hands omnipotent means of levelling the oligarchy—Cobbett, if his heart were sound and he had been gifted with integrity equal to his mind and physical impulses; Brougham, if not sucked into the whirlpool of the aristocracy, and if, instead of the notoriety of doing good, he had worshipped ' good for good's sake;' lastly, Thomas Attwood, if the legitimate ends of his public efforts were consistent with the powerful means of agitation he has organised, and if he had foresight and physical courage, and knowledge, of which he has none.  Now one man of mental superiority and determination, of independent means, might gain the confidence of the country and carry Reform by organising in London a centre of communication for the centralisation and spread of unions."[2]  Place, as might be expected, was already pulling the necessary wires.

The position was complicated in London by the fact that a rival organisation was already in the field, using the ill-famed Rotunda as its headquarters.[3]  It was descended from the British Association for Promoting Co-operative Knowledge, formed in May 1829 by a number of Owenite working men saturated with the ideals of community of property and the workman's right to the whole produce of his labour.  But, whereas Owen ignored the Reform movement, this society became gradually more political, till in March 1831 some of the members founded a schismatic body called the Metropolitan Trades Union, with the double object of securing the representation of the working class in Parliament and the shortening of hours of labour generally.  The leading spirit was Hetherington, champion of the Free Press movement, and shortly afterwards the new union was joined by William Lovett and other prominent members of the now expiring co-operative association.  About

[1] Place to Grote, October 26 ; Add. MSS. 35,149, f. 120.  Hume, said Place, was urging the formations of Unions in Scotland.

[2] Parkes to Grote, October 26 ; Add. MSS. 35,149, f. 117.

[3] The account of the National Union of the Working Classes is mainly taken from William Lovett's narrative in Add. MSS. 27,791, f. 243 ff. ; also from his published Autobiography.  See Wallas, *Life of Place*, chap. x.

this time the name was changed to " The National Union of the Working Classes and Others," but the society's small numbers made Carlile laugh at the ambitious title. It soon declared in favour of universal suffrage, annual parliaments, and ballot, and established twelve social meeting-places about London, where discussions were held, and the works of Paine, Godwin, Owen, and Ensor read. The Union was organised into classes under a leader, and there is little doubt it was illegal, had the Government troubled to prosecute ; the subscription was first a penny, but rose later to twopence. The members joined in all the democratic movements of the time, raising relief for the victims of the press laws, congratulating Poland on her early success, and violently attacking Melbourne's spring-gun and man-trap bill. Their general desire was " to rise in the scale of political importance and by means of a more just legislation better their social condition." In September Hetherington followed Cobbett's example in touring the country, but before this a large number of allied associations had been formed in various districts, notably one at Manchester, where a Political Union of the Birmingham type also existed.

Place had the heartiest dislike and contempt for the Union ; its sympathy with the economic views of the Ricardian Socialists shocked his intolerant orthodoxy, and he declared that many of the leaders " were perfectly atrocious." His depreciations of its influence must therefore be taken with caution ; yet even he admitted its wide hold on working men, particularly in the great manufacturing centres. But besides the extreme and doctrinaire nature of its republican views, which frightened off many of the saner working men, it suffered from the ignorance and folly of some leading members. One section caused scandal by decamping to Ireland with the funds ; others favoured Benbow's mad scheme of a national month's holiday ; others wished for a secret convention of delegates from all parts, while others preached open sedition. And above all by its ostentatious contempt for the Reform Bill, far the most extensive measure that could have any hope of becoming law, the Union cut itself off from the sympathy of the middle class, as well as from a large proportion of its own ; it disgusted sensible people, too, by its arrogant silliness, as when the Bethnal Green branch petitioned the King to abolish the House of Lords, or the Finsbury section urged the Commons to confiscate the estates of the 199 peers.[1]  Indeed throughout these exciting months the members of this Union occupied a pathetic, if most ineffective, position, forbidden as they were by principle to take part in the great democratic movement, believing that if the measure passed it would indefinitely block their own enfranchisement, boasting always that when the Government collapsed, as it shortly must, their own turn would come, yet, when the crisis occurred, doing nothing whatever, and finally shut out from the national jubilation.

Therefore in the eyes of Reforming politicians like Place, who realised the extreme danger, at a time of general excitement, of a divorce between the Ministerialists and the bill's supporters in the country, it was of vital importance to rescue the cause, so far as the working classes of London were concerned, from the hands of the only organisation at present existing.  This was the more urgent in that the Unionists were in process of arranging a mass meeting for November 7 ;  the proposed object was to explain to the respectable the views and peaceful character of the Union, but it was more than likely that inflammatory language would be used, such as seriously to prejudice the chances of Reform.  By the end of October the Union had given up any confidence in the Government it might ever have had ;  earlier in the month it had called for the formation of a Popular Guard, in case the " middlemen " formed a National Guard, and articles on the best methods of street fighting were frequent in the revolutionary press.  A meeting was accordingly held at the " Crown and Anchor " in the Strand, the centre of the Westminster Reformers, to found a more moderate association to unite middle and working classes to carry the Reform Bill.  Place's idea in fact was to do for London what Attwood had done for Birmingham.  Nevertheless the project was by no means welcomed even by such advanced Reformers as Burdett and Hobhouse, the two members for Westminster, and the Government greatly distrusted and disapproved of

[1] On September 27 a resolution was carried " that this meeting are anxious to declare to the House of Lords their unalterable and fervid devotion to the cause of Reform, and though they do not feel themselves much interested in the fate of the bill now pending, they solemnly pledge themselves never to relax their efforts until they have obtained for themselves and their fellow-countrymen the inestimable blessings of a full and free representation, by annual parliaments, universal suffrage, and vote by ballot."

it.[1] Joseph Hume, who joined as an ordinary member but refused to act as chairman, believed that the title chosen, the National Political Union, would suggest a connection with trade unions or the followers of Hunt and Owen.[2] Eventually Burdett consented to take the chair, and the first public meeting was held in Lincoln's Inn Fields on November 1.

It was a stormy occasion ; Place had insisted against Burdett's wish that, if the Union was to appeal to working men, some policy of general social improvement must be included in the prospectus, and not merely the Reform Bill.[3] He got, however, more than he bargained for ; for a strong detachment of Rotunda Radicals appeared on the scene, and attempted to capture the sense of the meeting for their own programme. In this they were foiled by the unscrupulous tactics of the Chair, but they succeeded in securing half the places on the Committee permanently for working men. Place was much disgusted, and Burdett, who lost his temper at the meeting, soon afterwards resigned. " I tell you what," he said to Hobhouse, " the more I see, the more I am convinced that there is no having to do with any but gentlemen ; that is, with men of education." [4] The Rotunda set were no less annoyed, and proceeded to denounce the new union as concocted in the Whig interest by secret agents of Government ; the question of forming a Popular Guard to counteract the middlemen was again mooted.[5] Still the Union had been formed, great as the difficulties were which it had to contend against ; and though its numbers might remain small while the people was sulky, it was certain to come into greater prominence on the revival of excitement, and to play a useful part in focussing and directing public opinion at a crisis.

In the meantime, news was arriving from the west which severely tried the faith of moderate Reformers, and provided arguments for or against political unions according to taste. The large majority of the city of Bristol was in favour of the Reform Bill, and at the last election, in spite of a Tory Corpora-

---

[1] *Recollections of a Long Life*, iv. 146 ; *Memoir of Althorp*, p. 366.
[2] Add. MSS. 27,791, f. 13.
[3] Place to James Mill, October 26 ; Add. MSS. 35,149, f. 120b.
[4] *Recollections*, iv. 151.
[5] Burdett had been specially cautioned by Melbourne not to allow the formation of a National Guard (*Melbourne Papers*, p. 138).

tion, the freemen had for once returned two Reforming members at a trifling cost. Partly for political, partly for municipal reasons, the magistrates were extremely unpopular, and it was largely to secure local protection for individual interests against corporate influence and corruption that a political union was founded in May 1831.[1] As the Reform struggle in Parliament went on, the city became highly excited, and resentment was caused by the presentation at Westminster of an anti-Reform petition purporting to come from the inhabitants generally. Disturbances were therefore feared on the occasion of the Gaol Delivery to be held by the Recorder, Sir Charles Wetherell, who all along had shown himself the bill's fiercest enemy in the Commons, and more particularly at his state entrance into the city, which was fixed for October 29.

The magistrates themselves were divided on the question of permitting the Recorder's visit, but finally sanctioned it ; they represented, however, to Melbourne that military assistance was desirable, and two troops of the 14th Dragoons and one of the 3rd Dragoon Guards were sent into the neighbourhood.[2]  Knowing this, the Bristol Union refused to take part in keeping the peace, and on October 25 its Council published a manifesto calling for the retirement of the Recorder and the Corporation. Thus feeling was running high before ever the Recorder arrived. The Corporation proceeded, possibly because no one else was available, to swear in young men of the upper classes, mostly anti-Reformers, as special constables ; these supplied a bodyguard to the procession entering the city.   The reading of the Recorder's commission was interrupted by hoots and cries for Reform, and the magistrates began to feel doubtful of the wisdom of continuing the Gaol Delivery.   However, no worse violence was offered than an occasional shower of missiles as Wetherell made his way to the Mansion House, where a Corporation banquet was provided.   Hitherto there had only been a few hundred citizens outside, shouting for the King and Reform ; but a large crowd was now assembling, and the irritating behaviour of the constables provoked a riotous mob to besiege the Mansion House.   After a tumultuous evening the troops with an effort succeeded in clearing the square.   In the meantime Sir Charles

[1] Ham to Place ;  Add. MSS. 27,790, f. 183.
[2] Cavalry regiments were at this time organised in three squadrons of two troops each.

Wetherell had made his escape over the leads, and the sessions were postponed.

The night passed off quietly, but early on the morning of Sunday, October 30, an assault was made on the Mansion House, ending in the complete sack of the building. The palisades were smashed, the furniture thrown out of the windows, and the contents of the Corporation cellars brought up and broached in the square with disastrous results. An appeal by the Council of the Union was of no avail to quiet the mob, who were now complaining that the " bloody bludgeon-men " began it, and preparing to have the prisoners out of the Bridewell.[1] Before this the squadron of the 14th had been actually sent back to their quarters outside the town by their commanding officer, Colonel Brereton, a well-meaning but lamentably weak man, who refused to take any action against the crowd on his own responsibility. As it was, the soldiers were compelled to fire in self-defence before they left. Meetings of private inhabitants were held at the Guildhall to proffer their help, but in the most unaccountable way the magistrates refused to act; fifty London police, so an eye-witness declared, could have settled the whole matter. No attempt was made to save the Bridewell, Brereton alleging that the military were " too tired to go out," even when called upon by the civil authorities. The mob next destroyed the New Gaol, though five thousand spectators, it is said, stood idly by watching a hundred rioters doing the work. Next came the Bishop's Palace. The first assault of the mob was repelled by the cavalry and a few constables, who between them cleared the premises ; immediately afterwards, however, this force was ordered to retire on the Mansion House, whereupon the rioters came back and set fire to the Palace, which was entirely gutted.

By the morning two sides of Queen's Square, the principal open place of the city, were burnt down, including the Mansion House and Custom Houses, besides three gaols and two toll-houses. Women and children who had escaped from the blazing houses were huddled together in the square,

---

[1] " Bristol General Union—The Council of the Union know that Sir C. Wetherell has left the city, and that the assizes are postponed. They earnestly entreat that every man will immediately return to his own home. Outrages only injure the cause of Reform " (Add. MSS. 27,790, f. 149).

while round about lay the charred bodies of men who in their drunken stupor had fallen easy victims to the flames. The remaining troop of horse, that of the 3rd Dragoon Guards, had been withdrawn for the night, horses and men being alike exhausted. In the morning they were received with joy, the apathy of the citizens having at last given way to fear, and a succession of charges with drawn sabres, though made without the command of Colonel Brereton, cleared the square and reasserted authority. Meanwhile the squadron of the 14th quartered at Keynsham, five miles outside the city, had been recalled, and at two in the morning a further troop had started for Bristol from Gloucester on urgent summons. The major in command went on by postchaise ahead of his troop, and arrived at seven. He went straight to the magistrates to induce them to come with him on horseback to the scene of the disturbances. They refused, on the ground that it would suggest to the mob to attack their property, but gave him written permission to restore order. In Queen's Square the mob had by now reassembled, but shortly afterwards the two troops of the 14th came in from Keynsham and dispersed the rioters, and by the time the third troop from Gloucester arrived order was restored. Nothing serious took place in the night, and the riots were at an end, though for some weeks the city remained under military protection.

All sorts of accounts of the rights of the affair were given in the local papers, and by report generally. A non-official committee of enquiry was appointed on the spot to take evidence, and in January a Special Commission came down to the city, and left five men under sentence of death. Besides this the unfortunate Colonel Brereton was court-martialled ; before the trial was over he took his own life in an agony of shame and grief. His conduct had been most strange ; it was agreed that a mistaken sense of humanity had prevented him from crushing the riot at first ; but afterwards he showed an incapacity and almost an apathy which suggested that he could not be of altogether sound mind. The most extraordinary points in this disastrous affair were the total lack of initiative and fear of responsibility on the part of the authorities, military and civil, and the indifference of the inhabitants to the destruction of their city. The magistrates acted boldly in approving the Recorder's visit at such a time, but having done so took no adequate precautions against disorder, and were afraid to make use of those they had taken. It would appear that the disturbance began as a result partly of political feeling and partly of the Corporation's unpopularity ; that the behaviour of the constables made riot easy ; that when matters had once become serious, the magistrates lost their heads and Colonel Brereton his nerve ; and that the absence of any confidence in constituted authority paralysed the respectable inhabitants.[1] The population of the great shipping place was no doubt a rough one ; but it is noteworthy that a large proportion of the rioters was said to have come in from the neighbourhood. " The greater number of our opponents," wrote Major Beckwith, the officer who arrived on the scene from Gloucester on Monday morning, " did not belong to Bristol, as was evident from the number of broken heads that were seen on almost every road leading from the town." [2] The Irish labourers were singled out for attack by one Bristol paper, but the accusation was denied. It was claimed by the General Union that they had done much to restore order, and indeed were the first of the citizens to come forward ; the statement was often repeated and used as a justification of political unions, but it was ridiculed by Major Beckwith. " As to the Political Union, after all was settled, their Commandant applied to know where he should place them, as they were willing to act in support of the troops. . . . No gentleman with a white band made his appearance till we had it all our own way, when numbers of those who had been active in plundering joined that squad in order to save themselves." It should be said in their favour that till the last moment they were forbidden by the magistrates to act in their corporate capacity, and so deprived of the advantage of acting in units under their recognised leaders.[3]

[1] Major Mackworth, the officer who took upon himself to order the cavalry to charge, wrote to Lord Fitzroy Somerset on November 3 : " The chief real faults were, a wretched police, public indifference until private houses were fired, want of arrangement, and personal fear. Party politics too had no mean share at first in countenancing if not encouraging the violence of the mob " (*H. O.* 40. 28).

[2] Major Beckwith's report ; *H. O.* 40. 28.

[3] The account of the Bristol riots is taken mainly from letters and reports to the Home Office in bundles 52. 12 ; 44. 24; 40. 28, 29. Information is also given by Place in Add. MSS. 27,790, and the picturesque description in Mr. Stanley Weyman's novel *Chippinge* is admirable.

It gives a curious idea of the condition of the west of England to notice the authorities' anxiety not to leave such a place as Gloucester for a night without military protection; trouble was also feared at Merthyr, in the absence of the troops at Bristol.   Riots had lately broken out at Yeovil and Tiverton, and an attack on the Palace and Cathedral of Wells was rumoured; scenes of disorder had also taken place, or at least been expected, at Exeter, Worcester, Coventry, Dudley, Bath, Kidderminster, and many other towns.   These disturbances, culminating in the riots at Derby and Nottingham and the three days' horror at Bristol, caused a feeling of insecurity in the country, and, though the outrages were as a rule committed by a rabble which in the frenzy of the moment had forgotten the little it ever knew about Reform, it was inevitable that opinions on that burning question should grow harder and more bitter.   Those already convinced of the justice of a measure may find in the violence of its extreme supporters only a reason for not delaying concession.   But such methods are hardly likely to win opponents from their belief in the unfitness for power of the classes demanding enfranchisement.   Certainly the peers of England were, if anything, confirmed in their hatred of the bill.   Tories accused the Government of having brought not peace but a sword, and of having set the example in dis-regard for the established order; Whigs almost felt kindly disposed to the Tories in their desire to dissociate themselves from the rioters; while Place and his friends published posters declaring that the best way of saving London from the horrors of Bristol was to join the National Political Union.

In this state of affairs nervous Londoners might well look forward with alarm to the mass meeting arranged for November 7 by the National Union of the Working Classes, a body which only did not approve the late riots, and was in fact preparing to assemble, armed with staves, for the promulgation of doc-trines almost certainly seditious.   This demonstration was to be imitated by allied societies simultaneously all over the country. The tenets of the Union, including a protest against hereditary legislators, were printed and distributed, and the branch unions spent the week in abusing the ministry and the moderate Radicals, and drawing democratic morals from the Bristol riots.[1]   Lord

[1] "The insurrection of Paris has no more analogy to the explosion at Bristol, than stabbing Julius Cæsar has to killing a pig; but it proves that

Melbourne, however, had received the opinion of the Law Officers of the Crown to the effect that Monday's meeting would be an unlawful and seditious assembly, if not treasonable ; [1] on Friday the 4th he communicated this to Wakley, the proposed chairman of the meeting. Wakley referred the matter to the Committee of the Union, who sent a deputation of five class-leaders to confer with Melbourne direct, and to represent that their intentions were peaceable. But Melbourne pointed out that the whole of the Union's declaration bordered on sedition, and at a further meeting of the Committee on Saturday night it was decided to cancel the meeting, much to the indignation and disgust of the less prudent members.[2]   Full precautions had been taken by the Home Secretary and the Commander-in-Chief to provide troops and special constables, and Wellington himself had supplied a scheme of defence for the capital ; [3] but the 7th passed off without any disturbance, and the Union was forced to admit defeat. Several of the provincial meetings, however, took place, but the idea had been on the whole a failure ; Monday the 21st was arranged for another attempt.[4]

The prominent feature of the month of November was the extraordinary growth of political unions, stimulated possibly by Hunt's north-western tour early in the month.   Liverpool, Leicester, Hull, Bath, Dublin, led the way, but many small villages had their unions, while at the other end of the scale was Manchester with two, of which the larger and more extreme had twenty-seven branch lodges, and altogether upward of 5000 members.   It was supported by similar associations in the great manufacturing towns of the surrounding district, and a meeting of delegates was appointed for the 28th, to form a " National Convention " for drawing up a Reform Bill to be presented to Parliament.[5]   This was in accord with Paine's doctrine that " the right of Reform is in the Nation, in its original character ; and the constitutional method would

what is called ' the mob ' is not always despicable " (*Radical Reformer*, November 26).

[1] *H. O.* 52. 14.   Althorp to Grey, November 4 ; *Althorp Papers*.

[2] J. R. Mansell to Curran, November 6 ; *H. O.* 44. 25.

[3] Wellington to Lord Fitzroy Somerset, November 3 ; *Despatches*, viii. 24.

[4] At Preston a riot ensued ; *H. O.* 52. 13.

[5] *H. O.* 52. 13.

be by a general convention, elected for the purpose." [1]   A pathetic apology for non-attendance came from the Radicals of Worcester.  " From there being so many Black Slugs living about the purlieus of the Cathedral, we have had a very uphill game to fight ever since the formation of our Union."

Scotland, too, was playing her part.  " Political unions have been very generally formed," wrote Cockburn.  " People are everywhere familiarised to great meetings in the open air, guided by men banded together and organised associations, and to hear things discussed—such as the use of bishops, the refusing to pay taxes, and the propriety of arming, which till now they would have started at even thinking of.  As yet, however, the unions are avoided by the prudent, and are chiefly composed of the poorer classes or wilder spirits.  They are useful at present, because whenever they have been established the peace has been preserved ; but they are most dangerous engines." [2]   Times had indeed changed since the days of Dundas and Braxfield.

The cause was promoted by the lectures of Detrosier, an ally of the Westminster Reformers,  " on the utility of Political Unions " ; he declared that the country generally was becoming more political, and that the dangers of the great moral revolution taking place in society could only be averted by union and wider knowledge. [3]   It seemed that for once ordinary dull men were waking up to an interest in public affairs and claiming their position as living members of the State.  The Huddersfield Union, which hoped to organise the whole labouring population of the district, declared, " We are proud to state that the people have now sufficient confidence in their own talents and energies, and are determined that no other Class shall be entrusted (or ought to be relied upon) to redress their wrongs or to obtain their rights.  The Age of Demagogues is gone ! "

There were rumours from some quarters that the unions were actually preparing to arm ; Nottingham was alleged to be laying in muskets at 16s. 8d. apiece, bayonets included, from Birmingham, and much the same was said of Birmingham itself, though without foundation.  It is not surprising to find a Manchester magistrate seriously alarmed for the peace of the country, and

---

[1] *Rights of Man*, Part I. p. 44.
[2] November 14; *Journal of Henry Cockburn*, i. 25.
[3] Add. MSS. 27,791, f. 223.

even middle-class Manchester Reformers were uneasy.[1] "We see no good," said the *Guardian*, "that can arise from the establishment of a mock Parliament in every corner of the kingdom, existing under no public responsibility, yet debating and acting upon every public question." "If Ministers give the least countenance to *armed* associations, I leave them," wrote the cautious Campbell. "Be your form of government what it may, republican or monarchical, it is preposterous to suppose that there can be a military force in the country not under the command of Government." Lord Eldon and many others wished the unions to be put down by law, as in 1789 and 1794; Peel believed that counter associations of the respectable classes must be formed for the defence of life and property.[2] It must be some instinctive dread of the collective conscience which fills Englishmen with so deep a distrust of all organised bodies of men, be they churches, companies, or trade unions. There is something strange and secret about their working, and they seem expected to fall below the level of individual morality. The political unions of 1831 were associated in Tory minds with the clubs of the time of the French Revolution, on both sides of the Channel, or with the mysterious Carbonari of the south. Their supposed connection with the just emancipated trade societies, and their apparent desire to rival Parliament as the exponents of the nation's will, smirched them with a suspicion of illegality which at a hint of violence was likely to darken into certainty.

From the beginning the political unions had had no more determined adversary than the King. Vehemently opposed to all attempts of trade societies to raise wages as illegal, he believed that even the Birmingham Union was tarred with the same brush, and in fact preferred that violent intentions should be avowed, as giving a pretext for prosecutions and arrests.[3] He saw in the corporate spirit of these bodies the makings of an "imperium in imperio," and, discrediting the idea that their iniquities would cease with the passing of the bill, looked forward to a permanent state of tyranny and anarchy. The opinion of Lord Grey and the Cabinet was much the same, though Grey laid stress on the action of the Lords as the immediate provocation, and on the

[1] *H. O.* 52. 13.
[2] *Life of Campbell*, ii. 2; *Life of Eldon*, iii. 158; *Peel Papers*, ii. 190.
[3] *Correspondence*, i. 401, 407.

certain abatement of the danger when Reform should be granted ;
if his next attempt should fail, he could not " be answerable for
the public peace." [1]  In any case the Bristol riots and the inflammatory placards of the Rotunda Radicals must have turned
the Government's attention seriously to the state of the country.
A proclamation against outrages was issued on November 2,
and the Cabinet agreed unanimously, in the absence of Lord
Durham at the Belgian Court, that " every possible discouragement should be given " to the unions, between the two varieties
of which they made no attempt to distinguish.[2]  There seems
absolutely no ground for the charge that ministers in any way
tried to excite the country in favour of the bill.  Radical
journalists may have found it difficult to ply their double task
of at once stirring up and allaying the passions of the people ;
but the Government's efforts, at least at this time, were entirely
occupied on the side of caution ;  they had much rather fall foul
of the unions than forfeit the confidence of their own class by
trafficking with them.[3]

From the first conception of the measure Grey had been
faced by an awkward contrast.  The people at large, who must
necessarily supply the driving force in case of a dissolution,
were eager for Reform on a broad basis, and anxious that it
should be carried through with all speed, knowing and recking
nothing of the dilatory meticulousness of parliamentary procedure.  But the only body which could constitutionally make
the Reform Bill law was not stirred by this surging impatient
desire ;  to it the bill was much as other bills, though infinitely
more important, and seemed to require, if anything, more than
ordinary care in the examination of its details.  For months the
boisterous torrent was cribbed within the narrow embankments
of routine, and fretted sorely.  Born parliamentarian as he was,
Grey's sympathies lay all with the banks ;  he would have liked
to let the current in with a rush at pleasure, as at the dissolution,
and then close the lock gates.  He found the people's ardour
most unreasonable and trying, if not ungrateful.  In this respect

---

[1] *Correspondence*, i. 412.

[2] *Ibid.*, i. 409.

[3] J. S. Mill to Fonblanque ;  *Life and Labours of Albany Fonblanque*,
p. 29.  Althorp wrote on November 2 :  " Revolutions do not originate as
riots like those at Bristol, but they may arise from such Unions as this of
which Burdett has put himself at the head " (*Memoir*, p. 366).

practically the whole of the Cabinet was with him ; and the situation arose which may be figured as the attempt to entice the freed winds back into their cave. The impotence of the rulers of England at this crisis has been often marked ; the great popular commotion was out of their experience, and soon showed that it was no less out of their control. Nowhere does this helpless alarm in face of the unfamiliar appear more strikingly than in the Government's attitude to the political unions. Unrecognised by the Constitution, their power could yet not be ignored as a determining force in politics. We may compare the spectacle of Cabinet and Commons waiting attentively in later days to hear the decisions of the Miners' Federation. Parliament was within measurable distance of abdicating its functions as the Great Council of the nation. Attwood, Place, Doherty, and Cobbett knew more of the real history of the country in those years than did Grey or Melbourne or Peel.

Nevertheless the Whig Cabinet was forced in November to consider the position of the unions seriously, and in one case actually appealed to one of them for help. On the 5th, at the height of the excitement regarding the proposed Radical meeting before White Conduit House, the Duke of Wellington wrote to the King, advising the suppression of the Birmingham Union, which, he declared, was arming and threatened to develop into a National Guard.[1] This letter, as the Duke admitted later to a friend, was in fact an intimation to the King that he was prepared to save him from his tyrant ministers, and form a new government. " I was certain," he wrote to Buckingham, " that nineteen-twentieths of the whole country would concur with me. I did it likewise at a period of the year at which I knew that, if the King wished to get rid of the bonds in which he is held, I could assist him in doing so. There was time to call a new Parliament." [2] The King, however, referred the somewhat unusual communication to his minister, who discovered that the Duke's evidence was faulty, and pointed out that, even should the supply of arms be actually taking place, it was impossible to forbid their use even to members of unions, unless they were acting as part of an organised force.[3]

But inaccurate as was the Duke's information, it turned out

---

[1] *Despatches*, viii. 30.
[2] *Ibid.*, viii. 143.
[3] *Correspondence*, i. 416.

that the scheme of organisation which alone could justify interference was a fact. A report was laid before the Council of the
Birmingham Union suggesting that the total force should be
formed into seven divisions with colours, each comprising
subdivisions, and below them hundreds and tens with appointed
leaders ; there were to be titles and gradations of ranks.[1]
It might seem that Attwood's boast about the two armies equal
to that which conquered at Waterloo was in the way of being
realised. Within a few days, however, the plan was seen by the
Cabinet ; it was condemned as illegal by the Law Officers of
the Crown, and the Government was prepared to take steps to
suppress it.[2] The ill-feeling, not to say danger, that would have
resulted from an open breach was avoided by the resourcefulness
of Lord Althorp, who, with the knowledge of his chief but certainly not of the King, communicated privately with Attwood.
Joseph Parkes, an able Birmingham attorney, was entrusted
with the facts of the case ; he went at once to Attwood and
induced him and his lieutenant Scholefield to cancel the drilled
meeting of the Union appointed for November 22 ; Parkes then
started for London, where he assured Althorp at a secret interview that all was well. " He says, as I suspected," wrote
Althorp to Grey, " that the Union is quite out of the control
of Attwood, but that Scholefield's influence is very great." [3]
Thus by a little tact an awkward corner was rounded, and
the dreaded organisation was never put into practice. This
manœuvre was suspected by the Duke of Wellington, who
denounced such collusion between the King's Government and
a body of potential criminals, but it did not become public
property.[4]

The Duke's suspicions had been aroused by the appearance
of a royal proclamation against unions organised as Attwood's
was to have been ; he took pleasure in the belief that his letter
to the King had produced it, but there is no reason to suppose
this. The proclamation was signed at a Council held on
November 21, and was the result primarily of the news from
Birmingham. From some evidence it would appear that the

[1] *Life of Attwood*, p. 182 ; *H. O.* 44. 25.
[2] *Correspondence*, i. 424.
[3] Althorp to Grey, November 20 ; *Althorp Papers*. Parkes to Grote,
November 28 ; Add. MSS. 35,149, f. 128.
[4] *Despatches*, viii. 85.

intention of certain of the Cabinet was to put down all or most political unions. A Home Office official wrote to Foster of Manchester : " With regard to the Political Unions, I am by his Lordship's direction to transmit to you the enclosed copies of a proclamation which has been issued by His Majesty, declaring all such associations to be unconstitutional and illegal ; and earnestly warning all His Majesty's subjects to abstain from entering into such unauthorised combinations." [1] The King too seemingly understood it in this sense. He was disgusted by a counter announcement by the astute Place that the proclamation did not apply to the National Political Union or indeed to most of those in existence.[2] Grey admitted its accuracy and agreed that there was no way of touching bodies not thus organised. In the country some unions obediently stopped arming ; we hear of men walking to Birmingham " to know what was to be done now the King had turned against them." [3] Others, not in a flourishing state, took advantage of the proclamation to dissolve ; others wrote to the Home Office to ask whether it applied to them. In most cases Melbourne left it to their own discretion ; an address of the Cupar union, pledged solely to support the Reform Bill, was endorsed thus : " Leaders of the Political Union extremely deceive themselves if they conceive that in forming an institution of so very doubtful a character they are acting in accordance with the views of H. M. Government." [4] It looks probable that Melbourne had expected the proclamation to apply to many more unions than it did.

Important though it was, the question of the political unions had only engaged part of the Government's attention during these weeks. Their main energies were concentrated on the " improved " Reform Bill to be introduced at the opening of next session, and all Grey's adroitness was needed to keep his Cabinet together. From the time of the rejection by the Lords the cleavage between the forward and conservative sections had been emphasised. Althorp, writing to his father on the day of the division, had declared the ministry must break up.[5] The rival policies were a creation of peers, and modification of

---

[1] *H. O.* 41. 10.    [2] *Correspondence*, i. 442.
[3] *H. O.* 40. 29.    [4] *H. O.* 40. 28 ; 102. 41.
[5] *Memoir*, p. 354.

the bill to win over a portion of the Lords. But the King's definite objection disposed, at any rate for the moment, of the first, and strong Reformers could only insist on the need of going straight ahead without making any concession that could alienate the people, their only strength. " Public support once withdrawn from you," wrote Durham, " you will not have that of the King for four-and-twenty hours. Do you think he keeps you in now because he likes you on Whig principles ? Far from it. He does so because the people would not sanction a Tory Government for an hour." [1]   True to his nature, Melbourne suppressed his conservative instincts in favour of a wise generosity. " It is a very dangerous way of dealing with a nation to attempt to retract that which you have once offered to concede." [2]

In truth a Cabinet pledged to the principle of the late bill had not left itself much latitude. But for what it was worth, and in redemption of his promise to the King, Lord Grey prepared to be conciliatory ; his correspondence with Lord Althorp suggests the difficulties faced. Russell had again been selected to outline the bill, and his first draft of it shows that he had received instructions to make any changes consistent with the ministers' pledge. According to this scheme, counties were not to be divided, and no boroughs were to have a single member —two great concessions to Tory feeling ; incidentally the Inns of Court would have returned four members. Althorp criticised the scheme and offered amendments, and for some weeks the two friends continued to work at the matter. [3]

Others of the Government went further, and sought for a settlement by consent of both parties. Lord Grey's attempt to approach the Duke of Wellington through Prince Leopold, who in the course of this year became King of the Belgians, is probably to be assigned to an earlier occasion ; in any case it was fruitless. [4]   Flushed by their late triumph and by Lord Ashley's victorious by-election in Dorset, the official Tories would have

---

[1] Durham to Graham, October 19 ;  *Life of Graham*, i. 128.

[2] Melbourne to Taylor, October 25 ;  *Melbourne Papers*, p. 135.

[3] *Althorp Papers*.

[4] King Leopold to Princess Victoria, February 3, 1837 : " If the Tory part of Parliament could have brought themselves to act without passion, much in the reform of Parliament might have been settled much more in conformity with their best interests. I was authorised, in 1831, to speak in this sense to the Duke of Wellington by Lord Grey ; the effect would have been highly beneficial to both parties, but passion made it impossible

no trafficking with the Jacobins of Downing Street. But negotiations were actually set on foot with Lord Wharncliffe, who had moved the rejection of the late bill in the Lords, but was prepared to vote for the second reading of the new one, if satisfactory concessions could be obtained. He and Lord Harrowby were the leaders of what came to be called the party of the Waverers. They had opposed the bill from conviction, but now agreed that something very like it must be passed.

The mediator in this matter was Lord Palmerston, who all along had distrusted the scope of the bill and usually exercised the privilege of a Foreign Secretary to keep away from the House of Commons. He began by approaching Wharncliffe's son, John Stuart-Wortley, who spoke to his father and Lord Harrowby ; Harrowby's son, Lord Sandon, was also canvassed by Edward Stanley. The two fathers with their sons proceeded to draw up a memorandum on the chances of compromise at Sandon, and on November 16 Wharncliffe called on Grey at East Sheen to discuss the matter.[1] Nothing definite was decided, but Wharncliffe agreed to accept these three principles : disfranchisement on the scale of the late bill, the enfranchisement of large towns, and the £10 qualification hedged with certain restrictions. Grey on the other side seemed willing largely to curtail Schedule B, and possibly to maintain the total numbers of the House. Among other debatable points were the division of counties, the retention of certain old rights of voting, and the possibility of spreading the measure over three bills. Wharncliffe also pleaded against enfranchising the metropolitan boroughs, as the King had already done without effect, but here Grey could offer no hopes ; he must hold by his pledge, he said, not to introduce a less efficient measure. As a matter of fact, this pledge should have been enough to show that no real compromise could be arrived at ; for the one thing the Tories wanted was a less efficient measure. Some good perhaps was done in clearing away misunderstanding, but it is difficult to see what advantage the two parties could really have expected ; they agreed, however, to meet again.[2]

to succeed." The Prince mounted the throne of Belgium in July ; it would appear therefore that the incident belongs to the spring (*Letters of Queen Victoria*, i. 61).

[1] *Greville Memoirs*, ii. 211 ; *Despatches*, viii. 83.

[2] A minute of the conversation, with Lord Wharncliffe's remarks, is printed in *Correspondence*, p. 464 ff.

In any case Lord Wharncliffe spoke without any authority to bind others. Wellington and Peel, who were consulted, looked askance at the proceedings, and the only good that most Tories thought likely to accrue from them was the irritation of the Radicals with the Government.[1] Strong Reformers were no less suspicious. " I see what Palmerston is driving at !" wrote Durham ; " he does not mind the disfranchisement of rotten boroughs, or the enfranchisement of great towns, provided he can get such an elective qualification as will make those large towns as little real representations of the people as the boroughs he has destroyed. And as a thorough anti-Reformer (which he is) he is right." [2]   Indeed the Government gained little but the approbation of the King, though William naturally refused Lord Grey's request that he should try to induce Spiritual and Lay Lords of Parliament to vote for the second reading of the new bill.[3]

In the meantime the Cabinet had to determine the important point as to when Parliament should reassemble. Advanced Reformers had wished this to be within a few days of the prorogation, but hope deferred now hardly looked for it earlier than Christmas. January 9 had in fact been the date provisionally fixed ; however, as Parliament stood actually prorogued only till November 22, it was time to come to a final decision. On the 13th Althorp wrote to Grey : " I have applications coming in upon me thickly to know when Parliament is to meet, and I do not know what to say. . . . As far as I can see of the question whether we ought to meet before Christmas or not, it appears very doubtful. Brougham is eager for it ; he says that in consequence of the false report of what passed at the interview you had with Mr. Carpell and his party the public have indissolubly connected the meeting after Christmas with the material alteration in the measure itself, and that if they find that Place was right when he said he inferred from what you said that Parliament would not meet till after Christmas, they will believe he was right also in his inference that great alterations were to be made in the Bill." [4]   Althorp was

[1] *Despatches*, viii. 87–91 ; *Peel Papers*, ii. 193–195 ; *Greville Memoirs*, ii. 213.

[2] *Life of Durham*, i. 269.

[3] *Correspondence*, i. 448.

[4] *Althorp Papers*.

desirous for these reasons to meet as soon as possible, though otherwise he would have preferred the later date. Grey was in no hurry either for the new bill, wishing probably to delay the time when the political unions would again take charge of it and stiffen the obstinacy of the Lords ; there was also the hope that their fervour might cool with delay.[1] In any case he must have hated the idea of giving way to the Radicals.

The decisive Cabinet was held on November 19. The chief argument for an early meeting of Parliament was based on the state of the country. Incendiarism had set in again, and special legislation against the unions might also be necessary. Eventually a division was taken ; Grey, Richmond, and Palmerston found themselves in a minority, but acquiesced in the decision to meet on December 6. Grey took the defeat so well that Althorp, so Brougham tells us, " fairly acknowledged that had he known how Lord Grey's excellent behaviour would have affected him, and how miserable (this was his expression) it would have made him, he should have been unable to vote the way he did." [2] Durham and Graham were away on the advanced side, Lansdowne and Stanley on the other. Palmerston was highly disgusted. " Were you aware yesterday," he wrote to Melbourne, " when you turned the scale in favour of meeting in a fortnight, what has been the nature of the communications between Wharncliffe and Grey ? . . . I am convinced that if time had been allowed for this negotiation it would have succeeded, and that by some modification in the bill, which from what Wharncliffe said need not have been great, we could not only have improved the measure, but have ensured a majority in the House of Lords for that and all other purposes *before* Parliament had met. How this is now to be done I hardly see. John Russell is to-morrow three weeks to expound what we call the principles, but what, as we well know from experience, will be all the *details* of the bill. From that moment negotiation is over. . . . It is evident that Brougham has pledged himself in conversation with Barnes and others that Parliament *should* meet before Christmas ; . . . and it is also equally evident that he fears that excitement about Reform could not be kept up in its present degree for six weeks longer." [3]

[1] Grey to Lansdowne, November 15 ; *Howick Papers.*

[2] *Correspondence*, i. 431 ; *Althorp Papers.*

[3] *Melbourne Papers*, p. 140. Grey asked Althorp : " I don't know

The announcement that Parliament would meet on December 6 was made on the 21st, and took off the edge of the proclamation against organised unions, which the King signed at the same Council. Unaware of the real reason for the early date, Reformers in the country were delighted ; uncertainty as to the fate of Reform was said to be causing stagnation of trade and unemployment. " I have known this district upwards of thirty years," said Potter of Manchester, " and I declare I never knew so much anxiety exist. . . . Manufacturers at present are continuing their business with little or no profit, many of them at an actual loss, and I feel convinced if the country is a second time thrown into alarm, numbers of the manufacturers, printers, bleachers, &c., will discharge their workmen, and a spirit of Democracy will be awakened which may eventually bring evils to all orders of men in the state." [1]

At this point the divided Cabinet was nearly destroyed by the threatened resignation of one of its leading members on the question of peer-making. From the point of view of those who desired a creation, the natural time to discuss it with the King was immediately after the loss of the bill in October, and there was opinion in favour of pressing it then, and resigning on its refusal. However, special circumstances at that time prevented such a proceeding. Serious tumults were feared in the country, which an anti-Reform ministry would only encourage. The King's request that the Whigs would continue in office over the anxious time appealed to their patriotism and chivalry ; in answering the royal letter Grey did not even allude to William's statement that he could never create peers to pass the bill. Since then, except for certain not very hopeful negotiations with a peer who could not claim to speak officially, and the possible conversion of a few bishops, nothing had occurred to make renewed failure unlikely.[2] Soon therefore after the early meeting of Parliament had been decided upon, Sir James Graham brought up the subject, and suggested to Althorp that it was desirable to come to an immediate understanding with

whether you were as much struck as I was by Brougham's manner. But of this when we meet." Brougham himself would have preferred the day to be December 1 (*Althorp Papers*).

[1] T. Muir to Durham, November 27 ; Potter to Bowring, November 29 (*Lambton Papers*).

[2] *Correspondence*, i. 364 443.

the King. Several of the Cabinet were convinced that Reform could not pass except by the creation of peers now or later. It was not fair to leave the King in ignorance of this, especially when he might assume the exact opposite from Grey's letter of October 8. If the proposal were eventually made to him and he refused, the ministry would have only themselves to blame. It was absurd to carry the bill laboriously through the Commons with the certain prospect of a second defeat in the Lords, and a defeat which would be alike fatal to the peace of the country and the ministers' own reputations. Graham pressed for a full explanation with the King before Parliament met, and wished the Government to resign unless they received a pledge that as many peers would be created as might be necessary to pass the bill.[1]

In the general principle of his request Graham had Durham and the Chancellor on his side. He met with little encouragement, however, from Althorp, who, unlike his father, was himself strongly opposed to a large creation, and was convinced that the sense of the Cabinet was against the proposal.[2] There was in fact considerable alarm in the moderate section at this time ; Stanley, one of their champions, was away in Ireland, while Lansdowne, Greville tells us, was always " gone to Bowood." [3] George Lamb wrote to Melbourne : " It seems clear that Grey is for moderation, but if nobody stands firmly by him he is sure to give way ; and it seems to me that the violent part of the Cabinet are put in continual communication upon this subject, and act in concert, while those who ought to check them do not understand each other." He was afraid of a yet more democratic bill being introduced, and to this he would have preferred the dissolution of the Cabinet. Melbourne himself feared that triennial parliaments would be demanded.[4] In these circumstances Graham determined to resign, and only Grey's representations that by doing so he would break up the Cabinet kept him in office ; he contented himself by drawing up a confidential paper in which he reserved the right to propose a creation of peers to the Cabinet at any future date.[5]

[1] Althorp to Grey, November 23 ; *Memoir of Althorp*, p. 370.
[2] Althorp to Grey, November 25 ; *Althorp Papers*.
[3] *Greville Memoirs*, ii. 217.
[4] *Melbourne Papers*, pp. 143, 146.
[5] *Life of Graham*, i. 130.

The decision to meet Parliament before Christmas made the need of shaping the new Reform Bill the more urgent. Althorp had submitted the result of his and Russell's labours to the Cabinet on November 19, and a week later Grey laid before it a memorandum from Lord Wharncliffe. The Waverers objected specially to the proposed metropolitan boroughs, to the uniform £10 franchise, and to the idea of single member representation, which offended the English spirit of compromise. The memorandum found little favour, and the Cabinet contented itself with reprieving eleven boroughs in Schedule B and allotting twelve more members to towns—thus maintaining the numbers of the House. These, however, and a few other changes were not enough, and on the 30th, after another ineffective conversation, Grey heard from Wharncliffe that negotiations must be considered as closed.[1] A meeting of city magnates called by the Governor of the Bank, in the hope of finding a basis of Reform on which moderate men might agree, was equally disappointing.[2] Gossip said that Grey's own anxieties were increased by the irritating behaviour of his son-in-law, whose return from the Continent must have been a sore trial to the moderates. There can be little doubt that Durham's great loss in the autumn had a bad effect upon his temper, at no time very forbearing ; Talleyrand deplored his " funeste influence sur Lord Grey," and in particular he caused grave scandal by a monstrous attack on his father-in-law at a Cabinet dinner. " If I had been Lord Grey," said Melbourne, " I would have knocked him down." It was commonly believed that Durham would have liked to turn out Palmerston and Melbourne, and that he himself wished for the seals of the Foreign Office.[3] It was under no very happy auspices that the ministers met Parliament.

They found the Opposition prepared for onslaughts on their government of the country during the recess. A cautious speech from the throne provoked no dissent, but Tory members were annoyed to find themselves summoned from the country

[1] *Correspondence*, i. 451–456, 478. Althorp to Grey, November 26 ; *Althorp Papers*.

[2] *Times*, November 23 ; *Correspondence*, i. 478.

[3] Althorp to Spencer, December 6 (wrongly dated) ; *Memoir of Althorp*, p. 374 ; *Greville Memoirs*, pp. 222, 226 ; *Brougham Memoirs*, iii. 468.

before Christmas simply for the purpose of the Reform Bill ; if any immediate administrative measures had been required, it would have been excusable. Riots and political unions were naturally the main topics, and Croker bitterly attacked the ministers for having assembled Parliament in deference to the commands of " their masters " without. Grey's interview with the " Crown and Anchor " politicians, and Melbourne's with the deputies from the Rotunda, were held to be degrading to the traditions of British statesmanship. " There ought not to be one government in Downing Street, another in the Strand, a third at Birmingham, a fourth at Manchester, and a fifth at Bristol." [1] Ministerialists, many of whom, Hobhouse tells us, had been sobered in their zeal by the late exhibitions of lawless violence, replied that all was due to the delay of Reform ; once grant it, and political unions and agitators would sink into their normal nothingness. Against Hunt's assertions that the people cared only for Radical Reform, Althorp produced a petition for the bill signed by 40,000 Yorkshiremen, and another with 22,000 names from Leeds. Behind the scenes a further vain attempt at an understanding was made by the moderates, On December 10 Grey, Brougham, and Althorp met Lords Harrowby, Wharncliffe, and Chandos in the hope of reaching some agreement on details. But the measure had by now been fairly thrashed out by ministers with suggestions from the King, and there was little room for concession or indeed debate. All along Lord Grey had objected to the use of the word " negotiations " or " mutual concession," insisting that his own course was already taken ; he was much annoyed at the *Standard's* allegation that he had sought the interview.[2]

The new bill was introduced by Lord John Russell on December 12. There were no startling changes, but what changes there were showed a conciliatory spirit ; several in fact of the Opposition suggestions, hitherto rejected, were now adopted. The numbers of the House were to remain the same, the condemned boroughs were no longer selected according to population, the new census of 1831 was preferred to the old one, and the Chandos clause formed part of the text. Those representing the Waverers in the Commons accepted the principle of the bill, while Peel declared that the changes in the new

---

[1] *Hansard* (3rd series), ix. 42 ff.
[2] *Correspondence*, ii. 21, 23, 28.

measure formed an ample justification for the resistance to the last.[1] In spite of his declaration of eternal hostility, and of an opposition which had lost nothing in vigour, the second reading was carried by 324 votes to 162, exactly two to one ; the Committee stage was left over to the new year.

In many ways the few months which followed the rejection of the bill by the Lords were dispiriting from a Reformer's point of view. " The first Reform Bill," wrote Albany Fonblanque, " had satisfied the country, closed all schisms, bound all people round the Government ; men flung away their favourite projects, and gratefully accepted the measure which Government had generously tendered. We received it as an instalment of a great debt, it is true, but it was an instalment offered in ready money. With the nation in this mood, the policy was rapid operation." But the summer was wasted, and the people received the third bill in comparative apathy.[2] The various outrages in the country, though only indirectly due to Reform, had taken off some of the glamour of the promised " bloodless revolution." Uncertainty and delay had shaken the confidence between ministers and people, and in many cases the dislocation of industry had been thus accounted for. The news of the early meeting of Parliament did indeed cause general relief, but latterly the Government's communications with the Waverers had become known, and the distrust of their sincerity this occasioned was not counterbalanced by any hope of additional strength in the Lords. It is true that several county meetings gave an encouragement they could not disdain, but the political unions were a doubtful benefit. Even those which confined themselves to supporting the ministry were heartily disliked by the King, and nearly all the ministers would have given anything to be saved from their friends. The unions themselves were by no means prospering. Parkes and Place both believed at this time that the people would have submitted to a Tory Government ; Place actually told Hobhouse that the Birmingham Union nearly collapsed from want of funds soon after the bill was thrown out, and the position of his own union

---

[1] *Cf.* a letter to Sir Robert Wilson : " The whole *number of the House is preserved*. . . . What a triumph for the Lords ! " (Add MSS. 30,112, f. 148).

[2] *Seven Administrations*, pp. 196–8.

was no less critical at the end of the year.[1] The unions of the baser sort were as usual actively hostile to Government ; in the middle of December a " National Convention " of delegates was engaged in drawing up a Radical Reform Bill at Manchester.[2]

But the political discontent was overshadowed by the general fear caused by the outbreak of the cholera at Sunderland towards the end of November. Beside this real plague, which confirmed the prophecies of those who believed that the last day was at hand, the mere " pestilence of revolution impiously unbound," as Wordsworth called the Reform agitation, seemed trivial and remote. The ravages of the cholera, being mainly confined to sordid hovels and slums, drew attention to the miserable condition of the poor. " The awful thing," wrote Greville, " is the vast extent of misery and distress which prevails, and the evidence of the rotten foundation on which the whole fabric of this gorgeous society rests." Besides this there were strike troubles in the north, and the distress of the Blackburn handloom weavers was said to be appalling. To crown all, incendiarism had broken out in the agricultural districts to a degree which showed how vain had been the severity of the Special Commissions.[3]

[1] Parkes to Grote, November 28 ; Add. MSS. 27,791, f. 121. *Broughton Recollections*, iv. 164.

[2] *Poor Man's Guardian*, December 10.

[3] County Fire Office to the Home Office, December 15 : " The burnings of the present season far outnumber those of last winter " (*H. O.* 40. 29). See *Twopenny Trash* of December and January.

# CHAPTER VIII

## PEER-MAKING

" Unus homo nobis cunctando restituit rem ;
Noenum rumores ponebat ante salutem ;
Ergo postque magisque viri nunc gloria claret."

ENNIUS.

THE failure of the negotiations with the Waverers made it plain that the discussion of the question of creating peers could not be much longer delayed. In spite of the conciliatory attitude of a few bishops and of Grey's attempts to convert the Primate, there was as yet no prospect of a Government majority on the second reading in the Lords ; on the other hand, Grey seemed rootedly opposed to a large creation, and except for sundry hints matters with the King stood just as they had in October.[1] In the country it was generally accepted that ministers had the assurance that the bill should pass, and rumours of an impending creation were well received by keen Reformers at the end of November ; they found encouragement in the example set by Louis Philippe in making a batch of thirty-six peers to swamp the Upper House in France.[2]

At the end of the year the matter was brought to a head by Brougham and Durham, the advanced members of the Cabinet, who wrote to Grey suggesting that a creation should no longer be put off.[3] Realising the improbability of concession on the enemy's part, they urged that it was absurd to expose themselves to certain defeat, and the country to no less certain disorder, by sending up the bill to the Lords with no means of securing its passage. The use of the prerogative would be alike constitutional and reasonable, considering the additions made to the peerage by Pitt and his Tory successors

[1] *Correspondence*, i. 439 ; ii. 63. Althorp to Spencer, December 20 ; *Memoir of Althorp*, p. 374.

[2] *Times*, November 23 ; Add. MSS. 27,791, f. 102.

[3] Brougham and Durham to Grey, December 29, 1831 ; *Brougham Memoirs*, iii. 151. *Life of Durham*, i. 271.

in nearly fifty years of power. Durham gave no details as to numbers or time,[1] but Brougham asked definitely for a preliminary creation of ten or twelve, the greater number to be merely "calls up," and for an arrangement with the King that more should be made if necessary ; it was likely, however, that the first batch would be enough, as opponents would infer from it that the ministers had full powers. "Rely on it, somehow or another, if he comes to some understanding with us, it will get out, and *render any considerable creation unnecessary*." Secrets shared by Brougham had a way of "getting out," as his sovereign and his colleagues knew only too well from the columns of the *Times*. "There is but one chance of safety," he added, "we must not lose the country. I would make no sacrifice of principle to the loudest clamour, yet when the principle goes with the cry nine parts in ten of the way, the cry may well take us on the remaining. By the nine-tenths I mean the necessity of carrying and preventing confusion, by the one-tenth I mean the doing it if need be by peer-making." [2]

Durham and Brougham were supported by that sturdy old Reformer, Lord Holland, who now begins to play a prominent part as calculator in chief to the ministry. "It is a strange quirk," he said, "to prefer the danger of having no House of Lords to a temporary enlargement of it." [3] He made the point that if the King waived his prerogative now, it would mean its abandonment for ever, and in fact bring in a state of affairs like that contemplated by the Peerage Bill of 1719. He too believed in the importance of having the King's unlimited support, and wrote to Grey : "I am an old tennis-player and like that way of counting, though it seems odd—15, 30, 40, Game—but the main point is to hang over our adversary with a *bisque ;* and the knowledge we have it will damp their exertions. That bisk, however, is 15 whenever we like." He enclosed a list of "peerables," adding : "I hope you will prove yourself (pardon the blasphemy) a famous Creator." [4]

[1] It appears from a letter of Stanley's that he advised forty or fifty (*Life of Graham*, i. 134).

[2] Brougham to Holland, quoted by Holland to Grey, January 1, 1832 ; *Howick Papers*.

[3] Holland to Brougham, December 31 ; *Brougham Memoirs*, iii. 454.

[4] Holland to Grey, January 1. On the 3rd the nephew of Fox wrote : "I shall tell the candidates for peerages to imitate the housemaid who enhanced her qualifications to old Davies, and say, ' and then, My Lord,

Lord Grey himself was veering in the same direction, and was actually inclined to Brougham's plan.[1] But he realised the strength of the opposition in the Cabinet, and the effect it would have upon the King. He wrote to the Chancellor on January 1 : " I have come nearer to your view of the matter of the peerage than I thought I ever could have done ; and am much inclined to new creations, at present, or before the meeting of Parliament, to the amount and in the manner you propose. But there will be a great difference of opinion in the Cabinet upon it. A letter from Lansdowne shows that his objections are not at all diminished. He comes to the Cabinet to-morrow. Palmerston and Melbourne are equally opposed to it. The Duke of Richmond also is against it, but I do not think his objections so insurmountable as they appeared to be some time ago. If this difference of opinion should go the length of producing resignations, you will perceive that it would be quite fatal.

" But there is another and a greater difficulty on the part of the King. You know how strong his objections were. Finding them supported by so many members of the Cabinet he is less likely to give way. He expresses great confidence too in our being able to carry the bill on the second reading, and, without any alterations that could be considered as affecting its principle, or real efficiency, through the Committee.

" This belief, proceeding as I conjecture from the general language that has been held to him by some of the antireformers, will encourage him at least in postponing any determination till we shall have better means of judging of the disposition of the House of Lords. In short, this question assumes a very embarrassing shape, and I hope it will not be long before we have you here to assist us with your counsel, for though your opinion is very fully and very clearly stated in your letter, there is nothing like personal discussion. . . .

" The Tories do not seem to lose heart. I hear their language, founded on an assumption that the King will not make peers, is as violent and as confident as ever, and Lyndhurst is be-besides all this, I'm a barrener,' since many are to be *barren* with an e as well as an o " (*Howick Papers*).

[1] *Correspondence*, ii. 58 (December 24) : " It is a matter for very serious consideration, whether we shall be justified in carrying the Bill on to that stage [the second reading] without something like an assurance, that the country would not be exposed to all the disastrous consequences of a second rejection."

coming more and more an avowed and prominent supporter of their views." [1]

Grey was to pay a visit to the Pavilion at Brighton on January 3, to discuss the political situation, and on Monday, the 2nd, a critical meeting of the Cabinet was held ; Althorp expected that it would result in the resignation of Richmond and other colleagues.[2] Of its proceedings we have two accounts, one from Lord Holland and one from Stanley.[3] The atmosphere was less thunderous than had been expected. The letters of Brougham and Durham were both read, and it was resolved to lay the matter fully before the King. There followed a discussion on the proposal to ask for an immediate creation of fifteen peers. Grey, Durham, Althorp, Russell, Holland, Grant, Carlisle[4] were in favour of this ; Lansdowne, Melbourne, Palmerston, Richmond, Stanley, against it. Stanley wrote : " Palmerston, I think, alone protested against being pledged even to consent to a large batch . . . . Lord Grey very desponding, Palmerston bored, Melbourne more hesitating than I ever saw him, Grant balancing which was the greatest danger till he came to no conclusion at all." Melbourne, Holland said, feared the precedent, while Lansdowne might perhaps be converted " if some of his great worthies, such as Whishaw or Minto, could with truth be quoted in favour of it." Brougham and Graham, both of course of the adventurous party, were away, and also Goderich. It was agreed as a compromise that Grey should propose a smaller number—probably two creations and eight calls up—to the King, stating that a larger batch might be required later. But this suggestion was to be merely tentative, nor would the life of the Government depend on its issue. The decision was really an indorsement of Brougham's plan ; there is no doubt that his weight in the Cabinet was very great, as was

[1] *Howick Papers* ; printed in *Brougham's Memoirs*, iii. 164. Lyndhurst, the Lord Chancellor of Canning's and Wellington's administrations, had been made Lord Chief Baron by the Whigs, as a non-party appointment ; the Reform Bill moved him to re-enter active politics.

[2] Althorp to Graham, December 29 ; to Brougham, January 3. Brougham replied that the Government must be carried on in spite of resignations, at least till the bill was passed (*Life of Graham*, i. 134 ; *Althorp Papers*).

[3] Holland to Brougham, January 2 ; *Brougham Memoirs*, iii. 455. Stanley to Graham, January 2 ; *Life of Graham*, i. 134.

[4] Lord Carlisle was in the Cabinet without office, but was frequently absent from illness.

only to be expected from his position in the country at the time he entered it. The contrast between the points of view of the two sections is interesting ; at the back of the minds of the peer-makers was the thought of the people—its indignation if the bill should miscarry and the real danger to peace and order ; the minority thought more of the constitutional aspect and the grave risk of so disquieting a precedent.

Thus armed, Lord Grey proceeded on the morrow to Brighton. The King had been naturally much grieved by the break-down of the attempts at conciliation.  But he was willing to take the fact that the attempt had been made as so much to the good, and throughout the last fortnight of the old year continued to urge on his minister the advantages of modifying the bill.  His chief objection at this point was to the addition of members to the metropolitan boroughs, which he feared would lead to constant election riots ; Grey did his best to soothe him, and much regretted that the King had thought fit to mention his opinion to the Archbishop of Canterbury at Brighton ; If it leaked out it would be likely to prejudice the Government.[1] William, however, had also let the Archbishop know his conviction that the bill ought to be allowed to reach the Committee stage in the Lords.  He was determined to do his duty as a constitutional King, but in truth a crisis was approaching in which the way was marked by no clear constitutional precedent. If William dreaded the Reform Bill, he dreaded a conflict between the two Houses more, and it was a cruel fate which led him at the outset of his reign to a point at which he might be forced, in the course of his constitutional support of a Government measure, to override the will of one of the three elements of the Constitution.  Hence his keen desire to break the threatened impact.  Nevertheless, as it became plain that his advisers saw no hope of securing a majority for the bill without the loss of honour, the King thought much on the hateful subject, and was prepared to meet his minister with an open mind on January 3.

The minute of their conversation, drawn up by Grey and accepted by the King as accurate, is extant.[2]  Grey mentioned the usual considerations, showing how unlikely it was that the bill could pass unscathed through Committee, even should it survive the second reading,—and an adverse majority of twenty

---

[1] *Correspondence*, ii. 38.                [2] *Ibid.*, ii. 68.

was still expected ; he laid stress on the commotions certain to break out in the country, and finally made the proposal sanctioned by the Cabinet. Without committing himself either way, the King asked to have the Cabinet's advice in writing, but agreed with Grey's suggestion as to the best way of making the creation, should it at last prove necessary. A letter dated January 5 showed more clearly the favourable bent of his thoughts ; the King expressed his confidence in his ministers and his grave doubt whether in the present state of the country they could be replaced ; but said that he would rather make twenty-one peers at once than run the risk of a " second edition " being necessary.[1] The Cabinet met again on January 7, but begged leave to defer their communication till the Lord Chancellor's arrival from Westmorland.[2] The King's letter was taken by ministers as a virtual compliance ; what with this and the unhoped for prospect of agreement in the Cabinet, Holland was sanguine enough to prophesy that they would have " no more trouble about it." [3] He and his friends were at this time delighted with the King, and no praises could be too much for his " kindness," his " directness," and his " candour."

Lord Grey's visit to Brighton was of course known to the Opposition ; they guessed its object, and fully believed he would be successful, though regarding the prospect with dismay.[4] Many Tories held that such a step would be an actual violation of the Constitution. The extreme view of its iniquity was thus stated by the Duke of Newcastle : " I do not question the King's prerogative to create peers, but I maintain, and will ever support fearlessly, that a creation of peers for a political purpose is and would be a criminal breach (it was so considered in Queen Anne's time), and would actually place the King and his ministers in the situation of traitors to their country. For what would such an act be, more or less, than the subversion of the Constitu-

---

[1] *Correspondence*, ii. 73.

[2] *Ibid.*, ii. 80.

[3] Grey to Lansdowne, January 5 ; *Howick Papers*. Holland to Brougham, January 7 ; *Brougham Memoirs*, iii. 459.

[4] Wellington to Lyndhurst, January 5. Martin, *Life of Lyndhurst*, p. 300. It was rumoured at Brighton that thirty-six peers were to be created at once (*Despatches*, viii. 154). Campbell, however, wrote from Brighton on January 9 : " Nothing is known here about the new peers. The Princess Augusta yesterday told Scarlett that she could learn nothing, and that the King never mentioned politics in the family " (*Life of Campbell*, ii. 4).

tion and fundamental laws of England ? . . . The King constitutionally has nothing to do with a bill until it has passed both Houses of Parliament, and that it is brought to him for approval or rejection. If the King does more, he does what he does not possess the right to do, and he acts unconstitutionally."

The more moderate opinion was that a creation was probably within the bounds of the Constitution, but must only be used in a most exceptional case. Even if the prestige of the Lords should survive this single case, a precedent would be set for adding ministerialist peers whenever the House refused to pass a Government bill in its entirety. " What becomes, then," asked Wellington, " of the independence of the House of Lords ? After such a precedent, it could be of no use to the existence of the monarchy, none to the democracy. It would be the ridicule of the public and a disgrace to itself." [1] This was in fact Lord Grey's own position. " It is a measure of extreme violence," he admitted to Althorp ; " there is no precedent for it in our history, the case of Queen Anne's Peers not being in point." [2] The distinction, though subtle, was correct. In 1711 the Tory ministry which brought about the Peace of Utrecht was faced by a Whig majority in the Lords. To obtain the sanction of both Houses of Parliament to the peace, they induced Queen Anne to create twelve peers ; this advice was made one of the articles of impeachment against Harley. When the thoughts of Reformers turned to a creation of peers in the autumn of 1831, as the sole hope of carrying the Reform Bill through the Upper House, the case of 1711 was the only precedent for such coercion. And when, after the rejection of the bill in October, the demand increased, the parallel was no longer exact. For on this occasion the Lords had actually declared against the bill, and there could be no disguise of the fact that the creation would be intended to pass a definite measure.

It was, however, plain that, if no means of coercing the Lords existed, they held a higher position than either of the other branches of the Constitution. For the Crown was dependent for supplies on the Commons, and the Commons were subject to a dissolution. The Lords alone would decide without appeal. The answer of their supporters was that the Constitution here, as elsewhere, trusted to the sweet reasonableness of the parties to avoid a deadlock. Grey said that in any ordinary case the

---

[1] *Despatches*, viii. 156.     [2] *Correspondence*, ii. 268.

Lords would have bowed to a demand of the Commons repeated after a general election.[1] The Tories said this was not an ordinary case ; the cry for " the bill, the whole bill, and nothing but the bill " showed an unconstitutional refusal to compromise. Moderate Tories would not again have thrown the bill out on the second reading, but expected the Government to submit to amendments favoured by the unfettered judgment of the House.[2] But the state of feeling on both sides was not propitious for conciliation, and the aid of the Crown was invoked. Not liking to admit the maxim that " Ministers govern through the instrumentality of the Crown,"[3] the Tories raised the cry that the ministers were dragging the Crown through the dirt, and using it for party purposes. It was of course extremely galling to them to see that institution, of which they considered themselves the special defenders, in this way turned against them. The strength of their indignation was increased by the immense respect in which the House of Lords was held by all the upper and middle classes. The King considered the Lords the bulwark of the Throne, and spoke of them as " that class of his subjects to whose support the Crown has, in every struggle, been chiefly indebted for its existence or its restoration."[4] Tory peers therefore made frantic efforts to save the King, while yet there was time, from becoming the engine of his own overthrow.

Wellington was actually urged by a brother Duke to go to the King and offer of his own accord to form a government.[5] Willing as he had been to take this step a couple of months back, he now refused on the ground that a new Parliament, which his acceptance of office would involve, could not meet in

---

[1] " In ordinary times the general and lasting and intense feeling of the public, after so much discussion, and so long an interval for consideration, and the increased majority in the House of Commons, would have been decisive : this is now more than doubtful " (*Correspondence*, ii. 44).

[2] Wellington to Wharncliffe, February 3, 1832 : " The House of Lords rejected *the bill*, and then the Minister, instead of modifying his measure, brings forward, as he boasts himself, a measure equally efficient ; that is to say, in substance and reality the same bill. Then the House of Lords are to be told, ' You must pass this bill, or be responsible for the consequences.' Is this fair ? Is it the House of Lords or the Minister, that is to say the Crown, that is responsible for the consequences ? " (*Despatches*, viii. 205 ; Gordon, *The Earl of Aberdeen*, p. 105).

[3] Anson, *Law of the Constitution*, vol. ii. Part I. 41.

[4] *Correspondence*, ii. 52.

[5] Buckingham to Wellington, January 1 ; *Despatches*, viii. 142.

time to renew the Mutiny Act, which would expire on March 25.[1] The Duke's reasons were characteristically practical; but we have the highest authority for believing that in any case the King considered a change of ministry impossible.[2] Nor was the attempt of Buckingham's son, Lord Chandos, to approach the King through Sir Herbert Taylor encouraging. Taylor showed the letter to Grey, and added a touch of comedy, which Althorp fully appreciated, by telling the disgusted Chandos that he presumed he had carried out his wishes in doing so.[3] The Waverers now took their turn, and Lord Wharncliffe saw the King on the 11th. He explained the ground of his objections to the bill, to wit the metropolitan boroughs and the representation of towns by single members, and pressed the King not to abandon hope that a settlement might yet be reached.[4] Various other Opposition peers claimed their privilege of private audience with the sovereign, some to present addresses from their counties; but the King was unwontedly discreet, and Grey was kept informed of his visitors.[5] Wellington, who was now recovering from a slight illness, still resisted the suggestion that he should himself demand an audience; his fine sense of honour forbade him to use a private and personal right for a political purpose, and at the same time he saw no hope of success. The King was acting with his eyes open, and had chosen his own disastrous course. He could not be treated as a mere puppet. For his own part the Duke did not greatly care by what means the bill was carried. By virtue of a general election following on an utterly unconstitutional dissolution and conducted amid violence and misrepresentation, the ministry had secured a majority which was riding rough-shod over the customary principles of English government. They had made the King their tool and the mob

---

[1] *Despatches*, viii. 143.

[2] Queen Adelaide to Earl Howe, January 18: " I am afraid [the King] has the fixed idea that no other administration could be formed at present amongst your friends, and thinks that they are aware of it themselves. How far he is right or not I cannot pretend to say, for I do not understand these important things, but I should like to know what the Duke of Wellington thinks " (*Despatches*, viii. 166).

[3] Chandos to Wellington, January 6; *Despatches*, viii. 147. Holland to Brougham, January 7; *Brougham Memoirs*, iii. 459. Althorp to Russell, January 7; *Early Correspondence*, ii. 30.

[4] *Correspondence*, ii. 93.

[5] Salisbury and Camden to Wellington, January 16, 21; *Despatches*, viii. 162, 166. *Correspondence*, ii. 126, 135.

their master, and the country was to be plunged in revolution simply that the Prime Minister's pledge to the canaille might not be broken. " We are governed by the mob and its organ— a licentious press." In the circumstances he preferred to wait till the King recovered his senses, and dare the ministers to do their worst.[1] The Duke of Buckingham was more sanguine or less scrupulous, and appealed to the King by letter not to create peers ; the letter was duly forwarded to the Prime Minister.[2]

While Tories thus bewailed their sovereign's infatuation, Whigs were anxiously calculating their chances of a majority on the second reading. Grey was encouraged by Lord Somers' declaration that he intended to vote for the bill, but the fear of possible resignations in the Cabinet was again in his mind, and ministered to his natural despondency ; he did not believe that in any case the King would consent to create more peers than twenty-five.[3]

However, the Cabinet meeting of January 13, which was attended by the Chancellor but not by Lansdowne or Holland, passed off without mishap, and a unanimous minute was presented to the King.[4] Taking his dislike to a double creation as final, it went straight to the heart of the matter, and said boldly that the number required must depend on circumstances ; an in-effective creation would be worse than useless. The Cabinet begged therefore to defer any such step for the present, in the confidence that when the time came the King would " allow them the power of acting at once up to the exigency of the case." This was indeed, as the King pointed out, widely different from the last modest request for ten peers, and involved in fact the surrender of the prerogative into the hands of the ministers, to be used to an extent depending on a third party and therefore as yet incalculable. Nevertheless he consented to allow his Government the power they asked for, qualifying his promise with the " irrevocable condition " that the creations of new peers should not be more than three, the rest to be com-

---

[1] Wellington to Strangford, January 12 ; to Exeter, January 14 ; to Montrose, January 21 (*Despatches*, viii. 155, 161, 168).

[2] *Correspondence*, ii. 139.

[3] Grey to Althorp, January 10 ; *Memoir of Althorp*, p. 386 ; *Althorp Papers*.

[4] *Correspondence*, ii. 96–105.

Y

posed of called up heirs and Scotch and Irish peers.[1]   Lord Grey replied, going over the ground of the King's letter, and merely suggesting that perhaps the ennobling of a few commoners of wealth and family might be better than the raising of Scotch and Irish lords to the peerage of the United Kingdom.[1]   Thus on January 15 the ministers had the King's promise to create peers, when the time came, to an extent sufficient to secure the passing of the bill.

On the 19th Parliament reassembled, and next day the Commons went into Committee on the Reform Bill; it was supported by strong petitions from Perth and from Manchester, where the unions of both kinds had agreed to its principle, though objecting to the £10 qualification.   A few days after this an incident occurred at Manchester which led to increased disaffection to the Government on the part of the extreme Radicals.   On Sunday, January 22, the Low Political Union gathered in St. George's Square to protest against the death sentences passed by the Special Commissions on some of the Bristol and Nottingham rioters, and probably also to support the Reform scheme of the "National Convention."[2]   On no other day of the week, they said, could they get out of the cotton mills in time to hold a meeting; nevertheless respectable opinion was much shocked.[3]   The meeting, which passed off perfectly quietly, was adjourned to the 29th;[4] the military authorities, however, decided to interfere, alarmed by reports that the union had been seen drilling by moonlight, and by the fact that some of the audience on the previous Sunday had been armed.   Accordingly, the adjourned meeting was broken up by the troops, who made eight arrests.   Three more men were arrested in London, where they had gone to address their friends of the National Union.   Four of the leaders were eventually sentenced at Lancaster to a year's imprisonment; they continued to write piteous letters from " the Lancaster

---

[1] *Correspondence*, ii. 113.   We know from a letter of Sir Herbert Taylor (*Correspondence*, ii. 333) that this condition was not thought of as a possible limitation of the total number.

[2] *Correspondence*, ii. 121.

[3] *H. O.* 40. 30, 41. 11, 52. 18 ;   Add. MSS. 27,791, f. 355.

[4] " The holding of these meetings on Sundays has proved too strong a measure for any but the most worthless and most reckless " (Bouverie to Melbourne).

Bastille" to their friends outside. Grey and Melbourne fully approved of the action of the Manchester magistrates.

This instance of "Whig despotism" caused much irritation, and many of the working classes were at this time in a very rebellious state. Benbow, whose approval of the Bristol riots had been generally disavowed, was urging his plan of a month's general "holiday" for the working classes. After a week the holiday makers were to lay hands on anything they could get, and so secure a more equitable readjustment of wealth ; the recent insurrection of the French artisans at Lyons and Grenoble had fired his imagination. "The leaders of all these unions," wrote Place contemptuously, "with but few exceptions, had succeeded in persuading themselves that the time was coming when the whole of the working men would be ready to rise *en masse* and take the management of their own affairs." He did not fail to point out that only an infinitesimal proportion of the working classes would ever hear of the proposal to rise, and further that working men had in no case "accomplished any national movement" without the help of the middle class.[1] Nevertheless Place had himself little expectation of benefit from the Reform Bill, except as a means of destroying the power of tradition and prescription. The £50 tenancy clause, and another which disqualified householders who had not paid up their rates, made it clear to him that the representation would still be divided between the old gentlemanly parties. And of these he expected the Tories to win, as alike more strenuous and more free handed in their electioneering methods. Writing some years after, he said that experience of the reformed Parliament had confirmed this forecast.[2] Still for the present the bill was worth supporting. On February 2 the National Political Union held its first general meeting, with Sir Francis Burdett for the last time in the chair. A petition to the Commons was proposed, begging the House to press on ministers the urgent need of passing the bill at once, owing to the restless state of the country. Burdett and Hume objected to the wording on the ground that ministers were already doing their utmost. An uproar followed, and the chairman left the room.[3] The same day the Birmingham Union declared their fitness for

[1] Add. MSS. 27,791, ff. 304, 333, 343.
[2] *Ibid.*, 27,790, f. 309.
[3] *Ibid.*, 27,791, f. 137.

action, 27,000 strong, by presenting an address which pledged their devotion to their leader.[1]

The King was in no way softened in his hostility to the unions by the late good behaviour of most of them, and soon after the provisional settlement of the peer question he communicated with Grey on the subject. His alarm was in fact almost the greater when the strength of the unions was shown in preserving tranquillity, and he looked forward with trembling anticipation to their dissolution as soon as the Reform Bill should pass.[2] As a matter of fact the country was at present more peaceful than it had been for some time, and the Midlands, where there had lately been riots, lay quiet under military supervision.[3] Lord Grey was anxious that the King should attribute this satisfactory state of things to the people's confidence that the bill was safe. In Parliament he considered that things were running less smoothly. A protest had been made against the expected creation of peers, and on one or two occasions in Committee the Government feared the result of a division ; on the 26th a motion on the Russian-Dutch loan, amounting to a vote of lack of confidence, was only lost by twenty-four votes. Sir Henry Parnell was turned out of his office of Secretary at War for not supporting the Government on this motion ; his place was filled by Hobhouse, one of the members for Westminster—a bold appointment, which Grey hardly expected his master to approve.[4] A debate in the Lords on the Belgian treaty seemed more dangerous in spirit than the figures of the division suggested.[5]

On the other hand the Waverers were working hard with the help and encouragement of Charles Greville, the diarist, now Clerk of the Council, who put himself in constant communication with Melbourne ; convinced that Grey had *carte blanche* to carry the bill, they had by this time determined

---

[1] Attwood to his wife, February 2 ; *Life of Attwood*, p. 191.

[2] The King wrote of the dangerous state of affairs " when the overthrow of all legitimate authority, the destruction of ancient institutions, of social order, and of every gradation and link of society are threatened, when a revolutionary and demoralising spirit is making frightful strides, when a poisonous press, almost unchecked, guides, excites, and at the same time controls public opinion " (*Correspondence*, ii. 78, 125).

[3] General Campbell's reports ; *H. O.* 40. 30.

[4] *Correspondence*, ii. 165.

[5] *Ibid.*, ii. 143, 155, 156.

to vote for the second reading rather than force the creation of peers, and were merely hesitating as to the best time for declaring their intentions. After some doubt they decided, with Melbourne's approval, to wait till the bill came up from the Commons, and so leave longer for negotiation.[1] Harrowby and Wharncliffe proceeded to canvass individual peers by letter, and even approached the leaders of their party. They laid stress on the determination of the people for Reform, the inability or refusal of conservatives to unite on a moderate alternative to the bill, and the almost certain power of the Cabinet to make peers to carry the second reading.[2] Nevertheless Peel and Wellington were both adamant, and declared for a die-hard policy. At a later stage of the bill the knowledge that Grey was authorised to create peers secured its passing without that necessity, but it was not so now.

The Duke, who was just realising that some Reform was required, refused to accept any responsibility for what might occur. Grey must bear the full odium of his crime. " As for the consequences of the bill being lost again by the vote of the House of Lords, they are worse than ridiculous ; they are contemptible. I know well the consequences of the union of the King and his Government with the majority of the House of Commons, all the Dissenters from the Church of England, the Radicals and the mob. But here the Government alone are responsible. I maintain, and will prove it whenever there is an opportunity, that the Government could restore and preserve tranquillity in all parts of this country ; ay, and in Ireland likewise." [3]

Peel, also admitting to the full the evil effects of a creation, yet held out as firmly for rejecting the bill at any price. Taking a higher and a longer view than his colleague, he judged that the loss of prestige the Lords would suffer by passing the bill against their expressed convictions outweighed the material injury of an inflow of Radicals to swamp them. " I assure you that my great object in public life for the last six months has been to vindicate the authority and maintain the character of the House of Lords. I think that it is the institu-

---

[1] *Greville Memoirs*, ii. 239, 241.

[2] Wharncliffe to Wellington, January 31 ; see also Harrowby's Circular ; *Despatches*, viii. 173–8.

[3] Wellington to Wharncliffe, February 3 ; *Despatches*, viii. 205.

tion most exposed to danger from the short-sighted folly of the times, and also the institution which, if it remain erect in character, is most likely to serve as a rallying-point for the returning good sense and moderation of the country." By virtue partly of his natural instinct, partly of his opinion that the Constitution was literally at an end, the Duke only considered the momentary effect. Peel looked to the bar of posterity ; a regenerate Tory party was doubtless already in his mind, and he preferred to bequeath it a tradition of unyielding loyalty to conscience than one of time-serving prudence. It was on a similar far-sighted principle that he justified the long hopeless resistance in the Commons. "Why have we been struggling against the Reform Bill in the House of Commons ? Not in the hope of resisting its final success in that House, but because we look beyond the Bill, because we know the nature of popular concessions, their tendency to propagate the necessity for further and more extensive compliances. We want to make the ' descensus ' as ' difficilis ' as we can—to teach young inexperienced men charged with the trust of government that, though they may be backed by popular clamour, they shall not override on the first spring-tide of excitement every barrier and breakwater raised against popular impulses ; that the carrying of extensive changes in the Constitution without previous deliberation shall not be a holiday task ; that there shall be just what has happened—the House sick of the question, the Ministers repenting they brought it forward, the country paying the penalty for the folly and incapacity of its rulers. All these are salutary sufferings, that may I trust make people hereafter distinguish between the amendment and the overturning of their institutions." [1] Granted the aristocratic position and the assumption that the bill was the result of temporary excitement, there could hardly be more statesmanlike argument than this. It is noteworthy that, in counselling the total rejection of the bill, Peel did not, any more than the Duke, take the threatened popular convulsion seriously. [2]

Thus thrown on their own resources, the Waverers could

---

[1] Peel to Harrowby, February 5 ; *Peel Papers*, ii. 200.

[2] Peel to Goulburn : " If the question lay between passing the present Bill and its rejection, I for one am prepared for all consequences of rejection, and I really do not believe that those consequences would be formidable " (*Peel Papers*, ii. 198).

only return to the task of organising a party of moderation. Wharncliffe explained the position at Brighton to Sir Herbert Taylor, declaring at the same time that, should peers nevertheless be made, he would oppose the Government at every stage of the measure.[1] Lord Grey was in a painfully anxious situation, not unnaturally considering the Waverers' attitude unreasonable. They knew he had no wish to make peers, but was pledged to carry the bill; if their and his joint efforts to secure an unforced majority failed, it would be surely mere vindictiveness on their part to penalise the Government by making its task even harder. Durham had held it inconceivable " that any peer having voted for the last Reform Bill, on the ground of its being a measure essential to the prosperity of the country and safety of the State, would vote against a similar Bill now, solely because to him had been added a sufficient number of colleagues to prevent his vote from being a second time rendered useless and inefficient." [2] These words, written on December 29, do not perfectly apply to the Waverers, but the principle is the same. However, the rules of logic are not the same as those of party politics. Grey's difficulties were increased by the fact that he did not know what was going on in the enemy's camp, whereas they, through Greville's communications with Melbourne, Richmond, and Palmerston, had a very fair idea of the state of affairs in his.[3] Disgusted by their factious opposition in the Lords, he could believe almost anything of them; Brougham had suggested that they might wish to create the impression that they would allow the second reading, and then at the last moment fall on the unsuspecting foe.[4]

Among these anxieties came a disquieting letter from Sir Herbert Taylor in the King's name, arising out of Grey's remark that a defeat in Committee might be no less fatal to the bill than its rejection on the second reading. The upshot was that the King hoped, supposing the second reading was carried in the Lords, that the Government would be willing to accept amendments in Committee, at least provisionally, and not stake their reputations on keeping the bill wholly intact. Then as to peers, the ominous words, " there must be some limit,"

---

[1] *Correspondence*, ii. 193.
[2] *Life of Durham*, i. 275; *Correspondence*, ii. 209.
[3] *Greville Memoirs*, ii. 254–8.
[4] *Correspondence*, ii. 184, 210; *Brougham Memoirs*, iii. 167.

were used, and stress was laid on the impossibility of knowing the amount necessary to keep on the safe side.[1]  Grey in reply stated that Schedule A, the £10 qualification, and the enfranchisement of large towns, must be held inviolable ;  as to other points he could make large concessions ;  he had further arranged a meeting with Harrowby for February 14, as there was little over a fortnight before the bill was expected to leave the Commons.

The King's answer was satisfactory ;  he believed prospects now looked brighter than ever before ;  Lord Wharncliffe expected the second reading would be carried by twenty votes ;  but if all failed, wrote Taylor, " your Lordship will not find the King fail you in the hour of need." [2]  It was stated, moreover, to Grey's secretary by Lord Sandon that twenty-five peers who had voted against the second reading in October had decided to come over.[3]  And finally just before the conference with Harrowby, now fixed for the 16th, Sir Herbert repeated that " the alternative " was at Grey's option. Thus, a month after the King's promise, his word held good to create peers if needed.  Harrowby and Wharncliffe assured Grey of their own good faith, but they could not speak for others, and were unable to express more than their " confident expectation and belief " that the second reading would be carried.  Grey had obtained leave, however, to show them Taylor's letter, which impressed them with the idea that he had " unlimited power " to create peers if necessary, and his moral position was accordingly strengthened.[4]  Henceforward the Opposition could be under no illusions.

It was no less understood on the Government side of the House of Commons that the Cabinet were empowered to create peers, and the general opinion, certainly in the advanced wing of the party, was that they ought to do so now.  " An army never looked for the appearance of the Gazette," said O'Connell, " with more anxiety than did the people at that moment." Lord Grey was deluged with advice from no mean counsellors to take the bold step, and his nearest and dearest began to doubt his wisdom.  The editor of his correspondence with the

---

[1] " Should forty or fifty be required (and His Majesty trusts he shall never be called upon to consider of an addition to that extent), the King wishes to know, whether there be any security that such a number will suffice " (*Correspondence*, ii. 205).  *Cf. Recollections*, iv. 181.

[2] *Correspondence*, ii. 220.

[3] *Ibid.*, ii. 222.

[4] *Ibid.*, ii. 225, 230 ;  *Greville Memoirs*, ii. 260.

King, the Lord Howick of 1832, quotes a letter of Sydney Smith to his mother, urging that Lord Grey ought to create or resign : " Mackintosh, Whishaw, Robert Smith, Rogers, Luttrell, Jeffrey, Sharpe, Ord, Macaulay, Fazakerley, Lord Ebrington—where will you find a better jury, or one more able and more willing to consider every point connected with the honour, character, and fame of Lord Grey ? There would not be among them a dissentient voice." Lord Howick adds that he himself spoke to his father in the same sense, but was satisfied by his answer.[1] Durham and Hobhouse thought seriously of resigning, and the latter, who believed that Wharncliffe and Harrowby were merely laying a trap, was with difficulty satisfied by Althorp's assurance that he and Brougham only held office on the certainty that the bill would go through.[2] In spite, however, of pressure and misrepresentation, Grey held to his resolve to " play the game his own way " and not create peers prematurely. In this there can be little doubt he was right ; the second reading in the Lords was a long way off, and it was impossible to calculate the amount necessary to make things safe ; nor would Grey have been acting fairly by the King, whose consent assumed that the request would not be made till the last possible moment. To us perhaps this seems obvious, after the event ; but at the time the general suspense and distrust of the enemy were great, and it needed no little firmness to hold out for Fabian tactics in the face of such authority.

A Mansion House banquet on February 18 gave Grey an opportunity of repelling the aspersions on his courage and good faith. He sought to keep up the spirits of the people by repeating his fixed resolve to carry the bill, which was still drearily passing through the Committee of the Commons. On the 28th the much debated clause enfranchising the metropolitan boroughs was approved by the strong Government majority of 80 ; but the less the bill was altered in the Commons, the fiercer, it was felt by many, would be the opposition of the Lords. Of the strength of this opposition there was still no certainty. Lord Holland, who could name 175 certain enemies out of 381 possible voters, was far from confident. Once again divisions in the Cabinet began to threaten the break-up of the Government, and put Grey's firmness to the test. Holland himself was for a prompt creation, which he

---

[1] *Correspondence*, ii. 195.     [2] *Recollections*, iv. 174 ff.

did not think would prove as distasteful to the King as was generally supposed.[1] Durham and Hobhouse of course agreed, and with them was the Reforming Duke of Sussex, the one real Liberal in the royal family.

Lord Althorp was of the same opinion, but, being what he was, groaned under the intolerable burden of difficulties mainly intellectual, but partly also ethical.[2] The late Duke of Devonshire once told a youthful audience that all through life it had been his lot to consort with men whose minds moved faster than his own. Lord Althorp's mind not only moved slowly but found motion of any kind torture. He himself felt no conviction that the second reading was safe, and that being so was tempted to resign unless the King were immediately asked to redeem his pledge. In either case—a large creation, or the resignation of the Cabinet—he believed the bill would be eventually passed. The one fatal chance was defeat on the second reading. On the other hand he knew that several of his colleagues were against him, including the Prime Minister; and beyond all doubt his own resignation would be followed by others and destroy the Government. His inclination was strongly to resign, unless the Cabinet consented, and " he had never sacrificed his own inclinations to a sense of duty without repenting it, and always found himself more substantially unhappy for having exerted himself for the public good."[3] In this case his inclinations went with the nearest way of saving his character; he admitted, however, that " a man under certain circumstances ought to sacrifice his character for the sake of his country."[4] In the agony of indecision he more than once spoke of shooting himself, and actually, so he said, removed his pistols from his bedroom for safety. He was faced by a crisis to which, as he pathetically complained, his faculties were not equal. Eventually, on March 10, he wrote to Lord Grey, declaring his belief that peers should be made before the second reading, and asking whether the threat of his own resignation would induce Grey to comply.[5]

The day before, Sir James Graham had written to the same

---

[1] Holland to Grey, February 24, 26 ; *Howick Papers*.

[2] *Recollections*, iv. 184, 188.

[3] *Life of Jeffrey*, ii. 244, quoted by Bagehot, *Biographical Studies*, p. 309 (Lord Althorp and the Reform Act of 1832).

[4] *Recollections*, iv. 195.

[5] *Memoir of Althorp*, p. 403.

effect. He held the present to be an opportunity which would never recur; even assuming the passing of the second reading, the opposition in Committee, and possibly on the third reading, would be no less uncompromising, while the ministers' own position with the King would be considerably weaker; the Tories would be in an ambush from which they could leap out at any moment to destroy the bill. He imagined the bitter contempt and indignation of the people when they realised the bill had been lost by the sheer negligence of the ministry to use a weapon actually put into their hands.[1]

At the decisive meeting of the Cabinet held on March 11, Durham, who shared the conviction of Birmingham Reformers that " to *risk* the passing of the Bill would irrecoverably destroy the character of the whole administration," embodied these views in four resolutions.[2] They were followed by a long discussion. Brougham was known to be in favour of an immediate creation, and it may well seem strange that Durham was left in a minority of one on a division. The force which prevailed against the appeal of four such men was the solemn judgment of Lord Grey, as given earlier in the day in a written reply to Althorp's letter.[3] This document is of extraordinary interest; it shows the reasons which to a constitutionalist of Lord Grey's experience and skill, at the supreme post of responsibility, appeared of sufficient force to outweigh his lieutenant's actual threat of resignation, and the opinions of Durham and the Chancellor—both of them more in touch with popular feeling than any others of the Cabinet—no less than of Holland, the partner of his traditions and career. Grey maintained that a majority on the second reading was practically certain; the Waverers were to declare their intentions at the introduction of the bill. In Committee, he confessed, the risk would be greater, though there was the hope of finding the Opposition divided; in any case the power of creating peers would remain. This being so he did not see the necessity which alone could justify so hateful a measure, to say nothing of the possibility of its failing after all.

" Here I confess my extreme repugnance to the measure

---

[1] Graham to Grey, March 9; *Life of Graham*, i. 138.

[2] *Recollections*, iv. p. 197. Joshua Scholefield to Durham, March 10; *Lambton Papers*.

[3] Grey to Althorp, March 11; *Memoir of Althorp*, p. 407.

makes me distrust my own judgment. I apply my reason to it with all the power I can, but I am conscious my feeling is stronger than my reason. It is a measure of extreme violence; there is no precedent for it in our history, the case of Queen Anne's Peers not being in point, it is a certain evil, dangerous itself as a precedent; and, with all these objections, in my opinion very uncertain of success.

" The majority against us was forty-one; the conversions, from which we now look for a more favourable result on the second reading, would turn against us almost to a man; many of those on whom we now depend would, I believe, certainly leave us; and there is no saying how far a defection, to which the natural feeling of the House of Lords would tend, might be carried. We should be exposed then to a great risk of failure even on the second reading. Would our difficulties be much diminished even in the Committee, when the whole body of the Opposition would be brought together, their mutual discontent composed, and their hostility to the Government increased and inflamed with additional rancour and acrimony? I really believe, therefore, that we should fail. . . ."

Even in the case of success, " would the Government have strength enough to go on without a further creation of peers? What has happened in France, allowing for all the dissimilarity between the two countries, may afford an example of what we might expect. The House of Lords would probably become unmanageable in our hands; and, if we should be displaced, the succeeding Government would be under the necessity of making a further addition to it; and then what would become of the constitutional character and efficiency of this branch of the Legislature? The result then is, that all these considerations press upon my mind with so irresistible a weight, that I really cannot bring myself to the adoption of a measure to which, as we now stand, there appear to me to be such insurmountable objections.

" With regard to the question which you put to me, I will take example by your frankness in answering it. As at present advised, I do not think anything would induce me to be a consenting party to a large creation of peers. The consequence of your resignation then would be, the immediate breaking up of the Government; for, if I refused to come in, I should now find it still more impossible to go on, without you."

It is not surprising that views so ably stated carried the day. Durham alone, whose conduct in the last few days is by no means flatteringly spoken of by Greville, left the Cabinet with the intention of resigning. He was persuaded to refrain, however, by Lord John Russell's determination to follow his example, and resolved not to force the break-up of the ministry.[1] The King was greatly pleased by the decision not to ask for peers before the second reading, and almost more so by the sentiments of Grey's letter to Althorp, which was laid before him; he allowed his minister to know that the powers promised him were not limited to the second reading, but extended " to carrying the Bill itself with such modifications as may be introduced in Committee, and reasonably admitted, without destroying the principle and the efficiency of the measure." [2] At the same time he promised to use his influence with the Archbishop of York and Lord Hill on the Government's behalf. Two months after his first promise the King's support was still firm.

Nevertheless there was as yet no certainty of a majority. The Die-hards were working as strenuously as the Waverers, and Wellington's prestige was very great; a consultation of Tory peers had been called by the Duke of Buckingham on February 20 to consider how best to fight the bill in the Lords.[3] The King could not even prevail on the Commander-in-Chief to vote for the Government, and every individual case was considered serious.[4] On the 16th Holland furnished Lord Grey with an elaborate calculation, pointing to a tie.[5] Keen Reformers might well hold that Grey was running it too fine. The next few days were extremely anxious and every peer's opinions

---

[1] " Richmond quarrels with Durham, Melbourne damns him, and the rest hate him. But there he is, frowning, sulking, bullying, and meddling, and doing all the harm he can " (*Greville Memoirs*, ii. 265); *Recollections*, iv. 198; *Life of Durham*, i. 278.

[2] *Correspondence*, ii. 261.

[3] Eldon to Wellington; Wellington to Eldon, February 17; to Aberdeen, February 19; to Newcastle and Lucan, March 13; *Despatches*, viii. 224-7, 260-1. Croker to Hertford, February 21; *Croker Papers*, p. 152.

[4] *Correspondence*, ii. 273.

[5] Holland to Grey, March 16. Of 415 peers he knew that 175 would vote for the bill, and 40 be absent. There remained 200, of whom 21 were doubtful: he subtracted 15 of these as unlikely to vote against the bill, and added 10 probable supporters to his own side. This gave a tie of 185 all (*Howick Papers*).

were eagerly canvassed ; it was felt that the smallest trifle might turn the scale, and Holland suggested the sending down of a batch of ministerialist Masters of Arts to Oxford to block an anti-Reform petition from the University.[1]

Meanwhile the bill had passed all its stages in the Commons. The third reading was carried on the 22nd, after a three nights' debate showing no decline of energy, though Peel, in the finest of all his speeches on the question, expressed the belief of practically the whole House in admitting that some Reform was necessary and desired by the people. On the 26th the bill was sent up to the Lords. Important statements were expected on the occasion of the first reading. To Grey's immense relief satisfactory declarations were made by Lords Harrowby and Wharncliffe and the Bishop of London ; they seemed to him " quite decisive of the success of the second reading," though ominous of evil in Committee.[2] The momentous debate was fixed for April 19.

March 21 had been the day for some time set apart for a general Fast, granted partly to satisfy the Saints, among whom Perceval, the son of the Prime Minister, cut a strange figure in the House by his wild ravings and denunciations of the iniquities of the time, and partly as a supplication against the cholera, which was taken as a special visitation of Divine Providence. The Radicals looked on the scheme with ridicule, if not contempt ; the working classes, they considered, were more in need of a feast than a fast.[3] The National Political Union decided after discussion not to celebrate the occasion by a dinner, but the Union of the Working Classes early arranged to hold a demonstration on the day. A mass meeting was to assemble at eleven in Finsbury Square, with a view to parading the streets in procession till four ; the members were then to go home and feast. The numbers of the procession were estimated at

---

[1] Holland to Grey, March 23 ; *Howick Papers.*

[2] *Correspondence*, ii. 286.

[3] A Birmingham paper quoted :—

"  We want no Fast, but Radical Reform,
   This, this alone, will check the threatening storm."

It added a " Reform Litany, for the General Farce day," which ran : " From the craft and assault of the Bishops, from their pride, vain-glory, and hypocrisy ; from their threatened death and destruction, good King, deliver us " (*H. O.* 52. 20).

100,000 ; their behaviour was perfectly peaceful, till on attempting to march westwards into the Strand they found Temple Bar held by a cordon of police ; the same obstruction met them in Holborn when they had turned up Chancery Lane. Eventually four of their leaders, including Lovett and Benbow, were arrested, but there was nothing in the nature of general disorder. A few days later the Government incurred further ridicule by the trial for unlawful assembly of six harmless workmen, accused of practising broadsword exercise with wooden swords in an obscure garret.[1] But worse than this could be borne from those who still had the Reform Bill in their charge.

Towards the end of March the feeling of newspaper readers, hitherto mainly a blend of impatience at the three weeks' delay in Committee and of desire to get the matter done with, began to swing back to something like the excitement of last October.[2] All thoughts were directed upon Lord Grey, whether as the silent strong man who could be trusted to save the State, or as the timid politician hesitating to put his fortune to the touch by insisting on a creation of peers. This was the all-absorbing question ; rumours had never been so frequent or so contradictory, and countless leading articles were devoted to the subject of peer-making in all its aspects, historical, constitutional, and ethical. The general opinion was still that Grey had unlimited power, and the *Times* spoke perhaps without irony in repelling the " stale scandal " that the King felt repugnance to the measure.[3] On April 9 it reminded its readers of the " one sure source of confidence, that the King is staunch, and resolved to create any number of peers which the ministers may think necessary." Place, however, said that the people " could not reconcile the studied silence, caution, and secrecy of ministers at so fearful a time with honest conduct on the part of the King. . . . Business slackened, a vague undefined notion of impending mischief was generally entertained. Apprehension of something worse than the suspension of manufacturing

---

[1] Add. MSS. 27,791, f. 399.

[2] *Morning Herald*, March 28. Thomas Arnold wrote on April 5, of himself and the poet Wordsworth : " Once and once only, we had a good fight about the Reform Bill during a walk up Greenhead Ghyll to see ' the unfinished sheepfold ' recorded in ' Michael.' "

[3] *Times*, April 7.

prevailed and would have risen to the highest possible pitch, and this alone would have produced a revolution, which, however much it was desirable that it should be prevented, became day by day less and less feared." [1]

As the fateful day of the second reading approached, and still no peers, it was felt by Reformers that either Grey must have unknown sources of information or else he was exposing the country to an unjustifiable risk, and he was devoted, body and soul, to damnation if he should turn out to be mistaken. There could be no forgiveness for one who had made the great refusal when the choice was his. Grey himself was fully conscious of this. "Things are in a very nervous state," he wrote, " and my personal responsibility, which the editor of the *Times* seeks to aggravate by direct excitement to assassination, is fearfully heavy. But I am satisfied I have done right; every day furnishing me with fresh proofs that a contrary course could not have been successful." [2] In the circumstances nothing remained for the people but to petition the Lords and calculate the strength of the army, encouraged by articles on street-fighting in the papers.[3]

From the Cabinet's point of view things had by no means gone smoothly since the first reading in the Lords. At that time matters had looked brighter, but they were now to learn how serious were the difficulties possible under a Constitution that still left ample room for the personal vagaries of the Prince. On March 27 the Cabinet met to discuss the line to be taken, according to the various possible results of the coming division. Omitting to decide definitely on their course if the bill should pass by a small majority, they unanimously recommended an instant prorogation for a few days, if it should be actually thrown out, and a creation of peers to follow.[4] The King's reply, dated March 30, shows the first signs of the cloven hoof. Victory by a very small margin might demand a creation " so extensive as His Majesty's confidential servants may not

[1] Add. MSS. 27,792, f. 37.

[2] Grey to Durham, April 4; *Lambton Papers*. On February 17 he had written to Taylor : "The rejection of the bill on the second reading would be to me such ruin as never fell upon a public man " (*Correspondence*, ii. 232).

[3] Add. MSS. 27,792, f. 38 ; *Poor Man's Guardian*, April 11.

[4] *Correspondence*, ii. 289. Althorp to Russell, March 27 ; *Early Correspondence*, ii. 30.

venture to recommend, nor His Majesty think fit to sanction."
As to the case of rejection, though holding his pledge " sacred,"
" subject to His Majesty's consideration of the nature and
extent of the addition," William was strongly in favour of a
greater modification of the bill than had yet been proposed,
to be arranged with its more conciliatory opponents before it
should be again introduced into the House of Commons.  He
suggested Schedule A and the extension of Scotch and Irish
representation as its basis.  It shows how little the King understood the popular feeling on the bill, that he seriously believed
that after the renewed mortification of a second defeat by the
Lords, after more than a year's interval since their hopes were first
raised, after Lord Grey had time and again pledged his honour
to introduce no measure less effective than the first, Englishmen
would consent to accept the mere shadow of the bill which
had long become a household word in the Three Kingdoms.[1]
Somewhat staggered by this new development, Lord Grey went
to Windsor to see the King on April 1 ; their conversation is
recorded in a minute.[2]

Lord Grey first made it clear that he was bound in conscience
to the principle of the current bill, interpreted again as Schedule
A, the enfranchisement of large towns, and the £10 qualification ;
he would propose nothing short of this.  Decision on the course
to be taken should the bill pass by a small majority was once
more postponed.  " His Majesty stated that he did not mean to
say that he would not consent to a creation," but he wished
the matter to be reserved.  Next, if the second reading should
be lost, Grey laid down that he could only continue to hold
office if the news of the bill's rejection should be accompanied
by the announcement of an immediate prorogation with a
creation of peers.  Delay might be avoided by the introduction

[1] *Correspondence*, ii. 292.   It is difficult to understand a statement in
Lord Broughton's *Recollections* (iv. 208) : he says how on March 28 he
met Lord Althorp just returned from a Levée : " It is all right," said he ;
" the King will do it.  If we are beaten the Parliament will be prorogued,
and we shall make eighty peers the next day.  The Cabinet are unanimous
on that point."  We learn from the King's letter described above that
the Cabinet Minute advising the creation was only put into his hands by
Lord Grey at the Levée.  He did not answer it till two days later.  Russell
was also cheerful (*Early Correspondence*, ii. 31).  Ministers seem to have
reckoned without their host.

[2] *Correspondence*, ii. 299.

Z

of the new bill in the Lords, but in any case there was fear of disturbance in the country and a renewed demand for Radical Reform ; he could not consider the King's suggestion of a session's respite. But the King did not definitely refuse to make peers, though, on Grey's confession that not less than fifty or sixty would be necesssary, he was deeply distressed and begged that the question might be still left open ; lists of proposed creations were to be submitted to him.

On April 3 another meeting of the Cabinet reaffirmed their previous decision. The King replied at immense length on the 5th.[1] After declaring the hesitation he felt " to commit himself to the extent which is now required from him," he proceeded to give an abstract of all he had said on the question of peer-making from January 4 and earlier. He alluded to the gradual increase in the number demanded ; he had first understood that twenty-one was the limit ; later it was agreed that the number must be indefinite ; he had once mentioned the proposal to create forty or fifty as hardly conceivable ; now fifty or sixty was suggested, an amount " upon which he would have placed a *positive* restriction " had the thought of it occurred to him as possible. But beyond all he stressed his original and " irrevocable " condition that, but for two or three special exceptions, the names proposed must be either eldest sons or collaterals of peers, or else peers of Scotland or Ireland ; to this he was " determined, under any circumstances, to adhere." As to the matter of the moment, he preferred to give no definite answer to a speculative question. This letter was sent in circulation to the Cabinet, and added not a little to the anxiety caused by the imminence of the all-important debate. Holland spoke of it as " very unsatisfactory and embarrassing—so much so that nothing but a majority on the second reading can give us a chance." [2] Lord Grey admitted its accuracy, but just suggested to Taylor that the elevation of some commoners would be extremely desirable.[3]

The King wrote again on the 7th.[4] He had studied the lists of " peerables " supplied by Grey, and agreed, if necessary, to raise to the peerage two commoners, whose creation was for special reasons overdue, together with thirty-four

---

[1] *Correspondence*, ii. 307, 311.
[2] Holland to Grey, April 6 ; *Howick Papers*.
[3] *Correspondence*, ii. 329.      [4] *Ibid.*, ii. 333.

eldest sons and collaterals and four others—forty peers in all.
This amount, considering the attitude of the bishops, could
not, he thought, fail to be sufficient, but he expressed his
surprise that the new list fell so far short of the numbers
of the last, which amounted to seventy-four, and hinted
that Whig lords ought to follow his own example in sacrificing
their personal preferences to the good of the party and the
nation. Grey admitted in reply that some possible names, such
as his own son's, were not on the list. But he declared there
were strong private reasons against it. The same held good with
respect to Palmerston ; it would have been a strange accident,
and one with far-reaching results on English and perhaps
European history, if Lord Palmerston had been moved to the
House of Lords to make a majority for the Reform Bill. The
Cabinet met the same day to declare that, though they hoped
forty would be enough, there could be no certainty ; they still
wanted their bisque.[1] And so the matter was left till the result
of the Lords' division created a fresh situation.

Ministers were naturally much disturbed by the turn the
King's communications had lately taken ; it was understood
outside the Cabinet that his aversion to the measure had increased.[2] To estimate whether the King actually went back
on his word is a delicate matter. The change, if change there
was, occurred in the last fortnight of March. On the 16th Grey
was assured that the power confided to him extended to every
stage of the bill. On the 27th the Cabinet asked for a promise
to create peers at once if the second reading were rejected. On
the 30th the King hinted that the number needed might be
greater than he could allow. This he said before he had heard
that fifty or sixty peers might be required ; Grey only told
him so two days after. Thus on the 30th he could not plead
the increased demand as his excuse, as he did in the letter of
April 5. On the other hand he declared that his pledge was
" sacred." This pledge would then seem to be that he would
create peers after a defeat, so long as the amount was not so
extensive that he should not think fit to sanction it. This
accords with the stipulation on the 5th that it must be " a reasonable number " ; also on February 12 Taylor had written that

[1] *Correspondence*, ii. 336.
[2] Grey to Durham, April 8 ; *Lambton Papers*. *Recollections*, iv. 209 ;
*Greville Memoirs*, ii. 284.

" there must be some limit." Nevertheless when, in deference
to the King's wish that there should not be two partial creations,
the ministers waived their first suggestion and refused the
King's offer to make twenty-one peers on the spot, they insisted
that the number to be made—if the step they were postponing
to the last moment should finally become necessary—must
depend solely on circumstances ; to this the King agreed. It
was absurd that he should now complain that the number was
excessive, admitting as he did that the responsibility lay with
the Opposition.

Nothing has so far been said of the " irrevocable condition "
as to positive new creations, which the King made from the
very first. The condition had never been revoked, but in the
interval the ministers had been led to understand that they
had absolute power to carry the bill, and Grey had been authorised to convey this impression to Lord Harrowby. In February
Taylor wrote, " Your Lordship will not find the King fail you
in the hour of need," and next month, as has been said more
than once, he assured Grey the promise was not confined to
the second reading. It is perhaps wrong to argue that the later
promise overruled the conditions of the former incomplete one ;
but it is rather futile to speak of not failing a friend in need if
the speaker still clings to conditions arbitrarily made by himself
which may render assistance vain. The fact is, the King did
not realise that the conditions he made were likely to be of
practical importance ; they were intended as restrictions on
quality, not on quantity.[1] Fifty peers was a very large increase
on Brougham's modest ten or on the twenty-one the King
himself suggested. But in his magniloquent promises of support,
of which the last was dated March 16, he should have remembered
the old stipulations and made it clear whether they were still in
force. But the matter does not rest solely on the construction
of the " irrevocable " condition ; for on April 5 the King further
limited himself to a "*reasonable*" creation, which might mean
anything he chose, if he was unwilling to trust his ministers to
that extent.

Certainly there does appear an altered tone in the King's
letters of March 30 and after. This is confirmed by very interesting external evidence. On April 11 Lord Holland wrote
to Grey : " Taylor told me he (the King) was another man

[1] *Correspondence*, ii. 333.

to-day—implied that he had never known him so near an unkind feeling to his present Government as within these few days. That at one time the extent of the pledge he had given to make peers in certain contingencies seemed to have *escaped his memory*, and that it was with a view of *reminding* him and keeping him to the letter at least of his engagement that he (Taylor) had recapitulated so minutely in the answer to the Cabinet minute but he hoped so accurately all that had passed on the subject— he implied (but he did not say) that but for the recollection of his past promises the King would have been disposed to reject peremptorily all notion of a creation of peers." After this there can be no doubt that some change in the King's sentiments had taken place ; and this, in a matter depending so much on the construction laid on indefinite promises made some time before, was almost equivalent to their withdrawal. The transactions between a constitutional King and his ministers must rest on a credit basis ; otherwise there will be something like the friction between George III and his Whig counsellors. Certainly there could be little hope of the delicate negotiations touching the Reform Bill being carried to a successful close if the Government could rely on nothing more than the letter of the King's promise.

The revival of confidence implied by the beginning of Taylor's statement was only temporary. A relapse followed, and a few days later a serious breach almost occurred. The King's behaviour was put down by Taylor to the worry and strain of the last fourteen months.[1] To a man of William's age and character the long argumentations, the incessant need of tact and reticence, and the inevitable approach of the crisis he had long foreseen and dreaded, were naturally upsetting. He thoroughly disapproved of the Reform Bill and the democratic movement which it typified ; to be represented as the patron of a measure which he detested must have been galling to a man of less prejudices than the Sailor King. The personal element may also have come in ; Lord Grey had perhaps got on his nerves, and there was always the hostility, implied or expressed, of most of his family. However, there is no evidence that he was specially got at by the Opposition in these weeks.

[1] *Correspondence*, ii. 371. Greville also, who was remarkably well informed on matters of high political gossip, had heard that the King was worried and out of sorts (*Greville Memoirs*, ii. 282).

The Queen, whom it would perhaps be in any case unworthy to suspect of any conscious influence, was at this time fully occupied with the illness of her niece, Princess Louisa.[1]

In these circumstances, it was under a heavy weight of anxiety that the ministers made ready for the second reading debate on Monday, April 9. Lord Grey himself was to open it ; the deep sense of responsibility he had long felt had been lately increased by the news that several peers had said their votes would be decided by " the tone and temper in which the business is opened," though of course also by the likelihood of concessions being made in Committee.[2] At the same time the Opposition leaders were far from confident, and bitterly denounced the treachery of the Waverers, but for which the bill would have been certainly and, as they believed, finally destroyed.[3] Before the debate began, the Duke of Buckingham gave notice of an alternative measure on the lines of enfranchising large towns, grouping rotten boroughs together to return two members, somewhat on the Scotch model, and extending the franchise. Nobody, however, took this scheme very seriously ; it was so obviously an eleventh hour vote-catching expedient, and in fact gave up the principle ; it was really intended for those who dreaded the odium of still opposing all Reform.

After a mild opening speech from Grey the debate centred largely, as usual, on the point whether or not the demand for Reform was really the offspring of the French Revolution of July, and might therefore be considered as a transient fad. This had always been the Duke's contention ; it was supported by Lyndhurst, for some time now a declared partisan, who asserted that at the 1830 election the main topic had been the slave trade until the news from Paris arrived. There

[1] *Correspondence*, ii. 283. " The Queen," said Princess Augusta, " is like my good mother—never interferes or even gives any opinion. We *may* think, we *must* think, we *do* think, but we need not speak." (Quoted in Greenwood, *Hanoverian Queens of England*, ii. 389.) Still the Queen was not afraid of speaking to Lord Howe (see above, p. 336).

[2] *Correspondence*, ii. 345.

[3] The Duke of Newcastle wrote of " those contemptible people the Waverers, or, as we should have called them at Eton, the *sneakers*." Wellington complained : " If they had not left us, we should have had a majority of not less than sixty, with all the gentlemen of England at our back, against the bill. We might have dictated our own alterations. As things are, they have ruined themselves and us " (*Despatches*, viii. 265, 271 ; Twiss, *Life of Eldon*, iii. 171).

had been no petitions for Reform in the years from 1824 to 1829. On the other side Brougham maintained that there had been a steady growth since 1782, only interrupted for a time by the French war. Durham, who aroused interest by furious denunciation of Phillpotts, the fighting Bishop of Exeter, admitted that the desire had been greatly strengthened in the last few years ; this he put down partly to the denial of the least and most obvious Reform, but mainly to the conversion of the great middle class, the bulwarks of the knowledge and property of the country. The Waverers justified their new attitude by the steady demand of the people and the impossibility of carrying on the Government without some concession. The Opposition speakers really ignored the consequences of a second rejection, and held that they did right in ignoring it ; if the Government did its duty, said Lyndhurst, there could be no insurrection.

Lord Grey ended the four nights' debate on a conciliatory note, declaring that even the disfranchisement of fifty-six boroughs and the £10 qualification were not essential parts of the bill, though he would do his best to maintain them. Jeffrey, writing an account of the debate to Cockburn, described the Prime Minister's speech as " admirable ; in tone and spirit perfect, and, considering his age and the time, really astonishing. He spoke near an hour and a half, after five o'clock, from the kindling dawn into full sunlight, and I think with great effect. The aspect of the House was very striking through the whole night, very full, and, on the whole, still and solemn (but for the row with Durham and Phillpotts, which ended in the merited exposure of the latter). The whole throne and the space around it clustered over with 100 members of our House and the space below the bar . . . nearly filled with 200 more, ranged in a standing row of three deep along the bar, another sitting on the ground against the wall, and the space between covered with moving and sitting figures in all directions, with twenty or thirty clambering on the railings, and perched up by the doorways. Between four and five, when the daylight began to shed its blue beams across the red candle light, the scene was very picturesque, from the singular grouping of forty or fifty of us sprawling on the floor, awake and asleep, in all imaginable attitudes. . . . The candles had been renewed before dawn, and blazed on after the sun came fairly in at the high windows, and produced a strange, but rather grand effect, on the red draperies and furniture and dusky tapestry on the walls." [1] The House divided 184 to 175 on Saturday morning—a Government majority of nine.[2] The Committee stage was postponed till after Easter.

The Opposition availed themselves of the privilege of recording their dissent. The Duke of Wellington and seventy-three other peers protested against the bill in a document which was published broadcast about the country by both parties for the next few weeks.[3] It proposed, they said, " a new form of government, incompatible with monarchy " ; it confiscated chartered rights, endangered other institutions, and struck a blow at the landed and moneyed interests ; worst of all, it opened the door to unchecked democracy. But it was not too late to rally forces for a final effort. The Tories spent the Easter recess intriguing to defeat the bill's main provisions.[4]

The ministers were jubilant in spite of the narrow majority, and congratulations poured in on Lady Grey. " The measure is now secure," Lord John Russell wrote to her, " and the country *for ever* Lord Grey's debtor." Grey's eloquence had long been considered one of the Whigs' chief assets in Parliament ; his defence of the Government on the Ancona question in March Holland had described as a speech " such as neither Pitt nor Canning nor my Uncle could have made with equal judgment and execution," and this final appeal in the early hours of Saturday, April 14, is said to have been a noble effort, worthy of a great occasion.[5] The carrying of the second reading without a creation of peers was a great personal triumph for Lord Grey,

---

[1] *Life of Jeffrey*, i. 329.

[2] The change from the minority of 41 in October is thus accounted for by the Annual Register (p. 146). The anti-Reformers gained three votes, and the Reformers lost three ; the 56 votes needed to outweigh this were composed of 34 from the turn over of 17 Waverers, 10 from the abstention of Tory peers, including the Canningite Dudley, and 12 from the support of peers who had not voted in October. Without proxies, there was only a majority of 2 (128–126) for the bill.

[3] Add. MSS. 27,792, f. 150. The protests of numerous other peers are given in condensed form in Grant and Robertson's *Select Statutes, &c.*, p. 212.

[4] Croker to Wellington, April 14 : " I have just had Haddington with me. He is confident of killing the bill " (*Despatches*, viii. 272).

[5] Holland to Grey, March 17 ; *Howick Papers. Broughton Recollections*, iv. 214.

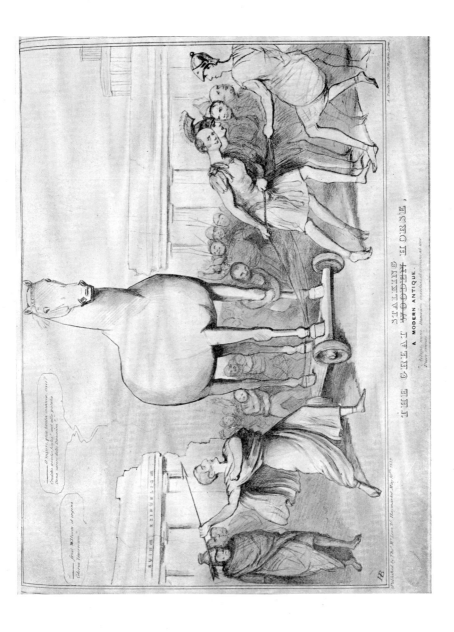

THE GREAT STALKING WOODEN HORSE,

**A MODERN ANTIQUE.**

Published by Tho.s McLean 26 Haymarket May 10th 1832

and no little compliment to the calculating skill of his advisers. He had brought Reform nearer to success than ever before, but no one knew better than he what dangers still lay in the way. Russell's optimism was far from universal ; on the first day of the debate Althorp had been told by Francis Baring that his party felt secure unless peers should yet be made ; [1] and this was certainly the opinion of keen Reformers in the country, though joy for the moment prevailed.

Vast meetings were held at Leeds, Glasgow, Newcastle, Manchester, Bolton, and many smaller places where unions had been formed. At Exeter crowds were waiting for the London coach ; on hearing the precious news they broke out into joyful cheers.[2] At Manchester, the evening before, John Bright, then a young man of twenty, had started by coach on his first journey to London. " It happened," he told a Rochdale audience nearly half a century later, " to be the very night when the House of Lords were discussing the second reading of the great Reform Bill, and during the 14th of April— I think it was as we were travelling along the road—some passenger observed something coming towards us, but still in the distance, and we all looked with great interest. We saw horses galloping and carriages coming at a speed which would quickly have left behind our coach if they had been going the same way. By-and-by we found they were chaises with four horses in each chaise, having two or three men inside, and they were throwing out placards from each window. These were express chaises coming from London, bringing the news to all the people of the country—for there were no telegraphs then— of the glorious triumph of popular principles even in the House of Lords." [3]

In London full gatherings of both the unions were held ; different as were the sentiments expressed with regard to the bill, there was a common note of defiance to the Lords, and men spoke freely of refusing taxes and rising in arms. " Though the unions of the working classes would not work with the political unions to obtain the bill, they would be one and all active in promoting and sustaining a revolution." [4] The *Poor*

[1] *Memoir of Althorp*, p. 415.
[2] Add. MSS. 27,792, ff. 147, 160 ; *Times*, April 21, 26.
[3] *Public Addresses by John Bright*, p. 415.
[4] Add. MSS. 27,792, ff. 151, 153 ; 27,796, f. 302.

*Man's Guardian* of April 14 answers a question put by the *Examiner* as to what the heroes of the Rotunda would do if the bill were rejected. " Feeling that an odious oligarchy (in which we include Whigs and Tories) have enslaved the many, we are prepared to act with the greatest number, for the general good, *whenever* an opportunity presents itself as the most likely to secure to the people their undoubted rights ; in case ' the bill ' should be rejected a second time, we hope the Union and its friends will ' stand at ease.' What do you recommend, Mr. Hume ? " " People of England," said the *Ballot,* " your share of the performance must now be executed."

While Reformers in the country made the most of the recess for purposes of organisation, Lord Grey was feeling a sense of relief he had not known for many weeks. " Altogether," he wrote to Taylor on the 16th, " I see things much more *couleur de rose* than I have done for a long time." The same day, however, he received from the King a letter almost amounting to a reprimand on the general course of the Government's foreign policy.[1] Especially in relation to France, but also in connection with the Polish and other questions, it had shown a spirit perilously verging on " *liberalism* " and contrary to the interests of authority and order. In future the King must ask that all instructions to be sent to ministers abroad should be first submitted for his approval. Lord Grey was much pained and surprised at this mark of his master's lack of confidence in him at a time when his full support was so sorely needed. The King had expressed " sincere satisfaction " at the result of the late division, and Lady Grey was informed on high authority that he had been most anxious concerning it beforehand.[2] Now he wrote in a manner implying not only disapproval but distrust, whereas Grey had always understood that except on certain points of the Reform Bill the King was fully at one with his ministers. He wrote in great distress to the King and Sir Herbert, justifying his attitude and offering his resignation.[3] The King in reply

[1] *Correspondence*, ii. 351.

[2] See an undated letter to Lady Grey : " Albemarle tells me the King did not sleep a minute all night owing to his anxiety, and that he is like a boy in spirits and delight to-day." Lord Albemarle was Master of the Horse. The letter is bound up with others of April 14 (*Howick Papers ;* see also *Creevey Papers*, p. 586).

[3] *Correspondence*, ii. 358, 365.

denied any withdrawal of his confidence, and declared that he had not in any way been swayed by outside influence. Matters were put right in an interview after the Levée on the 18th, but the incident did not tend to encourage the ministers.[1] Taylor wrote to say that the King's feeling on the matter of foreign policy had been for some time at the back of his mind; he excused his master's somewhat irritable and impatient manner by the nervous excitement from which he was only just recovering.[2]

There seems no reason to doubt the King's word, given in answer to a hint from Grey, that he had had no communication with any but his ministers. The Tory dukes had left the King alone for some time, and indeed he was too much of a Tory himself to need their exhortations. But there were constant rumours of a change in his opinions, which Grey deeply regretted. On the 18th he wrote to Sir Herbert Taylor: " I cannot help suspecting that some of those who have access to his Majesty's society assist in propagating these reports." This letter was shown to the King, and drew the following reply: His Majesty " thinks it more than probable, also, that some of these reports might be traced to individuals occasionally admitted to his society, and that feelings are often expressed by these and even by members of his own families (which your Lordship knows to be much split in opinion and feeling with regard to public men and public questions) which are calculated to produce and encourage the reports to which you allude. But, however he may regret and may admit the inconvenience of such a state of things and its consequences, his Majesty cannot prevent them." [3] By no means satisfied by this candid statement, Grey urged the Chancellor to go to Windsor, and impress on the King and his secretary the extreme awkwardness resulting from these rumours. Brougham went, but had little opportunity of pressing the subject; he was convinced, however, that the King was inclining his thoughts to the Tories.[4] It was impossible for Grey or Brougham to say more.

---

[1] *Correspondence*, ii. 366, 372. Hobhouse speaks of the King's peculiar graciousness to the anti-Reformers at this Levée, and writes: "That something has happened at headquarters I feel sure, and the Tories begin to lift up their heads again " (*Recollections*, iv. 216).

[2] *Correspondence*, ii. 371.

[3] *Ibid.*, ii. 374–378.

[4] Grey to Brougham, April 20; Brougham to Grey, April 21; *Brougham Memoirs*, iii. 180, 183.

In the meantime Grey had renewed communications with the Waverers through Palmerston, who arranged for a meeting between his chief and Wharncliffe in a few days. But Wharncliffe let Palmerston know that he, Harrowby, and Haddington were now treating with Lyndhurst and Ellenborough,[1] and that these two were in touch with the Duke himself. The prospect of an agreement seemed far from hopeful to Grey, who rather scented a Tory intrigue for office on the basis of moderate Reform—a suspicion to which Brougham also was inclined by the King's remarks at Windsor.[2] In the interval Richmond, Graham, and Wharncliffe met at Newmarket and entered into mild negotiations, while members of the Cabinet gave earnest attention to the drafting of the first clause of the bill.[3]

With the passing of the second reading, however, the ministers' control of the bill ended. As they had anticipated, they were now in the hands of a hostile majority ; that majority might include men of very different opinions, but it stood solid against democratic change. Apart from the enthusiasm outside Parliament, for which 175 peers had expressed their contempt by their votes, ministers had nothing behind them but the now doubtful support of the King. Their last dealings with him had not been such as to encourage the hope that he would construe his past promises very liberally in their favour.

Knowing less of the King's true attitude, anti-Reformers were hardly more sanguine. Wellington bitterly regretted the treachery of the moderate wing, but for which the party would have thrown out the bill by a comfortable margin. The vote of April 14 had sealed the fate of the country, which would henceforth groan under a revolutionary system, a mere parody of government, inevitable in whatever form the bill received the King's assent. Now it seemed hardly possible that it could be destroyed ; its principle approved by the House, ministers would be in a stronger position to ask for a creation of peers to carry it through. Still the Duke was not averse to forcing them to use such extreme methods. He wrote to Cumber-

---

[1] Lord Ellenborough (1790–1871) had been President of the Board of Control under Wellington.

[2] *Correspondence*, ii. 380. Grey to Brougham, April 21 (*Brougham Memoirs*, iii. 182); to Althorp, April 23 (*Althorp Papers*); to Holland, April 26 (*Howick Papers*).

[3] *Greville Memoirs*, ii. 290 ; *Howick Papers*, April 24.

land on April 27 : " My opinion is that we have no chance
of throwing out the bill. . . . The creation of Peers to carry
the bill after a majority of the House of Lords have determined
to adopt the principle, will be a very different measure from a
creation to force the principle upon the House. . . . At the
same time I must say that I can't give up trying if there should
be a chance of salvation ; and I intend to protest to the last
against the whole measure and its authors." [1]

But if the Duke admitted that the Reform Bill, or something
like it, must pass, he had no intention of allowing the Government
to dictate the precise form it should take. A few days earlier he
had written to Croker : " I think that we—that is to say, who
voted against the second reading—have at this moment the power
of making any reasonable alterations that we may think proper to
propose." [2] But secrecy of discussion was essential. Wharncliffe
was informed that he could not share the counsels of Whigs and
Tories at once ; if he meant to keep in touch with Lyndhurst and
Ellenborough, he must drop all negotiations with Grey. [3] The
Waverers had failed in bringing about any real conciliation
between the parties ; the passing of the second reading was
their one achievement. Henceforward party allegiance and the
Duke's prestige were too much for them, and though they yet
showed signs of insubordination they threw in their lot for the
future with the Tories. Theirs had been a most ungrateful
task. Winning little approval except from the King and their
own consciences, they were suspected of insincerity by both
sides, and won the contempt which is the usual reward of
moderates at a time when party passion runs high.

It remained to determine the lines on which the bill was to
be amended. The policy of the party was of course to keep the

[1] *Despatches*, viii. 284.

[2] Wellington to Croker, April 23 ; to Bathurst, April 27 : " If we are
to have the bill with the amendments such as the Government will agree to,
we must not be *gulled*. Let them who choose to take it do so with their
eyes open ; and those who do not, take their own " (*Despatches*, viii. 280,
286).

[3] Bathurst to Wellington, April 29 : " I am very glad that you desired
Lord Lyndhurst to tell Lord Wharncliffe that our party could have no
communication with him, if he had any with Lord Grey respecting the
amendments to the Reform Bill. I hope Lord Lyndhurst also reminded
Lord Wharncliffe that he was bound in honour not to communicate to
Lord Grey what had passed at the confidential meetings between him,
Lord Harrowby, Lord Lyndhurst, &c., &c. (*Despatches*, viii. 290).

franchise as far as possible out of the hands of the town voters, of whom the greater part might be presumed to be Radicals and Nonconformists. Large numbers of suggestions were made, and continuous correspondence was kept up between the party leaders. Croker, Aberdeen, and Bathurst were especially active.[1] The Duke of Cumberland wrote to Wellington for instructions, urging that a small committee of peers should be formed to frame a policy, which the rank and file should bind themselves to accept.[2] Answering on April 27, the Duke could give his royal pupil little definite information, but outlined his general view of affairs. " That upon which I think all agree is, that freeholders in towns returning members shall not vote for counties ; that there shall be no representatives for the suburbs of the metropolis, and no counties returning three members. . . . It appears to me absolutely necessary to get rid entirely of Schedule B ; that is to say, to allow all the boroughs in that schedule to continue to return two members. I should wish likewise, if possible, to mitigate the disfranchisement of the boroughs in Schedule A." But the only positive news he could give was that it had been resolved to propose the postponement of the two first clauses, dealing with disfranchisement.[3]

The Government were warned of this decision by Wharn- cliffe, who in spite of the Duke's disapproval persisted in his intention to try the effects of a meeting with Grey. It took place in London on Saturday, April 28, Palmerston and the Chancellor being also present.[4] As usual, nothing effective was done, but Wharncliffe was convinced that the Government were ready to make larger concessions than ever before ; this, however, was the end of negotiation between the parties. On May 5 Wharncliffe, Harrowby, and Haddington met to arrange final details with Lyndhurst and Ellenborough. It was then definitely fixed, against the wishes of the Waverers, to move the postponement of the disfranchising clauses, and the sugges- tion that Grey should be informed was overruled.[5] The con- clave believed the maxim that surprise is of the essence of war.

---

[1] See *Despatches*, viii. 272–298.

[2] *Ibid.*, viii. 282.

[3] *Ibid.*, viii. 283 ; *Greville Memoirs*, ii. 292.

[4] *Greville Memoirs*, ii. 293 ; *Correspondence*, ii. 382. Wellington to Croker, May 1 ; *Despatches*, viii. 292.

[5] Ellenborough to Wellington, May 6 ; *Despatches*, viii. 297. *Greville Memoirs*, ii. 293.

It would appear that the alternative bill of which notice was afterwards given by Lord Ellenborough was drafted on this same occasion. The five lords appointed to meet for the last time on the night of Sunday, the 6th, when it was hoped Lord Carnarvon would be also present.[1] Thus negotiations were going on among the Tories up to the very eve of the meeting of Parliament.

Reformers in the country had been by no means idle during the last few weeks. The renewal of the cry of Reaction had roused them for what was generally felt to be the crowning struggle. On April 24 a mass meeting, whose numbers were put at from forty to fifty thousand, was held at Edinburgh in the King's Park, to petition the Lords to pass the bill.[2] Though the Scotch Reform Bill was not yet out of the Commons, it was generally understood that the battle would be lost or won on the English bill, to which the others hung as corollaries. On the 27th the Council of the Birmingham Union met to draw up resolutions threatening an untiring demand for a more Radical measure than Lord John Russell's, if this should be rejected, and summoning a monster open air meeting for May 7. Reform Committees met in all the large towns, that of Manchester resolving to sit daily from the 9th onwards till the bill was carried.[3] Crowded meetings were held throughout Great Britain, and the press urged all classes to unite to overawe the Lords.

Colonel Jones thought fit to spur on the Government at this point by a letter to Durham, its main channel of communication with the Radicals. " The political feeling," he said, " that pervades Scotland generally is *aweful*. It exists more particularly in the west, where I am assured by those that possess the best local information, that some 60,000 men, and somewhat organised, are ready to turn out at 24 hours' notice and only require the occasion and a commander. My letters from Dundee and the Eastern district make the same report." In London there was the same excitement beneath a tranquil surface. " The quietude of the town must not deceive you ; there are all the germs of the most formidable resistance to Government ready to sprout. A few hundred pounds expended in getting up public meetings would at once bring into life a spirit much stronger than existed at the commencement of the first French Revolution. What

---

[1] *Despatches*, viii. 297.          [2] Add. MSS. 27,792, f. 181

[3] *Morning Chronicle*, May 5.

now only prevents any activity is that Burdett, Hume, some few others, and myself consider that it is not yet called for and would only be mischievous and throwing away unnecessarily our strength. But by-and-by if we won't move, others will." [1]

London did not long conceal her feelings. On May 4 the National Political Union met in full numbers, calling on the peers, under pain of non-payment of taxes and of the consequent " extinction of the privileged classes," to pass the bill unmutilated.[2] But the greatest impression was without doubt created by the Birmingham Union ; badly off as it was financially, it assembled a vast gathering, to which thirty neighbouring unions were invited, on the day Parliament met.[3] The Union had some time before resolved in the impatience of delay never again to petition the Lords ; but now personal respect for many peers and the desire to refute the charge of indifference persuaded them to try a last appeal. Under the auspices of Attwood the huge meeting pledged itself never to cease from agitation, should the bill be thrown out, till the country obtained a " more extensive restoration of the constitutional rights of the people." The Government measure was a " compromise which if not now accepted would never be offered again." [4] With hands solemnly uplifted, the crowd of 200,000 men repeated after its Chairman the dramatic vow : " With unbroken faith, through every peril and privation, we here devote ourselves to our country's cause." In London excitement was at its highest pitch, and placards in the streets reminded the people, " Seventh of May, Crisis day," while in several trades the suspension of orders had thrown numbers of men out of work.[5]

When the Lords met on Monday, May 7, the Duke of Sussex presented a petition in favour of the Reform Bill from the Common Council of the City of London ; Brougham presented another from the great meeting at Edinburgh. The House then went into Committee. After a conciliatory suggestion of Grey's had

---

[1] *Lambton Papers.*                                    [2] Add. MSS. 27,792, f. 188.

[3] Parkes to Place, May 2. The Union is £200 in debt, apart from the coming meeting. " £2000 has been spent in the cause " (Add. MSS. 27,792, f. 305).

[4] Add. MSS. 27,792, ff. 176, 181.

[5] *Recollections,* iv. 218 ; Add. MSS. 27,792, f. 203.

been accepted, Lord Lyndhurst rose to move the postponement of the two disfranchising clauses, on the ground that such order was more constitutional. The wisdom of Lyndhurst's step was much discussed ; it had been suggested over a fortnight before, when the Tories set themselves seriously to amend the bill. In the light of their anxiety to disfranchise as few boroughs as possible, it was natural enough to wait to see how many members must be transferred to the new constituencies which it was proposed to create. There was no doubt, on the other hand, that Schedule A was the most popular part of the bill. For these reasons to accept and to mutilate it were alike awkward ; the obvious remedy was to postpone it, nominally without prejudice, till other clauses had been dealt with. As early as April 24, however, Lord Bathurst had cautioned the Duke against letting it be supposed that the intention was to maintain the nomination boroughs. He reminded him of Brougham's misrepresentation as to the Commons stopping supplies a year before.[1] Certainly the step was not likely to please the people, and Brougham, like Greville, regarded it as a serious blunder in tactics. Ministers had feared, he said, that the Opposition would slowly whittle down the bill by amendments just on the border-line of importance, so giving those in charge of it very little on which to make a definite stand. They would gradually lose the confidence of the impatient people, while not liking to appeal to the King on points trifling in themselves. By Lyndhurst's action, on this theory, the Tories were delivered into their hands. This was true, no doubt, had the Whigs been secure of the King's support, and had most of them not been extremely unwilling to fall back on it in any case. But to Grey, who for every reason was anxious to proceed without friction, such opposition at the outset was most distasteful.[2] It showed, if nothing else, at least that the Opposition meant to take the control of the bill out of the Government's hands ; and this, in the case of so complicated a measure, virtually implied its dismemberment.

Though as late as Saturday Grey had no certain knowledge of the enemy's intentions, the ministers were aware on Monday of the attack that would be made ; just before the debate

[1] *Despatches*, viii. 282.
[2] All the same, if the clash had to come, Grey preferred it at once (*Creevey Papers*, p. 589).

2 A

began they received definite information from Wharncliffe.[1]
Anyhow it was too late for any counter-move, and Grey was
resolved to stand his ground. He therefore gave Lyndhurst
good warning that were the amendment carried he should be
obliged seriously to consider his proper course. Brougham and
Holland also made it clear that they considered the motion a
direct attack on the spirit of the bill. Without ulterior motives,
the Tories would not press a mere detail of procedure against
the ministers in chagre of the bill. The real intentions of the
leaders of the Opposition are not altogether clear. Some peers
were certainly moved by mere spite against the bill.[2] But the
Waverers as certainly were not ; Wharncliffe and Harrowby
had on Saturday both been against the postponement, and
probably aimed at nothing further than a display of strength
to humble the Government. Indeed Wharncliffe declared himself in favour of disfranchisement at least to the extent of
Schedule A.[3] The general idea was perhaps to assert the Lords'
right to discuss the bill on its merits, but different sections had
different motives. All, however, Waverers included, voted with
Lyndhurst, who carried his amendment by thirty-five. Thereupon Lord Grey moved that the Committee should report progress, and sit again on Thursday ; but Lord Ellenborough, representing those peers with whom he had been negotiating,
proceeded to give notice of amendments of his own ; they
accepted Schedule A but struck out all representation by a
single member. The pernicious uniformity of the £10 qualification was to be corrected by retaining the scot and lot boroughs.
Much hurt by what he considered the treacherous silence of the
Waverers, Grey refused to consider the rival scheme, and the
House adjourned.

The Tories were taken by surprise by Grey's action, and

---

[1] On the Saturday Grey wrote to Durham : " I have heard nothing
of the proceedings of the enemy that can be depended upon. No communication has been made, as was promised, by Lord Salisbury, and I
have written to remind him of his engagement to let me know, in time,
what he intended to do. It is said that they mean to move to put
off the Committee till the other Bills are brought up. . . . The general
expectation is that they will try some question before going into the Committee" (Lambton Papers). See also Russell's introduction to his own
Speeches, i. 73 ; Greville Memoirs, ii. 293.

[2] See Newcastle's speech ; Hansard (3rd series), xii. 709.

[3] Hansard (3rd series), xii. 713.

thought it must be due to a fit of temper.[1] Ellenborough, as fully expecting that the Committee would proceed, had intended to declare his scheme on Tuesday night ; he probably considered it quite immaterial whether he spoke before or after the division on Lyndhurst's motion, which was part of the concerted plan. Grey, not knowing how far Wellington was also implicated, believed the result of the division might have been different had Ellenborough explained his policy before it.[2] Altogether it seems to have been a night of surprises. Sir Denis Le Marchant, at this time Brougham's private secretary, writes :[3] " The Peers, with few exceptions—as usually happens when a question is imperfectly understood and the House is taken by surprise, voted according to party, and the Ministers were of course completely defeated." It has been mentioned above that the Tory scheme was uncompleted as late as Sunday, so this statement may well be true. Le Marchant goes on to say : " After the House had risen, Lord Althorp accompanied Lord Grey into the Chancellor's private room, where the leading members of the Cabinet soon collected and came to an unanimous resolution to resign, unless the King would create a sufficient number of peers to give them a working majority."

That night Grey wrote to Windsor asking for an audience next day, and announcing that a Cabinet would be held at eleven in the morning.[4] At this meeting all the Cabinet were present, except Lord Carlisle, who was unwell. It was decided to resign unless the King would create enough peers to " insure the success of the Bill in all its essential principles " ; the Tory Duke of Richmond alone dissented.[5] A minute to this effect was taken to Windsor by Grey and the Chancellor that afternoon ; they asked for a creation of not less than fifty peers.[6] The King asked for a night to think over his answer ; early on the morning of May 9 he wrote refusing " to consent to so large an addition to the peerage," and regretfully accepting his ministers' resignation, with every expression of gratitude and good-

---

[1] Greville said that Grey " threw up the Bill and the Government in a passion " (*Memoirs*, ii. 293).

[2] Ellenborough to Wellington, May 6 ; *Despatches*, viii. 298. *Hansard* (3rd series), xii. 727–732 ; *Correspondence*, ii. 391.

[3] *Memoir of Althorp*, p. 419.

[4] *Correspondence*, ii. 392.

[5] *Ibid.*, ii. 394.

[6] *Ibid.*, ii. 415 ; *Life of Campbell*, ii. 7.

will.[1]  He made some attempt later in the day, having come into town for a Levée, to induce Brougham and Richmond to remain in office to pass a Reform Bill of the scope suggested by Lord Ellenborough. Whether from loyalty or prudence, however, both declared that they must sink with the ship.[2]

Some surprise was caused by the Whigs' determination to make a stand on the postponement of the disfranchising clauses, which in itself was no mutilation of the bill.  Though the King's manner had of late been more propitious,[3] they had good reason for doubting his support, after recent communications, and in fact did not expect it ; it appears to have been matter for discussion whether it was worth while to advise the creation of peers at all.[4]  In the Cabinet, however, with the exception of Richmond, there seems to have been no difference of opinion. Greville, who certainly sometimes knew what had happened in the Cabinet, tells us that Palmerston actually proposed the step.[5]

Painful as must have been the disappointment to eager hearts among the ministers, and no less the foreboding that more was threatened than a mere change of administration, it must be admitted that few Cabinets have fallen from power in better spirits.[6]  The uncertainty and sense of impotence of the last few weeks had been almost intolerable.  To

[1] *Correspondence*, ii. 395.

[2] *Brougham Memoirs*, iii. 194; *Memoir of Althorp*, p. 423; *Broughton Recollections*, iv. 220; *Creevey Papers*, p. 588; *Greville Memoirs*, ii. 295. Brougham's statement in itself would hardly be sufficient evidence that the King had pressed him to form a government.  But the story is contemporary, and was never denied.  If false it might easily have been contradicted by gossips deriving their information from either the royal or the ducal source.

[3] Grey to Durham, May 5: "The King has got back to his former habit of great cordiality and good humour, and I never saw him in a more satisfactory temper of mind than this morning.  I have had three Royal dinners in succession, and thank God they are over.  The honour is very great, but the bore is equal to it" (*Lambton Papers*).

[4] *Correspondence*, ii. 392; *Brougham Memoirs*, iii. 191.

[5] *Greville Memoirs*, ii. 294.

[6] "Brougham . . . sprung from his chair and, rubbing his hands, declared that it was the happiest moment of his life" (*Creevey Papers*, p. 587; *Memoir of Althorp*, p. 423).  Hobhouse wrote (*Recollections*, iv. 220): "We were all very merry, for undone dogs as we were."  Yet for all his merriment he confessed to Durham : "Matters look very queer in our city, and I should be sorry to have to answer for the disappointment" (*Lambton Papers*).

Grey himself, after the incessant strain to a man of his years of a situation demanding at once the most extreme tact in soothing the anxieties of moderates and the most thick-skinned indifference to Radical abuse, any change was a relief ; though even now, it will be seen, he was not exempt from the attacks of ignorance and malice. But he stood in the public eye as one who had fought honestly and failed ; and even defeat is better than the hourly anticipation of it. To Althorp of course retirement was an unmixed pleasure. Jeffrey relates how, in going to Downing Street to learn the King's answer, he had a characteristic scene with " that most honest, frank, true, and stout-hearted of all God's creatures. He had not come down-stairs, and I was led up to his dressing-room, where I found him sitting on a stool, in a dark duffle dressing-gown, with his arms (very rough and hairy) bare above the elbows, and his beard half shaved, and half staring through the lather, with a desperate razor in one hand, and a great soap brush in the other. He gave me the loose finger of the brush hand, and with the usual twinkle of his bright eye and radiant smile he said : ' You need not be anxious about your Scotch Bill for to-night, for I have the pleasure to tell you *we are no longer his Majesty's Ministers.*' " Jeffrey had good enough cause to be anxious about Scotland, however. " Do what you can," he implored Cockburn, " to *keep peace,* and with your last official breath exhort and conjure lovers of liberty to be lovers of order and tolerance. I tremble for Scotland, and think there is greater hazard there than in any other quarter." [1]

If anything, ministers showed too little reluctance at the surrender of their power to carry a measure which they had declared so necessary for the public good. But at moments of crisis it is generally the personal thought which first suggests itself, though it may not last the longest. And, on a larger view, each section of the Cabinet had its own solace. For the more timid can hardly have looked on the loss of the " Revolution Bill " with deep sorrow, with Ellenborough's milder measure now in the field ; while the bolder spirits, thinking more of their sup-porters outside Parliament, probably saw victory still in sight.

The King, no less than other people, was taken by surprise. He was altogether unprepared for matters coming to a head so soon after the meeting of Parliament, though Grey's note on

[1] Jeffrey to Cockburn, May 9 ; *Life of Jeffrey,* i. 330.

Tuesday morning showed that the Government treated their defeat as serious.[1] The definite proposal to create peers was made to him that afternoon, and his answer was given on Wednesday morning. When at length the news became public, opinion was divided. Some, inferring that Grey could never have had any assurance of passing the bill, blamed him severely for having played so carelessly with the people's fortunes and for not resigning as soon as he discovered the King would not support him. Others, knowing more, but not all, of the truth, cried out bitterly at the King's betrayal of the ministers. In either case the shock was great, for nearly all Reformers had taken it for granted since October that Grey had the King's pledged word to create peers in such numbers and at such time as circumstances should ordain. Treachery was freely imputed ; it was the universal opinion among Reformers that Lyndhurst's motion was part of a definite plot, and many believed that it would not have been made without encouragement from Court.[2] The King was commonly accused, in Creevey's words, of having " permitted the Duke of Cumberland to tell his friends that he would make no peers." [3] Of this there is no evidence ; it is on the face of it unlikely ; for, though the King was lamentably indiscreet in his conversation—how indiscreet will appear later—, nothing in the rest of his conduct suggests that he could be so utterly base as to intrigue against his own ministers. William IV was not his father, and Grey was not Fox. And it is im-

---

[1] *Correspondence*, ii. 392, 393.

[2] " That the combination of forces among the Opposition was no casual one is proved by the fact that intelligence of the anticipated defeat of ministers had been conveyed to Edinburgh even before it was whispered in London, and by the promptitude of the Horse Guards in ordering all officers absent on furlough to join their regiments, in the expectation no doubt that the risings consequent on the division would render their services indispensable " (*Spectator*, May 12).

[3] *Creevey Papers*, p. 587. Creevey adds: "and then the rats were in their old ranks again at once." He speaks also of "our perfidious Billy." Place wrote in 1837 : " It is also very probable, if indeed not certain, that the King was playing false with ministers, and that he had made known to the Duke of Wellington his resolve not to make peers to carry the Bill " (Add. MSS. 27,792, f. 247). The *Manchester Guardian* said : " It was the treacherous disclosure by some of the Fitzclarences that the King would not create peers that led to the discomfiture of the Bill. . . . We ask whether a letter was not shown to the bishops a few hours before the division on Lord Lyndhurst's motion, which convinced them that peers would not be created."

probable that the King had definitely set his face against a creation of peers until a special case forced him to decide.

The question of the King's honesty to the Whigs must of course be judged in the light of their former communications. As matters were left on April 7, the King had reluctantly consented to make forty peers, of whom only two were to be other than eldest sons and collaterals. The Cabinet had gratefully accepted this offer, though not concealing their belief that the number might yet be insufficient. The King's consistency up to this point has been already discussed, and, so far as any definite conclusion can be reached on a matter so elusive, it was suggested that the Whigs might fairly have expected, at least from the spirit of the King's promises, a stronger support than he was prepared to give.[1] For even apart from the condition stated on April 13, that no permanent increase was to be made to the peerage, William had limited his former gallant promise not to fail his ministers in their hour of need, by declaring that the number must be " reasonable." In fact it was the growing extent of the demand, combined with its uncertainty, which had induced the King to hesitate. So it was now. For it is impossible to believe, in view of previous calculations, that forty-eight eldest sons and collaterals of peers could not have been procured at dear need; and this, or slightly more, was the amount fixed by the two ministers on May 8.[2]

This view is confirmed by the curious apologia for his years of kingship which the King handed to Sir Robert Peel in 1835. On the failure of the attempt at conciliation, the Memorandum runs: " Lord Grey and his colleagues brought forward a proposition for an increase in the peerage which appeared to his Majesty so unreasonably extensive, so injurious to the character of that branch of the Legislature, and so degrading in its effects to the aristocracy of the country, that he refused to acquiesce

---

[1] See above, p. 357.

[2] After the list of forty had been approved by the King on April 7, some discussion followed with Lord Grey ; the King pointed out that the list submitted to him on January 9 contained fifty-two eldest sons, fifteen collaterals of childless peers, and seven Scotch and Irish peers unlikely to have children. Grey replied that many of these were ineligible for various reasons ; however, the Cabinet minute of April 7 admitted : " It might be possible, out of the lists before submitted to your Majesty by Earl Grey, and from those of Irish and Scotch peers, to add a further number, if your Majesty should be disposed to consent to it " (*Correspondence*, ii. 335, 338).

in it."[1]   And later in the month of May, when defending himself against the common charge of treachery, the King reminded Grey that he and Brougham had been forced to admit "that his Majesty had *never* encouraged them to expect that he would consent to so extensive a creation."[2]

The reply to both statements is the same.   Though the King had never contemplated fifty creations, he had in January acquiesced in the ministers' proposal that the number should be left indefinite.   For this concession they agreed to dispense with the immediate creation of twenty-one peers.   The King pledged himself beyond question : " he will not, after having allowed that the resource should be effectual, and having, indeed, insisted upon the absurdity of incurring any risk by an insufficient addition to the House of Lords, if resorted to at all, deny to his Ministers the power ' of acting at once up to the full exigency of the case.' "[3]   This pledge was repeated several times in the spring ;  it was used, at the King's suggestion, to influence the Waverers ;  and it was idle after that to complain that the amount had become unreasonable.   The ministers were no more responsible for it than was William himself :  for he admitted that the principles of the bill could not be violated.   Peel, after seeing the correspondence, told Croker on May 14 " that it was obvious that his Majesty's case was a bad one."[4]

It should be said on the King's side that the Whig leaders do not seem to have shown any resentment or sense of injury ; irresponsible politicians in and out of Parliament of course proclaimed the King's falsehood angrily, but they were not possessed of the evidence on which to form a fair judgment. Still allowance must be made, at least in Grey's case, for the superstitious devotion to the throne which was at this time no monopoly of Toryism.

On Wednesday evening, May 9, Grey and Althorp announced in both Houses that his Majesty had been graciously pleased to accept their resignations, and that they only held office till their successors could be appointed.   But before this it was known that Lord Lyndhurst was with the King.

[1] *Memoirs of Baron Stockmar*, i. 320.   [2] *Correspondence*, ii. 415.
[3] *Correspondence*, ii. 113.   [4] *Croker Papers*, ii. 165.

# CHAPTER IX

## THE DAYS OF MAY

" See, see, we come ! no swords we draw
   We kindle not war's battle-fires ;
By union, justice, reason, law,
   We'll gain the birthright of our sires,
And thus we raise from sea to sea,
Our sacred watchword, Liberty ! "
                              —*Call of the Unions.*

FROM the defeat of the Government in the House of Lords the
action moves on from day to day at a breathless pace.  For
eleven days London and the whole of England, with a great part
of Scotland, were shaken by a storm of political excitement
utterly outside the experience of the fiercest partisan to-day.
Men at the time were swept along by an enthusiasm they could
not stop to analyse ; impulse took the reins from reason, and
led Englishmen a dance they are proud to believe more congenial to southern temperaments.  The Days of May were
England's response to the Days of July, and that no blood
flowed in the streets of London was put down to the superior
excellence of her institutions and the greater reasonableness
of her sons.  Nevertheless the air was charged with talk of
pikes and barricades and swords rough-sharpened for the first
time since Waterloo.  Subtler weapons were borrowed from the
lore of finance, and City men took pride to think how scientific
a revolution might be made in the nineteenth century.  To
many of the middle classes it was the great week of their lives ;
gathered in eager groups outside the closed shops and factories
to meet the morning coach and spend the day in discussing how
soonest to make the people's will prevail, they tasted in the
delicious excitement an intensity of life unknown before or
after.  But in others, gauging better the capacities of the untried
masses, there was deep anxiety lest the folly of the governing
class should force power into hands less fitted to use than to

acquire it. Convinced that the Reform Bill must in no long time abolish the old monopoly of rule, they had rather that the change should come by gradual necessity than by the uncontrollable violence of the moment, and worked hard to keep their marshalled forces within the bounds of law till war should be actually declared.

Here the press did a useful work. Though their pages were constantly disgraced by virulent attacks on the innocent, the newspapers kept on the side of order, partly no doubt from prudent fear. But by crowding their columns with accounts of meetings all over the country they created a corporate feeling of joint effort, which was the surest base for confidence and peace. Practically nothing but political matter appears in the papers of these days. Serious trouble was feared from the strike of pitmen in the Tyne and Wear collieries, amounting possibly to a " simultaneous rising," but hardly any attention is given to it by the press ; [1] and it is constantly stated that eight pages do not half suffice for the petitions, the resolutions, and even brief mention of the innumerable assemblages held about the country.

For eleven days the ordinary business of the nation was suspended, and men's eyes and ears were turned to Westminster and St. James's. Almost alone, and in vivid contrast to the general unrest, stands the calm figure of Robert Owen, who a few days before had held a co-operative congress in London ; he looked with pity on the struggling whirlpool of wasted effort, and wrote in his paper the *Crisis :* " At a season like the present, when the people are running in all directions, exclaiming ' What must we do to be saved ? ' . . . they present an affecting spectacle to the philosopher." [2] But men believing in the value of parliamentary rule were not capable of such detachment. To Tories looking back on this period the Days of May were a hideous dream, in which the powers of order and ancient right had been eclipsed by all the evil that lurks in the blind passions of the people and in the perverted brains of leaders who have sold their principles for power. But to Liberals they were the birth-pangs of Government by consent.

The last act of the Reform drama is divided into two scenes, of which the first ends with the Duke's announcement to the King on Tuesday, May 15, of his failure to form a ministry.

---

[1] *H. O.* 52. 19; 41. 11.          [2] *Crisis,* May 19.

The other culminates with the King's agreement to yield to
his ministers on the Friday following. It was not till then,
and barely then, that matters were finally settled, but Monday
night was no less a critical point, and the renewal of difficulties
was totally unexpected.

Most Reformers had a presentiment that the bill could
hardly get through Committee in a form the ministers could
honestly accept. Therefore on the news of Lord Lyndhurst's
successful amendment opinion was prepared. No one believed
that the postponement of the disfranchising clauses was a mere
Gulliverian question of beginning at the big or little end.[1]
The press urged the country to unite, and a Westminster
meeting was held on Tuesday evening, May 8, to address the
King and demand a creation of peers. Various speakers openly
stated that they had refused to pay the tax-collector, and this
move was generally approved. Nothing, however, was said
in either House of Parliament that night, and there had been
rumours during the day that seventy peers were to be created.
But on Wednesday morning the *Morning Chronicle* came out
with a furious attack against the royal ladies, now assuming
that the bill was as good as dead.[2] These charges were kept up
during the whole of the excitement and were one of its most
painful features; they served, however, to shield the King himself
from much of the hatred he would otherwise have incurred.
Those who had tossed up their caps in April for King Billy,
the honest tar, found it easier to think him weak than wicked.
The usual pretence was that the King was hedged round by a
band of lying advisers, who deceived him as to the true wishes
of his loyal people; foremost among these were the foreign
queen, the princesses, the hated Cumberland, and the troop of
royal bastards. The definite announcement of the ministers'

---

[1] *Morning Chronicle*, May 8.

[2] " The Queen and the Princesses have in fact never ceased tormenting
his Majesty with all manner of sinister reports and forebodings as to the
evils which will result from Reform. It is proper that the nation should
know, without disguise or reserve, that the Queen has done more injury
to the cause of Reform than any person living " (*Morning Chronicle*, May 9).
" The Queen's fixed impression," wrote Creevey in 1834, " is that an
English revolution is rapidly approaching, and that her own fate is to be
that of Marie Antoinette, and she trusts she shall be able to act her part
with more courage " (*Creevey Papers*, p. 624).

resignation was not made till the Houses met, but it was generally understood that peers would not be created, and in any case the bill was for the moment lost.

The National Political Union justified its foundation by assembling that evening a meeting of several thousands to raise the standard of resistance. " It was not a mere struggle for any particular measure of legislation, it was a question as to the means and source of legislation itself." Some attempts were made here, as elsewhere, to condemn the ministers for having presumed to raise the people's hopes so high without the assured means of fulfilling them ; " it was impossible that Lord Grey could have expected to carry the bill without creating peers " ; nothing had happened which had not been foretold once and again from the day the bill was introduced in the House of Commons. But to most minds the prompt resignation of ministers absolved them from all blame, if indeed it was not childish to linger apportioning guilt to those who were at least the champions of Reform, when all energies were needed to combat its bitter opponents. And there was a strong belief that Grey had at one time held a certain pledge that peers should be made.[1] It was his " base desertion " by the Reforming king which had defeated the bill ; all abuse of the minister was drowned in denunciation of that king's backstairs counsellors, who richly deserved the block. There were monarchs in history who had listened to the despotic advice of a foreign woman ; in the issue it had not been well for them nor for their wives. The people were now thrown on their own resources ; they would take no Reform from its enemies' hands, nor would they fear coercion when all the troops in England were less in number than those which one city of French working men had put to flight. One constitutional act remained. They had petitioned the Lords to pass the bill. The Lords had rejected it. They had petitioned the King to create peers to overrule the Lords. The King had denied their prayer. They would now petition the Commons to revive the undoubted right they had exercised two hundred years before, when a tyrannous Government

---

[1] The papers published a letter purporting to be written by the King to Lord Grey, on January 15, from the Brighton Pavilion, in which full means to carry the bill were promised. This was the date on which the King did give Grey his first provisional permission, so it is likely the forger did not forge entirely at random.

thwarted the liberties of the people. In 1642 the Commons of England had appointed Commissioners of their own to receive the moneys with which the Treasury could not be trusted. So now the National Union would petition the Commons to refuse supplies to the enemy and bring both King and Lords to their knees. A committee was chosen to draw up the petition, and the meeting dispersed with three groans for the King and the German Queen.[1]

On Thursday the Common Council of the City, in these years always a Radical body, also proceeded to petition the Commons to stop the supplies. All the wards and parishes of London were meeting, and resolutions to pay no taxes were universal, placards to that effect being displayed in windows openly.[2] Above all the unions were finding their real place, and at last fulfilling the purposes for which they had been devised. When the public opinion was apathetic, they were forced to depend on the support of enthusiasts and could only hope to create interest gradually and by the arts of the propagandist ; it has been shown how even the greatest found difficulty in keeping their heads above the waters of bankruptcy. But when public opinion was at length roused and political keenness became fashionable, there was a spontaneous inflow of members to the unions, as the known centres of all that might be doing. The agents of the National Political were kept busy from morning till night enrolling recruits, and the ranks of country unions were also swelled.[3] Some places, hitherto politically unenterprising, were moved now at the eleventh hour to follow the example of the strenuous. In the general stoppage of business, men collected round the offices of their union to discuss or carry out policy, and thus opinion was formed and discipline made easy.

All the unions founded on Attwood's plan were legal bodies, at least since November, and therefore not subject to the con-

---

[1] *Morning Chronicle*, May 10 ; Add. MSS. 27,792, f. 263.

[2] " I, ——, householder, do solemnly declare that I will pay no more taxes or other Government impositions, except Poors' Rates, unless the Reform Bill, with the £10 or a less property qualification, and enfranchisement to the Metropolitan districts, is secured whole and unmutilated to the nation " (*Morning Chronicle*, May 11).

[3] Add. MSS. 27,793, f. 23. Three thousand new members joined on May 9, 10, 11 ; *Morning Chronicle*, May 12.

tempt felt by the respectable for the Unions of the Working Classes, which most certainly were not.[1]   At this crisis, however, both varieties came nearer together than ever before, and at meetings of both held on Thursday, resolutions were passed to withhold taxes.  The National Political again denounced " false, fleeting, perjured Clarence," and petitioned the Commons to bring Lord Grey back to power.[2]   The Rotunda Radicals had no such plain objective.  Forbidden to express any regret for the Reform Bill, they were spoiling for a fight with those who had rejected it.  Nevertheless their leaders foresaw that the fruits of the campaign would go to the middle classes, and the word to the workmen was to " stand at ease."[3] Though the refusal to pay taxes and the withdrawal of cash from banks by Benefit Societies were to be welcomed as tending to shake credit, members of the Union were cautioned not wantonly to embroil themselves with the " red-coated bullies," and so act the part of cat's-paws.  But if the middle classes took up arms, then their chance had come, and they must fight for their own ends and no one else's.[4]   As matters turned out, however, for all their brave words and brave ideas, the Reform struggle of May 1832 brought no direct benefit to the Unions of the Working Classes.  The " middlemen " pulled up the ladder after them, leaving to the working people less hope of political importance than before, and only the memory of a great surrender by their common enemies to tactics they might themselves one day repeat.  It was this disappointment in large measure which drew off great numbers of the working class from politics, after the passing of the Reform Bill, into a more hopeful field of effort, as represented by the " Consolidated National Trades Union," quaintly called the Grand National.

[1] Place said :  " The difference between the Political Unions and the Unions of the Working Classes was that the first desired the Reform Bill to prevent a revolution, the last desired its destruction as a means of producing a revolution " (Add. MSS. *27,792*, f. 248 ;  *27,793*, f. 76.

[2] *Morning Chronicle*, May 11.

[3] *Poor Man's Guardian*, May 12.

[4] " To those excluded from the Bill—Assist the Bill-men in the cause ; but should you take up arms in defence of Reform, do business on your own account.  Defend the good cause, and claim equal rights.—L." (*Republican*, vol. ii., No. 4, edited by J. H. B. Lorymer.)  " One word of advice—let us be sober—no joining mobs—no window breaking—no scuffles—no beastly drinking—be reserved—be prepared for the worst " (*Poor Man's Guardian*, May 12).

The remainder waited a few years, and then, as the unsatisfied unionists returned to their ranks, wasted their faith and strength in the wild emprise of Chartism.[1]

The distinguishing feature of the Days of May, as the last action in an English political campaign, was the excellence of the communication and co-operation established between the middle class societies in London and the provinces. This was only made possible by the enterprise of Francis Place and Thomas Attwood. Delegates had met, of course, during the Yorkshire Reform movement of the eighties, but their decisions had nothing like the same practical importance. Excited crowds were not waiting for their orders to leave their homes and march on the capital. Brief mention has been made of the revival of political interest in the country when the Lords met after Easter. Large numbers of meetings had assembled on May 7 and 8 to urge the peers not to presume to mar the perfection of the people's bill. The enthusiasm caused by these had not had time to die down when the news of the Lords' precipitate action and the resignation of the Whigs burst upon the country in quick succession. Immediately the furnace was heated one seven times hotter than before. Most provincial towns heard of the fall of the Government on Thursday morning. At Liverpool business was at once suspended on the Exchange, for events were taking place which made even money-making seem tame.[2] The news reached Manchester soon after mid-day. " We have no recollection," said the *Manchester Guardian*, " of any former public event whatever, which produced so complete a stoppage of business in this town, as that caused by the resignation of Earl Grey's administration. Orders were forthwith countermanded ; merchants suspended their operations ; buyers from a distance went, or were recalled, home, without effecting their purchases, and a large number of our manufacturers and warehousemen state that, for anything they really have to do, they might just as well actually close their establishments." In the morning a meeting was held, at which the chairman, while cautiously refusing to put a motion against paying taxes to the vote, declared that he would pay none himself, and that others might follow his example if they liked. Between two and five o'clock a petition to the Commons to stop the supplies was signed by

[1] Lovett's *Autobiography*, p. 86.
[2] *Morning Chronicle*, May 14.

over 20,000 names, and that evening three deputies started with it for London.[1]

Birmingham naturally heard earlier ; many windows already showed the placard : " No taxes paid here until the Reform Bill is passed." The news put an end to business, and the mother of unions was joined by men of a higher class than most of its members. It is said that five hundred inhabitants prominent in business also enrolled themselves, besides a number of Roman Catholic priests and Quakers.[2] A vast meeting of many thousands assembled in the afternoon at Newhall hill, the site of last Monday's impressive demonstration, when the solemn act of devotion was performed and the Union war-chant sung. Attwood dissuaded the meeting from deciding to refuse taxes as yet. Wishing to hear on authority how the land lay, he held his forces well in hand, and despatched a deputation that evening to Westminster with a petition from the meeting praying the Commons to stop the supplies. In the meantime he sent the fiery cross round the neighbourhood, and wrote especially to his brother Charles at Newcastle-on-Tyne, the headquarters of the Northern Political Union, and to Wallace, chairman of the Glasgow and Greenock Unions, urging them to hasten to Birmingham to give their advice in framing a national plan of campaign ; they were to face the hard facts of physical coercion.[3] A touch of romance was added by the arrival of Count Czapski, fresh from the struggle for Polish nationality, who promised his military knowledge in the service of the Union. The Council determined to sit daily henceforth ; they circulated copies of a manifesto against the Duke of Wellington, and, wise in their generation, issued a badge to be worn by members. This was a vast success, and appealed strongly to the middle class imagination. We are told that " Union " mugs, pipes,

[1] Add. MSS. 27,793, f. 87 ; *Manchester Guardian*, May 12.

[2] Add. MSS. 27,793, f. 88 ; *Century of Birmingham*, p. 617. A Birmingham clergyman wrote to the Duke of Wellington declaring that these proceedings had been much exaggerated. The meeting of the Unions on May 7 did not number more than 50,000 ; the placards refusing taxes were in very few houses of more than £10 rent ; of the 500 respectables who joined, some had really put down their names long before, while others only joined in a panic and had already repented. The Union was nothing but a rabble (*Despatches*, viii. 318).

[3] " Expresses were leaving Birmingham all day to the various Unions and bodies of Reform of the United Kingdom, urging them to ' stand fast ' and unite to obtain Reform " (*Morning Chronicle*, May 11).

and jugs, bearing Attwood's head, were to be seen everywhere in Birmingham and in the villages round, where branch unions flourished.[1] Birmingham considered the Reform question her special subject; she had long been identified with it, since the days when the "Legislatorial Attorney" was sent to Westminster; she had virtually started its practical discussion by the founding of the Union, in January 1830, and now in 1832, "the great year of Birmingham," the capital of the Midlands was chosen as the centre of resistance to coercion.[2] A bold band of inhabitants actually offered the Political Council a bodyguard of 1500 men with muskets. The brave part played by the town was not forgotten by the leaders of Reform, and Durham declared a few days after this that it was to Birmingham that the country owed its salvation.[3]

For the moment the defence of the bill had been taken out of the hands of its official champions. But when the ministers' announcement on Wednesday, May 9, left no doubt of their fall from power, the Whigs in Parliament rose up to maintain their principles no less in defeat, and the House of Commons entered on a course of action assertive of its highest claims of supremacy. As soon as Althorp entered the House, and again after he had made his official statement, he was greeted by loud cheering, and Lord Ebrington promptly gave notice, as on the parallel occasion in October, of a motion of confidence for the next evening. The party leaders had taken the refusal of their advice with extraordinary meekness, and did their best to prevail on Ebrington to abandon a measure that could only lead to excitement; an unusual delicacy persuaded them that it was their duty in no way to obstruct the King's attempts to form a new administration. Such an attitude is more surprising in Althorp, for all his anxiety to leave office, than in Grey, who certainly had no idea of appealing to the sovereign people. One gathers that his feeling was that he had done his duty and was thankful to be rid of it. The rank and file, however, had more spirit than to acquiesce in such self-denial, and Grey reluctantly yielded.

[1] Recollections of Edwin Thornton, quoted in *Life of Attwood*, p. 185.

[2] "Birmingham was by circumstances placed in the front of the battle, . . . on the formation of the new ministry the first blow would probably be struck there" (*Life of Attwood*, p. 196).

[3] Parkes to Mrs. Grote, May 18; Add. MSS. 27,794, f. 262.

2 B

Ebrington's resolutions, as finally framed, were fairly strongly worded; [1] they were in the form of an address to the King, declaring the House's confidence in the late Government and the hope that the King would " call to his Councils such persons only as will carry into effect, unimpaired in all its essential provisions, that Bill for reforming the Representation of the people which has recently passed this House." [2]   The address also urged the belief " that any successful attempt to mutilate or impair the efficiency of the Bill will be productive of great disappointment and dismay."   It amounted in fact, as Peel pointed out in a speech of great force, to a claim by the Commons to override alike the amending powers of the Lords and the Crown's right to select its ministers. [3]   Early in the debate Althorp was induced to admit openly that the advice tendered to the King had been to create a sufficient number of peers to carry the Reform Bill; this confession was received with long and loud cheering, which committed the Whig party, had their approval been in doubt, to the bold policy. [4]   Althorp's statement naturally fixed the line of the debate; the Opposition violently attacked ministers for having dared to counsel so revolutionary a step on the mere ground of conjecture, when not a syllable of the bill had been struck out.   Even on their own side, the ministers' action was a strong dose for some weak stomachs; the Reforming Colonel Davies said on May 9 that, while he could approve of a demand for fifty or seventy peers, it was unconstitutional to ask for such a transfer of the prerogative as would be implied in an unlimited number. Macaulay replied with a constitutional argument on the rights of peer-making.   In a matter so closely touching the personal action of the monarch, expression had to be very guarded; yet, for all the Commons' adherence to etiquette, the veil of ministerial responsibility had been drawn aside in a way which showed how ill reality and constitutional

[1] Grey to Taylor, May 10 : " In the House of Commons, too, a feeling prevails which we have no power of controlling.  It is in vain that it has been represented both by Lord Althorp and myself, that nothing could be more unpleasant to us personally, than any proceeding which might tend to throw difficulties in the way of the formation of a new Administration. . . . I was interrupted here by Lord Duncannon, who assures me that Lord Ebrington's motion was unavoidable " (*Correspondence*, ii. 400).

[2] *Hansard* (3rd series), xii. 788,

[3] *Ibid.*, xii. 839.

[4] *Recollections*, iv. 222.

theory accorded. The division resulted in a Whig majority of eighty, which both sides took as a triumph—the Tories because it showed a fall of fifty on the similar vote in October, and the Government because of the stronger character of the resolutions.[1] Even Hunt, though declaring his indifference to either party, spoke at last of the bill as " the best measure of Reform that could be obtained." As it turned out, however, Lord Ebrington's resolutions were beside the mark, if intended, as Macaulay understood, " as a recommendation to his Majesty to retain his present Ministers " ; it did not follow that if the Reform Bill was to be passed, it must be passed by the Whigs.

After the Levée on May 9, when Brougham and Richmond had refused to continue in office, the King sent for Lord Lyndhurst to St. James's. He asked him as his former Chancellor to take stock of the position of parties in the country, and consider whether an administration could be formed on the basis of moderate, but yet " extensive," Reform. It is plain that a measure embracing all the essential features of the Reform Bill was meant. He was to report to the King at Windsor on Thursday night. Lyndhurst communicated first with the Duke of Wellington, who agreed to support the project ; next with Sir Robert Peel, who refused ; then with a few other men whose judgment he could trust. Croker, whose diary of these days is of unique interest, describes a conversation at Apsley House on the Thursday morning, at which he, the Duke, Lyndhurst, and Peel were present. The question of the premiership was discussed. Peel, who had been intended for it, was obdurate, and Croker then suggested Lord Harrowby, as morally bound to save the party from the difficulties he had created. Certain as Lyndhurst felt that Harrowby would decline, the Duke refused even to make the offer till he had sounded a number of Tory peers who were to meet at his house next day.[2] Lynd-

---

[1] It is interesting to compare this debate with that on Mr. Balfour's vote of censure on the Government's handling of the Parliament Bill, on August 7, 1911. Then it was known, of course, that the King had consented to act on the advice of his ministers, but in both cases the Opposition accused the Government of not having taken the people's opinion fairly. The 1910 election was said to have been fought on a divided issue ; that of 1831 was said to have been held under intimidation and in circumstances that made a calm judgment impossible. In neither case had the King been two years on the throne.

[2] *Croker Papers*, ii. 155.

hurst therefore, though feeling strongly that circumstances pointed to the Duke as Premier, had nothing decisive to report when he described the result of his efforts to the King at the time arranged.   He returned with a message summoning the Duke to an interview with the King in London on Saturday.[1]   This was the extent of Lord Lyndhurst's mission ;  he was not to form a government, nor even to ask anyone else to form one—simply to prospect for the King's benefit.

Wellington, however, was directly commissioned to form an administration, though not necessarily to be at the head of it, and with soldierly promptitude he set about the task made so difficult by Peel's desertion.   Peel had been designed, he told Parliament, for " that office which in political life is supposed to be the highest object of ambition " ;[2]  why he refused it and Wellington was willing to accept it is one of the most interesting points in the history of the Reform Bill.   Peel's attitude is perhaps more intelligible at first sight than Wellington's ;  indeed the puzzle can hardly be stated better than in the words of Disraeli, that cunning strategist, written less than twelve years after : " The future historian of the country will be perplexed to ascertain what was the distinct object which the Duke of Wellington proposed to himself in the political manœuvres of May 1832.   It was known that the passing of the Reform Bill was a condition absolute with the King ;  it was unquestionable, that the first general election under the new law must ignominiously expel the Anti-Reform Ministry from power, who would then resume their seats on the Opposition benches in both Houses with the loss not only of their boroughs, but of that reputation for political consistency, which might have been some compensation for the parliamentary influence of which they had been deprived." [3]

Both statesmen were at one in their genuine belief that the bill was not only bad and pernicious in every detail but in-

[1] Lyndhurst to Wellington, May 10 ; *Despatches*, viii. 303.   See also Lyndhurst's speech in the Lords on May 17 ; *Hansard* (3rd series), xii. 1000.

[2] *Hansard* (3rd series), xii. 1073.   Peel, however, was able to say on May 11 : "I have received no invitation, from any person authorised to make one, to accept office " (*Hansard* (3rd series), xii. 887).   The inconsistency is explained by the subtlety that Lyndhurst only sounded him.

[3] *Coningsby*, Book I. chap. vii. ; published in 1844.

compatible with the existence of a mixed form of government, and indeed anything short of mob-rule and anarchy ; neither ever wavered in this opinion, though each was forced to admit, at least by the spring of 1832, that some Reform was necessary to the country. They had considered the bill so bad that on two occasions—in November 1831 and February 1832—they had refused to join in an attempt to amend it, though nothing more was asked of them than to allow it a second reading. In February they had clung to this uncompromising attitude in spite of the belief that the King would create peers on the advice of his ministers. Both considered that advice a crime against the State, and as such refused to participate in it even to the extent of making it unnecessary by compliance. The Duke, admitting that a creation would render the House of Lords " contemptible in its own eyes, and in those of the public," held that this part, and all other parts, of the Constitution would be no less irreparably damaged by the passing of the bill.[1] Peel, equally horrified by the idea of a creation, insisted equally on the duty of the Lords to refuse the second reading.

Such was their attitude before the bill was presented to the Lords ; and it remained much the same after the passing of the second reading had limited their efforts to amendment. It was not till the Whigs' resignation that their policies diverged. Even now both understood that " everything that is really important and really dangerous " in the bill must pass in any case ; nor had the situation been altered by the Government's positive demand for peers ; for the Tory discussions of the last few months had assumed that the demand would be made, and Tory disgust could hardly wax keener than before. The actual change of circumstances amounted to this ; there was a chance of turning out the Whigs, and the King had appealed to the Tories to do it.

Peel was earnestly besought by Croker not to let the opportunity slip ;[2] but his refusal to Lyndhurst was final, and was grounded on the same profound and far-sighted considerations which had guided his previous policy of no surrender. " I look beyond the exigency and the peril of the present moment, and I do believe that one of the greatest calamities that could befall

---

[1] Wellington to Wharncliffe, February 3 ; *Despatches*, viii. 206.
[2] Croker to Peel, May 11, *Croker Papers*, ii. 177 ; *Peel Papers*, ii. 204, where it is misdated May 4, 1831.

the country would be the utter want of confidence in the declarations of public men which must follow the adoption of the Bill of Reform by me as a Minister of the Crown." He justly argued that the Catholic question was no parallel.[1] He had on that occasion, when once convinced of the necessity of yielding to the Irish, been most anxious to resign. But the matter was urgent ; it was doubtful whether the King could be persuaded to sanction Relief ; certainly no one could persuade him but the Duke of Wellington ; the Duke saw no hope of carrying the measure without Peel's help ; the majority of the Lords were hostile ; the majority of the country were decidedly so ; it may probably be said that the bill could not have been passed except by the Tories ; civil war was threatening. It was utterly against his own wishes that Peel consented to stand by his chief in carrying through a measure deeply repugnant to both of them.[2] There was no such necessity now. The King had sanctioned the bill ; the country—at any rate its temporary majority—was wildly in favour of it ; the Duke and Peel were not in office ; they had refused indignantly to bear any responsibility for the state of the country. It was a matter of " personal honour " to Peel's mind, and, much as he would have liked to come to the King's rescue, he felt he could not in conscience.

It is perhaps natural to wonder whether Peel, consummate parliamentarian as he was, had not at the back of his mind the idea that a Tory administration formed in such circumstances was doomed to an early and not very glorious end, and whether he did not therefore shrink from committing his fortunes to a vessel water-logged from the very start. Such a suggestion was hinted by Disraeli and given as a certainty by Holland.[3] No doubt it was to Peel's personal

---

[1] Peel to Croker, May 12 ; *Peel Papers*, ii. 205. Peel's apologia in the House of Commons was made on May 18 ; *Hansard* (3rd series), xii. 1073.

[2] Peel to Wellington, January 12, 1829 : " If my retirement should prove, in your opinion, after the communications which you may have with the King or with those whom it may be necessary for you to consult, *an insuperable obstacle* to the adoption of the course which, upon the whole, I believe to be the least open to objection, under all the circumstances of the time, in that case you shall command every service that I can render in any capacity." Wellington to Peel, January 17 : " I tell you fairly that I do not see the smallest chance of getting the better of these difficulties if you should not continue in office " (*Peel Papers*, ii. 80).

[3] Holland to Grey, May 15, 16 : " The Duke's tergiversation and Peel's white feather " (*Howick Papers*. Cf. Greville, ii. 296 ff.).

interest to keep out of any responsible position till Reform was passed, now that it could no longer be moderate, and he himself declared in February that he had not the slightest wish to resume office. A man may of course be subconsciously biassed by influences he does not recognise, but we can go no further than this ; " in as distinct words as one man is capable of using in contradicting another," Peel denied that he had been swayed by any such considerations.[1] There may have been matters on which Peel was willing to drift with public opinion ; [2] but on Reform his line was taken. Nevertheless he gave the Duke of Wellington full credit for acting from the highest possible motives in a direction exactly opposite to his own.[3]

The Duke, like many other men of action, felt loyalty to persons a nearer duty than loyalty to ideas. His defence of his conduct is given in various letters as well as in his speech in the Lords on May 17. As he viewed it, the ministers had tendered to the King unnecessary, unconstitutional, and positively criminal advice.[4] They were the slaves of the mob and declared enemies to the institutions of England. The King, as a last resource, had appealed to his chivalry to save him from the need of obeying the unholy counsel. Had he failed his master, he would have been " ashamed to show his face in the streets." He therefore sacrificed his unshaken opinions to serve the King.[5]

It is very easy to pick holes in the Duke's defence. In the first place, he might have prevented peer-making by inducing

[1] *Hansard* (3rd series), xii. 1078.

[2] " Peel has an idea about currency, and a distinct impression about it, and therefore on that point I would trust him for not yielding to clamour ; but about most matters, the Church especially, he seems to have no idea, and therefore I would not trust him for not giving it all up to-morrow, if the clamour were loud enough " (Arnold to Whately, *Life of Arnold*, p. 425).

[3] *Hansard* (3rd series), xii. 1075.

[4] "When I first heard of this Bill being proposed to be carried by a creation of Peers I said it was quite impossible. . . . For, my Lords, I do maintain, that the just exercise of the prerogative of the Crown does by no means go to the extent of enabling his Majesty to create a body of Peers with the view to carry any particular measure " (*Hansard* (3rd series), xii. 998, 999, and *Despatches*, passim).

[5] *Hansard* (3rd series), xii. 997. Wellington to Lyndhurst, May 10: " I am perfectly ready to do whatever his Majesty may command me. I am as much averse to the Reform as ever I was. No embarrassment of that kind, no private consideration, shall prevent me from making every effort to serve the King " (*Despatches*, viii. 304).

his party to abstain from voting, as he had induced them to vote for Catholic Emancipation : " My Lords, right about face, quick march." To this his answer was that to abstain under the threat of a creation was to become accomplice in the crime.[1] Surely to act contrary to one's principles under the threat of a creation was so no less ; it was simply one further turn of the screw. For in either case the Duke's action was forced by Lord Grey's "unconstitutional" menace; he could not escape from that. Secondly, he had himself declared more than once that the Reform Bill was no less destructive to the Constitution than a creation of peers ; this had been his main reason for adopting a die-hard position.[2] Now the peers were to vote for it—a suggestion he had once scouted as outrageous.[3] However, against the honour of the Lords he set the appeal of the King, and it was possible that in some small points the bill might be amended.[4] Thirdly, his position was unconstitutional. He said in the House of Lords : " I do not think that, under the influence of this measure, it is possible that any Government can expect to overcome the dangers to which this country must be exposed. But, my Lords, this was not the question before me ; I was called on to assist my Sovereign in resisting a measure which would lead to the immediate overthrow of one branch of the Legislature. . . ." And yet, as the Duke had said just before, " His Majesty insisted that some extensive measure of Reform (I use his Majesty's own words) should be carried." [5] This contention strikes at the whole doctrine of ministerial responsibility. The King can do no wrong, and the Duke was of course ready to bear the full burden of criticism for his conduct. But it would

---

[1] " And, my Lords, my opinion is, that the threat of carrying this measure of creating Peers into execution, if it should have the effect of inducing noble Lords to absent themselves from the House, or to adopt any particular line of conduct, is just as bad as its execution : for, my Lords, it does by violence force a decision on this House. . . . But, I say, my Lords, that the effect of any body of men agreeing publicly to such a course, will be to make themselves parties to this very proceeding . . ." (*Hansard* (3rd series), xii. 995).

[2] Wellington to Lord Exeter, January 14 : " I confess that, injurious as I think that this supposed creation of Peers would be, I cannot think that it will tend more immediately to the destruction of the House of Lords than carrying the Reform Bill " (*Despatches*, viii. 162).

[3] Wellington to Wharncliffe, February 3 ; *Despatches*, viii. 207.

[4] Wellington to Gleig, May 21 ; *Despatches*, viii. 340.

[5] *Hansard* (3rd series), xii. 996.

be little satisfaction for a House of Commons to impeach or remove offending ministers, knowing that they believed it to be their duty to carry out the orders of the Sovereign contrary to their own judgment. A minister must feel himself morally, as well as legally, responsible for his policy, if Cabinet government is to rest on a basis of confidence. We can hold this view without disparaging the Duke's splendid and soldierlike devotion to the distracted old King, whose line of behaviour he had by no means approved, in the face of certain obloquy and possible danger.[1] Fourthly, the Duke's intention was not quite so single-hearted as he apparently believed. He was to some degree biassed by his anxiety to turn out the Whigs, and so give the country " the benefit of some government." He wrote on May 21 : " I think that the mistake made by my friends is this : first, in not estimating the extent of the advantage of taking the King out of the hands of the Radicals. . . . In my opinion the advantage first mentioned more than compensates for all that would have been lost by our having anything to say to the Reform Bill." [2] This thought perhaps necessarily followed on his reprobation of Grey's peer-making advice, but it is, correctly speaking, distinct from it. It showed a dangerous state of mind to turn out the Government for attempting to pass their Reform Bill by the only means open to them, and then to pass it, or the essential parts of it, with their support. But the Duke acted with a clear conscience, and his acknowledged sacrifice to duty won him much heart-felt admiration.

Such being his feelings, he immediately set about the task of constructing an administration, whether or not he was himself to form part of it. Peel's loss was of course a very severe blow, and really wrecked the scheme, though Lyndhurst was at first extremely sanguine. Again Croker reveals the secret negotiations of the Tories. The peers who assembled at Apsley House on Friday morning ratified the Duke's decision by the momentous resolution " to support the King's Government even in passing the present Bill with some amendments." They were constrained alike by the King's words to Lyndhurst

---

[1] Wellington to Strangford, January 12 : " This King in particular has lived in the world, has taken a part in Parliament, and knows as well as any one of us the consequences of his actions. . . . I conclude—indeed I *know*—that he has *chosen* the course he has taken " (*Despatches*, viii. 156).

[2] Wellington to Gleig ; *Despatches*, viii. 340.

and by the vote of the Commons the night before.  Thus encouraged, the Duke was willing on Saturday morning to assume
the premiership if necessary.   It had been already offered to
Lord Harrowby, to the wealthy financier Alexander Baring,
and, after the precedent of Addington, to Charles Manners Sutton,
the Speaker, but all with one voice had refused it.[1]  At one
o'clock the Duke waited on his sovereign at St. James's.   The
fact that such steps were being taken was vaguely known to
the London Reformers, though the chance of their success did
not seriously alarm them.   On Friday night Peel stated in the
Commons that he had not been invited to take office, and next
morning it was confidently announced in the press that the
Duke was to be the First Lord of the Treasury, and Baring
Chancellor of the Exchequer ; but there was no official news.[2]

Place has recorded that Althorp's plain statement that the
Government had gone out on the rejection of their advice to
create peers set the final seal on the union between the Whigs in
Parliament and the people outside.[3]  The desire of Rockingham
and Fox was for a glorious moment realised.   But, though the
objects of the two wings of the Reforming party were the same,
their actual methods hardly overlapped ;  Grey would have been
as much disgusted by the plans now being laid at Charing Cross
as Wellington himself.   On Friday morning, May 11, the deputies
from Birmingham and other places, who had travelled through
the night, met for a council of war in Place's library.   In harmony
with Attwood's policy, they decided that should the Duke become
Premier a stand must be made at Birmingham.[4]  In the meantime
the deputies were to remain in London and establish communications with the leading Reforming bodies.   They were received with
rapturous welcome by a great meeting of Westminster electors
held at the " Crown and Anchor," which petitioned the Commons
to grant no supplies except to the Whig Government ; shouts
for a republic mingled with personal abuse of the Queen.   The
deputies then visited a gathering of the Livery of London in
Common Hall ; here, too, as at the Common Council on Thursday, a petition was carried for the stopping of supplies ; it was

---

[1] *Croker Papers*, ii. 157.

[2] *Morning Chronicle*, May 10, 12.

[3] " It exalted Earl Grey even above the height on which his own most
ardent admirers had hoped to place him.   The House of Commons and the
people were as one body pulling together " (Add. MSS. 27,793, f. 73).

[4] Add. MSS. 27,793, f. 99.

" not time yet to take up arms, but to be provided." [1] Many of the London parishes also assembled, and about the country enthusiastic Reform meetings cried for peers and stoppage of supplies.[2] It was a great period for public meetings, as *Pickwick* testifies. A portly middle-aged gentleman would be voted to the chair amid deafening applause ; after his expression of deepest gratitude and conscious unworthiness, other portly middle-aged gentlemen would luxuriantly declaim on the sacred principles of liberty and British independence ; a long string of pompous resolutions would be moved, seconded, and carried, and the chairman would be thanked for his able and impartial conduct. But most of the meetings during this fortnight show a graver tone, as though the speakers felt that they might be called to put their sentiments into practice.[3]

Saturday, the day when weekly papers came out, was also passed in preparing resistance ; it was becoming more certain that a Tory government would be formed, and a rumour grew up that a surprise dissolution of Parliament would take place on Monday, demanding Reformers' more strenuous efforts.[4] A meeting of influential Reformers was held at noon in Covent Garden ; " all were fully resolved not to submit to a Tory administration." The meeting seems to have been united by the corporate feeling of great purpose. " The persons present were all men of sub-

[1] Add. MSS. 27,793, f. 100 ; *Morning Chronicle*, May 12.

[2] *E.g.* at Preston, Lincoln, Portsmouth, Brighton, Exeter, Banbury, Sheffield, Bolton, Lewes, Liverpool, Blackburn, Wigan, Leigh, Chorley, Warrington (Add. MSS. 27,793, f. 153), &c.

[3] Place enumerates 290 petitions to the Commons to stop supplies, actually presented between May 8 and May 23 ; many more, he says, were not presented. Forty-nine memorials actually presented to the King were recorded in the *Gazette ;* 201 public meetings were held in eleven days. Place also gives the number of signatures attached to five different petitions from the city of Perth at five stages in the Reform struggle, and the length of time during which they were collected. The list rises from 1200 in ten days in November 1830 to 5300 in a day and a half in May 1832 (Add. MSS. 27,794, ff. 58, 344, 347).

[4] The *Morning Chronicle* of May 12 stated that the Reform Committee who organised the last election had met, and urged that the people must keep an eye on the boroughs in Schedule A. No non-resident burgage-holder must be allowed to enter. An election committee also met in Manchester; Durham received a letter from James Losh, dated May 13 : " I conclude that the Duke of Wellington must be the Prime Minister . . . and then of course we shall have a dissolution. I have written to Lord Howick as to what I think about Northumberland. I do not believe that there will be a contest " (*Lambton Papers*).

stance, some were very rich men, all were persons of influence and whom circumstances had made of considerable importance. Some were only known to others by name, some not in any way, but it seemed to be concluded that all who were present were good men and true." [1] Later in the day the scot and lot electors of Southwark protested in violent language against the supposed influence of the Queen and the Earl of Munster, who was actually accused of scheming for his father's throne. [2]

More important was a second meeting of the deputies held in the afternoon at Place's house, to discuss strategy. It was resolved, as soon as the Duke's administration should be officially proclaimed, to send home all the deputies but three, " to put the people in open opposition." All the great towns were to be barricaded and held as in a state of siege till further orders came from London. [3] In the meantime the Reformers on the spot were to remain quiet and play a waiting game. They were at all costs to prevent the people meeting the troops in open battle, and at the same time to show such a threatening face that the Duke would not dare to move the troops out of London. If matters should come to violence, which he hoped they would not, Place relied on a large number of soldiers of all ranks, who had declared their readiness to lead. The military part of the plan was closely bound up with the financial. The desperate efforts of the house of Rothschild, and no doubt of the Barings and other anti-Reform magnates, had kept the Funds from falling as much as had been expected on the news of Grey's resignation. [4] They dropped, however, from 85 on Tuesday to $83\frac{1}{2}$ on Wednesday, and now stood at $83\frac{1}{4}$. [5] For two days the Bank of England had been besieged by crowds, but as much, it would appear, from curiosity than from a general desire to withdraw cash. [6] Place now hit on his famous placard: " To stop the Duke, go for Gold." The meeting, which included several bankers,

[1] Add. MSS. 27,793, f. 143.

[2] *Ibid.*, f. 149; *Morning Chronicle*, May 14. George Fitzclarence, William IV's eldest son by Mrs. Jordan, was created Earl of Munster in 1831.

[3] " Communications had been had, as well personally as by other means, between the leaders of the National Political Union and many influential men in nearly all the large towns in England and Scotland and many other places " (Add. MSS. 27,793, ff. 141, 146).

[4] Arbuthnot to Wellington, May 12 ; *Despatches*, viii. 308.

[5] *Morning Chronicle*, May 9, 10, 12.

[6] *Ibid.*, May 14.

approved, and a large number of copies were printed off, some to be distributed over the country, and others to be posted about London in the small hours of Sunday morning. At Birmingham £2000 was withdrawn from the saving's-bank alone, and on Monday and Tuesday the Bank of England paid out several hundred thousand pounds.[1] It was calculated that the refusal of taxes, the demand for gold, and the general stoppage of industry and trade, would produce all the consequences of rebellion, if it did not at once make an anti-Reform ministry impossible. The streets would be full of unemployed and foodless workmen and their families, though the leaders were to prevent bloodshed as far as possible. The Tories would be bold men if they were prepared to face an angry and starving population.

The Duke of Wellington, who knew nothing of these preparations and would probably have ignored them if he had known, kept his appointment at the palace on Saturday afternoon with a brave heart. The King and Queen drove in from Windsor through a hissing crowd.[2] The Duke was now formally commissioned to form a government, but for some hours doubt as to his exact position produced a comedy of errors. Croker heard at the " new Club," [3] much to his astonishment, that he had actually kissed hands as Prime Minister ; this was untrue, but it sounded probable from the accounts that Peel and Sutton gave of the audiences to which they had been summoned by the King later in the afternoon. Both had apparently expected again to be offered the chief place, and Sutton was surprised when the King asked him merely to lead the Commons.[4] However, it seems plain that Wellington was intended at this time to be Prime Minister, though, as will be shown later, he never kissed hands. That evening he wrote to the King on the prospects of success.[5] He had secured Sir George Murray and Sir Henry Hardinge, of his former ministry ; probably also Lord

---

[1] Add. MSS. 27,793, f. 148; *Morning Chronicle*, May 15. It is probable that Place, with an inventor's partiality, rather exaggerated the effect of his placard, but there is no doubt that the run on the Bank was considerable, and was believed to be greater.

[2] *Morning Chronicle*, May 14.

[3] The Carlton.

[4] *Croker Papers*, ii. 159–161.

[5] *Despatches*, viii. 306.

Aberdeen;[1] he was to try another conversation with the Speaker.

The next forty-eight hours were spent by the Duke in a ceaseless round of interviews with possible ministers, several of whom refused to give a definite answer; they were no doubt anxious not to commit themselves prematurely. Many suggestions, likely and unlikely, were made by Lyndhurst on Saturday night;[2] but Peel's refusal carried great weight, and Goulburn, Herries, and Croker—all of them members of the old Government—followed his example. The Duke's report to the King, dated midday on Sunday, was not hopeful; the Speaker had again refused.[3] Manners Sutton's qualifications were rather respectability and personal influence in the House than actual talent; nevertheless the consent of Alexander Baring to act as Chancellor of the Exchequer was believed to depend on his decision, and Baring's weight and prestige in the City were felt to be worth an effort.[4] So much was this so that the Duke, his hopes now running low, made yet another attempt to secure the Speaker, now again as Prime Minister, and he and Lyndhurst were closeted for a long space with Sutton and Baring on Sunday afternoon.[5] "The arrangement proposed," said Baring in the House of Commons afterwards, "would have excluded the noble Duke from power, and probably from office." Sutton, however, could not make up his mind that night; his shilly-shallying did much to ruin the Tories' prospects, and was in fact given as the reason why no government was formed. Next morning the Duke and Lyndhurst were impatient for an answer; they had only agreed to offer Sutton the premiership as a last resource, and his delay was intolerable.[6] Eventually on Monday after-

[1] Sir A. Gordon, *Earl of Aberdeen*, p. 106.
[2] *Despatches*, viii. 307.
[3] *Ibid.*, viii. 314.
[4] Hardinge to Wellington, May 13; *Despatches*, viii. 312.
[5] Wellington to the King, May 13, 6.30 P.M.; *Despatches*, viii. 314.
[6] See two letters dated May 14 (*Despatches*, viii. 316), referring to the Apsley House meeting on Sunday and the consequent negotiations. Lyndhurst writes to the Duke: " I confess I don't like the affair in which I found you engaged to-day. . . . Will our anti-reforming friends consent to be thus handed over to other hands ? However, it seems too late to retreat. We must therefore, if the offer should be accepted, make the best of it. I incline to think the answer will be favourable. If it should be otherwise, we must assemble some dozen of the best of our young friends in the House of Commons, and ask them whether they will under-

noon the Speaker wrote to Wellington accepting, " though with fear and trembling," the proposal made to him on Sunday, but only if no other arrangement was possible ; he asked, however, for an interview after the House had risen ; he had no time to call on the Duke earlier, as his presence was needed in the Chair.[1] When the House rose that night it was too late.

The Whigs understood on Saturday that an administration had been formed ; but they did not realise at once that it was to carry the Reform Bill.[2]  It was with utter amazement they discovered that what Althorp had suggested in October as possible was really to be a fact.[3]  The proper line for the party to take was discussed at a meeting at Brooks's on Sunday ; the fiercer spirits were eager to oppose so flagrant a negation of principle tooth and nail, and Lord Ebrington had ready another address to the King.  Hume was actually for refusing supplies. But it was felt that violence must force a dissolution, and Althorp, supported by a fiery harangue from Stanley, carried a resolution pledging the party " to accept a Tory Reform Bill and if necessary to carry it further,"—thus showing that the party cared more for measures than for men.[4]  Yet preparations were made to show the new ministry what was thought of them.

take the fight. . . ."  The Duke replies: " I confess that I did not like all that passed yesterday ; and I had reason to believe afterwards that many of our friends will not approve of the arrangement.  This may be flattery or vanity."

[1] Sutton to Wellington, May 14 ; Wellington to Sutton, 3 P.M., in reply ; *Despatches*, viii. 315.

[2] *Recollections*, iv. 223.

[3] Holland to Grey, Saturday evening : " Is it possible that Wellington has announced his adhesion to the bill, the whole bill, and nothing but the bill ?  We should well consider our line and act up to it in entire concert. . . ."  Sunday evening: "What is to be our cue in the Lords if Wellington brings in the bill—et sunt qui credere possunt " (*Howick Papers*).

[4] *Life of Campbell*, ii. 10; *Recollections*, iv. 224; *Croker Papers*, ii. 164; *Life of Graham*, i. 143, where a letter of Palmerston is given : " I am delighted with the decision of last night.  It is infinitely wise, because it is perfectly honest, and will place our conduct and motives in a most honourable contrast with those of our opponents.  The idea of standing over the new Ministry with the rod of adjournment in one hand and the physic-boat full of Reform in the other, and compelling them to swallow the dose properly is excellent."  Russell, in the introduction to his *Speeches*, i. 79, wrongly gives the date of this meeting as Saturday, but he admits that he was not present.

Sunday passed off without disturbance in London, except for the mobbing in church of Bishop Ryder, Lord Harrowby's brother.[1]  For Monday a mass meeting of the three parishes of Marylebone, St. Pancras, and Paddington had been arranged under Hume's auspices.  There was no violence, but in fear of it the troops in London had been held " in readiness to turn out at a moment's notice in aid of the Civil Power."  However, they were wisely kept in barracks, and no provocation was given.[2] The Common Council of the City again took the field, preparing an address to the King, and over the three kingdoms the tale of protest meetings showed no decline.[3]  At Birmingham excitement was increased by the return of two of the deputies from London ; Scholefield had seen Lord Grey, who told him that all was over.  Attwood urged a run on the banks ; the crisis was felt to be too serious for mere rioting.[4]  There was a rumour in the town that the Union was to march for London, presumably to take part in a vast meeting on Hampstead Heath, expected to number millions, which had been one of the schemes of the London Committee.  Some of the Scots Greys, quartered in Birmingham, understood that they were to be used to stop the march.  Alexander Somerville, then a trooper in the regiment, tells us how on that Sunday the barrack-yard gates, contrary to custom, were shut, and how the troops, who for the last three days had kept their horses saddled and bridled, were ordered to rough-sharpen their swords that afternoon. There seems no reason to suppose that anything more was meant than to have the men ready, as was the case in London, to check any disturbance which might break out in the crowded streets.  But Somerville and his friends were deeply impressed, especially as some of them had actually joined the Union, while others had written letters to the Duke and Lord Hill declaring " that, while the Greys would do their duty if riots and outrages upon property were committed, they would not draw swords or triggers upon a deliberative public meeting, or kill the people of Birmingham for attempting to leave their town with a petition to London."[5]

[1] Add. MSS. 27,793, f. 187 ; *Hansard* (3rd series), xii. 984.
[2] War Office reports, May 13, 14 ; *W. O.* 3. 84;  3. 486.
[3] Add. MSS. 27,793, f. 197.
[4] *Morning Chronicle*, May 16, and G. Attwood's narrative.
[5] *Autobiography of a Working Man*, p. 244 ; *Memoir of Althorp*, p. 433.

The sitting of the House of Commons on Monday night, May 14, was on all hands admitted to have been unique in the history of Parliament, so bitter and so violent was the tone of the speeches.[1] The presentation of the petition from the Livery of the City, praying for the refusal of supplies, gave Lord Ebrington his opportunity. Referring to the prevalent rumours that the Duke of Wellington was taking office to pass the equivalent of the Reform Bill, he declared that, though he would support the measure by whomsoever proposed, he considered such conduct to be an act of gross public immorality. He was followed in the same style by Duncombe, Macaulay, and Lord John Russell, who spoke of " those who, in carrying that measure, would stand in the face of the country publicly dishonoured." [2] Baring made a feeble resistance ; he besought the House to suspend judgment till an accredited minister of the Crown stood before it, and defended compliance with the sovereign's appeal. He was finally crushed by the speech of Sir Robert Inglis, the High Tory who had turned Peel out of his seat for Oxford University. Inglis avowed that, if the reports were true, " he could not but regard the measure with the greatest pain, as one of the most fatal violations of public confidence which could be inflicted." [3] For once official policy was altered by criticism in the course of a debate. Baring threw up the sponge and suggested that the Whigs should remain in office to pass the bill without creating peers, on the understanding that the Lords should not touch Schedule A.[4] Others of the Tories agreed that it was absurd that, if the bill was to be passed after all, it should not be passed by its friends.

Sir Henry Hardinge wrote to the Duke at ten o'clock, telling him of the change of events and urging that he should speak with those who had been present. The Duke replied that he failed to see why speeches or a vote in the Commons should affect him, " unless it should be found that a government cannot be formed for the King in the House of Commons." [5] This, however, is just what was found. When the House rose, even Hunt having agreed that the Whigs alone could pacify the

---

[1] *Recollections*, iv. 225. *Greville Memoirs*, ii. 299 : "Such a scene of violence and excitement as never had been exhibited within those walls."

[2] *Hansard* (3rd series), xii. 932.  [3] *Ibid.*, xii. 947.

[4] *Ibid.*, xii. 957.  [5] *Despatches*, viii. 317.

country, Peel, Croker, Baring, and the Speaker drove to Apsley
House.   It was decided that the Duke must resign his commission
to form a government, and promise to refrain from attacking the
bill in future; early next morning he went to St. James's and
told the King that he was unable to help him.   In spite of assertions to the contrary, it appears that the break-down of proceedings was due solely to the events of the night before in
Parliament, and especially to the speeches of Inglis and the
other Tories.[2]   There is no evidence that the Duke gave
so much as a thought to the agitation of the country.   No
further official communications took place between the King
and the Duke of Wellington.

Thus baffled at the eleventh hour in his hope to escape
from his Whig advisers, the King had nothing better than to
write to Grey with the suggestion, on the lines of Baring's
later speech, that the bill might yet be passed by agreement,
without a creation of peers.[3]   Grey replied that he would submit
the new proposal to the Cabinet.   The ministers met in Downing
Street that afternoon; they agreed unanimously, not even
Richmond dissenting, that the Reform Bill must be passed " as
nearly as possible in its present form "; unless they saw some
security that this would be so, they could not remain in office;
and they must demand the right to create peers " if it should be

---

[1] *Greville Memoirs*, ii. 300; *Croker Papers*, ii. 167.

[2] Wellington to Buckingham, May 15; *Despatches*, viii. 322.   In the
" Lyndhurst Recollections " at the end of Monypenny's *Life of Disraeli*,
i. 388, it is said: " It was the original intention not to have given the
House time to come to this vote, but to have prorogued it that morning.
The hesitation of Manners Sutton and Baring, and the unwillingness of
Peel to act without their adhesion, lost everything."   Peel, as we know,
would not act in any case.   As to the intention to prorogue, the statement is in accord with popular belief of the time; but we have no direct
evidence, and indeed, seeing he was to pass the bill, the Duke had no
need to dissolve.   It would have been very dangerous to peace.   It was
before this that the King made his one recorded venture in poetry:

" I consider dissolution
Tantamount to revolution,"

but it was no less applicable now (*Peel Papers*, ii. 192).

[3] *Correspondence*, ii. 406; Hobhouse wrote: " I called on Lord Althorp,
when in came the Duke of Richmond, and said: ' Well, I have bad news
for you; no shooting this year.   Pack up your guns again. . . . The Duke
of Wellington has been with the King this morning, and given up his commission altogether ' " (*Recollections*, iv. 226).

required to give additional strength to your Majesty's Government in the House of Lords." [1] The King had in fact asked them gratuitously to put themselves back into the miserable position they held before May 7, with no additional guarantee but the vague hope that the foiled Opposition would prove more conciliatory. And this after a week of wild meetings throughout the country calling for a large creation of peers, stoppage of the supplies, and almost the abolition of the monarchy itself. Things were in this state when it was moved in both Houses to adjourn over Wednesday, Grey simply saying that he had received a communication from the King.

The Tuesday papers had seized on Baring's hint of conciliation, and urged Grey to beware of an enemy's gifts. They had heard that almost the first act of the " embryo administration " had been to draw up a proclamation declaring all unions illegal and ordering the arrest of their members.[2] Everywhere meetings continued with increased boldness. At Manchester a great gathering was held on Monday on the historic field of Peterloo. Hetherington of the Rotunda happened to be present ; he was prepared for the moment to forego universal suffrage if the bill were granted, and rejoiced to see rich and poor for once united. Brokers were known to have agreed not to buy goods distrained for refusal of taxes, and a run to some extent was made on the banks.[3] On Tuesday some 30,000 Edinburgh Reformers assembled outside the walls of Holyrood ; there were vast meetings too at Glasgow, but Scotland refrained from violent outbreaks. " I never before," wrote Cockburn, " actually *felt* the immediate presence of a great popular crisis. I advise nobody to create it. The fearful part of it was the absence of riot. There was nothing to distract the attention, or to break the terrible silence—nothing but grave looks and orderly public proceedings, unconquerable resolution, and the absolute certainty that, if any accident had made resistance begin anywhere, it would have run like an electric shock in a moment." [4] The same day as the Edinburgh demonstration, a Lambeth meeting resolved to address the King, " praying that

---

[1] *Correspondence*, ii. 411.

[2] *Morning Chronicle*, May 15.

[3] Add. MSS. 27,794, f. 55 ; *Morning Chronicle*, May 17. The *Manchester Correspondent* said 620 depositors had given notice to withdraw £16,700 (*Poor Man's Guardian*, May 19).

[4] *Journal of Henry Cockburn*, i. 30.

if he had not resolution to check a proud and selfish aristocracy, he would abdicate his throne." The Reformers of Newcastle reminded the Queen of the fate of Marie Antoinette. Hume, in Kensington, declared the soldiers would not fight. Rumours of a dissolution were in the air.[1]

But on Tuesday afternoon it became known that the King was in communication with the Whigs ; it was assumed that they were back in office on their own terms. The demand for gold slackened, consols went up a point.[2] Joe Parkes, the one Birmingham deputy remaining in London, started for home that night, and published the good news along the road. He arrived early, and proceeded without delay amid an exultant crowd to Attwood's house. The great man was in bed and had to be awoken to hear the tidings. The excitement of this surprise visit and the beauty of the May morning made a great impression on all concerned in the joyful event. Parkes sent at once to all places within fifteen miles, urging them to call meetings and let him have their resolutions in Birmingham by four o'clock. At one a great open-air meeting was held on the familiar ground of Newhall hill. In the evening a second deputation, this time including the Founder of Unions himself, started in pomp for London, with a sheaf of resolutions ; they stopped at Coventry to harangue the crowd.[3] The second scene of the last act was fairly begun.

The raptures of Birmingham were emulated in many towns about the country. At a meeting of the Hull Political Union a speaker said that he had thought to come that evening in a revolutionary and republican frame of mind ; many had believed, and he among them, that William IV would be the last of his house to wear the crown of England.[4] " Such was his opinion

---

[1] Add. MSS. 27,794, ff. 15-30.

[2] *Ibid.*, f. 84 ; *Morning Chronicle*, May 16.

[3] Parkes to Mrs. Grote, May 18 ; Add. MSS. 27,794, f. 262 ; *Life of Attwood*, p. 214. There is reason to believe that Parkes purposely exaggerated the prospect of success, in order to create a dramatic contrast between the moods of the people before and after his arrival.

[4] *Cf.* the following tirade in the *New Weekly Messenger :* " We are monarchists, . . . but if monarchy can only subsist with Wellingtons, Cumberlands, Lyndhursts, ambitious bastards, and German women for its ministerings and its love, and with rotten boroughs, enormous pensions, and desolating taxes for its appendages . . . let Monarchy go to the right about, and the lesser evil of Republicanism become dominant in England " (*Poor Man's Guardian*, May 19).

that afternoon. But he had changed that opinion. He believed that republicanism was now thrown back half a century." [1]

But at headquarters matters were by no means going smoothly. The King was still as much disinclined as ever to create peers, and hoped a means might be found of passing the bill without them. Grey was not pleased with an answer still indefinite, and another Cabinet was summoned for Wednesday evening. A feeling was now growing up among the more advanced Whigs that a creation of peers was in itself desirable, partly as a means of strengthening the party in the Lords, and partly as a token of victory in the country's eyes.[2] Grey was naturally not of this opinion himself, but the Cabinet's answer of May 15 looks like a compromise between those who did and did not want peers to be made.[3] At length, on Wednesday, they replied that the only alternative to a creation was a pledge on the part of the Tories to let the bill pass. Grey had discussed the possibility of this with Sir Herbert Taylor at St. James's in the afternoon, but there were felt to be many difficulties. Sooner, however, than force a creation, the Cabinet would postpone their final answer till Friday, the 18th, when the intentions of the Lords might have been declared.[4]

The King was much embarrassed, and it was by no means held certain that he would yield even now.[5] We have it on the

---

[1] *Hull Advertiser*, May 18.

[2] Holland to Grey (endorsed May 15, 16) : " I don't know what you mean by your fears of their failure, and your wishes for the success of their pride and obstinacy—for my part I wish for the triumph of my friends and the failure of my enemies, and long to see you brought back with double power and glory on the shoulders of the Commons and the people, and with a good lot of peers of more than three denominations in your pocket. . . . Use your victory with temper, moderation, and even tenderness if you like, *but use it*. If the proposition be, pass the bill but without Peers—I answer *No*, Peers I will have, and peers some of whom shall be taken from rich respectable Whig commoners, to show that my power in that respect is unfettered and unrestrained " (*Howick Papers*).

[3] *Correspondence*, ii. 411.

[4] *Ibid.*, ii. 419.

[5] Sir Denis Le Marchant (*Memoir of Althorp*, p. 434) says that in this interval the Queen wrote, even after the King had seen Lord Grey, to an intimate friend, " I do not despair yet." Place mentions a curious piece of palace gossip. On the evening of the 15th Hobhouse told him " there had been a hitch of a most extraordinary nature." . . . " The ' hitch ' was a project of the Queen's, to which after much persuasion the King had acceded, to leave the country clandestinely and run away to Hanover. He very seriously assured me that some step had been taken

authority of Lord Munster that on Wednesday he was positively determined not to make peers. This nobleman now proceeded to play a most dishonourable game. Taking advantage of his relationship with his father, most indiscreet of men, he kept the leaders of the Opposition almost hourly informed of the progress of affairs at the palace.[1] Late on Tuesday night he told the Duke of Buckingham " that the King was up to that hour firm and decided, but had had up to that hour no answer from Lord Grey." [2] " His (Lord Munster's) idea was, that if Lord Grey would make no concession, the King would make an appeal to his people, to his Peers, and to the Commons, to support him." Next Munster writes to Wellington : " After thirteen hours since the King's answer, last night, to Lord Grey, his Lordship is *come*.[3] I know not what has passed, but the King repeated to me, five minutes before Lord Grey came in, *that nothing should make him create Peers*. He is *most stout*. For God's sake be sure, if the King is driven to the wall, of *Peel*." Again later : " I have just seen the King, and he has *not any answer* yet from Lord Grey, and nothing whatever passed between him and the King." In the evening Munster called on Buckingham, after which he wrote to Wellington : " *Pray depend* upon the King. *Not* ten minutes before he saw Lord Grey, when, as I have written you word, *nothing* passed, he said in reference to something I said, ' Why, you know very well, George, as well as I do, that I never will make Peers.' He is buoyed up with the hope of Peel's aid in case of difficulty." Writing just before midnight, Buckingham tells the Duke of Wellington that " the person "—obviously Munster—" is to see the King again to-night, and means to

with a view to the departure of the King and Queen, when their intention became known and was consequently frustrated " (Add. MSS. 27,794, f. 88).

[1] This remarkable correspondence is given in the Duke's *Despatches*, viii. 329, 326, 329, 274, 260, 329, 306—seven notes in all. Most are dated May 16, some with the hour also. One only has " May " ; another is undated, but the covering note from Lord Chandos is dated 9.30, Wednesday evening. A third is dated 4.50, April 16. This is clearly a mistake ; everyone knows how easy it is to misdate a letter by the month which has just passed ; it fits in admirably with the other notes, and seems to be referred to in one of them. If so, all the notes were written on Wednesday, May 16, and tell a continuous story, harmonising with evidence given in Lord Grey's Correspondence.

[2] *i.e.* to the letter of May 15 ; *Correspondence*, ii. 411.

[3] This interview was to be at 1 o'clock ; *Correspondence*, ii. 417.

press him to put the case on this footing[1] into your hands."
After these disclosures it is impossible not to sympathise with
the Radical attacks on Munster, which came extremely near
the truth; the Queen herself can hardly be acquitted of indiscretion, but she never approached this disgraceful backstairs
attempt of Munster's to supplant the ministers with whom
his father was in official communication. If the Tories were
not warned on May 7 that William would not make peers, it
was not from want of will or scruple on the part of the son he
had ennobled.[2]

Wellington, who on the 15th had honourably suggested to
Taylor that all correspondence between himself and the palace
should cease, seems to have paid no attention to the intrigue.[3]
But the Duke of Buckingham was anxious to make use of it,
and showed an ignorance of constitutional propriety strange,
perhaps, in any but his father's son, by suggesting that Peel's
scruples might be overcome by an " appeal to his *allegiance* as
a subject."[4] This from a leader of the " constitutional " party.
He stated also to Wellington the amendments which he should
feel bound to make to the bill in the House of Lords, if, as he
hoped, the King would allow the battle to be fought out there
without weighting either scale. Thus the Duke of Buckingham
was convinced till the last minute of Wednesday that no peers
would in any circumstances be made.[5] Lord Londonderry had
gathered the same from a personal interview with the King,
who still hoped that the Opposition would let the important
parts of the bill through.[6] But Wellington cherished no such
illusions; he had shot his bolt, and now, loyal in defeat as when
victory was possible, had told the King he would take no more
part in the discussions on the Reform Bill.[7] On Thursday,
however, a further demand was made upon his patriotism, with
which he felt unable to comply.

The King had determined to intervene actively in hopes of

---

[1] *i.e.* that no peers are to be made.
[2] See above, p. 374, *n.* 3.
[3] *Despatches*, viii. 325.
[4] His father was the Earl Temple who helped George III to destroy
Fox's East India Bill in the Lords.
[5] Buckingham to Wellington, May 16, 11.45; *Despatches*, viii. 329.
[6] Londonderry to Wellington, May 16; *Despatches*, viii. 328.
[7] Wellington to Buckingham, May 17; to Eldon, May 22; *Despatches*,
viii. 331, 341.

freeing himself from the odious necessity of peer-making.  He
ordered Sir Herbert Taylor to write to a number of influential
lords of Parliament, informing them that all difficulties would
be removed by the declaration in the House that night by " a
sufficient number of peers " that they had decided to drop
their opposition to the bill.  The Duke was further asked to
communicate with Lyndhurst, Ellenborough, and any other
peers he thought likely to comply.[1]  Lord Grey was informed
of this move and told that a number of peers had already
promised the King to abstain, if that should relieve him from
the dreaded alternative.  If declarations to this effect were
made in the Lords, Grey was authorised to announce his continuance in office.[2]  But one of the Duke's strange scruples
stood in the way ; willing to assure his master privately that
he would no longer oppose, he felt that to say so in public would
make him a party to the ministers' iniquitous threat.  He
was moved partly by pride, partly by a sense of fitness, triumph-
ing over reason.[3]  Knowing nothing of this, ministers believed
that all was settled, and Althorp said as much that night in the
Commons.  But in the other House Grey and his colleagues
were amazed to hear nothing but fierce denunciations of themselves ; Wellington and Lyndhurst explained and defended their
own conduct in the last few days, but no statement in the least
resembling a declaration of peace was forthcoming.  The other
Opposition peers followed suit.  Those in the King's secret could
hardly believe their ears.  Hobhouse writes : " I was satisfied
that all was over, and I went to the Commons.  I sat down next
to Althorp, and told him what had passed.  He said : ' Well,
so much the better ; but it is rather a bore for me to have spoken
with so much confidence, though I was quite justified in so
doing.  Now I shall have my shooting.'  ' You may,' I said ;
' so shall we.  The pitchforks will be here.'  ' Not here,' he
replied, ' the other House.' "[4]  Lord Grey, who had been forced

---

[1] *Correspondence*, ii. 420.  The other letters were to the Dukes of
Cumberland and Gloucester, the Archbishop of Canterbury, and Lords
Verulam, Mansfield, Brownlow, Rosslyn, Skelmersdale, and Farnborough
(*Howick Papers*).

[2] *Correspondence*, ii. 420.

[3] Wellington to Taylor, May 17 ; *Despatches*, viii. 332.  The attitude
of those Conservative peers may be compared, who in August 1911 followed
Lord Lansdowne's advice so far as not to vote against the Parliament
Bill, but not to the extent of voting for it.

[4] *Recollections*, iv. 230, 231.

to withhold his announcement, wrote in great distress to the King and Sir Herbert Taylor to tell them that a Cabinet had been summoned for noon next day. He asserted that "as the Peers were leaving the House Lord Strangford said to somebody near him, ' You see Sir H. Taylor's famous letter did no good.' " This was an overstatement, but it is true that the letter left the vital question still undecided.[1] Its failure had resulted in a complete deadlock, and the question of peer-making had to be opened once more. The King was deeply disappointed that a mere question of form should have caused a hitch, but still hoped that peers might come forward ;[2] the advanced Whigs prepared addresses asking for peers, to be moved that night ;[3] and Tory peers began to reconsider their proper course if a creation should yet be made.[4] The final crisis was at hand.

Meanwhile the short-lived confidence of the people had died down. In London the National Political Union, which in the course of the day had enrolled 1200 recruits, held another great meeting on Wednesday night ; it was attended by delegates from Manchester and Dublin, where 50,000 Reformers had assembled a few days before.[5] " I saw the Duke," said Potter, " in October last, in company with another gentleman from Manchester, when we brought up the petition to the House of Lords. . . . We told him that the people of the north of England were one and all Reformers and bent on obtaining the bill. . . . The Duke's reply was this : ' The people of England are very quiet if they are let alone ; and if they won't, there is a way to make them.' " [6] The inference was not difficult to draw. Certainly Jeffrey drew it. " It will only require," he

[1] *Correspondence*, ii. 423, 424. On this point nearly all the authorities are misleading. Even Sir William Anson (*Law of the Constitution*, vol. i. (1911), p. 356) is not correct. The editor of the *Taylor Papers* seems also to have confused the unsuccessful letter of May 17, which the King did authorise, with the later successful announcement of May 20, which, so far as we have evidence, he did not (*Taylor Papers*, p. 340).

[2] *Correspondence*, ii. 430.

[3] *Recollections*, iv. 231, 232. Grote to Durham, Thursday : " It is clear that the necessity of creating Peers stands just as it did before the debate took place " (*Lambton Papers*).

[4] *Despatches*, viii. 331.

[5] A Dublin paper wrote : " It is almost impossible that any political event could have produced such a thorough union among the parties who have been quarrelling about a repeal of the Union."

[6] Add. MSS. 27,794, f. 164 ; *Morning Chronicle*, May 17.

wrote in this anxious interval, " twelve or fifteen desperate men to be got together in a room—a Chancellor and Home Secretary to be created—a commission made for proroguing Parliament at two o'clock, and a proclamation for dissolving it for the *Evening Gazette*—an insulting answer proposed to the address of the Commons—and the country is on fire before Sunday morning ; aye—inextinguishable fire, though blood should be poured out on it like water. Then would follow the dispersion of unions, and meetings, and petitions, by soldiery ; and vindictive burnings ; and massacres of anti-Reformers in all the manufacturing districts ; and summary arrests of men accused of sedition and treason ; and shoals of persecutions for libels, followed by triumphant acquittals ; and elections carried through amidst sanguinary tumults ; and finally, a House of Commons returned to put down that brutal administration, but *too late* to stay the torrent it had created." [1]

On Thursday morning there was great uneasiness ; it was seen that the jubilations had been premature ; and fears crept about the town that the ministers were the victims of foul play. The Duke and that " cunning cad " Peel might yet have some *coup d'état* in hand.[2] The rage for meetings showed no abatement, and it was arranged that, should matters still be unsettled on Monday, resolutions should be passed at the London Tavern by the National Political Union, to set the tone to the country. The overflow outside would provoke the Duke to take some drastic step.[3] As for the Rotunda Radicals, they were in a state of great excitement over the acquittal the day before of their Fast-day leaders, Lovett and Benbow.[4] The Friday papers, with accounts of last night's scene in the Lords, turned the anxiety of Reformers into bitter resentment. Althorp's words in the Commons argued some hope which had not been fulfilled. All hung on the King's expected decision, which must be declared before nightfall. Otherwise England was " on the eve of the barricades." [5]

It was perhaps the day of the dissolution which really settled that the Reform Bill must become law. The night of May 14, 1832, may have decided that it would become so without a change of ministers. But in the eyes of the people of the Three

---

[1] Jeffrey to Cockburn, May 17 ; *Life of Jeffrey*, i. 331.
[2] *Morning Chronicle*, May 17.   [3] Add. MSS. 27,794, f. 259.
[4] Add. MSS. 27,796, f .306.   [5] *Morning Chronicle*, May 18.

Kingdoms it was May 18 on which the battle was won and which brought the country nearest to a revolution. The Cabinet were to sit at twelve, and Ellice had summoned a meeting at the Treasury at one ; in the hope of convincing his colleagues of the true state of affairs Hobhouse induced Place to write him a letter which might be shown to others.[1]  Place was in his glory at such a moment, and evidently with great gusto put the following menaces on paper : " Lists containing the names, addresses, &c., of persons in every part of the country likely to be useful have been made. The name of every man who has at any public meeting showed himself friendly to Reform has been registered. Addresses and proclamations to the people have been sketched, and printed copies will, if need be, be sent to every such person all over the kingdom—means have been devised to placard towns and villages, to circulate handbills, and assemble the people. So many men of known character, civil and *military*, have entered heartily into the scheme, that their names when published will produce great effect in every desirable way. If the Duke come into power now, we shall be unable longer to ' hold to the laws '—break them we must, be the consequences whatever they may, we know that all must join with us, to save their property, no matter what may be their private opinions. Towns will be barricadoed—new municipal arrangements will be formed by the inhabitants, and the first town which is barricaded shuts up all banks." [2]

Such was the business-like plan of rebellion over which advanced Reformers were gloating, while the Cabinet sat in high council in Downing Street. They resolved that, in view of the failure of the first alternative suggested in their minute of Wednesday, there was no course open but to recommend a creation of peers. They reminded the King of his former promise to make forty-one, and asked for " full and indisputable security " to carry the Reform Bill. A minute to this effect was carried to St. James's in the afternoon by Lord Grey and the Chancellor ; [3] they remained some time urging their cause with the King.

In their absence the tension outside grew terrible. Place tells us that he gathered from many callers of all descriptions that London generally expected the Duke to take office.

[1] Add. MSS. 27,794, ff. 278, 280.     [2] *Ibid.*, f. 278.
[3] *Correspondence*, ii. 432.

Meetings were held about the town, and the various deputies were ready to start for home the instant the news was declared. They were to summon meetings which should send representatives to a central congress in London and proceed to barricade their towns, Birmingham taking the lead. There was a plan to kidnap the families of Tories as hostages, but " no proceedings beyond those of causing a general demand for gold were to be taken in the first instance. The evening papers had prepared to insert the statements in Parliament in second editions, which were to be immediately forwarded to all parts of the country." [1] As the afternoon drew on the Houses met, but ministers knew nothing more than the strangers who packed the galleries. In the Commons Lord Milton was ready with an address to the King, and a call of the House was nearly over, when Stanley came in with a message. About five o'clock Lord Althorp rose and announced that the Government had secured a guarantee sufficient to convice them of their power to carry the bill.[2] Lord Grey made a similar statement in the Lords. After what Brougham describes as a most painful interview, the two ministers had obtained the King's verbal consent to make peers if required ; it was confirmed that evening in writing : " His Majesty authorises Earl Grey, if any obstacle should arise during the further progress of the Bill, to submit to him a creation of peers to such extent as shall be necessary to enable him to carry the Bill, always bearing in mind that it has been and still is his Majesty's object to avoid any permanent increase to the peerage." Possible eldest sons and collaterals were to be called up before any actual creations took place.[3]

Place gives a highly interesting account of the circumstances which immediately led to the King's yielding. He was informed of them, he says, next morning by a man in office of high consideration. " At about two o'clock a gentleman came

---

[1] Add. MSS. 27,794, ff. 281–6.    [2] *Recollections*, iv. 232.
[3] *Correspondence*, ii. 434 ; *Brougham's Memoirs*, iii. 199. The King, says Brougham, was in great distress : it was " the only audience I ever had in which he kept his seat, and did not desire us to sit down." Brougham adds that it was he who insisted on the King giving his consent in writing, and that Grey was " perfectly shocked " at his audacity. The Brougham tradition is followed by Roebuck (*History of the Whig Ministry of* 1830, ii. 331–3) and Molesworth (*History of the Reform Bill*, p. 333). For an exposure of the spurious letter of the King's, dated Windsor, May 17, see the *Edinburgh Review*, vol. cxxv. p. 544.

to Earl Grey privately ; he was commissioned by the Bank Directors to inform him that if nothing was settled in time to be forwarded to the country by the mails, they apprehended that the depositors in Savings Banks would generally give notice to withdraw their deposits and convert the amount into cash ; that this being known other persons would also demand gold for paper, and that the run upon all the banks would in four days compel them to close their doors. That Earl Grey requested the gentleman to proceed to the Duke of Wellington and make the communication to him, that he did so, and the Duke having immediately made a similar communication to the King, Earl Grey was restored to office with the power he desired." [1] Much of this may of course be true. The incident must have taken place, if so, between the meeting of the Cabinet and the two ministers' audience at the palace. But it is difficult to believe that Grey would have sent on such an informant to the Duke of Wellington, who had no official position and, as Grey knew, had already decided for his own part to abstain from the further discussion of the bill. Brougham says nothing of the matter, and the King's consent is perfectly intelligible without such explanation, his own scheme having broken down on Thursday night.

In Brougham's *Political Philosophy*, written in 1843, the following remarkable statement occurs : " I have often since asked myself the question, whether, if no secession had taken place, and the Peers had persisted in really opposing the most important provisions of the Bill, we should have had recourse to the perilous creation ? Well nigh twelve years have now rolled over my head since the crisis of 1832. I speak very calmly on this as on any political question whatever, and I cannot, with any confidence, answer it in the affirmative. . . . I much question whether I should not have preferred running the risk of the confusion that attended the loss of the Bill as it then stood ; and I have a strong impression on my mind that my illustrious friend would have more than met me half-way. . . . My opinion of Lord Grey's extreme repugnance to the course upon which we felt we were forced, has been confirmed since he read the above passage." [2] This is a strong statement, and no doubt Brougham believed it at the time when

---

[1] Add. MSS. 27,794, f. 286.
[2] *Political Philosophy* (2nd edition), iii. 308.

he wrote it.   But to say correctly what one would have done in a hypothetical case twelve years before would be a difficult feat for a memory more accurate than Brougham's.   The influence of time may be seen by comparing the above passage with the even stronger form of words which the writer allowed himself twenty years later.[1]   We know too that Grey's conservative instincts reasserted themselves at the end of his life.  In 1843 he was nearly eighty, and his inclinations may well have coloured his memory.   Brougham admits that his colleague and he were thoroughly convinced *at the time* of the necessity, and certainly all contemporary evidence goes to show that the creation would have taken place.

For some days it seemed that the King might be called upon to redeem his pledge.   The Opposition lords were much disorganised ;   their leader kept away from the House, and made no attempt to influence opinion.[2]   Grote impressed on Durham the danger that peers might lie in ambush to mutilate the bill when occasion offered.   " The tenor of the speeches of Noble Peers distinctly implies that there can have been *no tacit understanding* between the two parties ;   it also proves that the Opposition Peers *do not know* that the power of new creation is positively and peremptorily lodged with the Ministry.  . . . It seems absolutely certain that nothing but an infusion of new Peers can carry the Bill."[3]   Lord Grey, completely knocked up by the strain of the last few days, was still inclined to be despondent, and believed that resistance might yet be made in Committee ;   he implored Sir Herbert Taylor to do all he could to prevent it.[4]   Taylor wrote on the 20th that he had the names of twenty-four peers who had agreed not to vote ;  the same day he admitted that he had allowed the fact of the King's unlimited consent to make peers to become known.[5]  Though Taylor's action came in for much criticism, and was taken without their knowledge or the King's, the ministers gladly assumed the responsibility for it.[6]   Henceforward their

---

[1] *Brougham Memoirs*, iii. 206–8.   *E.g.* " I much question whether I should not " becomes " I am persuaded I should."

[2] Elgin to Wellington, May 19 ;  *Despatches*, viii. 336.

[3] *Life of Durham*, i. 287.

[4] *Correspondence*, ii. 439.

[5] *Ibid.*, ii. 444 ;  *Taylor Papers*, p. 358.

[6] *Life of Graham*, i. 145 ;  *Brougham Memoirs*, iii. 202.   See above, p. 409, *n*. 1.

course lay clear, though for some time the open triumph of the political unions, many of which showed no signs of dissolving, caused trouble with the nervous and unhappy King. The Government were advised on the one hand to suppress the unions by law, on the other to persuade them to disband by passing the bill at once, preferably by a creation of peers.[1] Both suggestions were equally distasteful to Grey.

Whether or not as the result of Taylor's purposed indiscretion, the bill passed rapidly through Committee ; for the next fortnight Tory peers " skulked in clubs and country houses," and the Duke did not encourage suggestions that they should muster to kill it on the occasion of the third reading. The measure would become law in any case ; the only difference would be the addition of sixty Whig peers.[2] On June 4 the third reading was carried by 106 votes to 22, and next day the Commons agreed to the Lords' trifling amendments. Only one hitch, and that a slight one, occurred. As the result of the Days of May the Court had become extremely unpopular ; William IV had created more republicans in a week, said a Radical paper, than Paine's writings had in twenty-five years.[3] The ministers urged that, by giving the Royal Assent to the Reform Bill in person, the King might regain the people's favour. But William refused to gratify those who had disgraced themselves by insulting their sovereign, and still more, by " villainous and indecent attacks " on " his amiable, beloved, and truly respectable consort." [4] Accordingly a commission was made out in the usual way, and on June 7 the Reform Bill became law.[5]

When the news came that the Government were restored to power, for most Reformers party bitterness was sunk for the moment in a deep sense of relief and of gratitude for a

[1] *Correspondence*, ii. 469. Holland to Grey, May 19 ; *Howick Papers.*

[2] Wellington to Eldon, May 22 ; to Falmouth, May 25 ; *Despatches*, viii. 341, 346.

[3] *The Republican*, May 26.

[4] The King to Althorp, May 23 ; *Althorp Papers.*

[5] *Correspondence*, ii. 466, 467. The Reform Act is 2 & 3 Will. IV, cap. 45. The Scotch and Irish Reform Bills became law in the course of the summer. A flysheet of the time pictured the Queen and the Duke of Wellington retiring to Germany. The Queen remarks :

" My cranky old sailor is worse than a Taylor,
 His bill by commission was signed t'other day ;
I'm a Germany stormer, I hate a reformer,
 Confusion to Billy, his Broom, and his Grey."

great deliverance, which had surpassed the revolution of July.[1] Even Francis Place allowed himself that Sunday a few minutes of meditation on the nearness of the avoided danger. " We were within a moment of general rebellion," was his considered judgment.[2] It is so easy to speak loosely of the country being on the verge of revolution, and such language is so apt to be used in an indefinite and metaphorical sense, that it is important, however difficult it may be, to come to some understanding of what was, and what was not, likely to happen in England in May 1832.

First, it is essential to remember that no Tory administration was ever formed ; it is inaccurate to speak of the Duke " resigning office " or resigning anything except his commision to form a government. The Whig ministers never actually gave up their seals of office ; they attended, or should have attended, to their departmental work all the time. Melbourne was still Home Secretary on May 12 when the King refused to receive the address of the Council of the Birmingham Union.[3] This is also true of the War Office ; Hobhouse was there on May 12, and George Lamb said in the House of Commons, in answer to a question, " that there had been no movement of troops except under the sanction of Ministers." [4] Secondly, as far as the Duke of Wellington was concerned, the crisis was over on the night of Monday the 14th. He took leave of the King next morning, and had no further communication with him except on the 17th, when Taylor wrote suggesting that he should make an announcement in the Lords. Of course the King's refusal to create peers on Friday might possibly have led to the Duke making another attempt to form a government, but no such negotiations were in the air. The Duke was merely a spectator at the finish.

The ground thus partly cleared, an attempt may be made to estimate the true state of things. For the Reformers' arrangements Place's account, written about five years later but interspersed with contemporary letters and documents, is the main authority. Though no safe guide as to events occurring in Downing Street or at St. James's, he was absolutely at the

---

[1] *Morning Chronicle*, May 19.
[2] Add. MSS. 27,795, f. 27.
[3] Melbourne to Durham, May 13 ; *Lambton Papers*.
[4] *Recollections*, iv. 223 ; *Hansard* (3rd series), xii. 1090.

heart of the middle class political arrangements in the capital, and corresponded with Radicals in the great towns. Familiar with the industrial conditions of London from his youth up, he had given his life to the study of questions affecting the working people, and had been brought by his labours into close contact with many of them engaged in different trades and in different places. Only eight years before, he pulled the principal wires in the agitation against the Combination Laws. He had also become acquainted with the intellectual Radicals in and out of Parliament, such as Bentham, Hume, Burdett, Hobhouse, and Grote ; his rooms at Charing Cross were the political centre of middle class London. He was the founder of the National Political Union and a member of its council. Therefore he had every means of knowing the plans he describes. He had more-over a remarkably accurate mind, very little biassed by emotion ; he was much more inclined to irony than to exaggeration. Where his knowledge was not at first hand, he usually gives his authority. Hence there is every reason for accepting his evidence on matters of fact, and his conjectures were based on wider knowledge than is usual concerning popular politics.

Something has been already said of the strategy adopted. The provincial delegates were to hurry home as soon as a Tory ministry was announced ; they were to be replaced at head-quarters by deputies from the towns, who were to form a per-manent committee of public safety. The first blow would be aimed at the nation's credit. It was hoped that the Commons would refuse supplies ; in any case no taxes would be paid, and a run would be made on all banks. As to the former, it is true that the great part of the revenue did not come from direct taxation ; but a general refusal on the part of the Reforming bourgeoisie would be very serious, as Melbourne admitted,[1] and distrained goods would not be easily sold. As to the strength of the demand for gold, there is much mystery ; be-tween three and four hundred thousand pounds were said to have been withdrawn from the Bank on Monday and Tuesday, and Place said this was " a mere demonstration " ; provincial banks must assuredly have collapsed.[2] It was hoped that this

---

[1] *Melbourne Papers*, pp. 130, 134.

[2] Francis (*History of the Bank of England*, ii. 67, 68) says that "£1,500,000 were paid in a few days." " In one day £307,000 were paid. . . . That the demand was political was proved from the trifling nature of the applications from the country bankers."

would be enough for the Duke. If not, provisional governments would barricade all the towns, beginning with Birmingham. The troops would be kept from leaving London by the threat of disturbance there.[1] Above all the general stoppage of business would throw vast numbers of ill-organised men out of employment ; however little they might know of what the Reform Bill meant, they would have a vague idea that it would bring lower prices and better wages. Place hoped that funds would be forthcoming " to feed and lead the people " ; but even if they were not the excitement would be no less dangerous to the Government.[2]

In these circumstances he did not expect there would be serious fighting with the troops ; if there should be, he had no fear of the event. The days of revolution in Paris were big in men's minds during these months, and it was not held possible that Englishmen could fail where Frenchmen, and even Belgians, had succeeded. The great scheme of a mammoth meeting of several millions had been given up, but we have it on Croker's authority that some thousands of Manchester operatives had been marched up to London ; on the first news of Wellington's failure they had been withdrawn and quartered in neighbouring villages, where they were supporting themselves by begging.[3] " At the election of 1868 an old labourer in the agricultural Borough of Woodstock told a Liberal canvasser from Oxford that in his youth arms had been stored in his father's cottage so as to be in readiness for the outbreak which was to take place if Lord Grey's Reform Bill was finally defeated." [4] To lead these irregular forces the Reformers had secured, Place tells us, " a large number of able

[1] Place writes : " An old guardsman, a General Officer, told me that he had seen his friend Lord Melbourne at the Home Office, and had told him the Duke could do nothing with the army since he dared not move any part of it away from the Metropolis, and that he could not use it with any effect in London " (Add. MSS. 27,794, f. 283).

[2] Add. MSS. 27,794, f. 278 : " If we have money, we shall have the power to feed and lead the people, and in less than five days we shall have the soldiers with us." The Reformers' balance-sheet for May 1832 would be an interesting document. They certainly had some very rich men, such as Grote, among them.

[3] *Croker*, ii. 169 : " They confessed that they had come up *many thousands* to carry the Reform Bill, which was to put down machinery, and enable the poor man to earn a livelihood."

[4] G. W. E. Russell, *Collections and Recollections*, p. 108,

officers." [1]  Unfortunately we have little but this meagre statement.  In December General Sir G. Cockburn wrote to Grey
suggesting the enrolment of a National Guard, organised by
parishes, as a possible means of overawing the Lords.[2]  Parkes
also mentions a few names, but it is hardly surprising that such
secrets should not have been made public property.[3]  On the
whole Place was convinced the commotion—he would not call
it a civil war—would not last over a few days, though in that
time much irreparable damage would be done.[4]

It would be most interesting to know what part the leading
Whigs would have taken—whether Durham, for instance,
would have sanctioned a fighting policy, or even drawn the
sword himself.  The position of Hobhouse, as the late Secretary
at War, would have been yet more delicate.  It is most unlikely
that any others of the Cabinet would have sympathised with
forcible revolution ; indeed they hardly realised that any such
thing was contemplated.  It must also be held extremely
doubtful whether the Commons would have refused supplies
when it came to the point.  The Government majority on
Ebrington's motion approving the advice to create peers fell
to eighty—a decline of fifty on the corresponding vote in October
—and this would have been a far stronger step, amounting in
fact to defiance of the King's personal wish.  The idea was
favoured openly by several speakers in the House, but it would
appear that a motion to this effect was beaten at Brooks's on
Sunday night, the party agreeing to support the bill in any
case, even if proposed by the Duke.[5]  It is practically certain
that the House would not have consented to destroy the King's

---

[1] Add. MSS. 27,792, f. 39.

[2] *Ibid.*, 27,790, f. 270.

[3] Parkes to Mrs. Grote, May 18 : " If we had been overreached this
week by the borough-mongers, I and two friends should have made the
revolution whatever the cost.  I had written to General Johnstone, and
had got a cover to Colonel Napier, and would have had both in Birmingham, and a Count Chopski, a Pole, by Monday, and I think we could have
prevented anarchy, and set all right in two days " (Add. MSS. 27,794, f. 262).

[4] Place to Hobhouse, June 2 ; Add. MSS. 35,149, f. 154.

[5] *Croker Papers*, ii. 164 ; see above, p. 399.  Parkes, writing to Grote
on May 14, gives on Durham's authority a most inaccurate story.  Durham
recommended ministers " to meet the Duke in the House of Commons
with an open vote of *no confidence*.  The dirty fellow Stanley moved at
Brookes' and carried merely to oppose supplies, and the Duke is too wily
to propose supplies " (Add. MSS. 27,794, f. 10).

Government. The people would have fought their own battle.

On the other hand most Tories seem to have made light of the thought of resistance, had the Duke accepted office. Croker was sure the Government might be carried on with the Duke at the Horse Guards,[1] and the *Standard* believed that " a fortnight's firm government would put down the unions and the meetings without bayonet or blood," adding : " The present excitement is not so great as that which prevailed in 1810 or 1817—nothing to be compared with that which raged in 1820 about the Queen—and yet there was no difficulty found in suppressing these riots." [2]   The difference was that in the present case the excitement was organised.   This conviction tallies with the universal idea of the advanced Reformers that the Duke would use force to quiet the country.   There was a tradition in Attwood's family that warrants had actually been prepared for his arrest and that of other leading unionists, but that Grey on returning to power found them still unsigned.[3]   It is difficult to believe this as stated ; however, the Duke's reported remark that he knew a way to keep the people quiet turned attention to the army, and any unusual incident was jealously noted.   It has been said before that Hobhouse was at the War Office during the entire period, and it is hardly possible that any orders could have emanated from the Duke.   The fact that Lord Fitzroy Somerset, military secretary to Lord Hill, called at Apsley House is not sufficient.[4]   He was a friend of the Duke's and had consulted him as to military arrangements with regard to the intended meeting in White Conduit Fields in November 1831.   The rough-sharpening of swords by the Greys at Birmingham can hardly be supposed, without direct evidence, to have been intended to suppress a peaceful crowd, nor was the holding of the Guards in readiness on May 14 a political move.   The *Poor Man's Guardian* held Hobhouse, not Wellington, responsible for the gathering of troops towards " the Wen."

[1] *Croker Papers*, ii. 163.

[2] Quoted Add. MSS. 27,794, f. 74.

[3] *Life of Attwood*, p. 216.   It is possible that the Duke may have had warrants made out to be used in the event of his accepting office ; if so, it was before Attwood came to London.   But the Duke never moved from Apsley House, and it is not clear where Grey could have found the warrants.   *Cf.* Jeffrey's letter, quoted on p. 410.

[4] *Morning Chronicle*, May 14.

So any opinions that may be formed of the Duke's probable policy, had he taken office and found himself faced by an insurrection, must be pure guesses. And, as a matter of fact, at the supreme moment of popular excitement, the Duke had no intention whatever of taking office. Genuine therefore as the Reformers' preparations were, their suspicions of him were unfounded after Monday night. The revolution was most completely organised four days after the probability of its occurrence had practically disappeared. But if Manners Sutton had not delayed his acceptance, and if the formation of a Tory ministry had been announced, as Lord Carnarvon wished, on Monday, an insurrection on the plan described by Place must almost certainly have broken out.

The difficulty of conjecturing its probable issue is enhanced by the fact that most of the upper classes seem to have had no conception of what was going on beneath the surface. The aristocracy, says Place, " could not imagine that any real danger could result from the rejection of the Reform Bill, in any way to affect themselves." They apprehended nothing more serious than a common riot.[1] Hobhouse was content to receive his information from Place. If, as seems certain, Place's descriptions are correct, it is a most memorable case of a Government utterly incapable of understanding or coping with a critical situation. The zeal of the people was a force quite apart from, and undirected by, the leaders of the popular party in Parliament. Reformers had no doubts of their success, even if the army should remain loyal ; and this they thought unlikely. When in November 1831 the Duke drew up a scheme for the defence of London in case of riot, the forces at the disposal of the War Office consisted of four regiments of cavalry in London, with a regiment and a squadron from the south near by ; twelve guns, five battalions of Foot Guards, and 500 marines.[2] It is improbable that a much greater force was available in May, though troops were said to be converging on London from the provinces.[3] England was at the

---

[1] Add. MSS. 27,792, f. 38.

[2] *Despatches*, viii. 22. The Duke said St. James's Park ought to be the centre of operations; communications should be kept up with the royal palaces, with the City Road by Regent Street, and with the Bank and the Tower on both sides of the river ; the instructions are most elaborate.

[3] " Military in all parts of the country were during the last week put into active motion—all, or nearly so, stepping out for ' the Wen.' Of

time divided into four military districts ; [1]   the troops in all of
them had been occupied in maintaining order at various times
in the last few months, and during these very weeks Sir Henry
Bouverie had his hands full in keeping the peace among the
strikers in the Durham coal-field.   In the whole of the Northern
District, which included Cheshire and Nottingham, there were
three cavalry regiments ; one of these was responsible " for the
whole of the Clothing district of Yorkshire, and for the Coal
district on the Tyne and Wear." [2]   At Birmingham there were
two troops of the Greys—about 150 effective men. [3]   There can
be no doubt that the constant employment of the military in
industrial disputes and ordinary disturbances must have done
something to lessen the awe they inspired among working men.

As to the loyalty of the army, there were rumours that the
troops in London had promised to fire high, while we have
Alexander Somerville's direct testimony as to the temper of
many in the ranks at Birmingham.   They would quell a riot,
but would not interfere for merely political reasons. [4]   The
Hertfordshire Yeomanry sent in their resignations to Hatfield
as soon as the fall of the Whig Government was announced. [5]
From the inability of any force, civil or military, to prevent
riots at various places earlier in the history of the bill, it seems
very unlikely that an organised attempt, at each great centre,
to take over the control of the town could have been resisted.
Most certainly 150 troopers, tinged with disaffection, could
not have coerced the populace of Birmingham.   In London
the Duke would have been prepared " to lay open in a minute
any house or church " with artillery fire, [6] but success must
have been extraordinarily difficult in the face of a population
predominantly Radical and fired by the story of the French
barricades, with a hostile House of Commons too sitting at
Westminster, and the Bank very probably suspending pay-

course now ' Sancho ' [Hobhouse] knows nothing of the matter " (*Poor
Man's Guardian*, May 26).

   [1] Northern : South-west : West : Inland.   *Army List*, May 1832.
   [2] Bouverie (O. C. northern district) to Home Office, April 12 ;  *H. O.*
40. 30.
   [3] Cavalry Monthly Returns, *W. O.* 17. 449.   There were also two
troops of the Greys at Coventry.
   [4] *Autobiography of a Working Man*, p. 248.
   [5] Martineau, *History of England*, ii. 46.
   [6] *Despatches*, viii. 25.

ment.   Had the people won, it is doubtful what would have happened.   Place himself hazarded no more than the certain " establishment of a representative government in all its parts." [1] All along the Revolution of July was the model ;  it was even ironically suggested that the Duke of Sussex, who had been forbidden the Court in consequence of his behaviour during the crisis, might play the part of Louis Philippe.[2]   But doubtless King William was safe enough, and it would not have been the winners of the victory who would have controlled its results.

The securing, and still more the passing, of the bill was followed in the country by the customary orgy of bell-ringing, illuminations, and public banquets.   On May 23 Thomas Attwood was presented with the Freedom of the City at the Guildhall—the first private person, he proudly claimed, ever to have received that honour.   His return to Birmingham, " upon which town the eyes of Britain and of Europe were fixed," [3] was a triumphal progress through streets bright with bunting, and set the tone to middle class rejoicing throughout the Three Kingdoms.[4]

But long after the tumult and the shouting had died, the struggle for the Reform Bill lived in the minds of those who remembered it as an event quite distinct from anything else in British history.   It was in truth a revolution, no less decisive than that which subdued the Crown to Parliament.   To Whigs of the old school it was the supreme glory of their party to have brought a warfare against such odds to a successful end, and to have steered a straight course between Radicalism and reaction.   To younger men, of the Macaulay stamp, it was the conforming of politics to the new ideas which in other ways of life promised an **era** of light and progress.   But it meant most

[1] Place to Hobhouse, June 2 ;  Add. MSS. 35,149, f. 154.

[2] *Cosmopolite*, May 26.

[3] *Autobiography of a Working Man*, p. 247.

[4] A flysheet headed " Reform and Victory," composed in praise of " the Grey Horse and the Union Coach " is typical of many.   " Why, Sir," says an admirer, " one of the wheels was made at Birmingham, and the spokes of that wheel is made of Attwood, the finest wood in the world ; there was another wheel made in London, another in Manchester, and the other in Edinburgh." . . . " Pray, who drives the coach, neighbour ? " he is asked, and answers, " Why, friend, she runs by steam now, but old Bill King, a sailor chap, drove her first."

of all to democrats.   Since before the time of the French Revolution they had vainly striven to wake a sleeping people to the
consciousness of its power.   " The impending mischief has
passed over us," wrote Place in the flush of victory, "thanks
to the enlightened state to which large masses of the people have
attained ;   thanks indeed to their foresight, the steady conduct
of their leaders, and the unlimited confidence the people felt in
themselves, and that which they placed in the men who came
forward in the common cause.   But for these demonstrations
a revolution would have commenced, which would have been
the act of the whole people to a greater extent than any which
had ever before been accomplished."   " This was indeed the
first time," he claimed, " they ever combined of their own free
will for a really national purpose." [1]

Often of course popular feeling had influenced the politics
of Westminster ;   but never before had pressure, organised
at all so scientifically, been brought to bear.   This had been
done by union on a large scale.   Vague excitement had been
fused into a weapon capable of striking a winning blow.   There
had been discipline and corporate effort in a class as a rule
contemptuously ignored as " the mob."   This was the secret
of the enthusiasm centred round the name of Attwood, a man
with no remarkable gifts—as appeared when he took his seat
in the Reformed Parliament,—except a personal attraction for
the middle class.[1]   " He has taught the people," said Grote at
the Guildhall banquet, " to combine for a great public purpose,
without breaking any of the salutary restraints of law, and
without violating any of their obligations as private citizens.
He has divested the physical force of the country of its terrors
and its lawlessness."   For the future it was earnestly hoped
that the same popular control might be maintained ;   henceforth
all institutions must stand the utilitarian test, and the victory
must be pressed unfalteringly home.   To democrats the inevitable decline of interest was most heartbreaking.   But for
the moment the greater part of the country was satisfied.   " There

---

[1] Add. MSS. 27,795, ff. 26, 28.

[2] *Life of Attwood*, p. 225.   " To the prompt, energetic, and determined
—but peaceable—conduct of these unions, it is now very generally
admitted, by all but those who hate popular liberty, that we were indebted
for the preservation of the country from anarchy and civil war . . ."
(*Political Unionist*, No. 1, June 30).

was an agreement," said the *Westminster*, " between the sounder part of the aristocracy and what are called the Radicals, that a trial should be given to the working of the Reform Bill, before any further innovation was demanded."

There remained the Tories, doubting whether in future politics would be a fit pastime for gentlemen, and the Rotunda Radicals, sincerely hoping that they would not. The complaints of the old rulers of England make really pathetic reading. " All my feelings," wrote the aged Eldon, " satisfy me that my time is very short. I am grateful to God that such is the case ; being very confident that, if the bill passes, the monarchy and the Peers of the realm will not, as such, survive me long. I have *long* been sure that the work of destruction of both has been going on in this country, and I am now sure that it will be, very speedily, fully accomplished." [1] But there was one who did not altogether despair of the State, and Peel's sustained effort, against enormous odds, to reconstruct a conservative party was a noble feat of statesmanship. On the other hand the leaders of the working men, caring nothing for the Reform Bill as such, believed that the example set by its achievement could never cease to inspire. " When the Bill is safe . . . we cannot think so ill of human nature as to think that those who will then have gained their own freedom, will not aid us to gain ours. We must, as they have done, endeavour to show by our own conduct, that we deserve to enjoy our rights." [2] The working men were disappointed ; those who had " gained their own freedom " had other things to do than to enfranchise the poor, and so far the Reform Bill brought little benefit to labour. But incomplete as it was, it left enough of the middle class without the vote for a union to be formed once more, strong enough to storm the walls of privilege. Again a class had failed, and it was found needful to try the nation.[3]

[1] Eldon to Wellington, May 22 ; *Despatches*, viii. 343. There is a tablet in Harrow Church commemorating an Irish judge " who died of the first Reform Bill." " He sunk beneath the efforts of a mind too great for his earthly frame, in opposing the Revolutionary Invasion of the Religion and Constitution of England " (G. W. E. Russell, *One Look Back*, p. 44).

[2] *Poor Man's Guardian*, May 26.

[3] John Bright, October 16, 1866. " The real state of the case," said Bright, " if it were put in simple language, would be this—that the

But it was the Reform Act of 1832 which showed that the fortress could be stormed, and which marked out the line of assault. Though it in fact only enfranchised part of a single class, it established a precedent of permanent force for enfranchising all classes when they should reach the stage of political consciousness and social power. It determined that those who have power outside Parliament must have power inside it, and sanctioned a readjustment of the Constitution for this purpose, even at the price of ancient forms and individual interests. It decided against government by a ruling class irresponsible to the people, however efficient by descent and training. On the other hand the existence in Parliament of a party, whose leaders had long prepared the minds of the aristocracy for Reform, made it possible for the change to take place without a breach of continuity in the national life. It was fortunate for the country that many of the Whigs did not see the consequences of their courage. For it can hardly be believed that, had they not acted as they did, England could have survived the years between 1830 and 1848 without some violent rebellion of the classes outside the pale. The events of May 1832 showed how intense a resolution could be displayed by men of little organisation and experience. That memory of the people in act to strike, yet quietly dispersing when victory was assured, had a great and sobering influence on the generations following. Much remained undone, as the working classes knew to their cost ; but for many years the guiding opinion of the country found expression in Parliament ; it was felt that should further change be needed the Constitution was equal to provide it ; and the stage was cleared of political encumbrance for the working out of the destinies of Victorian England.

working men are almost universally excluded, roughly and insolently, from political power, and that the middle class, whilst they have the semblance of it, are defrauded of the reality." Quoted in Trevelyan's *Life of John Bright*, p. 365.

# BIBLIOGRAPHICAL NOTE

BESIDES the private papers mentioned in the Preface, the following authorities throw light on the passing of the Reform Bill. This list is not meant to be complete, and in particular it does not cover the ground of the first and third chapters—that is to say, the Reform movement before 1830 and the social condition of England.

## I. MS. SOURCES

In the Public Record Office :
> Home Office Papers, under the following headings : Disturbances, Domestic, Municipal and Provincial, Scotland, Ireland. These are in bundles, and there is no means of referring to an individual document.
> Home Office Entry Books, under the same headings.
> War Office Papers.

In the British Museum :
> Correspondence of Sir Robert Wilson, chiefly with leading Whigs.
> Correspondence of Lord Broughton ; very little, however, of importance for 1830–32 is to be found.
> Place MSS. ; of unique importance for the history of the movement outside Parliament. Place wrote his *History of the Reform Agitation* between 1836 and 1839 ; valuable extracts are given in his Life by Graham Wallas, chapters ix.–xi.
> Political Caricatures of 1830–32, and Cartoons by Richard Doyle.

## II. PUBLISHED CORRESPONDENCE, &c.

Creevey, T. *Papers.* 3rd ed. 1905.

Croker, J. W. *Correspondence and Diary.* Vol. ii. 1884.

Grey, Charles, Earl. *Correspondence with King William IV and Sir Herbert Taylor.* 2 vols. 1867.

—— *Correspondence with Princess Lieven.* Vols. i., ii. 1890.

Hansard. *Parliamentary Debates* (3rd Series). Vols. i.–xii.

Melbourne, Viscount. *Papers.* 1889.

Peel, Sir R. *Papers.* Vol. ii. 1899.

Russell, Lord J. *Early Correspondence.* 2 vols. 1913.

Wellington, Duke of. *Despatches, &c.* (Civil Series). Vols. vi.–viii. These contain much valuable correspondence of the Tory leaders. 1878, &c.

### III. MEMOIRS, REMINISCENCES, &c.

Brougham, Lord. *Life and Times.* Vol. iii. 1871. Brougham's memoirs were written when he was over eighty, and are by no means accurate, but they contain valuable letters.
Broughton, Lord. *Recollections of a Long Life.* Vol. iv. 1910.
Buckingham and Chandos, Duke of. *Courts and Cabinets of William IV and Victoria.* Vol. i. 1861.
Cockburn, H. *Journal.* Vol. i. 1874. Valuable for opinion in Scotland.
*Edinburgh Review.* Articles in numbers of April 1867, April 1871 (attributed to Lord Howick), April 1872.
Greville, C. G. *Journal of Reigns of George IV and William IV.* Vols. i., ii. 4th ed. 1875. Greville was Clerk of the Council, and had excellent information.
Lovett, W. *Life and Struggles.* 1876.
Malmesbury, Earl of. *Memoirs of an ex-Minister.* Vol. i. 3rd ed. 1884.
Mill, J. S. *Autobiography.* 1873.
*Retrospect of the Events of* 1831–2. By a Contemporary Witness. 1878. The writer quotes letters of Grote and Parkes.
Russell, Lord J. *Speeches and Despatches.* Vol. i. 1870. The Introduction is autobiographical.
—— *Essay on the English Government and Constitution.* New edition. 1873. Contains the first draft of the Reform Bill.
—— *Recollections and Suggestions.* 1875.
Somerville, A. *Autobiography of a Working Man.* 1848.

### IV. BIOGRAPHIES

*Aberdeen, Earl of.* By Sir A. Gordon (*The Queen's Prime Ministers*). 1893.
*Abinger, James, First Lord : Memoir.* By P. C. Scarlett. 1877.
*Althorp, Viscount : Memoir.* By Sir Denis Le Marchant. 1876. The author was Brougham's private secretary, and gives valuable first-hand evidence as well as extracts from the Althorp papers.
*Arnold, T. : Life.* By A. P. Stanley. Teachers' edition. 1901.
*Attwood, T : Life.* By C. M. Wakefield. Privately printed. 1885.
*Campbell, John, Lord.* By Mrs. Hardcastle. 2 vols. 1881.
*Cobbett, W : Life.* By E. I. Carlile. 1904.
*Durham, J. G. Lambton, Earl of : Life and Letters.* By S. J. Reid. 1906.
*Eldon, Earl of.* By Horace Twiss. Vol. iii. 1844.

*Fonblanque, A.: Life and Labours.* By E. Fonblanque. 1874.

*Graham, Sir James: Life and Letters.* By C. S. Parker. 1907.

*Hanoverian Queens of England: Lives.* By Alice Greenwood. Vol. ii. 1911.

*Jeffrey, Lord: Life and Correspondence.* By Lord Cockburn. 1852.

*Lyndhurst, Lord: Life.* By Sir Theodore Martin. Vol. i. 1874.

*Macaulay, Lord: Life and Letters.* By Sir G. O. Trevelyan. Popular edition. 1901.

*Macaulay, Z.: Life and Letters.* By Viscountess Knutsford. 1900.

*Melbourne, Viscount: Memoirs.* By W. M. Torrens. 2 vols. 1890.

*Owen, Richard: Life.* By Frank Podmore. 2 vols. 1906.

*Palmerston, Viscount: Life.* By Lord Dalling. Vols. i., ii. 1870.

*Place, Francis: Life.* By Graham Wallas. 1898. An excellent account of the Radical side of the movement.

*Smith, Sydney: Memoir and Letters.* By Lady Holland. 2 vols. 1855.

—— By G. W. E. Russell. (English Men of Letters.) 1905.

*Stockmar, Baron: Memoirs.* By E. von Stockmar. (English translation.) 2 vols. 1872.

There is no Life of Lord Grey except one by his son, General Charles Grey, published in 1861, which goes down no further than 1817. This deficiency is soon to be made good by Mr. G. M. Trevelyan.

## V. Histories, &c.

Bagehot, W. *Biographical Studies.* 1880. Excellent sketches of Lord Althorp and Sir Robert Peel.

Kent, C. B. R. *The English Radicals.* 1899.

Martineau, Harriet. *History of England during the Thirty Years' Peace.* Vols. i., ii. 1849, 1850. The author knew and admired Durham and Place, and writes from the Radical point of view.

Molesworth, W. N. *History of the Reform Bill.* 1865. " The point to which the author has especially directed his attention . . . is the influence exercised by the people on the character and success of the measure. . . . He believes that in its main features the Reform Bill was virtually their work." Long extracts from speeches in Parliament. Acknowledgment of information received from Brougham and Russell. Misleading account (from Brougham) of the 1831 dissolution and of the final crisis.

—— *History of England.* Vol. i. 1874. In his account of the Reform struggle the author seems to have made no use of Lord Grey's correspondence with the King. The errors of his earlier work are not corrected.

Porritt, E. and A. *The Unreformed House of Commons.* 1903.

Roebuck, J. A. *History of the Whig Ministry of* 1830. 2 vols. 1852. Anti-Whig : " That the Whigs, as a party, sought more than their own party advantage, I see no reason to believe." The author received information—often misleading—from Brougham, and Brougham and Peel were his heroes; he believed William IV to have been " very weak and very false." He gives long *précis* of the speeches in Parliament.

Stephen, L.  *The English Utilitarians.*  Vols. i., ii.  1900.

Temperley, H. W. V.  Chapter xviii. (Great Britain, 1815–32) in vol. x. of the *Cambridge Modern History*, with bibliography.  1907.

Walpole, Sir Spencer.  *History of England from the Conclusion of the Great War.*  Vol. ii.  1878.

The two last works give the best short accounts of the Reform struggle.

# INDEX

ABERDEEN, 4th Earl of, on Grey and Wellington, 53; on Wellington's declaration, 98; attitude to Reform Bill, 366, 398

Addington. *See* Sidmouth

Adelaide, Queen, 79, 185; outfit, 191; and Lord Howe, 289, 336; rumours unfounded, 209, 358; her unpopularity, 379, 381, 394, 396, 404; rumours, 405; press attacks, 415

Agricultural labourers, unrepresented in Parliament, 12, 245; revolt in 1830, 95, 114, 130–4, 163; their condition, 110–4

Agriculture, its condition in 1830, 51, 59, 112; new methods, 107

Airlie, 6th Earl of, 208

Albemarle, 4th Earl of, 217, 362

Althorp, Viscount, 3rd Earl Spencer, 143, 144; advanced Whig, 24, 42; refuses to join Canning, 44, 45; on Wellington administration, 52; votes against it (1830), 65; moves Reform amendment, 68; attempts to unite Whig party, 69, 70–2, 75, 79; supports Hume, 80; congratulates Brougham, 89; discusses Reform with him, 96, 105; speech on the Address, 99; takes office under Grey, 142–4; views on Brougham, 149; suggests plan of Reform, 179; favours Ballot, 180; goes to Brighton (1831), 185; as speaker, 190; his Budget, 192, 193; presents petitions, 194; speech on Reform, 199; advises dissolution, 215; wishes as to new bill, 229; has charge of it in the Commons, 277, 278; against peer-making, 280, 287; offends Palmerston, 288; writes to Birmingham Political Union, 290, 293; on Political Unions, 314; communicates with Attwood, 316; expects Government to break, 317; drafts third Reform Bill, 318; views on meeting of Parliament, 320, 321; on peer-making, 323; meets Waverers, 325; on peer-making (1832), 331; pacifies Hobhouse, 345; his indecision, 346; his delight at leaving office, 373; announces his resignation in Parliament, 376, 385; statement of May 10, 386, 394; carries resolution at Brooks's, 399; statement of May 17, 408, 410; of May 18, 412

American War, its effect on demand for Reform, 6

Anglesey, 1st Marquis of, 213

Anne, Queen, 334

Antwerp, 100

Apsley House, preparations for defence (November 1830), 102; windows broken (April 1831), 219; meeting (May 10, 1832), 387; (May 11), 393; (May 13), 398; (May 14), 402

Arkwright, Sir R., 13

Army. *See* Military

Arnold, T., on Revolution of July, 86; on Reform, 253, 257; his Liberalism, 259, 263; on trade unions, 264; on the "Day of the Lord," 273; discusses Reform with Wordsworth, 351; on Peel, 391

scribes to Loyal and Patriotic Fund, 221 ; as coal-owner, 226 ; Croker's opinion, 249 ; death of his son, 280 ; on Palmerston, 318 ; his behaviour, 324, 349 ; advises creation of peers, 329, 331, 343, 345–7 ; dissuaded from resigning, 349 ; speech on second reading, 359 ; on Birmingham, 385 ; on meeting at Brooks's, 419

THE END

Printed by BALLANTYNE, HANSON & Co.
at Paul's Work, Edinburgh

# THE
# POLITICAL HISTORY OF ENGLAND

Edited by the Rev. WILLIAM HUNT, D.Litt., and
REGINALD LANE POOLE, M.A., LL.D.

(*Editor of "The English Historical Review"*)

Complete in 12 volumes. 8vo. Price £4, 10s. net, but each volume
can be had separately, price 7s. 6d. net

Each volume has its own Index and Two or more Maps

Vol. I. FROM THE EARLIEST TIMES TO THE NORMAN
CONQUEST (to 1066). By THOMAS HODGKIN, D.C.L., Litt.D., Fellow of the
British Academy. With 2 Maps.

Vol. II. FROM THE NORMAN CONQUEST TO THE DEATH
OF JOHN (1066 to 1216). By GEORGE BURTON ADAMS, Professor of History in
Yale University. With 2 Maps.

Vol. III. FROM THE ACCESSION OF HENRY III TO THE
DEATH OF EDWARD III (1216 to 1377). By T. F. TOUT, M.A., Professor
of Mediæval and Modern History in the University of Manchester; Fellow of the
British Academy; formerly Fellow of Pembroke College, Oxford. With 3 Maps.

Vol. IV. FROM THE ACCESSION OF RICHARD II TO THE
DEATH OF RICHARD III (1377 to 1485). By C. OMAN, M.A., LL.D.,
Chichele Professor of Modern History in the University of Oxford; Fellow of the
British Academy. With 3 Maps.

Vol. V. FROM THE ACCESSION OF HENRY VII TO THE
DEATH OF HENRY VIII (1485 to 1547). By H. A. L. FISHER, M.A., Fellow
and Tutor of New College, Oxford; Fellow of the British Academy. With
2 Maps.

Vol. VI. FROM THE ACCESSION OF EDWARD VI TO THE
DEATH OF ELIZABETH (1547 to 1603). By A. F. POLLARD, M.A., Fellow
of All Souls' College, Oxford; Professor of English History in the University of
London. With 2 Maps.

Vol. VII. FROM THE ACCESSION OF JAMES I TO THE
RESTORATION (1603 to 1660). By F. C. MONTAGUE, M.A., Astor Professor
of History in University College, London; formerly Fellow of Oriel College,
Oxford. With 3 Maps.

Vol. VIII. FROM THE RESTORATION TO THE DEATH OF
WILLIAM III (1660 to 1702). By RICHARD LODGE, M.A., LL.D., Professor
of History in the University of Edinburgh; formerly Fellow of Brasenose College,
Oxford. With 2 Maps.

Vol. IX. FROM THE ACCESSION OF ANNE TO THE DEATH
OF GEORGE II (1782 to 1760). By I. S. LEADAM, M.A., formerly Fellow of
Brasenose College, Oxford. With 8 Maps.

Vol. X. FROM THE ACCESSION OF GEORGE III TO THE
CLOSE OF PITT'S FIRST ADMINISTRATION (1760 to 1801). By the Rev.
WILLIAM HUNT, M.A., D.Litt.. Trinity College, Oxford. With 3 Maps.

Vol. XI. FROM ADDINGTON'S ADMINISTRATION TO THE
CLOSE OF WILLIAM IV's REIGN (1881 to 1837). By the Hon. GEORGE C.
BRODRICK, D.C.L., late Warden of Merton College, Oxford, and J. K. FOTHER-
INGHAM, M.A., D.Litt., Fellow of Magdalen College, Oxford; Lecturer in Ancient
History at King's College, London. With 3 Maps.

Vol. XII. THE REIGN OF QUEEN VICTORIA (1837 to 1901).
By SIDNEY LOW, M.A., Balliol College, Oxford; formerly Lecturer on History
at King's College, London; and LLOYD C. SANDERS, B.A. With 3 Maps.

LONGMANS, GREEN AND CO.
LONDON, NEW YORK, BOMBAY, CALCUTTA, AND MADRAS

# STANDARD HISTORICAL WORKS

## WORKS BY JAMES A. FROUDE

THE HISTORY OF ENGLAND, from the Fall of Wolsey to the Defeat of the Spanish Armada. 12 vols. Crown 8vo, 3s. 6d. each.

THE DIVORCE OF CATHERINE OF ARAGON. Crown 8vo, 3s. 6d.

THE SPANISH STORY OF THE ARMADA, and other Essays. Crown 8vo. 3s. 6d.

ENGLISH SEAMEN IN THE SIXTEENTH CENTURY. Crown 8vo, 3s. 6d. Illustrated Edition. With 5 Photogravures and 16 other Illustrations. Large Crown 8vo, 6s. net.

THE ENGLISH IN IRELAND IN THE EIGHTEENTH CENTURY. 3 vols. Crown 8vo, 10s. 6d.

## WORKS BY WILLIAM EDWARD HARTPOLE LECKY

HISTORY OF ENGLAND IN THE EIGHTEENTH CENTURY. Library Edition. 8 vols. 8vo. Vols. I and II, 36s. Vols. III and IV, 36s. Vols. V and VI, 36s. Vols VII and VIII, 36s. Cabinet Edition. ENGLAND. 7 vols. Crown 8vo, 5s. net each. IRELAND. 5 vols. Crown 8vo, 5s. net each.

LEADERS OF PUBLIC OPINION IN IRELAND: FLOOD, GRATTAN, O'CONNELL. 2 vols. Crown 8vo, 5s. net.

## WORKS BY SAMUEL RAWSON GARDINER, D.C.L.

HISTORY OF ENGLAND, from the Accession of James I. to the Outbreak of the Civil War, 1603-42. 10 vols. Crown 8vo, 5s. net each.

HISTORY OF THE GREAT CIVIL WAR, 1642-49. 4 vols. Crown 8vo, 5s. net each.

HISTORY OF THE COMMONWEALTH AND PROTECTORATE, 1649-56. 4 vols. Crown 8vo, 5s. net each.

THE STUDENT'S HISTORY OF ENGLAND. 378 Illustrations. Crown 8vo, 12s.

CROMWELL'S PLACE IN HISTORY. Crown 8vo, 3s. 6d. net.

OLIVER CROMWELL. With Frontispiece. Crown 8vo, 5s. net.

## WORKS BY SIR SPENCER WALPOLE, K.C.B.

HISTORY OF ENGLAND FROM THE CONCLUSION OF THE GREAT WAR IN 1815 TO 1858. 6 vols. Crown 8vo, 6s. each.

THE HISTORY OF TWENTY-FIVE YEARS (1856-80) Vols. I and II. 1856-70. 8vo. (Out of print.) Vols. III and IV. 1878-80. 8vo, 21s. net.

---

A HISTORY OF ENGLAND. By J. FRANCK BRIGHT, D.D. Crown 8vo.
Period I.—MEDIÆVAL MONARCHY: the Departure of the Romans to Richard III. From A.D. 449-1485. 4s. 6d.
Period II.—PERSONAL MONARCHY: Henry VII to James II. From 1485-1688. 5s.
Period III.—CONSTITUTIONAL MONARCHY: William and Mary to William IV. From 1689-1837. 7s. 6d.
Period IV.—THE GROWTH OF DEMOCRACY: Victoria. From 1837-80. 6s.
Period V.—IMPERIAL REACTION: Victoria. From 1880-1901. 4s. 6d.

THE CONSTITUTIONAL HISTORY OF ENGLAND since the Accession of George III. By Sir THOMAS ERSKINE MAY, K.C.B. (Lord Farnborough). Edited and Continued by FRANCIS HOLLAND. 3 vols. 8vo. Vols. I and II, 1760-1860. 15s. net. Vol. III, 1861-1911. By FRANCIS HOLLAND. 12s. 6d. net.

LONGMANS, GREEN AND CO.
LONDON, NEW YORK, BOMBAY, CALCUTTA, AND MADRAS

UNIVERSITY LIBRARY NOTTINGHAM